T0210413

Test Driven

Test Driven

PRACTICAL TDD AND ACCEPTANCE TDD FOR JAVA DEVELOPERS

LASSE KOSKELA

MANNING
Greenwich
(74° w. long.)

For online information and ordering of this and other Manning books, please visit www.manning.com. The publisher offers discounts on this book when ordered in quantity. For more information, please contact:

Special Sales Department
Manning Publications Co.
20 Baldwin Road
PO Box 761
Shelter Island, NY 11964
Email: orders@manning.com

♾ Recognizing the importance of preserving what has been written, it is Manning's policy to have the books we publish printed on acid-free paper, and we exert our best efforts to that end.

Manning Publications Co.
20 Baldwin Road
PO Box 761
Shelter Island, NY 11964

Copyeditor: Laura Merrill
Typesetter: Gordan Salinovic
Cover designer: Leslie Haimes

ISBN 9781932394856
Printed in the United States of America

To my colleagues,
for bugging me to finish this project.

And to my love Lotta,
who gave me the energy to do it.

brief contents

contents

PART 3 BUILDING PRODUCTS WITH ACCEPTANCE TDD 321

preface

Seven years ago, in the midst of a global IT boom, programming shops of all shapes and sizes were racing like mad toward the next IPO, and the job market was hotter than ever. I had been pulled into the booming new media industry and was just starting my programming career, spending long days and nights hacking away at random pieces of code, configuring servers, uploading PHP scripts to a live production system, and generally acting like I knew my stuff.

On a rainy September evening, working late again, my heart suddenly skipped a beat: What did I just do? Did I drop all the data from the production database? That's what it looked like, and I was going to get canned. How could I get the data back? I had thought it was the test database. This couldn't be happening to me! But it was.

I didn't get fired the next morning, largely because it turned out the customer didn't care about the data I'd squashed. And it seemed everyone else was doing the same thing—it could have been any one of us, they said. I had learned a lesson, however, and that evening marked the beginning of my journey toward a more responsible, reliable way of developing software.

A couple of years later, I was working for a large multinational consulting company, developing applications and backend systems for other large corporations. I'd learned a lot during my short career, thanks to all those late nights at the computer, and working on these kinds of systems was a good chance to sharpen my skills in practice. Again, I thought I knew my stuff well when I joined the ranks.

And again, it turned out I didn't know as much as I thought. I continued to learn something important almost every day.

The most important discovery I made changed the way I thought about software development: Extreme Programming (XP) gave me a new perspective on the right way to develop software. What I saw in XP was a combination of the high productivity of my past hack-a-thons and a systematic, disciplined way to work. In addition to the fact that XP projects bring the development team closer to the customer, the single biggest idea that struck a chord with me was test-driven development (TDD). The simple idea of writing tests before the code demolished my concept of programming and unit-testing as separate activities.

TDD wasn't a walk in the park. Every now and then, I'd decide to write tests first. For a while, it would work; but after half an hour I'd find myself editing production code without a failing test. Over time, my ability to stick with the test-first programming improved, and I was able to go a whole day without falling back on my old habits. But then I stumbled across a piece of code that didn't bend enough to my skills. I was coming to grips with how it should be done but didn't yet have all the tricks up my sleeve. I didn't know how to do it the smart way, and frequently I wasn't determined enough to do it the hard way. It took several years to master all the tricks, learn all the tools, and get where I am now.

I wrote this book so you don't have to crawl over the same obstacles I did; you can use the book to guide your way more easily through these lessons. For me, catching the test-first bug has been the single most important influence on how I approach my work and see programming—just as getting into agile methods changed the way I think about software development.

I hope you'll catch the bug, too.

acknowledgments

Taking an idea and turning it into a book is no small feat, and I couldn't have done it without the help of the legion of hard-core professionals and kind souls who contributed their time and effort to this project.

First, thanks to Mike Curwen from JavaRanch, who started it all by connecting me with Jackie Carter at Manning in early 2005. Jackie became my first development editor; she taught me how to write and encouraged me to keep going. Looking back at my first drafts, Jackie, I can see that what you did was a heroic act!

I'd also like to thank the rest of the team at Manning, especially publisher Marjan Bace, my second development editor Cynthia Kane, technical editor Ernest Friedman-Hill, review editor Karen Tegtmeyer, copy editor Laura Merrill, proofreader Tiffany Taylor, and project editor Mary Piergies. It was a true pleasure working with all of you.

I didn't write this book behind closed doors. I had the pleasure of getting valuable feedback early on and throughout the development process from an excellent cast of reviewers, including J. B. Rainsberger, Ron Jeffries, Laurent Bossavit, Dave Nicolette, Michael Feathers, Christopher Haupt, Johannes Link, Duncan Pierce, Simon Baker, Sam Newman, David Saff, Boris Gloger, Cédric Beust, Nat Pryce, Derek Lakin, Bill Fly, Stuart Caborn, Pekka Enberg, Hannu Terävä, Jukka Lindström, Jason Rogers, Dave Corun, Doug Warren, Mark Monster, Jon Skeet, Ilja Preuss, William Wake, and Bas Vodde. Your feedback not only made this a better book but also gave me confidence and encouragement.

My gratitude also goes to the MEAP readers of the early manuscript for their valuable feedback and comments. You did a great job pointing out remaining discrepancies and suggesting improvements, picking up where the reviewers left off.

I wouldn't be writing this today if not for my past and present colleagues, from whom I've learned this trade. I owe a lot to Allan Halme and Joonas Lyytinen for showing me the ropes. You continue to be my mentors, even if we no longer work together on a day-to-day basis. I'd like to thank my fellow moderators at JavaRanch for keeping the saloon running. I've learned a lot through the thousands of conversations I've had at the ranch. And speaking of conversations, I'd especially like to thank Bas Vodde for all the far-out conversations we've had on trains and in hotel lobbies.

Special thanks to my colleagues at Reaktor Innovations for their encouragement, support, enthusiasm, and feedback. You've taught me a lot and continue to amaze me with your energy and talent. It's an honor to be working with you.

I'd also like to thank my clients: the ones I've worked with and the ones who have attended my training sessions. You've given me the practical perspective for my work, and I appreciate it. I wouldn't know what I was talking about if it weren't for the concrete problems you gave me to solve!

My life as a software developer has become easier every year due to the tools that open source developers around the world are creating free of charge for all of us. Parts 2 and 3 of this book are full of things that wouldn't be possible without your philanthropic efforts. Thank you, and keep up the good work. I hope to return the favor one day.

Finally, I'd like to thank my family and loved ones, who have endured this project with me. I appreciate your patience and unfailing support—even when I haven't been there for you as much as I should have. And, most important, I love you guys!

about this book

Test-driven development was born in the hands and minds of software developers looking for a way to develop software better and faster. This book was written by one such software developer who wishes to make learning TDD easier. Because most of the problems encountered by developers new to TDD relate to overcoming technical hindrances, we've taken an extremely hands-on approach. Not only do we explain TDD through an extended hands-on example, but we also devote several chapters to showing you how to write unit tests for technology that's generally considered difficult to test. First-hand experiences will be the biggest learning opportunities you'll encounter, but this book can act as the catalyst that gets you past the steepest learning curve.

Audience

This book is aimed at Java programmers of all experience levels who are looking to improve their productivity and the quality of the code they develop. Test-driven development lets you unleash your potential by offering a solid framework for building software reliably in small increments. Regardless of whether you're creating a missile-control system or putting together the next YouTube, you can benefit from adopting TDD.

Our second intended audience includes Java programmers who aren't necessarily interested in TDD but who are looking for help in putting their code under test. Test-driven development is primarily a design and development technique; but writing unit tests is such an essential activity in TDD that this book will lend you a hand during pure test-writing, too—we cover a lot of (so-called) difficult-to-test technologies such as data-access code, concurrent programs, and user-interface code.

Whether you're simply looking to get the job done or have a larger goal of personal improvement in mind, we hope you'll find this book helpful.

Roadmap

You're reading a book that covers a lot of ground. In order to structure the material, we've divided the book into three parts with distinct focuses. Part 1 introduces the book's main topics—test-driven development and acceptance test-driven development—starting with the very basics.

Chapter 1 begins with a problem statement—the challenges we need to overcome—and explains how TDD and acceptance TDD provide an effective solution in the form of test-first programming, evolutionary design, test automation, and merciless refactoring.

Chapter 2 gets our hands dirty, extending our understanding of TDD through an in-depth example: a homegrown template engine we test-drive from scratch. Along the way, we discuss how to manage the tests we want to write in a test list and how to select the next test from that list.

Chapter 3 finishes what chapter 2 started, continuing the development of the template engine through an extensive design change, starting with a spike—a learning experiment—and then proceeding to make the change to the template engine in a controlled, disciplined manner.

Chapter 4 brings our perspective back to a higher level to explain the strategies in our toolkit, from selecting tests to making them pass. We also talk about essential testing concepts such as fixtures, test doubles, and the differences between state- and interaction-based testing. After giving some guidelines for creating testable designs, chapter 4 ends with an overview of a number of key test patterns and a section on working in a test-first manner with legacy code.

Part 2 is about getting dirty again, demonstrating through working examples how we can apply TDD when working with a variety of technologies that are sometimes referred to as being "difficult to test-drive." After part 2, you'll know that folks who say that don't know what they're talking about!

Chapter 5 starts our journey through the trenches of web development. We learn to test-drive request/response-style web layers using plain old Java Servlets and Spring Controllers, and we learn to test-drive the presentation layer built with JavaServer Pages and Apache Velocity templates. The chapter also contrasts these request/response examples with test-driving web applications using a component-based framework, Apache Wicket.

Chapter 6 explains how to test-drive the data-access layer behind our web components. We'll see examples of test-driving data-access objects based on raw JDBC code, the Spring Framework's JdbcTemplate API, and the de facto object-relational mapping (ORM) tool, Hibernate. We'll also discuss how to deal with the database in our unit tests and how to fill in the gaps with integration tests. Finally, we share a few tricks for dealing with the file system.

Chapter 7 takes us to the land of the unknown: nondeterministic behavior. After first examining our options for faking time, we turn our attention to multithreading. We begin with a discussion of what we can and should test for, exploring topics such as thread safety, blocking operations, starting and stopping threads, and asynchronous execution. Our trip to the world of the unpredictable ends with a tour of the new synchronization objects from `java.util.concurrent` that were introduced in Java 5.

Chapter 8 is about face—the face of Java Swing applications, that is. Again, we begin by figuring out what we should test for when test-driving UI code. Then, we look at three design patterns that make our test-driven lives easier, and we briefly introduce two open source tools—Jemmy and Abbot—for unit-testing Swing components. We finish chapter 8 (and part 2) with an extended example, test-driving the face and behavior for a custom Swing component.

Part 3 is a change of tempo. We move from the concrete world of test-driving objects and classes into the fuzzier world of building whole systems in a test-first manner with acceptance TDD.

Chapter 9 gets us going with an introduction to user stories for managing requirements, and to the essence of acceptance tests. Once we're up to speed with the *what*, we focus on the *how*—the process of acceptance TDD and what it requires from the team. We also crystallize the benefits of and the reasons for developing software with acceptance TDD. The chapter ends with a discussion of what kinds of aspects our acceptance tests should specify about the system we're building and an overview of some of the tools in our disposal.

Chapter 10 makes acceptance TDD more concrete by taking a closer look at Fit, a popular acceptance-testing tool. Our Fit tutorial begins with a description of how the developer can use Fit to collaborate with the customer, first sketching acceptance tests in a tabular format and then touching them up into syntax recognized by Fit. We then see how to implement the backing code that glues our tabular tests into interaction with the system, first going through the three standard fixtures built into Fit and then looking at additional utilities provided by the FitLibrary, an extension to Fit. Finally, we learn to run our precious Fit tests from the command line and as part of an Apache Ant build.

Chapter 11 expands our perspective by looking at a number of strategies for implementing our acceptance tests independent of the tools in use. After going through our options for connecting tests to the system we're developing, we discuss the kinds of limitations and opportunities that technology puts in our way. We also share some tips for speeding up acceptance tests and keeping complexity in check.

Chapter 12 ends part 3 as a black sheep of sorts—a chapter on ensuring the success of TDD adoption. We begin by exploring what ingredients should be in place for us to achieve lasting change, both for ourselves and for our peers. We then focus on resistance: how to recognize it and how to deal with it. Finally, we go through a long list of things in our toolbox that can facilitate the successful adoption we're seeking.

Because writing unit tests is so central to test-driven development, we've also provided three brief tutorials on some of the essential tools; you can use them as cheat sheets. Appendices A and B are for the JUnit unit-testing framework, illustrating the syntax for versions 4.3 and 3.8, respectively. Appendix C does the same for EasyMock, a dynamic mock-object framework we can use to generate smart test doubles.

Test-driving code in the comfort of our favorite IDE is cool, but we need to make those tests part of our automated build. That's why we've included appendix D: a brief tutorial for running JUnit tests with Apache Ant, the standard build tool for Java developers.

Code conventions

The code examples presented in this book consist of Java source code as well as a host of markup languages and output listings. We present the longer pieces of code as listings with their own headers. Smaller bits of code are run inline with the text. In all cases, we present the code using a `monospaced` font, to differentiate it from the rest of the text. In part 2, we frequently refer from the text to elements in code listings. Such references are also presented using a `monospaced` font, to make them stand out from plain English. Many longer listings also have numbered annotations that we refer to in the text.

Code downloads

The complete example code for the book can be downloaded from the Manning website page for this book, at http://www.manning.com/koskela. This includes the source code shown in the book as well as the omitted parts-everything you need to play and tinker with the code, taking it further from where we left off, or tearing it into pieces for a closer autopsy.

The download includes a Maven 2 POM file and instructions for installing and using Maven (http://maven.apache.org) to compile and run the examples. Note that the download doesn't include the various dependencies, and you need to have an Internet connection when running the Maven build for the first time—Maven will then download all the required dependencies from the Internet. After that, you're free to disconnect and play with the examples offline.

The code examples were written against Java 5, so you'll need to have that installed in order to compile and run the examples. You can download a suitable Java environment from http://java.sun.com/javase. (To compile the code, you'll need to download the JDK, not the JRE.)

We seriously recommend installing a proper IDE as well. The example code comes in the form of an Eclipse project, so you may want to download and install the latest and greatest version of Eclipse (http://www.eclipse.org). Other mainstream tools such as IntelliJ IDEA (http://www.jetbrains.com/idea) and NetBeans (http://www.netbeans.org) should work fine, too—you'll just need to configure the project yourself.

Online chapter

There's one hot topic that we don't cover in the 12 chapters that made their way into the final manuscript: test-driving Enterprise JavaBeans. Instead, we've provided more than 40 pages of detailed advice for developers working with this technology in the form of an extra chapter that's only available online.

This bonus chapter covers Enterprise JavaBeans, ranging from regular session beans we use to encapsulate our applications' business logic to the persistence-oriented entity beans to the asynchronous-message-driven beans and the Timer API.

Although we focus on covering the latest and greatest EJB 3.0 specification, we show some key tips and tricks for both 3.0 and the older 2.x API. We do this because many legacy systems continue to use the 2.x version of the EJB specification, regardless of the massive testability and design improvements introduced in the EJB 3.0 specification.

You can download the bonus chapter from http://www.manning.com/koskela.

What's next?

This book should give you enough ammunition to get going with test-driven development, but there's bound to be a question or two that we haven't managed to answer in full. Fortunately, Manning provides an online forum where you can talk to the authors of Manning titles, including the one you're reading right now. You can reach Lasse at the Author Online forum for *Test Driven* at http://www.manning-sandbox.com/forum.jspa?forumID=306.

Test-driven development is a technique and a methodology that can't be described perfectly in a single written document, be it a short article or a series of books. This is partly because TDD is a technique that evolves together with the practitioner and partly because writing tests—a central activity in TDD—varies so much from one technology domain to the next. There are always new twists or tricks that we could've included but didn't. Thus, it's good to know where to go for further assistance. The *testdrivendevelopment* Yahoo! group is an excellent resource and frequently features interesting discussions about TDD and related issues. If you have a burning question and aren't sure who to ask, ask the mailing list!

If tapping into the Yahoo! group isn't enough to satisfy your need for passive information-gathering about what's happening in the community, I also suggest subscribing your feed reader to http://www.testdriven.com, a web portal focused on TDD. This portal gives you a heads-up about any relevant new article, blog entry, or development tool that appears on the scene. And, of course, many of the industry conferences on agile methods feature content about or related to TDD, so why not start attending those if you haven't already?

I'm looking forward to seeing you join the TDD community!

Author Online

Purchase of *Test Driven* includes free access to a private web forum run by Manning Publications, where you can make comments about the book, ask technical questions, and receive help from the author and from other users. To access the forum and subscribe to it, point your web browser to http://www.manning.com/koskela. This page provides information on how to get on the forum once you are registered, what kind of help is available, and the rules of conduct on the forum.

Manning's commitment to our readers is to provide a venue where a meaningful dialogue between individual readers and between readers and the author can take place. It is not a commitment to any specific amount of participation on the part of the author, whose contribution to the book's forum remains voluntary (and unpaid). We suggest you try asking the author some challenging questions, lest his interest stray!

The Author Online forum and the archives of previous discussions will be accessible from the publisher's website as long as the book is in print.

about the cover illustration

The figure on the cover of *Test Driven* is a *Franc Comtois*, an inhabitant of the Free County of Burgundy in northeastern France. This territory of Burgundy was an independent state for a large part of its history, becoming permanently ceded to France only in the seventeenth century. The region has its own traditions and language, called Franc-Comtois, which is still spoken today.

The illustration is taken from a French travel book, *Encyclopedie des Voyages* by J. G. St. Saveur, published in 1796. Travel for pleasure was a relatively new phenomenon at the time and travel guides such as this one were popular, introducing both the tourist as well as the armchair traveler to the inhabitants of other regions of France and abroad.

The diversity of the drawings in the *Encyclopedie des Voyages* speaks vividly of the uniqueness and individuality of the world's towns and provinces just 200 years ago. This was a time when the dress codes of two regions separated by a few dozen miles identified people uniquely as belonging to one or the other. The travel guide brings to life a sense of isolation and distance of that period and of every other historic period except our own hyperkinetic present. Dress codes have changed since then and the diversity by region, so rich at the time, has faded away. It is now often hard to tell the inhabitant of one continent from another. Perhaps, trying to view it optimistically, we have traded a cultural and visual diversity for a more varied personal life. Or a more varied and interesting intellectual and technical life.

We at Manning celebrate the inventiveness, the initiative, and the fun of the computer business with book covers based on the rich diversity of regional life two centuries ago brought back to life by the pictures from this travel guide.

Part 1

A TDD primer

Part 1 is a test-driven development (TDD) primer, giving you a kick start in the art of test driving. In chapter 1, you'll learn about both TDD and its big brother, acceptance TDD, from the very basics, getting an overview of both techniques. Chapter 2 takes you deeper into the test-first realm through a hands-on tutorial that you can follow on your computer, editing and running actual code as we go along. Chapter 3 continues on this path, developing the hands-on example further by throwing in a larger-scale refactoring that introduces significant changes to our design.

While teaching TDD to dozens and dozens of programmers over the years, I've learned that practice is a better teacher than I am. By the time you've implemented a fully capable template engine through chapters 2 and 3, you'll be ready to add some heavily guarded trade secrets to your toolbox. Chapter 4 expands our idea of TDD with a number of tips and tricks, from selecting the next test to different ways of making it pass. Design guidelines and testing tools will get the coverage they deserve, too.

1 The big picture

I can stand brute force, but brute reason is quite unbearable.

—Oscar Wilde

"Only ever write code to fix a failing test." That's test-driven development, or TDD,[1] in one sentence. First we write a test, then we write code to make the test pass. Then we find the best possible design for what we have, relying on the existing tests to keep us from breaking things while we're at it. This approach to building software encourages good design, produces testable code, and keeps us away from over-engineering our systems because of flawed assumptions. And all of this is accomplished by the simple act of driving our design each step of the way with executable tests that move us toward the final implementation.

This book is about learning to take those small steps. Throughout the chapters, we'll learn the principles and intricacies of TDD, we'll learn to develop Java and Enterprise Java applications with TDD, and we'll learn to drive our overall development process with an extension to the core idea of TDD with what we call acceptance test-driven development (acceptance TDD or ATDD). We will drive development on the feature level by writing functional or acceptance tests for a feature before implementing the feature with TDD.

As a way of applying tests for more than just verification of the correctness of software, TDD is not exactly a new invention. Many old-timers have stories to tell about how they used to write the tests before the code, back in the day. Today, this way of developing software has a name—TDD. The majority of this book is dedicated to the "what" and "how" of test-driven development, applied to the various tasks involved in developing software.

In terms of mainstream adoption, however, TDD is still new. Much like today's commodities are yesterday's luxury items, a programming and design technique often starts as the luxury of a few experienced practitioners and then is adopted by the masses some years later when the pioneers have proven and shaped the technique. The technique becomes business as usual rather than a niche for the adventurous.

I believe that mainstream adoption of TDD is getting closer every day. In fact, I believe it has already started, and I hope that this book will make the landing a bit less bumpy.

We'll start by laying out the challenge to deliver software using the current state of the practice in software development. Once we're on the same page about what we'd like to accomplish and what's standing in our way, we'll create a roadmap for exploring how TDD and acceptance TDD can help resolve those problems, and

---

[1] The acronym TDD is sometimes expanded to Test-Driven Design. Another commonly used term for what we refer to as TDD is Test-First Programming. They're just different names for the same thing.

we'll look at the kinds of tools we might want to employ during our journey becoming to master craftspeople.

1.1 The challenge: solving the right problem right

The function of software development is to support the operations and business of an organization. Our focus as professional software developers should be on delivering systems that help our organizations improve their effectiveness and throughput, that lower the operational costs, and so forth.

Looking back at my years as a professional software developer and at the decades of experience documented in printed literature and as evidenced by craftsmen's war stories around the world, we can only conclude that most organizations could do a lot better in the task of delivering systems that support their business. In short, we're building systems that don't work quite right; even if they would work without a hitch, they tend to solve the wrong problems. In essence, we're writing code that fails to meet actual needs.

Next, let's look at how creating poorly written code and missing the moving target of the customer's actual needs are parts of the challenge of being able to deliver a working solution to the right problem.

1.1.1 Creating poorly written code

Even after several decades of advancements in the software industry, the quality of the software produced remains a problem. Considering the recent years' focus on time to market, the growth in the sheer volume of software being developed, and the stream of new technologies to absorb, it is no surprise that software development organizations have continued to face quality problems.

There are two sides to these quality problems: high defect rates and lack of maintainability.

Riddled with defects

Defects create unwanted costs by making the system unstable, unpredictable, or potentially completely unusable. They reduce the value of the software we deliver—sometimes to the point of creating more damage than value.

The way we try to get rid of defects is through testing—we see if the software works, and then we try to break it somehow. Testing has been established as a critical ingredient in software development, but the way testing is traditionally performed—a lengthy testing phase after the code is "frozen"—leaves much room for improvement. For instance, the cost of fixing defects that get caught during testing is typically a magnitude or two higher than if we'd caught them as they were introduced into the code base. Having defects means we're not able to deliver. The slower and the more costly it is to find and fix defects, the less able we become.

Defects might be the most obvious problem with poorly written code, but such code is also a nightmare to maintain and slow and costly to develop further.

Nightmare to maintain, slow to develop

Well-written code exhibits good design and a balanced division of responsibilities without duplication—all the good stuff. Poorly written code doesn't, and working with it is a nightmare in many aspects. One of them is that the code is difficult to understand and, thus, difficult to change. As if that wasn't enough of a speed bump, changing problematic code tends to break functionality elsewhere in the system, and duplication wreaks havoc in the form of bugs that were supposed to be fixed already. The list goes on.

"I don't want to touch that. It'll take forever, and I don't know what will break if I do." This is a very real problem because software needs to change. Rather than rewrite every time we need to change existing code or add new code, we need to be able to build on what we have. That's what maintainability is all about, and that's what enables us to meet a business's changing needs. With unmaintainable code we're moving slower than we'd like, which often leads to the ever-increasing pressure to deliver, which ends up making us deliver still more poorly written code. That's a vicious cycle that must end if we want to be able to consistently deliver.

As if these problems weren't enough, there's still the matter of failing to meet actual needs. Let's talk about that.

1.1.2 Failing to meet actual needs

Nobody likes buying a pig in a poke.[2] Yet the customers of software development groups have been constantly forced to do just that. In exchange for a specification, the software developers have set off to build what the specification describes—only to find out 12 months later that the specification didn't quite match what the customer intended back then. Not to mention that, especially in the modern day's hectic world of business, the customer's current needs are significantly different from what they were last year.

As a result of this repeated failure to deliver what the customer needs, we as an industry have devised new ways of running software projects. We've tried working harder (and longer) to create the specification, which has often made things even

[2] A sack. Don't buy a pig in a sack.

worse, considering that the extended period of time to a delivered system leaves even more time for the world to change around the system. Plus, nailing down even more details early on has a connection to building a house of cards. Errors in the specification can easily bring down the whole project as assumptions are built on assumptions.

Our industry's track record makes for gloomy reading. There's no need to fall into total depression, however, because there are known cures to these problems. Agile software development,[3] including methods such as Extreme Programming (XP) and Scrum, represents the most effective antidote I am aware of. The rest of this book will give us a thorough understanding of a key ingredient of the agility provided by these methods—being test-driven.

1.2 Solution: being test-driven

Just like the problem we're facing has two parts to it—poorly written code and failure to meet actual needs—the solution we're going to explore in the coming chapters is two-pronged as well. On one hand, we need to learn how to build the thing right. On the other, we need to learn how to build the right thing. The solution I'm describing in this book—being test-driven—is largely the same for both hands. The slight difference between the two parts to the solution is in *how* we take advantage of tests in helping us to create maintainable, working software that meets the customer's actual, present needs.

On a lower level, we test-drive code using the technique we call TDD. On a higher level—that of features and functionality—we test-drive the system using a similar technique we call acceptance TDD. Figure 1.1 describes this combination from the perspective of improving both *external* and *internal quality*.

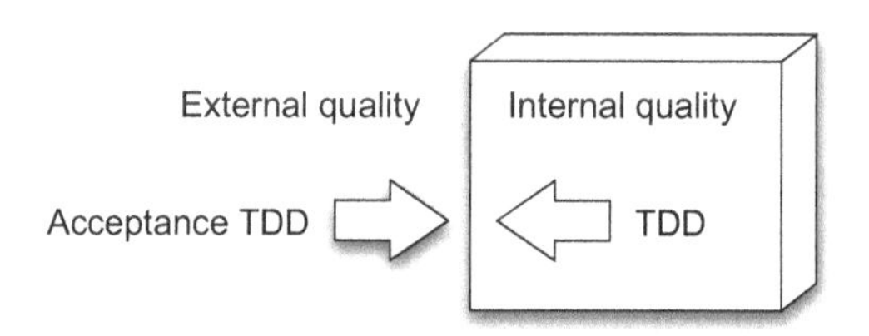

Figure 1.1
TDD is a technique for improving the software's internal quality, whereas acceptance TDD helps us keep our product's external quality on track by giving it the correct features and functionality.

[3] Refer to *Agile & Iterative Development: A Manager's Guide* (Addison-Wesley, 2003) by Craig Larman for a good introduction to agile methods.

As we can see from figure 1.1, these two distinct levels on which we test-drive the software collectively improve both the product's internal quality and the external, or perceived, quality. In the following sections, we'll discover how TDD and acceptance TDD accomplish these improvements. Before we dig deeper into the techniques, let's first concentrate on how these techniques help us overcome the challenge of being able to deliver.

1.2.1 High quality with TDD

TDD is a way of programming that encourages good design and is a disciplined process that helps us avoid programming errors. TDD does so by making us write small, automated tests, which eventually build up a very effective alarm system for protecting our code from regression. You cannot add quality into software after the fact, and the short development cycle that TDD promotes is well geared toward writing high-quality code from the start.

The short cycle is different from the way we're used to programming. We've always designed first, then implemented the design, and then tested the implementation somehow—usually not too thoroughly. (After all, we're good programmers and don't make mistakes, right?) TDD turns this thinking around and says we should write the test first and only then write code to reach that clear goal. Design is what we do last. We look at the code we have and find the simplest design possible.

The last step in the cycle is called *refactoring*. Refactoring is a disciplined way of transforming code from one state or structure to another, removing duplication, and gradually moving the code toward the best design we can imagine. By constantly refactoring, we can grow our code base and evolve our design incrementally.

If you're not quite sure what we're talking about with the TDD cycle, don't worry. We'll take a closer look at this cycle in section 1.3.

To recap what we've learned about TDD so far, it is a programming technique that helps us write thoroughly tested code and evolve our code with the best design possible at each stage. TDD simply helps us avoid the vicious circle of poorly written code. Prong number one of the test-driven solution!

Speaking of quality, let's talk a bit about that rather abstract concept and what it means for us.

Quality comes in many flavors

Evidenced by the quality assurance departments of the corporate world of today, people tend to associate the word *quality* with the number of defects found after using the software. Some consider quality to be other things such as the degree to which the software fulfills its users' needs and expectations. Some consider not just the externally visible quality but also the internal qualities of the software in question (which translate to external qualities like the cost of development, maintenance, and so forth). TDD contributes to improved quality in all of these aspects with its design-guiding and quality-oriented nature.

Quite possibly the number one reason for a defect to slip through to production is that there was no test verifying that that particular execution path through our code indeed works as it should. (Another candidate for that unwanted title is our laziness: not running all of the tests or running them a bit sloppily, thereby letting a bug crawl through.)

TDD remedies this situation by making sure that there's practically no code in the system that is not required—and therefore executed—by the tests. Through extensive test coverage and having all of those tests automated, TDD effectively guarantees that whatever you have written a test for works, and the quality (in terms of defects) becomes more of a function of how well we succeed in coming up with the right test cases.

One significant part of that task is a matter of testing skills—our ability to derive test cases for the normal cases, the corner cases, the foreseeable user errors, and so forth. The way TDD can help in this regard is by letting us focus on the public interfaces for our modules, classes, and what have you. By not knowing what the implementation looks like, we are better positioned to think out of the box and focus on how the code should behave and how the developer of the client code would—or could—use it, either on purpose or by mistake.

TDD's attention to quality of both code and design also has a significant effect on how much of our precious development time is spent fixing defects rather than, say, implementing new functionality or improving the existing code base's design.

Less time spent fixing defects

TDD helps us speed up by reducing the time it takes to fix defects. It is common sense that fixing a defect two months after its introduction into the system takes time and money—much more than fixing it on the same day it was introduced. Whatever we can do to reduce the number of defects introduced in the first place, and to help us find those defects as soon as they're in, is bound to pay back.

Proceeding test-first in tiny steps makes sure that we will hardly ever need to touch the debugger. We know exactly which couple of lines we added that made the test break and are able to drill down into the source of the problem in no time, avoiding those long debugging sessions we often hear about in fellow programmers' war stories. We're able to fix our defects sooner, reducing the business's cost to the project. With each missed defect costing anywhere from several hundred to several thousand dollars,[4] it's big bucks we're talking here. Not having to spend hours and hours looking at the debugger allows for more time to be spent on other useful activities.

The fact that we are delivering the required functionality faster means that we have more time available for cleaning up our code base, getting up to speed on the latest developments in tools and technologies, catching up with our coworkers, and so forth—more time available to improve quality, confidence, and speed. These are all things that feed back into our ability to test-drive effectively. It's a virtuous cycle, and once you're on it, there seems to be no end to the improvements!

We'll soon talk about further benefits of adopting and practicing TDD—the benefits for you and me as programmers—but before we go there, let's talk a bit about the second prong of our solution to the aforementioned challenge of being able to deliver: acceptance TDD.

1.2.2 Meeting needs with acceptance TDD

TDD helps us build code with high technical quality—code that does what we expect it to do and code that's easy to understand and work with. The correctness of the code we develop with TDD, however, is tested for isolated blocks of logic rather than for features and system capabilities. Furthermore, even the best code written test-first can implement the wrong thing, something the customer doesn't really need. That's where acceptance test-driven development comes into the picture. The traditional way of adding features into a system is to first write a requirements document of some kind, proceed with implementation, have the development team test the feature, and then have the customer acceptance-test the feature. Acceptance TDD differs from this method by moving the testing function before the implementation, as shown in figure 1.2. In other words, we translate a requirement into a set of executable tests and then do the implementation against the tests rather than against the developer's interpretation of a verbal requirement.

Acceptance TDD provides the missing ingredient to delivering a good product by bridging the gap between the programmer and the customer. Rather than working off of arbitrary requirements documents, in acceptance TDD we strive for close collaboration and defining explicit, unambiguous tests that tell us exactly what it means when we say a feature is "done." By defining the desired functionality in very

[4] http://www.jrothman.com/Papers/Costtofixdefect.html.

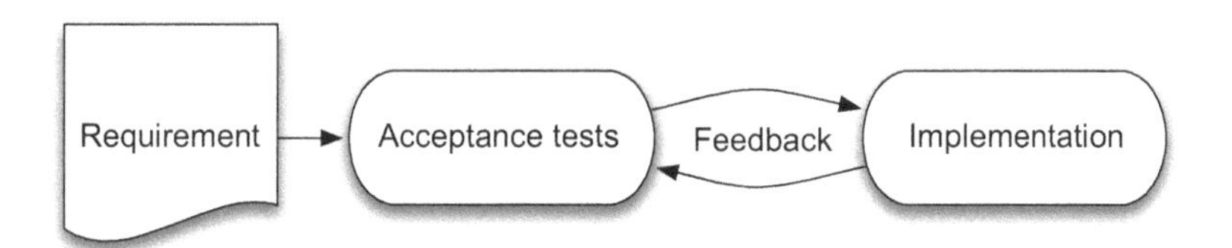

Figure 1.2 Acceptance test-driven development drives implementation of a requirement through a set of automated, executable acceptance tests.

concrete terms—via executable tests—we are effectively ensuring that we're delivering what the customer needs.

The process is much like the TDD cycle on the code level. With acceptance TDD, we're just talking about tests for the behavior of a system rather than tests for the behavior of objects. This difference also means that we need to speak a language that both the programmer and the customer understand.

TDD and acceptance TDD often go hand in hand. On the system level, we run our development process with acceptance TDD; and inside the implementation step of each feature; we employ TDD. They are by no means tightly coupled, but they are powerful in combination and they do fit together seamlessly.

We should now have an idea of how TDD and acceptance TDD team together for a solution to the challenge of being able to deliver high-quality software that targets the right need. We'll soon study in more detail what TDD is, how it helps us create high-quality code, and how to build it right. In section 1.4, we'll talk more about how we can let tests drive our development on a higher level to help us meet our customers' needs—to build the right thing—with acceptance TDD. Before going farther, though, let's talk a bit about how we, as programmers, benefit from working test-first.

1.2.3 *What's in it for me?*

We don't buy a new car for no reason, and we definitely shouldn't adopt a new development technique just because it exists. There has to be something valuable—something that improves our productivity—in order for it to make sense for us to take on learning a new way of doing our job. We already know that TDD and acceptance TDD help us produce higher-quality software that meets our customers' needs. Let's spell out to ourselves how these techniques make our personal work experience more enjoyable.

I can easily identify at least three clear benefits I have personally gained from having adopted TDD back in the day:

- I rarely get a support call or end up in a long debugging session.
- I feel confident in the quality of my work.
- I have more time to develop as a professional.

Let me explain what I mean by these benefits.

No more long debugging sessions

I still remember a particular programming task a few years back. I got the task of fixing a defect in a homegrown parser for a proprietary file format. I read hundreds and hundreds of lines of code, going back and forth as I was trying to come to grips with the design; eventually figured I knew what needed to be done.

Not yet having adopted TDD at that time, I started molding the parser toward the new design I had envisioned that would get rid of the defect and make the parser easier to understand as a nice bonus. It took a couple of hours to get the new design in place and the code base compiling. Full of excitement about my ultra-smart design, I tabbed to a terminal window to install the parser to a test server. And? The darn parser didn't work. It just did not work, and I had no idea why. I ran the code in a debugger, but I still couldn't figure out the problem. I'm pretty sure it took more than a couple of hours of stepping through the code again and again with the debugger before I found and fixed the problem. And it turned out to be a rather trivial one. Tired, hungry, and slightly pissed off, I left the office cursing my blindness for the error.

It was much later that I realized the problem was not with my blindness but the way I approached the task—the process, if you will—by taking way too big a step, effectively losing sight of the tree from the woods. If I had written small, focused tests along the way as we do with TDD, I would've spotted the error immediately after writing the flawed branching construct.

As if the deadly debugging session wasn't enough, Murphy's Law[5] proved itself yet again. I soon got a rather angry call due to the parser crashing in a customer's production environment. It turns out that I had introduced at least one major defect into the parser as I changed its design. It's one thing to know that your code could exhibit a better design. It's another thing to be awakened at 3:00 a.m. from sleep by an angry account manager who was just awakened by an even angrier customer.

I would've slept at least two hours more that night—and better—if only I had used a technique like TDD or, at the very least, written proper tests for the parser.

[5] Murphy's Law: If something bad can happen, it will happen.

That particular incident raised my interest in testing my changes significantly because I was suddenly painfully aware of having had false confidence in my work. And I like to feel confident with my work.

Feeling confident with my work

Deep down, we want to write code that works. Our job might be at stake if we deliver code that's too buggy. On the other hand, we want to write code as fast as possible. Our livelihood might also be at stake if we take too long writing the code. As a result, we often have to decide when we are confident enough about the code we're writing to release it and move on to our next task.

For a moment, let's take a trip down memory lane. Think about a programming session you've experienced, writing some piece—any piece—of code that needed to work or bad things would happen. Take a minute to reminisce about that moment.

How did you go about writing that code? Did you design it first on a notepad? Did you write the code in one burst, getting it right the first time, or did you go back and start over? Did you spot an obvious error in your loop? Did it compile at first try?

How did you verify that the particular piece of code worked? Did you write a `main` method just for testing? Did you click through the user interface to see that the functionality was there? Did you spot errors in your tests? Did you step through the code in a debugger? Did you have to go back multiple times to fix some small issues? Overall, how long did it take to test it compared to writing the code itself?

Whatever your answers were for these questions, I hope you've got some idea right now of the kind of things and activities you have done in order to crank out code that you trust—code that you're confident works. With this in mind, I have a question for you.

What if you could be confident that any code you release contains *exactly* zero defects? If you could know that your code works *exactly* how the specification says it should, would your stress level come falling down? Mine has. What if you could speed up the slow parts of that programming session you were thinking about—while increasing your confidence in the code's correctness? Could you envision working that way *all the time*?

I cannot promise that adopting TDD would make your software defect-free. In the end it's you who's writing the code, and it's up to you to avoid injecting bugs into your code base. What I can promise, though, is that practicing TDD will make you more confident about your software by letting you know exactly what your code does in which situations.

This added confidence does wonders to the internal quality of our software as well. You might say it's a virtuous cycle. The better your test suite is, the better the quality of your code and the more confident you can be about any changes you make. The more confident you are about the changes you make, the more changes you dare to make. The more changes you make, the better your internal quality becomes, the easier it is to write tests for your code, and so on. Clearly a good thing!

More time for other stuff

TDD and acceptance TDD don't make us type any faster, but they help us cut time from less productive activities such as debugging and cursing at unreadable code, or rework due to misunderstandings regarding requirements. As we proceed in small steps, accumulating tests and becoming more confident about our code, we no longer feel the need to repeat the same tests over and over again "just in case the computer would do something different this time," or feel unsure whether we've checked that odd combination of data that could break things.

The more confidence we have, the faster we can move on to other tasks. Sure, our confidence can sometimes be false, but the occasion when that happens is, in my experience, outweighed by the diminished time we spend pondering whether we have tested the code enough to pass it on or check it in and whether the feature is implemented correctly or not.

TDD and acceptance TDD aren't silver bullets, but they are one of the closest things to that legendary shiny projectile we've seen since the invention of time-sharing machines. In the next section, we'll talk about TDD in more detail. After that, we'll do the same for acceptance TDD.

Let's go.

1.3 Build it right: TDD

So test-driven development is a development and design technique that helps us build up the system incrementally, knowing that we're never far from a working baseline. And a test is our way of taking that next small step.

In this section, we'll learn what makes TDD tick, and we'll elaborate on why it works and what kind of benefits we get from using the technique. It all begins with the TDD cycle, which is the heartbeat of our work. After exploring the TDD cycle, we'll talk about the meaning of having working software all the time, starting from day one. An essential part of building the system incrementally is to design for the present, rather than try to go for a design of the whole system up front. We'll also talk through how TDD helps us do just that. Then, we'll continue with a discussion of what makes this approach feasible—how to keep our software in good health and working, all day, every day.

Let's get going. Next stop, the TDD cycle of *test-code-refactor.*

1.3.1 Test-code-refactor: the heartbeat

As we learned in the first paragraph of this chapter, test-driven development, or TDD, is a programming technique based on a very simple rule:

> *Only ever write code to fix a failing test.*

In other words, write the test first, and only then write the code that makes it pass. This rule is controversial to many of us who have been schooled to first produce a thorough design, then implement the design, and finally test our software in order to find all those bugs we've injected during implementation. TDD turns this cycle around, as illustrated in figure 1.3.

Test first, then code, and design afterward. Does the thought of "designing afterward" feels awkward? That's only natural. It's not the same kind of design we're used to in the traditional design-code-test process. In fact, it's such a different beast that we've given it a different name, too. We call it *refactoring* to better communicate that the last step is about transforming the current design toward a better design. With this little renaming operation, our TDD cycle really looks like that in figure 1.4: *test-code-refactor.*

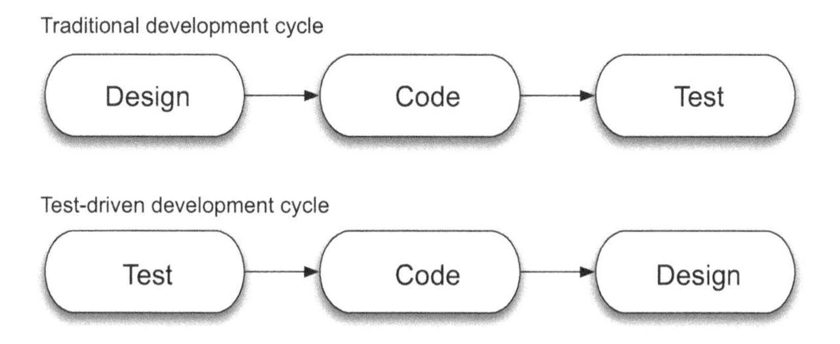

Figure 1.3 TDD turns around the traditional design-code-test sequence. Instead, we test first, then write code, and design afterward.

Figure 1.4 Test-code-refactor is the mantra we test-driven developers like to chant. It describes succinctly what we do, it's easy to spell, and it sounds cool.

In its deceptive simplicity, this little cycle, test-code-refactor, encompasses a significant power to improve the overall quality of our personal software process and, subsequently, that of the whole team, project, and organization.

Red-green-refactor

Red-green-refactor is an alternative mnemonic for the *TDD cycle* of writing a test, making it pass, and making it pretty. What's with the colors, you ask?

When we begin the TDD cycle by writing a test, it fails. It fails because our system is broken right now; it doesn't have all the functionality we want it to have. In some development environments, it fails by displaying a red bar—thus the *red* in the mnemonic.

In the second step, making it pass, we implement the missing functionality so that all tests pass—both the one we just added and all the ones we had already. At this time, the red bar turns to green, which takes us to *green* in the mnemonic.

The last part of the cycle, *refactor*, is just that—refactoring. As we improve the design of the code without altering its external behavior, all tests should pass and, thus, we should remain green.

Red, green, green. Red, green, refactor. Quite catchy, isn't it?

We'll take a closer look at this cycle in chapter 2, but let's do a quick overview of what we do in each of these three steps and why we do them. Then we'll explore further the rationale and dynamics behind the technique.

First we write a test

When we write a test in the first step of the TDD cycle, we're really doing more than just writing a test. We're making design decisions. We're designing the API—the interface for accessing the functionality we're testing. By writing the test before the code it's testing, we are forcing ourselves to think hard about how we want the code to be used. It's a bit like putting together a jigsaw puzzle. As illustrated by figure 1.5, it's difficult to get the piece you need if you don't know the pieces with which it should connect.

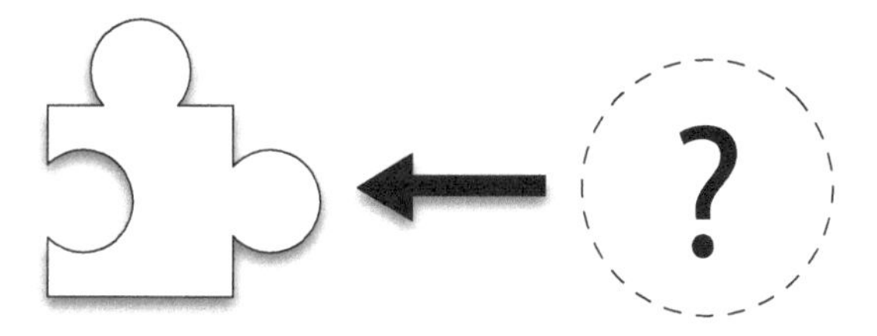

Figure 1.5
How do we know what our interface should be like if we don't try to use it? We don't. Writing the test before the code makes us think about our design from the code user's (the developer's) perspective, leading to a usable API.

That's not something to be taken lightly. You may have heard user-interface specialists talk about how important it is to design user interfaces for the user. Why should things be any different for the internals of our software? Aren't we—the programmers—users of our code just like end users are users of our software?

This way of thinking about code can sometimes make a huge difference. I've often looked at the API of some third-party library and wondered how the heck I'm supposed to use it. I'm pretty confident that many of those APIs haven't been designed with the user in mind, but rather on the terms of the programmers developing the library. One of the fundamental lessons in designing an interface is that we only evaluate a design effectively and objectively when we try to use it. By writing the test first, we are ensuring that we will not miss that feedback.

NOTE Granularity of the tests we write is also something to pay attention to. We strive to write just enough test code to have a failing test rather than write an epic-sized test for a piece of functionality that'll take an hour to implement. Depending on the domain, tools, and technologies in question, writing the test might be a matter of a few seconds or it might take a couple of minutes. The implementation for a test should generally be within that time range, too. Using complex technologies might push our granularity and rhythm toward the longer end of the range, but, as we will see in part 2, most of the time all the talk about the complexity associated with stuff like Java Servlets or data access code is really just that: talk.

It's not easy to create simple-to-use APIs. That's why we need all the help we can get. As it turns out, driving our design with tests is extremely effective and produces modular, testable code. Because we're writing the test first, we have no choice but to make the code testable. By definition, the code we write *is* testable—otherwise it wouldn't exist!

The design of software is not just about structure. It's also about the suitability of the software for the current needs. Software that knows how to boil water, cook rice, deep-fry vegetables, and marinate a chicken is not the perfect match for someone who's only interested in getting a cup of tea. While it probably doesn't bother you that your car's engine has two extra valves on stand-by for those occasions when extra acceleration is needed, it certainly would bother you if you needed to change all the valves from your engine. That's the cost of over-engineering software.

You're spending money on developing stuff that's not really needed, and you're spending money on having to deal with the added complexity while working on that over-engineered piece of code. You aren't going to need it yet, so why put it in? Instead, put those extras on a list somewhere so you don't forget them. It might be that many of them never end up in the software—and for a good reason.

One way tests drive the design in TDD is that they tell you exactly what your software needs to be able to do *now*. Not tomorrow, not yesterday—now. Proceeding in these small steps, implementing just enough functionality to get that next test passing, we are in control of our software and its design. We have the safety net of automated tests to make sure we don't stumble in the dark, we have the clear sight of where we need to go, and we have the confidence that we're implementing stuff that matters and stuff that we need right now.

This theme of focusing on the present is central to TDD. Indeed, the theme repeats itself in the second step of the TDD cycle, writing just enough code.

Then we write just enough code

The second step of the TDD cycle is to write just enough code to make the test pass. Why just enough code? The test we've written is a test that's failing. It's pointing out a gap between what the code does and what we expect it to do. It's a small gap, which we should be able to close in a few minutes, which, in turn, means that the code is never broken for long.

One of the fundamental ideas behind the concept of test-first development is to let the tests show you what to implement in order to make progress on developing the software. You're not just coding away, oblivious to the requirements of the piece of code you're writing. You're satisfying an explicit, unambiguous requirement expressed by a test. You're making progress, and you've got a passing test to show for it.

It's worth noting that when we write just enough code, our main goal is to make the test pass as quickly as possible. That often means an implementation that's not optimal. And that's OK. We'll take care of all that after we have the desired behavior in place—and tests to prove it. With the tests as our safety net, we can then proceed to improving the design in the last step of the TDD cycle: refactoring.

And then we refactor

The final step of the TDD cycle of test-code-refactor is when we take a step back, look at our design, and figure out ways of making it better. The refactoring step is what makes TDD sustainable. We could consider TDD without refactoring to be a good way of producing ugly code. Thoroughly tested ugly code, but still. The ugliness is directly proportionate to our productivity in working with and further developing the code, which makes it pretty darn important to not forget to refactor. In fact, it's so important that we'll dedicate a whole section to talking about refactoring in more detail.

Before we go there, though, let's explore the big picture of developing software in small increments.

1.3.2 Developing in small increments

A common tenet of agile methods is that they all suggest producing a potentially deployable product as soon as possible—regardless of how little functionality it has—and to keep on cranking out those deployable versions every day (some projects have reported building a release package of their software several times a day) until the project is finished. This practice makes sure that when the deadline comes, you have something you can deliver and that works. It might not have all the features the customer asked for, and it might not have everything your iteration plan said it would, but at least you've got something—and something that works.

Figure 1.6 shows an incremental progression of working, tested functionality where the inventory of non-integrated, unfinished work is very small at any given point in time.

Too many projects have pushed back their deadline again and again, eventually getting canceled, without delivering a single line of working code. By building your product in small increments, iteration by iteration, you don't have to worry about not making the deadline because you have a working (albeit not feature-complete) system starting from the first iteration. Similarly, too many projects have delivered buggy code as a result of a last-minute rush of getting it together for the deadline.

TDD removes this problem by proceeding in small steps, each of which results in a working product that's one small step closer to the desired behavior. Because these steps are so small (calculated in minutes rather than hours or days), we don't end up with a pile of random code we need to quickly stitch together. We keep the software working by never letting it go too far away from that state. Likewise, we keep the software lean and mean by designing for the present moment rather than looking too far ahead.

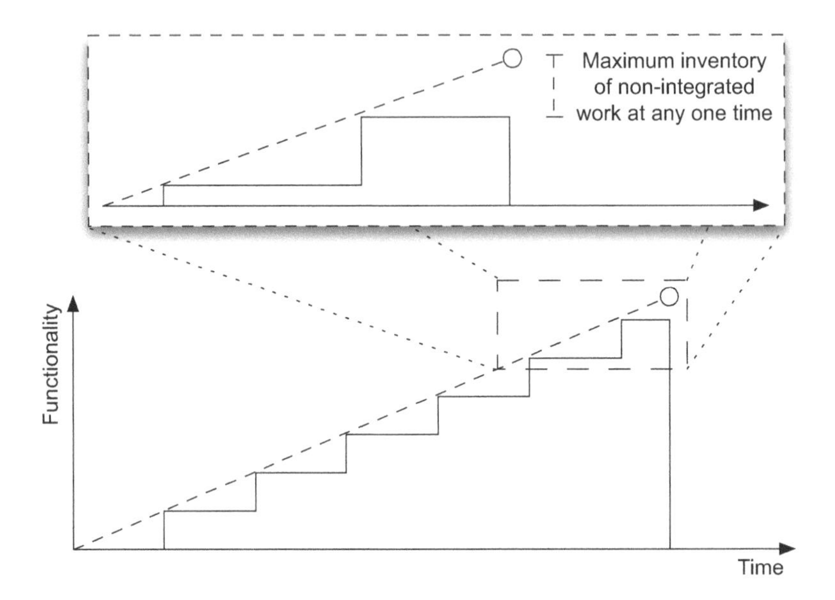

Figure 1.6 With incremental development—building the whole system in small increments—we are never far from an integrated, working code base. This reduces risk, because the inventory of unfinished work remains small. As we'll learn later on, incremental development also enables effective learning through early feedback based on the customer and developers constantly seeing actual, working software.

Building software in increments and, especially, in increments dictated by the perceived cost and benefit of business functionality, is not something you can do with the traditional "design everything up front, considering every possible twist, so that the architecture is rock solid and supports all the features the product will have" approach to design. We can't build the complete, perfect architecture for the envisioned end product in a single run. Only the simplest or most thoroughly understood project makes it possible to get the architecture right early on. We need to iterate, adding to our design a small step at a time.

Figure 1.7 shows how this iterative, incremental process moves back and forth between the small step of adding functionality and adjusting our design—and architecture—to properly accommodate that added functionality.

This is incremental and evolutionary design. Instead of designing as much as we possibly can up front, we design as much as we deem necessary in order to make progress. Instead of thoroughly analyzing all the possible scenarios imaginable before finalizing the design, we opt for making our design decisions based on knowledge—not assumptions—acquired during implementation.

The degree of up-front design necessary before diving into the implementation of the specific feature or capability varies from situation to situation, between

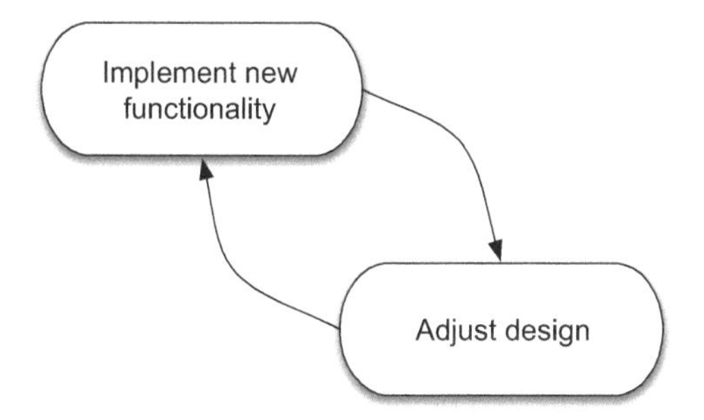

Figure 1.7
Incremental design is about adjusting the code's structure in small increments as more behavior is added. At any stage during the lifetime of the code base, the code exhibits the best design the developers could conceive for supporting the present functionality. This way, we evolve an empirically proven architecture.

teams, between individuals, and between technologies. The key is to keep an eye on whether you're going in the right direction. Big part of your design didn't work out? Cut back on up-front design. Ended up with a design that doesn't scale enough? Turn the up-front design lever up a notch.

You've probably noticed that we keep talking about taking *small* steps. Let's take a closer look at why small is good for us.

Small enough to fit our heads

The rationale behind slicing a bigger goal into small tests is two-fold. First of all, many tasks we face out there in the field are far too big, ambiguous, or outright complex to be manageable. Thus, we need to split them into smaller pieces so they fit our heads better. I don't know about yours, but my mind doesn't handle those big monsters well, and I've heard others say the same thing (I'm hoping they weren't just being polite). Figure 1.8 shows how a complex problem can be simplified into smaller, simpler problems to be solved one at a time.

Let's face it. The majority of people can handle up to five to seven concepts simultaneously in their working memory. Overloading your brain beyond its

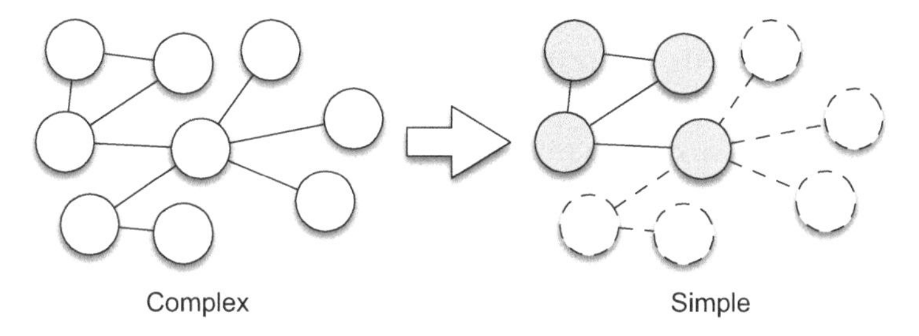

Figure 1.8 We are much better able to grasp complex problems by giving our attention to smaller pieces one at a time.

capacity is bound to result in something getting overlooked while we're swapping things back and forth between the working and long-term memory (or a written document). Having a sequence of smaller steps toward the end goal lets us measure our progress in terms of something concrete, assuming that we will know when each of those steps gets finished—which we do know because we've sliced our overall task into a sequence of small tests that make measurable progress toward the ultimate goal.

TDD by its nature encourages such small steps with evolutionary design. We're constantly improving, changing the design in small increments. In practice, we'll have to build *some* architecture as we go—we'll just need to take that task into consideration when estimating the work.

Let's take a closer look at how evolutionary design works, how it creates a living code base, and what kinds of implications it has for our way of working.

Evolutionary design

Many programmers are familiar with a situation where a piece of code screams for someone to fix it but nobody does. Why? Because that piece of code happens to be part of the interface between two components and is, thus, that much harder to change, so nobody ends up changing it. Evolutionary design is a mindset that requires us to make that change—nurture the living and growing code base instead of protecting it from the bad, bad world that wants change—and thus improve the quality of our design and, indirectly, the quality of the whole system.

So, how does this evolutionary design work? It works in small steps. The suggested amount of up-front design varies from one agile method to another, but the common idea is that you'll only implement architecture that you know you're going to need. In one extreme, you know this only when you start working on a feature that requires, say, an email server. At that point, you know you'll need an email server, so you implement that email service architectural component, install the email server, and so forth. Typically, this kind of architectural change can be added just in time without too much pain. Sometimes, it's not that easy.

Software systems can have certain needs—typically related to performance and/or networking capabilities—that may not be easy to add into the architecture after the fact. For example, splitting a single-user desktop application into a desktop client talking to a multi-user server over the network is something that's bound to take plenty of effort. Similarly, making a batch-processing application support real-time updates on the side might not be the easiest task the team will face.

Then again, these needs don't tend to come to developers as a complete surprise. Although changes in requirements are generally something we cannot anticipate,

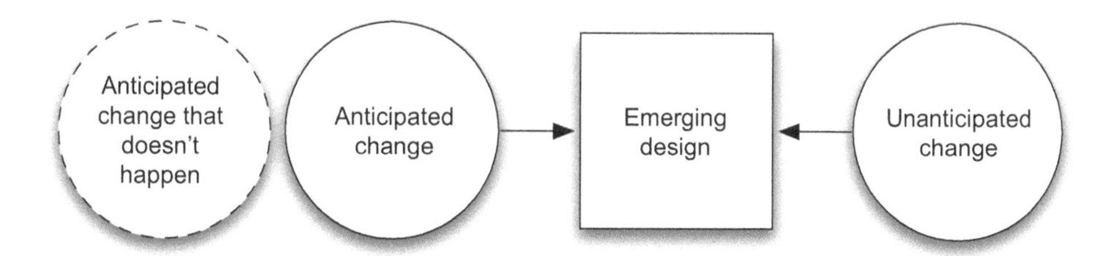

Figure 1.9 The emerging, evolutionary design of a system is influenced by both anticipated and unanticipated change. It's worth noting, though, that a significant amount of anticipated change doesn't happen—or happens in a different form than expected, essentially making it unanticipated change. Our job is to apply common sense and good judgment when preparing for change that we know will happen. A lot of such change never does.

the developers often see beforehand that certain evolution is going to take place at some point, in light of the known requirements. We could call this *anticipated change*. As figure 1.9 points out, though, anticipated change is not *guaranteed* change. Some anticipated change never happens, and some may quickly turn to unanticipated change as the various unknowns reveal surprises.

Evolutionary design does not mean using common sense is prohibited. The developers should make use of what they know within the limits of common sense, with awareness of the uncertainty of change itself, and while keeping in mind what the priorities are.

For example, consider a situation where we know that while the system now needs to handle an hourly batch update over the network from the company's customer relationship management (CRM) system, in a few months it will likely be developed further into real-time integration, passing web service messages over the hypertext transfer protocol (HTTP). With this information, what should we do to accommodate the possible future requirement for real-time integration?

Should we separate the data-processing logic from the data-receiving logic? Definitely! Should we already build the first, batch-based release on top of an application server so that we've got out-of-the-box web services support when the issue of handling web service messages becomes relevant? Perhaps we should, perhaps we shouldn't.

The point here is to make a trade-off between avoiding unnecessary work on something that we don't need and avoiding taking shortcuts now that will come back to bite us. History has shown time and time again that for the most part, evolutionary design is less expensive than trying to get the final design on paper in the beginning.

Discipline required

Again, the amount of up-front work varies from project to project (and it should—one size doesn't fit all), but evolutionary design means that in any case you'll be doing a lot of changes to existing code to make room for the new features you're adding into the system as the iterations go by. With a lot of change happening all the time, we cannot afford having poorly written code. As such, we need plenty of discipline on the part of developers to keep our code from rotting.[6] The good news is that together with its supporting practices, evolutionary design will also help us weed out those problems and eventually stabilize our bug count closer to zero[7] instead of letting us build on a foundation of lurking defects.

What are these supporting practices? In short, it's all about keeping your software in good health—at all times. An essential part of achieving this is refactoring. We already mentioned refactoring in passing as the last step of the TDD cycle of test-code-refactor. For a longer explanation of how refactoring fits into the big picture, read on.

1.3.3 Keeping code healthy with refactoring

Proceeding in small increments means that we're constantly extending the system to do something that its current design might not support. Consequently, we're constantly extending the system's design in ways that might break existing concepts as well as introduce new ones. This, in turn, means that we're bound to end up with a broken design that's inconsistent, unbalanced, difficult to understand, difficult to extend, or otherwise having a bad hair day. If we're out of luck, all of them. And that would seriously hamper our ability to keep delivering software to our customers. Not to worry, though. There is a way to practice evolutionary design without letting the design rot—that way is called *refactoring*.

Quoting Martin Fowler, the author of *Refactoring: Improving the Design of Existing Code* (Addison-Wesley, 1999), refactoring is "a disciplined technique for restructuring an existing body of code, altering its internal structure without changing its external behavior." That description manages to pack a lot of information into such a short sentence. Let's spell it out and see what it's actually telling us about refactoring, shall we?

---

6 http://www.objectmentor.com/resources/articles/Principles_and_Patterns.pdf.

7 No, I'm not going to talk about whether zero-defect software is feasible. Feel free to voice your opinion, though.

Refactoring is disciplined

When *refactoring* (verb), we are not just altering the code's structure but improving the design by altering it in a controlled manner—by applying small behavior-preserving transformations that are called *refactorings* (noun). In other words, refactoring is about applying refactorings on code in a controlled manner. This restructuring can be a significant change to the existing design, but it is always performed in small steps, verifying at each stage that the little transformations we've made have not changed existing behavior.

We don't just change code. We first identify specific problems in the design, and then we select appropriate refactorings and apply them carefully and thoughtfully. We wait until a problem begins to present itself, and only then do we solve it. We don't predict design problems beforehand and prepare for them—that would increase the possibility of creating more problems with our system's design than solving them.

Refactorings are transformations

A refactoring can also be thought of as a transformation between two *states*. The starting state has some characteristic you'd like to get rid of or otherwise improve on, and the target state represents a design that would incorporate that improvement. Figure 1.10 shows an example of a refactoring called Replace Inheritance with Delegation (also documented in Fowler's book) that, as its name implies, moves our design from an inheritance-based solution to a delegation-based solution.

The reason for doing this refactoring might be, for instance, that the subclass is only extending the superclass in order to reuse a small part of its functionality and, as an unwanted side effect, inherits a whole bunch of data and functionality we don't care for.

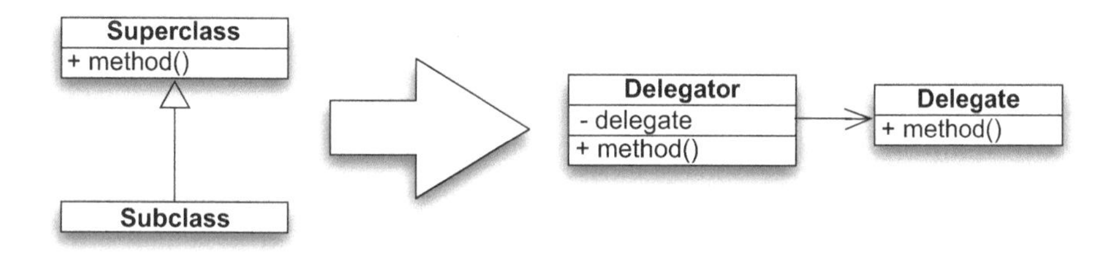

Figure 1.10 Refactorings are transformations between two functionally identical states or structures of the code. Here we see a transformation from using inheritance hierarchy to using a delegate to provide the same functionality while improving the design's fitness for our current needs. These transformations are not absolute improvements—they're simply disciplined transitions from one possible design to another. In fact, for many refactorings there exists a reverse refactoring, making the same transformation in the opposite direction.

Some of these refactorings are so well defined that modern development tools have automated them. This automation has made refactoring evolutionary designs feasible for applications and systems of pretty much any size and complexity. (Can you imagine yourself renaming a method for clarity if that would mean manually checking out some five dozen source files from version control, doing a search-and-replace, and then checking in?)

Refactoring to patterns

Sometimes, one or both of the states we move between with our refactorings are known *design patterns*,[8] or known solutions to common design problems. Although most of the refactorings people apply on a daily basis are operating on a level much smaller than that of design patterns, every now and then we do, in fact, spot signs of a hidden pattern in our code and decide to move the design toward that pattern, making it explicit. To read more about the relationship between refactoring and design patterns, I heartily recommend Joshua Kerievsky's *Refactoring to Patterns* (Addison-Wesley, 2004).

Refactorings alter internal structure

So these transformations are applied to the system's internal structure—the code—which means that many of the refactorings are very low-level. For example, one of the most common refactorings is called *rename method*. Renaming a method or a local variable might not seem like too significant a change in the system's design, but renaming a method from something ambiguous to something clear and concise can make a world of difference to someone new to the code and needing to understand the existing code.

Also, such low-level refactorings are the fundamental building blocks to achieving larger refactorings. These "larger" refactorings are typically those that deal with moving the responsibilities around in your code, introducing or removing an inheritance hierarchy, or making other similar changes that (usually) involve more than one class. In the end, all refactorings can be reduced into a series of smaller steps, such as renaming a variable; adding a new, empty class; changing the return type of a method; and so forth.

---

[8] A good Java-oriented reference for classic design patterns is *Software Architecture Design Patterns in Java* by Partha Kuchana (Auerbach, 2004).

Although technically the most common refactorings are things like renaming a method, the number-one reason for refactoring is *duplication.* It might be duplication in terms of having two similar pieces of code in two methods or classes—something that could be extracted into a single method invoked in both places—but the duplication could also be in terms of responsibilities. Duplication, of course, is bad for a code base because it makes the system more difficult to change. Having logic and responsibility duplicated in multiple places is a guaranteed way to introduce defects due to us forgetting to make the change in all necessary corners of the code base.

In addition to not introducing defects with our changes to the code's internal structure, we also don't want our refactorings to add functionality. That is, refactorings should preserve behavior.

Refactorings preserve behavior

The latter part of the earlier quote by Martin Fowler says, "without changing [code's] external behavior." What does that mean? It means that whatever transformations you apply to the existing code, those transformations should only affect the code's design and structure—not its externally visible behavior or functionality. In other words, client code that uses the code you're refactoring should not notice any difference in how the refactored code behaves.

Renaming a method that's part of a class's public interface will obviously have to ripple through to client code as well, but the behavior of that method should not change in any way. Similarly, restructuring the code behind the public interface should not in any way change the behavior visible through the public interface.

NOTE Now that we know what refactoring is, it's worth mentioning what it isn't. In the past few years, I have started hearing the word *refactoring* a lot. Much to my disappointment, in most cases, it seems, the correct word would've been *rewriting* or *editing* without the discipline associated with refactoring.

So we think we've been successful at altering internal structure without changing external behavior. Cool. But how can we be sure that our refactorings haven't changed the code's external behavior? By running tests against our code, of course! We want to keep our software working, and tests are the tool for ensuring that.

1.3.4 Making sure the software still works

It's easy to say that we should deliver working software from day one, but it can seem like a daunting task to be constantly refactoring the design, all the while making sure that whatever we're changing does not break existing functionality. Yes, it is daunting. It is daunting to such a degree that we're likely to slip if we don't have any help. Although the main purpose of tests in TDD is to help us design and develop working software, they also have a role to play in keeping it that way in the future.

Contrary to popular belief, testing does not need to be a burden.[9] However, it's true that manual testing can be slow and error-prone, which is what turns developers off about testing in general. Experience has shown that developers (and dedicated testers as well for that matter) tend to skip some aspects of manual tests, relying on their intuition that those tests could not have been broken by whatever change it is they're testing. Luckily, we're in the business of automating stuff with software so we're best positioned to help ourselves by making the computer turn testing into something that's fast and automated!

Protection with automated tests

Regression in general is about moving back to a less developed state. In the case of software, regression is existing, once-working functionality getting broken. That is, it regresses from a working state to a non-working state, as illustrated in figure 1.11.

Regression doesn't just happen, though. It's we developers who trigger regression by introducing defects with our changes. As professional software developers,

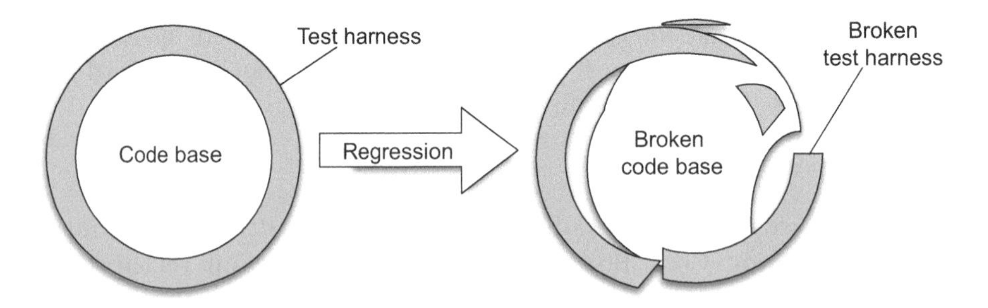

Figure 1.11 Our test harness forms a mold around the code base. As a change is introduced that breaks the code base, the mold no longer fits, so it breaks and lets us know that we've been bad.

[9] In fact, writing tests is fun when you're programming test-first!

we want to know that our changes are not breaking anything and we want to know as soon as possible. This can only be accomplished by having an automated *test harness* that we can execute at will and that alerts us to any failures during the test run.

This is called *regression testing* and is about executing tests repeatedly throughout the project to verify that defects that once existed are not reappearing undetected as the software evolves through thousands and thousands of changes—in other words, testing that the software hasn't regressed since the last time these tests were run. Furthermore, the regression tests are likely to catch a whole bunch of new bugs that would otherwise appear.

There are a number of characteristics that are important for a test harness, one of which is that the tests must be easy to run—otherwise we'll be tempted to skip the tests and check our changes in, hoping that they won't break anything. Another essential property is that the tests run fast—otherwise we'll be tempted to run the tests less frequently, again skipping an important verification step.

Not running tests immediately risks pouring precious time into fixing a bug later on without the advantage of knowing which change had introduced the bug. Immediate feedback with the right context does enormous things to speed up development, practically no time is spent on detective work trying to figure out the exact context in which the bug surfaced. If we run our test suite after every tiny change, we'll know exactly which couple of lines caused the tests to fail.

Getting fast feedback

Sometimes, though, it is not possible to run all tests fast enough. A common culprit for slowness of a test harness is a set of tests that access an external resource such as a database, a shared drive, a web server on the Internet, or a directory service. Even local file-system access can push your test runs beyond several minutes. Furthermore, sometimes there are so many tests that running all of them takes too long for a single developer to wait idle, even if the tests have been optimized over and over again.

In these situations, it often makes sense to run a subset of the tests (a subset that's most likely to catch any bugs introduced by the change), check in, and leave a build server crunching through the rest of the tests in the background while we move on with our next task. These build servers are sometimes referred to as *continuous integration servers* due to the fact that they are often used in conjunction with the practice of *continuous integration*[10]—developers integrating their changes frequently in such small increments that it's almost continuous.

---

[10] For more details on continuous integration, please refer to Martin Fowler's seminal article at http://www.martinfowler.com/articles/continuousIntegration.html.

> **Continuous integration is not about having a continuous integration server**
>
> Continuous integration servers should not be equated with the *practice* of continuous integration. Continuous integration servers provide machinery for automated builds and fancy reports. If the developers aren't integrating their changes frequently, the continuous integration server will sit idle while the developers continue diverging their private workspaces from each other, building up more conflicts to merge!

This approach basically trades in some of the confidence that the last change didn't break anything for speed of development, relying on the assumption that most of the time the change doesn't break those parts of the system that weren't covered by the developer's chosen subset of "fast" tests.

You can think of it as a form of optimistic locking for getting fast feedback. If no tests broke, we're proceeding at maximum pace, not spending time running the full set of tests only to find that none of them broke. If one of the tests we left to the build server breaks, however, we'll end up paying extra to get it fixed since we've already lost the context, having moved on to our next task. That's the trade-off we're making—losing the context can easily mean a magnitude of difference in the time and effort it takes to correct a mistake.

An essential property of a regression test is that it's being executed repeatedly. This means that we either need to pay for someone to spend a significant amount of time running and re-running our regression tests—of which we may have hundreds or thousands—or we can choose to automate some or all of them and have the computer execute them automatically or upon request with minimal involvement on behalf of a human.

We now have an idea of what TDD is about, what it's made of, and why we should use it. Before we dive head first into the details of doing test-driven development in the remaining chapters of parts 1 and 2, let's explore the feature-level technique of acceptance test-driven development a bit further and discuss how we can let acceptance tests drive us toward the product that meets our customers' needs.

1.4 Build the right thing: acceptance TDD

Testing has always been an integral part of software development. However, the way testing has been carried out has changed significantly throughout the decades. As programmers, we have always been interested in knowing that our software works before handing it over to users. The means with which we obtain this knowledge, however, has evolved quite a bit with the rise of agile software development processes such as Extreme Programming.

Furthermore, the role of tests themselves has morphed into other areas of software development than plain verification of conformance to specification. In fact, the solution to the second half of our problem of code that fails to meet actual needs is to let tests drive our development on the level of features and functionality of the system we're building. That is what practicing acceptance test-driven development is about. In short, *we only ever start test-driving a feature into the system when there is a test calling for it.*

In essence, this means that tests are no longer merely a verification tool, but also an integral part of requirements and specification as well as a medium for customer collaboration. In this section, we'll go into more detail about these new roles for tests, starting with examining their part in nurturing close collaboration between developers, testers, and customers, and then discussing the use of tests as the shared language facilitating this collaboration.

Before discussing the collaboration-oriented aspects of the technique, let's first figure out the relationship between acceptance test-driven development and TDD. After all, their names are almost identical, so there must be something to it.

1.4.1 What's in a name?

The name *acceptance test-driven development* implies that acceptance TDD is likely something similar to "regular" TDD. The suffix is obviously coming from TDD, but where is the rest coming from? What is an acceptance test? In short, *acceptance tests* are indicators of the completion of a requirement or feature. When all acceptance tests for a requirement or feature are passing, you know you're done.

Acceptance TDD as a technique is not coupled to any specific format for expressing requirements. The same ideas can be applied much to the same effect whether you're implementing use cases, user stories, or some other equivalent medium for documenting what needs to be done. It's worth noting, though, that teams using user stories to manage their requirements tend to talk about *story test-driven development* instead—which is a different name for the same technique. Yet others prefer to call it *customer test-driven development*, which is also appropriate considering the tests' nature of being customer-owned.

NOTE Although TDD and acceptance TDD have much in common and the big brother certainly borrows a lot from its little brother, both TDD and acceptance TDD can be adopted without the other. Programmers who have no user story in sight or who don't write tests for a feature before implementing it can still adopt TDD and reap its benefits; teams who aren't programming test-first can still build features test-first. Having said that, these techniques do reinforce each other, and adopting both is likely to yield a lot more improvement than using either of them alone.

Regardless of what specific format or tool we use to manage requirements, the primary goal of acceptance TDD is to support close collaboration between the customer and the development team. Let's see how being test-driven helps us with that.

1.4.2 Close collaboration

Close collaboration is essential for any complex endeavors involving people, and software development with acceptance TDD is no exception. In practice, we want to have an integrated project team instead of separate development, business analysis, and testing teams, let alone a distant QA department.

The fundamental idea is that the way to achieve the best possible level of productivity for the whole team is to nurture rapid feedback and effective, face-to-face communication around concrete, working software instead of passing around test plans, requirements specifications, and bug reports between customers, testers, business analysts, and developers. With acceptance TDD, we are able to collaborate effectively by bringing together the knowledge, skills, and abilities required for doing a good job.

Let's see how this close collaboration helps us deliver the right product by improving our interactions and reducing the likelihood of misunderstood requirements and costly rework.

Seeing concrete, working software

Very few customers have been completely satisfied with what the contractor delivers to them after several months of silence. By feeding the customer with completed functionality as a continuous stream, we're making sure that, if there's something wrong or missing, we'll know about it right away. This early feedback reduces our risks and costs. Furthermore, by not keeping an inventory of supposedly "completed" items that the customer hasn't seen yet, we're avoiding the usual illusion of progress that is built on assumptions and that is supported by document-driven methods and meaningless statements such as "development is 90% complete."

Building trust and confidence

Another significant benefit of delivering working software early and often is that we're building trust and confidence both between the team and the customer and within the team itself. By showing the customer (and ourselves) that we can deliver, we're making life a lot easier for our whole team.

Customer in control

There's one key difference in the role and power of the customer between incremental development and the traditional waterfall, big design, up-front style of development. With incremental development, the customer gets to choose which features they get first. Similarly, they also get to choose which features are dropped if the team is not able to implement all of them within the project's allocated time or budget.

The customer's decisions are, of course, influenced by the cost of the features, which the developers estimate—including the cost of delaying, the cost of building things in a different order, and so forth.

The ability of the customer to decide what their money is spent on can really change the way they look at software projects. Finally, the customer is in control of what their money is spent on. Talk about motivating the customer!

Evolving a shared language

By encouraging close collaboration between testers, developers, and customers, we are effectively facilitating a situation where the information needed is obtained as quickly as possible—in all directions. Furthermore, this continuous exposure within the team is likely to increase the efficiency of communication as people get to know each other better and begin to evolve a shared language. Software development is a people business, after all, and we shouldn't neglect that fact.

Let's contemplate for a while the possibility of using acceptance tests as the foundation for that shared language between the whole team—including customers, testers, and developers.

1.4.3 Tests as a shared language

One of the biggest problems of developing software for someone else is the prevalent ambiguity in requirements. It is far from child's play to express and communicate requirements in such a way that no information is lost and that the original idea is transmitted fully intact. Some would go as far as saying it's impossible to do so. After all, we can't read minds.[11]

[11] If you can, please get in touch. We've got a job opening for a Senior Customer Mind Reader.

This problem is highlighted when the medium used for this communication is written documentation—a requirements specification, for example—which is far from being a perfect way to transfer information and understanding. If we were able to transform the requirements into executable tests that verify whether the system conforms to each particular aspect of the specification, there would be many fewer problems with ambiguity and less room for interpretation on behalf of developers. This is the wonderful premise of *tests as specification*.

Tests as specification

Tests as specification provides a way to look at tests as something that's essentially derived from requirements; therefore—in theory at least—a system that passes the tests should by definition conform to the specification. This, however, assumes perfect test coverage, which is rarely—if ever—the case in the so-called "real world" software projects.

Defects get through testing every now and then. That is hardly news to anyone who's lived through a couple of commercial software projects. In part, this is due to our having missed a test that we should've considered. In part, this is due to our human nature and our deceptive intuition, which manages to talk us out of running some of the tests to "save time."

This begs the question, are we really better off using tests as specification if the tests we have tend to leak in one way or another? Is it really feasible to use tests as specification, effectively redefining the meaning of these concepts? Using tests as specification is not a silver bullet either, but it does have a number of clear advantages that makes it worth considering:

- Faster feedback through automation
- More reliable test execution
- One less translation step

First of all, there's no denying that having automated, executable tests would get rid of a lot of grunt work and would accelerate our feedback loop enormously compared to manually executed test cases. Second, executable tests would effectively prevent our inherent laziness from getting us into trouble, because we would be able to exploit the fact that the computer doesn't suffer from the same problems of character that we humans are born with. Finally, we are already making the same errors in translating the true requirements into writing with our current practice, so would it really be any worse if we'd just change the format and medium we're using to document our test cases?

There are still plenty of opportunities to err while transforming the requirements into tests, of course, but the less knowledge transfer and human interpretation is involved in running the tests, the less chance there is that something falls into the gaps after the test has been crafted.

Specification by example

Furthermore, one of the most striking benefits of using tests as the specification driving development is that tests typically employ *specification by example* instead of abstraction or prose (although there should almost invariably be some amount of prose involved—things are not black and white in this respect either). In other words, instead of the traditional "the system shall calculate tax" pattern familiar in requirements documents, specification by example promotes expressing the requirement through examples such as "for a $20 subscription with a tax rate of 10%, the system charges a total of $22 from the user's account."

For this simple requirement, the difference between the traditional "system shall" and an example-based version might not be that significant—after all, we all know how to calculate tax in such a trivial case. However, the requirements we meet at work are typically not as trivial, and the risk of misunderstanding is much higher. For instance, applying multiple taxes for a given transaction might need to employ different calculation rules in different locales, which can be clarified enormously through concrete examples.

Specification by example is a natural fit for our intuition and makes it easier to relate the requirements to the concrete world and our software. Specification by example can also be seen in TDD. Whereas acceptance tests specify by example the desired behavior of the system, the examples and the desired behavior specified with unit tests are specifications about the desired implementation rather than about the functionality delivered.

Higher quality inside and out, better confidence in our work, and the customer loving us for giving them software that meets their needs—who wouldn't like these improvements, especially if it's not just talk? After all, in theory, anything and everything is possible. We'll soon make our own transition from talking the talk to walking the walk in the rest of the book; but before that, let's talk about the tools at our disposal.

1.5 Tools for test-driven development

Tools are important. Without tools like compilers, editors, and operating systems, software development would be difficult compared to where we have ended up over decades and decades of technical advancements. Test-driven development is no exception in this regard—as a code-intensive development technique, good tools can make a huge difference. We'll next take a condensed tour of three fundamental or otherwise useful categories of tools and techniques: unit testing frameworks, continuous integration with its supporting machinery, and code coverage.

1.5.1 Unit-testing with xUnit

A number of years ago, Kent Beck created a unit-testing framework for SmallTalk called SUnit (http://sunit.sf.net). That framework has since given birth to a real movement within the software development community with practically every programming language in active use having gotten a port of its own.[12] For a Java developer, the de facto standard tool—also based on the design of SUnit—is called JUnit, available at http://www.junit.org/. The family of unit-testing frameworks that are based on the same patterns found in SUnit and JUnit is often referred to as *x*Unit because of their similarities: If you know one, it's not much of a leap to start using another (provided that you're familiar with the programming language itself).

What exactly does a *unit-testing framework* mean in the context of xUnit? It means that the library provides supporting code for writing unit tests, running them, and reporting the test results. In the case of JUnit, this support is realized by providing a set of base classes for the developer to extend, a set of classes and interfaces to perform common tasks such as making assertions, and so forth. For running the unit tests written with JUnit, the project provides different *test runners*—classes that know how to collect a set of JUnit tests, run them, collect the test results, and present them to the developer either graphically or as a plain-text summary.

We'll be using JUnit and Java in this book. In fact, we'll be using plenty of extensions to JUnit as we go about test-driving different kinds of components. If you're not familiar with JUnit, please refer to the appendices for an introduction to this wonderful little tool. Don't get too immersed in the details of JUnit, though, because we've got a couple of additional categories of tools to talk

[12] There are more or less direct ports of SUnit and JUnit for ColdFusion, C#, C and C++, Delphi, ActionScript, Haskell, JavaScript, Visual Basic and JScript, Lingo, LISP, Lua, Objective-C, PL/SQL, Perl, PHP, PowerBuilder, Python, Ruby, Scheme, Tcl/Tk, Korn Shell—and that's not even all of them! Ron Jeffries maintains a list of xUnit frameworks at http://www.xprogramming.com/software.htm.

about—for example, the kind of tools we might look to for support in implementing acceptance TDD.

1.5.2 Test frameworks for acceptance TDD

Although the unit-testing framework scene has developed strongly around the xUnit concept, it's not so homogeneous in the world of acceptance testing. The main reason for this difference is that the idea of test-driving on the feature level is relatively new, and the incumbent record-and-replay style of test automation tools don't work well when there's nothing to record.

Another thing to think about in the fragmented market is the fact that two systems rarely have the exact same interfaces. The exception to the rule is web applications, which can all be accessed with standard technologies such as the HTTP protocol and the HTML markup language. What's more important than the technologies involved, however, is how the tools aim to support our primary interest with acceptance TDD—close customer collaboration.

There are tools like Fit and Fitnesse, which are table oriented and employ a visual format to aid developers, testers, and business analysts in collaborating with nontechnical stakeholders. In addition to the tabular format championed by the Fit family of tools, another popular approach to describing executable tests is to represent tests as statements in plain text. Perhaps the best-known example of tools from this category is Exactor. Sometimes it's sufficient for a given project's purposes to use a more technical medium such as an actual scripting language for describing tests. In many cases, however, and despite of existing acceptance testing frameworks being readily available, the best option can also be a homegrown framework.

We'll take a closer look at some of these tools in part 3 when exploring acceptance test-driven development further. For now, let's move on to the next tooling-related topic we have yet to cover—continuous build servers.

1.5.3 Continuous integration and builds

Working in a team that's constantly changing code here and there creates pressure on the developers to integrate their changes significantly more often than some are used to in more traditional environments. Teams using TDD are almost by definition[13] employing collective code ownership, meaning that everyone is authorized to change any code in the code base.

[13] How well would the test-code-refactor cycle work out in an environment where developers would need to ask the owner of a given class to implement a refactoring? Not too well, I think. It doesn't have to be strictly black and white, however. There have been reports of teams successfully using a variety of hybrid code-ownership models.

In practice, this means that as long as the team is refactoring mercilessly as part of their test-code-refactor cycle, there will be a constant stream of small changes to the source repository. With this in mind, waiting for two days before checking in your changes is likely to require manual merging—an activity that at least I don't like too much.

All this leads us to adopting a process of synchronizing our changes to the source repository much more frequently than before. This highly frequent integration of developers' workspaces with the centralized source repository—*continuous integration*—is generally considered to involve not just the integration of source code ("it compiles!") but also the verification of the integrated source code by running automated tests ("it works!"). In practice, however, this full verification sometimes requires certain practical trade-offs, which we'll discuss next.

Practical trade-offs

A common pattern with teams implementing continuous integration is to run only a relevant subset of all tests before checking in their changes and to delegate the running of the full test suite (including unit, integration, and functional tests) to a dedicated build server, also known as a *continuous build server*. Figure 1.12 illustrates a basic setup with a continuous integration server polling for changes from the source repository.

In essence, this is a practical trade-off many teams decide to make. On the one hand, running the full test suite often takes too long (several minutes—even

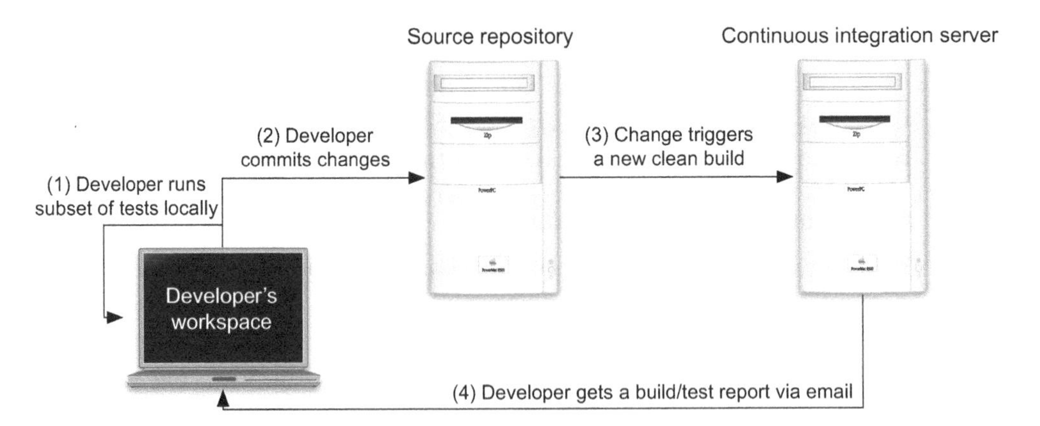

Figure 1.12 This is a typical scenario of a developer (1) running a relevant subset of automated tests locally before (2) committing the change to the source repository. In the third step (3), the change triggers a new build on the continuous integration server (using a commit-hook in the repository or by frequently polling the repository for changes). Finally, after running a clean build with the latest changes (4), the continuous integration server sends a build report to the developer via email.

hours) for a developer to wait for the green bar. On the other hand, most of the tests are unlikely to have been affected by the developer's recent changes; that is, they are unlikely to reveal new information to the developer. Thus, having the developer run only a selected subset of the tests (lasting some seconds) before checking in can make a lot of sense.

In the (we hope) rare case of the changes breaking some tests that the developer hadn't run on their machine before checking in, the build server will eventually (often within 5–15 minutes) notify them and the rest of the team that the code base was broken by the recent changes.

By now, if you're anything like me and you're new to continuous integration, you've started wondering about the technical implementation of such a build server. The short story is, there's no need to write your own.

Build servers galore

Fortunately, and perhaps not surprisingly, you don't need to write your own tools to run a build server, because a selection of open source as well as commercial products offer the required functionality. Some of the more popular ones include CruiseControl (http://cruisecontrol.sf.net), AntHill (http://www.urbancode.com), Continuum (http://maven.apache.org/continuum), and Bamboo (http://www.atlassian.com/software/bamboo/), and more are popping up all the time.

If you are interested in learning more about the philosophy behind continuous integration and the associated tools, please refer to Martin Fowler's article "Continuous Integration".[14] James Shore has also done some great writing on the difference between doing continuous integration and using continuous build servers.[15]

1.5.4 Code coverage

Many developers are familiar with static code analysis tools such as Lint and its variants (http://www.splint.org). Java developers, in particular, might have experiences running the PMD tool (http://pmd.sf.net) to detect anomalies regarding the illegal use of certain constructs or to calculate complexity measurements. The increased attention to automated testing and, especially, unit testing has also created a number of tools over the years for measuring *code coverage* (also known as *test coverage*). In short, code coverage is a measurement of how thoroughly our

---

[14] http://www.martinfowler.com/articles/continuousIntegration.html.

[15] http://www.jamesshore.com.

automated tests exercise the production code and its source code statements, branches, and expressions.[16]

The main benefit of incorporating code-coverage measures into our builds, for example, is that we are constantly aware of how thoroughly our test suite exercises our software. This can be especially helpful when a team is just starting to write unit tests or adopting TDD, because it helps pointing out areas of the code base that are not getting tested as thoroughly as other parts of the code.

Just like most other technical source code measurements,[17] however, code coverage does have its potential risk of misuse. Blindly running after perfect code coverage would be a dubious thing to do. Sometimes, due to the APIs our code uses, going from 99% to 100% means testing for conditions that cannot happen. So, if you do decide to add code coverage to your toolbox, be careful not to shoot yourself in the foot.

What degree of code coverage should I aim for?

When we bring up the topic of code coverage, someone is bound to pop the question, "How high should I set the bar for code coverage?" Should it be 100%? Or maybe 90%? 80%?

The answer is, it depends. It depends on the specific technologies, languages, and tools in use, and often a host of other things. What seems typical for Java and J2EE projects is an average code coverage of 85%. That is not due to some parts of the code missing tests—the biggest source for the difference from 100% coverage is the warts and idioms of the language and APIs being used.

To quote a private conversation with fellow consultant and author J. B. Rainsberger, "Aim for 100% while learning—you'll understand why 85% is nicer."

We are not going to look into code-coverage tools here, but some of the more popular tools for measuring Java projects include Cenqua Clover (http://www.cenqua.com/clover), Cobertura (http://cobertura.sf.net), and EMMA (http://emma.sf.net).

---

[16] See my article, "Introduction to Code Coverage" (http://www.javaranch.com/newsletter/200401/IntroToCodeCoverage.html), for a more thorough introduction to the theory and some of the code coverage tools available.

[17] Ever heard of people getting paid by the number of lines of code they've written? It has happened and didn't work out too well.

I think that's about enough of tooling. You'll bump into a slew of useful tools as you learn about testing components implemented with different technologies, but for now it's enough that we have an idea of the basics of unit testing frameworks such as JUnit and how they relate to test-driven development.

Let's wrap up this chapter with a quick summary. It's about time we see some action, so start pulling up your sleeves!

1.6 Summary

We started this chapter with an overview of the challenge of delivering software to support our organizations' business and operations. Our traditional methods of developing systems have a lot to improve in this aspect: producing systems with high defect rates, that are hard and costly to change, and that don't fulfill their primary purpose of meeting the customer's actual needs.

Test-driven development is a development and design technique that helps us build working software starting from day one, add functionality and behavior in small increments, and keep the software working all the way. This is made possible by adopting an evolutionary approach to design and by employing refactoring to maintain the best possible design at each step—not letting the living code base rot over time. TDD helps us build the product right.

In return for this disciplined way of working in small steps, we can lower our defect rates and generally deliver higher-quality software that's maintainable and ready for change. In the process, we gain confidence in our code and we are able to move faster and faster because we have less code to write, we spend less time fixing defects, and we have more time for doing useful things.

In order to build the right product, we employ a technique we call acceptance test-driven development. Acceptance TDD is not a testing technique but a powerful development tool facilitating effective collaboration between different roles within the project, including customers, testers, and developers. Acceptance TDD supports this collaboration by providing incrementally developing, concrete software described by customer-oriented tests as the basis for discussion and feedback. By seeing concrete features implemented throughout the project in a customer-defined priority order, we build trust and confidence, further supporting effective collaboration using a shared language.

In the following chapters of part 1, we will learn the ins and outs of test-driven development—a technique that carries enormous potential in aiding us toward successful software projects with low defect counts and projects that deliver on schedule. Part 2 will show us ways to apply TDD in the context of specific Java and

J2EE technologies that are sometimes considered a challenge for test-driving—which is by and large a false assumption!

Once we have a grasp of TDD, we will go for the same kind of understanding of acceptance TDD in part 3. We will dissect the process and build an understanding of how it delivers the most value possible in a given situation with user stories and acceptance tests as the magic ingredient.

I hope you'll enjoy the journey!

2 Beginning TDD

Experience is a hard teacher because she gives the test first, the lesson afterward.

—Chinese proverb

Something big airports are generally very good at is using signs. No matter which airport I fly from, I never have to worry about not knowing which way to turn from a corner. Whenever I no longer know which way to walk, I look up and there it is: the sign that says, "Gate 42: continue straight forward."

It wasn't like that when I started writing software for a living. There was just one sign outside the terminal building saying, "Good luck." Figuring out what I should change and ending up with a correct solution was a bit like trying to find your way to the right gate at Heathrow without the hundreds of signs and displays. For software development, test-driven development with its simple rules and guidance is like those signs at the airport, making sure I end up where I need to be—and in time.

We already created a somewhat shallow idea in chapter 1 of what TDD is and talked about the forces in play, such as incremental and evolutionary design, and the "reversed" cycle of development. As we learned in chapter 1, TDD is both a design and programming technique that's essentially based on the simple rule of only writing production code to fix a failing test. TDD turns the usual design-code-test sequence of activities around into what we call the TDD cycle: test-code-refactor, illustrated in figure 2.1 and reproduced from chapter 1.

We talked about TDD being a simple and effective technique for developing higher-quality software that works and stays malleable through the continuous design we perform via frequent, merciless refactoring. Thanks to the enhanced confidence we have in our code, along with lower defect rates and a thorough test suite combined with better design, we become more productive and our work is much more enjoyable than in the times where a go-live was followed by an undetermined period of late nights and angry customers.

In this chapter, we'll develop further our understanding of what TDD is and what the secret (and not so secret) ingredients are that make it work. We'll do that by writing code test-first, learning by doing. We will be writing small tests, squeezing out the desired behavior step by step, and refactoring our code mercilessly. We're going to

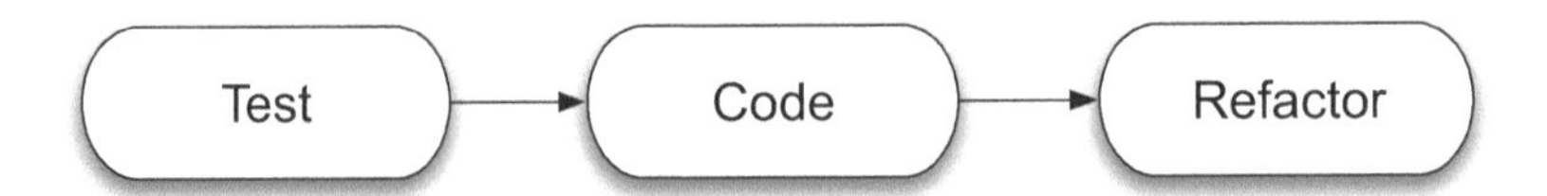

Figure 2.1 The TDD cycle is a three-step process of writing a test, making it pass by writing just enough production code, and finally improving the design by disciplined refactorings.

be adding and removing code, and we're going to be changing code so that we can remove code. Along the way, we'll introduce an increasingly robust and capable implementation of a template engine, including some exception-handling functionality to accompany the "happy path" behavior we're going to begin with. We will also discuss how there are often two possible paths, *breadth first* and *depth first*, to the ultimate goal of a feature-complete system.

It'll be intensive, and there will be code listings after one another. Once we're through all that, you should have a much better understanding of how TDD works in practice and what kinds of sometimes awkward-seeming tricks we pull in order to keep moving fast.

We'll soon begin developing actual software using TDD. We're going to develop a template engine capable of rendering templates containing variables to be populated dynamically at runtime. Because the first step in TDD is writing a failing test, we need to figure out what desired behavior we'd like to test for. So, before getting our hands dirty, let's have a quick chat about how to get from abstract requirements to concrete tests.

2.1 From requirements to tests

Imagine you are implementing a subsystem for the corporate collaboration software suite[1] that's responsible for providing mail-template functionality so that the CEO's assistant can send all sorts of important, personalized emails to all personnel with a couple of mouse-clicks. How would tests drive the development of the said subsystem? You're going to know the answer to that question by the time you've finished reading this chapter; but, as with any system, it starts with decomposing the requirements into something smaller and more concrete.

2.1.1 Decomposing requirements

With any requirements you may have envisioned for the subsystem, you've probably already sliced and diced them into some kind of a set of "things we need to do"—let's call them tasks—that will, when completed, lead to satisfying the original requirement. Now erase those tasks out of your head and do it all again, this time slicing the requirements into a set of tests that, when passing, lead to the requirements being satisfied. Can you think of such tests? I'll bet you can. It might be difficult at first, but I'm confident that you've already thought of a number of little tests that would verify some tiny part of the whole.

---

[1] Now that's a fancy way to say "email application"!

"A mail template without any variable data is sent off as is." "The placeholder for the recipient's first name in a greeting should get replaced with each individual recipient's name, respectively." Soon, you'll have a whole bunch of those tests, which together verify more than just a tiny part of the whole. Eventually, you'll have covered most if not all of your expectations for the product's behavior and functionality.

To clarify the difference between tasks and tests, table 2.1 contrasts a few of the possible decompositions of the mail-template subsystem into tasks and tests, respectively. Decomposing into tasks (left-hand column) leads to items that do not represent progress in terms of produced software. Contrast this with the right-hand column of tests, which have a clear connection to capabilities of the produced software.

Table 2.1 Alternative decompositions of a mail-template subsystem

Mail template subsystem decomposed into a set of tasks	Mail template subsystem decomposed into a set of test(s)
Write a regular expression for identifying variables from the template.	Template without any variables renders as is.
Implement a template parser that uses the regular expression.	Template with one variable is rendered with the variable replaced with its value.
Implement a template engine that provides a public API and uses the template parser internally.	Template with multiple variables is rendered with the appropriate placeholders replaced by the associated values.
...	...

Translating requirements into tests is far superior to merely decomposing requirements into tasks because tasks such as those in table 2.1 make it is easy to lose sight of the ultimate goal—the satisfied requirement. Tasks only give us an idea of what we should *do*. Without a more concrete definition of *done*, we're left with a situation that's not that different from saying we've won the lottery simply because we purchased a lottery ticket.

We'll see more examples of decomposing requirements into tests rather than tasks later in this chapter. There are a couple of topics I'd like to discuss before that, though.

2.1.2 What are good tests made of?

So tests are generally better than tasks for guiding our work, but does it matter what kind of tests we write? Sure it does. Although there's no universal definition for what constitutes a good test, there are some guidelines and heuristics we can use to assess whether we're writing good tests. There are plenty of rules for the technical implementation of a (unit) test,[2] but from the perspective of decomposing requirements into tests, two properties of a good test can be identified as especially important:

- A good test is atomic.
- A good test is isolated.

What these properties are saying is that a good test tests a small, focused, atomic slice of the desired behavior and that the test should be isolated from other tests so that, for example, the test assumes nothing about any previously executed tests. The atomicity of a test also helps us keep our eye on the ball—a small but steady step toward the goal of a fully functional, working system.

As long as we represent our steps in the language of unambiguous tests, the mental connection between the individual steps and the ultimate destination remains much stronger and much clearer, and we're less likely to forget something.

Speaking of steps, we don't just pick tests at random until we're done. Let's talk about how we pick the next step or test to tackle.

2.1.3 Working from a test list

Armed with an initial set of tests, we can proceed to making them pass, one by one. To start with, we need to pick one of the tests—often the one we think is the easiest to make pass or one that represents the most progress with the least effort. For now, we forget that any of those other tests exist. We're completely focused on the one test we picked. We'll also come back to the question of which test to tackle next several times in the remaining chapters in part 1. After all, it's a decision we need to make every couple of minutes when test-driving with small tests.

So, what next? We'll start by writing the test code. We'll go as far as to compile and execute the test before even thinking about writing the production code our test is exercising. We can't write the test because it doesn't compile? We can't write a test for code we don't have? Oh, yes we can. Let's discuss how to do that.

---

[2] Such as "tests should be isolated and order independent," "tests should run fast," "tests shouldn't require manual setup," and so on.

2.1.4 Programming by intention

When you're writing tests before the production code they're supposed to test, you inevitably face a dilemma: how to test something that doesn't exist without breaking our test-first rule. The answer is as simple as the rule was—imagine the code you're testing exists!

How's that possible? What are we supposed to imagine? We imagine the ideal shape and form of the production code from this particular test's point of view. Isn't that cheating? Yes, it is cheating, and we love it! You see, by writing our tests with the assumption that the production code is as easy to use as we could imagine, we're making it a breeze to write the test and we're effectively making sure that our production code will become as easy to use as we were able to imagine. It has to, because our tests won't pass otherwise.

That's what I call the power of imagination! And it has a name, too. It's called *programming by intention*. Programming by intention, the concept of writing code as if another piece of code exists—even if it doesn't—is a technique that makes you focus on what we could have instead of working around what we have. Programming by intention tends to lead to code that flows better, code that's easier to understand and use—code that expresses what it does and why, instead of how it does it.

Now that we know that we should split our requirements into small, focused tests rather than tasks, and now that we understand how to progress through the list of tests by programming by intention, it's time to get busy developing a world class template engine test-first.

2.2 Choosing the first test

As promised, we're going to develop a template engine using test-driven development. In order to not take too big a bite at once, we'll restrict our focus to the business logic of the template engine and not worry about the whole system within which the template engine is being used for rendering personalized emails and what not.

> **TIP** At this point, I highly recommend launching your favorite IDE and following along as we proceed to develop the template engine one small step at a time. Although I have done my best to write a chapter that helps you understand what we're doing and why, there's nothing more illustrative than doing it yourself!

The template engine we're talking about needs to be capable of reading in a template, which is basically static text with an arbitrary number of variable placeholders mixed in. The variables are marked up using a specific syntax; before the template engine is asked to render the template, it needs to be given the values for the named variables.

Everything clear? Let's get going. The first thing we need to do is process the description of the template engine into an initial list of tests and then choose one of them to be implemented.

2.2.1 Creating a list of tests

Before we can come up with an initial list of tests, we need to have some requirements. For our example, let's use the following set of requirements for the mail template subsystem:

- The system replaces variable placeholders like ${firstname} and ${lastname} from a template with values provided at runtime.
- The system attempts to send a template with some variables not populated will raise an error.
- The system silently ignores values for variables that aren't found from the template.
- The system supports the full Latin-1 character set in templates.
- The system supports the full Latin-1 character set in variable values.
- And so forth...

Those are detailed requirements, aren't they? Are they tests? No. They're requirements smaller and more detailed than "implement a mail template subsystem," but they're not tests. Tests are typically much more explicit, describing the expected behavior for specific scenarios rather than articulating a generic description of that behavior.

Here's one attempt at turning the mail template subsystem's requirements into proper tests:

- Evaluating template "Hello, ${name}" with the value "Reader" for variable "name" results in the string "Hello, Reader".
- Evaluating template "${greeting}, ${name}" with values "Hi" and "Reader", respectively, results in the string "Hi, Reader".
- Evaluating template "Hello, ${name}" with no value for variable "name" raises a `MissingValueError`.

- Evaluating template "Hello, ${name}" with values "Hi" and "Reader" for variables "doesnotexist" and "name", respectively, results in the string "Hello, Reader".
- And so forth... (We could, for example, include some specific examples that would serve as proof that the system handles Latin-1 characters.)

See the difference? The requirements have been transformed into something that's clearly a degree more concrete, more executable, more example-like. With these tests as our completion criteria, there's no question of whether we're there yet or not. With these tests, we don't need to wonder, for example, what it means to "raise an error" and, assuming it means throwing an exception, what kind of an exception it should be and what the exception message should say. The tests tell us that we should throw a `MissingValueError` exception and that we're not interested in the specific error message.

With this kind of test, we are finally able to produce that binary answer for the question, "am I done?" The test list itself is never done, however. The test list is a working document to which we add new tests as we go. We're bound to be missing some tests from our initial list, and we'll likely think of a bunch of them while we're deep into implementing some other test. At that time, we write those tests down and continue with what we're working on.

We've got a list of tests that tell us exactly when the requirements have been fulfilled. Next, we start working through the list, making them pass one by one.

2.2.2 Writing the first failing test

Let's take another example and practice our programming by intention a bit before continuing with our journey to test-driven development. Why don't we take the first test from the list and see how we might go about writing the test before the code?

Here's our test again:

Evaluating template "Hello, ${name}" with the value "Reader" for variable "name" results in the string "Hello, Reader".

NOTE At this point, we're pulling out the IDE to write some code. We'll be using JUnit 4, the latest version of the de facto unit-testing framework for Java today (http://www.junit.org). If you're not already familiar with JUnit, take a peek at appendix A for a short introduction. You won't need to do that quite yet, though, if you don't feel like it. The JUnit stuff is not essential here—the purpose is to see programming by intention in action—so just focus on the code we're writing inside the methods and pay no attention to the weird annotations we're using.

Because we're going to implement the test first, let's start by giving a name for our test class, in listing 2.1.

Listing 2.1 Creating a skeleton for our tests

```
public class TestTemplate {
}
```

Next, we need a test method. Let's call it `oneVariable`, as shown in listing 2.2.

Listing 2.2 Adding a test method

```
import org.junit.Test;
public class TestTemplate {
    @Test
    public void oneVariable() throws Exception {
    }
}
```

We're making progress. Can you feel the wind? No? Well, that's all right, because we know that small steps are good for us. Besides, we're just about to get into the interesting part—programming stuff by intention. The code in listing 2.3 is what we might feel like writing for the test, *assuming* that the implementation is there (even though it isn't), exercising our freedom to design the template feature in a way that makes it easy to use.

Listing 2.3 Writing the actual test

```
import org.junit.Test;
import static org.junit.Assert.*;

public class TestTemplate {
    @Test
    public void oneVariable() throws Exception {
        Template template = new Template("Hello, ${name}");
        template.set("name", "Reader");
        assertEquals("Hello, Reader", template.evaluate());
    }
}
```

In the test method in listing 2.3, we first create a `Template` object by passing the template text as a constructor argument. We then set a value for the variable "name" and finally invoke a method named `evaluate`, asserting the resulting output matches our expectation.

How does that feel? Is that the way you'd like the template system to work? That's the way I felt like it should work. I'm a bit undecided about the name of `set` because `put` would be consistent with the ubiquitous `java.util.Map` interface. I do think `set` sounds better to my ear than `put`, however, so let's leave it like that for now. Let's proceed and see how we can make the compiler happy with our imagination-powered snippet of code.

Making the compiler happy

Now, the compiler is eager to remind us that, regardless of our intentions, the class `Template` does not exist. We'll have to add that. Next, the compiler points out that there's no such constructor for `Template` that takes a `String` as a parameter. It's also anxious to point out that the methods `set` and `evaluate` don't exist either, so we'll have to add those as well.[3] We end up with the following skeleton of a class, in listing 2.4.

Listing 2.4 Satisfying the compiler by adding empty methods and constructors

```
public class Template {

    public Template(String templateText) {
    }

    public void set(String variable, String value) {
    }

    public String evaluate() {
        return null;
    }
}
```

Finally, the code compiles. What's next? Next, we run the test, of course.

[3] Modern IDEs provide shortcuts for generating missing methods in a breeze, making our test-driven life that much easier.

Running the test

When we run our freshly written test, it fails—not surprisingly, because none of the methods we added are doing anything. (You didn't implement the methods already, did you?)

I like to run the test at this point and see it fail before I proceed to making the test pass. Why? Because then I know that when I'm clicking that Run button in my IDE, the test I'm working on is indeed executed, and I'm not looking at the result of running some other test. That would be confusing. I know. I've done that. And not just once or twice. Plus, seeing the test fail tells me that the functionality I'm testing for doesn't exist yet—an unexpected green bar means that an assumption I have made about the code base doesn't hold!

> **A failing test is progress**
>
> If you're thinking we haven't even gotten started yet—after all, we haven't implemented a single line of code for the behavior we're testing for—consider the following: What we have now is a test that tells us when we're done with that particular task. Not a moment too soon, not a moment too late. It won't try to tell us something like "you're 90% done" or "just five more minutes." We'll know when the test passes; that is, when the code does what we expect it to do.
>
> I wouldn't be surprised if you're thinking I've got a marble or two missing. I'm pretty confident that you'll figure out on your own exactly how significant a change this way of looking at things is for you, personally—we're not all alike, and certain techniques help some more than others. Oh, and we'll be writing a lot more code test-first during the first half of the book, so there will be plenty of opportunities to evaluate how well the technique works in practice.

Running the test, we get the output in figure 2.2, complaining about getting a `null` when it expected the string "Hello, Reader".

We're in the red phase of the TDD cycle, which means that we have written and executed a test that is failing—and our IDE indicates that by showing a red progress bar. We've now written a test, programming by intention, and we have a skeleton of the production code that our test is testing. At this point, all that's left is to implement the `Template` class so that our test passes and we can rest our eyes on a green progress bar.

Figure 2.2
Our first failing test. What a precious moment. What we see here is the Eclipse IDE's JUnit runner. But all major IDEs have something similar to a red bar, some kind of hierarchical list of tests run, and access to the detailed error—the stack trace for failed tests.

2.2.3 *Making the first test pass*

We don't have much code yet, but we've already made a number of significant design decisions. We've decided that there should be a class `Template` that loads a template text given as an argument to the constructor, lets us set a value for a named placeholder, and can evaluate itself, producing the wanted output. What's next?

We had already written the skeleton for the `Template` class, shown in listing 2.5, so that our test compiles.

Listing 2.5 Stubbing out methods of the `Template` class to make compilation succeed

```
public class Template {

    public Template(String templateText) {
    }

    public void set(String variable, String value) {
    }

    public String evaluate() {
        return null;
    }
}
```

All the constructors and methods are in place to make the compiler happy, but none of those constructors and methods is doing anything so far. We've written a single failing test to show us a path forward, we've added just enough production code to make the test compile, and the next thing to do is the often most brain-tickling part of creating the functionality our test is asking of us.

There's more to making the test pass than just that, though. We want to make the test pass in the easiest, quickest way possible. To put it another way, we're now facing a red bar, meaning the code in our workspace is currently in an unstable state. We want to get out of that state and into stable ground *as quickly as possible.*

Here's an interesting decision. How do we make the test pass as quickly and easily as possible? Evaluating a template that simple, "Hello, ${name}", with a string-replace operation would be a matter of a few minutes of work, probably. There's another implementation, however, of the functionality implied by our failing test that fits our goal of "as quickly as possible" a bit better. Listing 2.6 shows us what that could look like.

Listing 2.6 Passing as quickly as possible with a hard-coded return statement

```
public class Template {

    public Template(String templateText) {
    }

    public void set(String variable, String value) {
    }

    public String evaluate() {
        return "Hello, Reader";      <-- It couldn't get much simpler than this
    }
}
```

To save space, from now on we'll omit the two `import` statements from the test listings, but you'll still need them to access the JUnit library.

Yes, I am serious. Hard-coding the `evaluate` method to return "Hello, Reader" is most certainly the quickest and easiest way to make the test pass. Although it may not make much sense at first, it's good to push ourselves a bit to squeeze out the wanted behavior with our tests.

In this case, we're making use of neither the actual variable nor the template. And that means we know at least two dimensions on which to push our code toward a proper implementation. Let's extend our test to squeeze out the implementation we're looking for.

2.2.4 Writing another test

Let's say we want to first drive out hard-coding on the part of the variable's value. Listing 2.7 presents one way to do this by extending the existing test through another assertion.

Listing 2.7 Forcing out the hard-coded return statement with another test

```
public class TestTemplate {
    @Test
    public void oneVariable() throws Exception {
        Template template = new Template("Hello, ${name}");
        template.set("name", "Reader");
        assertEquals("Hello, Reader", template.evaluate());
    }

    @Test
    public void differentValue() throws Exception {
        Template template = new Template("Hello, ${name}");
        template.set("name", "someone else");
        assertEquals("Hello, someone else", template.evaluate());
    }
}
```

Triangulate with a different value.

We've added a second call to `set`—with different input—and a second assertion to verify that the `Template` object will re-evaluate the template with the latest value for the "name" variable. Our hard-coded `evaluate` method in the `Template` class will surely no longer pass this test, which was our goal.

This technique is aptly named *triangulation*, referring to how we're using multiple bearings to pinpoint the implementation toward the proper implementation.

We could call it *playing difficult*, but it really can help in avoiding premature optimization, feature creep, and over-engineering in general.

Now, how could we make this enhanced test pass? Do you see a way around having to parse the actual template? I guess we could hard-code some more and push the need for the real implementation a bit farther. Let's see where that would take us, as illustrated by listing 2.8.

Listing 2.8 Making the second test pass by storing and returning the set value

```
public class Template {

    private String variableValue;

    public Template(String templateText) {
    }

    public void set(String variable, String value) {
        this.variableValue = value;
    }

    public String evaluate() {
        return "Hello, " + variableValue;
    }
}
```

Our test passes again with minimal effort. Obviously our test isn't good enough yet, because we've got that hard-coded part in there, so let's continue triangulating to push out the last bits of literal strings from our code. Listing 2.9 shows how we alter our test to drive out not just the hard-coding of the variable value but also the template text around the variable.

Listing 2.9 Applying triangulation for the static template text

```
public class TestTemplate {
    @Test
    public void oneVariable() throws Exception {
        Template template = new Template("Hello, ${name}");
        template.set("name", "Reader");
        assertEquals("Hello, Reader", template.evaluate());
    }

    @Test
    public void differentTemplate() throws Exception {      <-- Rename test to match what we're doing
        Template template = new Template("Hi, ${name}");
        template.set("name", "someone else");
```

```
        assertEquals("Hi, someone else", template.evaluate());
    }
}
```

Squeeze out more hard coding

Red bar. Obviously our hard-coded return statement doesn't cut it anymore. At this point, we're facing the task of parsing the template text somehow. Perhaps we should first implement the parsing logic and then come back to this test. What do you think?

I'm thinking it's time to discuss breadth and depth.

2.3 Breadth-first, depth-first

The software we build today is not something trivial that can be built in a matter of a couple of hours. I've worked with systems with tens of thousands of lines of code. One system had over a million lines of code. And I know there are plenty of people out there who have developed and maintained systems that have had many more millions of lines of code than the one I had the privilege of being involved with. Just like it'll get messy if we try to swallow a muffin as a whole, taking too big a bite talking about code will surely backfire as well.

In our template engine example, we just reached a point where we uncovered a muffin-size bit of complexity that we haven't yet taken care of. At the same time, the test we were working on—evaluating a template—cannot work without that particular bit of complexity being tackled first. Or can it?

As you may remember from the algorithms course in school, there is more than one way to traverse a tree. We can either traverse breadth-first or we can traverse depth-first. The same holds true for test-driven development. Well, sort of. Figures 2.3 and 2.4 compare these two alternatives side by side.

We could decide to go breadth-first, writing tests against the public interface of the `Template` class; making them pass by faking the internals, the lower-level functionality; and only then proceed to writing tests for (and implementing) the layer beneath the original one. Figure 2.3 illustrates this approach.

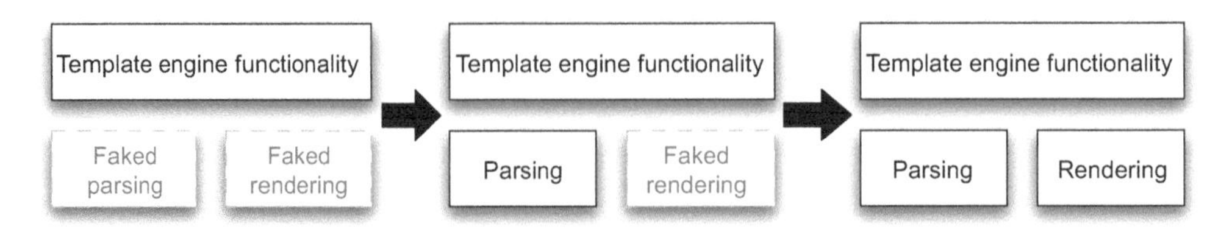

Figure 2.3 With a breadth-first strategy, we implement the higher-level functionality first by faking the required lower-level functionality.

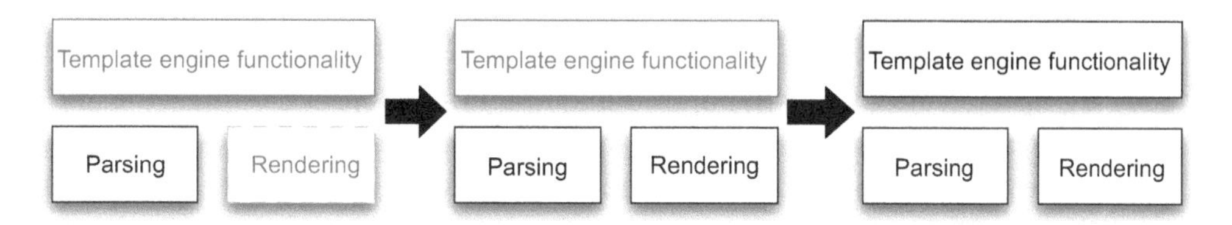

Figure 2.4 With a depth-first strategy, we implement the lower-level functionality first and only compose the higher-level functionality once all the ingredients are present.

The other option would be to back out to a working state and start writing tests for the template-parsing logic instead—and come back once we've got the template-parsing stuff in check. That is, traverse functionality depth-first and implement the details first for one small vertical slice before moving on with the next slice. Figure 2.4 shows what this approach might look like.

In the case of our template engine having to deal with "Hello, ${name}", we can fake the lower-level functionality—parsing the template—a little longer before we add more functionality (more tests, that is) and see where that'll lead us.

2.3.1 *Faking details a little longer*

First, we'll need to start storing the variable value and the template text somewhere. We'll also need to make `evaluate` replace the placeholder with the value. Listing 2.10 shows one way to get our test passing.

Listing 2.10 Our first attempt at handling the variable for real

```
public class Template {

    private String variableValue;

    private String templateText;

    public Template(String templateText) {
        this.templateText = templateText;
    }

    public void set(String variable, String value) {
        this.variableValue = value;
    }

    public String evaluate() {
        return templateText.replaceAll("\\$\\{name\\}", variableValue);
    }
}
```

Some might say what we're doing here is cheating—we're still hard-coding the regular expression to look for "${name}". It's not really cheating, however. We're being disciplined and not giving in to the temptation of "just write the code and be done with it." We'll get there eventually. Baby steps, remember? All tests are passing, we're on stable ground—with a green bar as evidence—and we know exactly where that ground is. What's next?

Refactoring is what's next. Do you see anything to refactor? Spot any duplication that's bothering you? Any less-than-ideal code constructs? Nothing strikes my eye, so I'll go on and proceed to enhancing our test. Specifically, I'd like to drive out that hard-coded variable name. What better way to do that than by introducing multiple variables into the template?

2.3.2 Squeezing out the fake stuff

It's time to write a test for multiple variables on a template. This, by the way, is test number 2 on our test list. We're proceeding almost at light-speed, aren't we? Adding the following snippet to our test class should give us more to think about:

```
@Test
public void multipleVariables() throws Exception {
    Template template = new Template("${one}, ${two}, ${three}");
    template.set("one", "1");
    template.set("two", "2");
    template.set("three", "3");
    assertEquals("1, 2, 3", template.evaluate());
}
```

This test fails right now, telling us that `evaluate` returns the template text as is instead of "1, 2, 3" (which is hardly a surprise because our regular expression is looking for just "${name}"). The big question now is how to deal with this added level of variability in the template.

One way that comes to mind—to get the test passing as quickly as possible—would be to do the search-and-replace operation for each of the variable name-value pairs the `Template` knows about. That could be slow, and there could be some issues with variable values containing substrings that look like a "${variable}", but that should be good enough for us right now. Usually, when I think of worries or deficiencies like the one with the regular expression approach we're talking about here, I write them down as new tests on the list. Let's do that right now:

Evaluate template "${one}, ${two}, ${three}" with values "1", "${foo}", and "3", respectively, and verify that the template engine renders the result as "1, ${foo}, 3".

When we find that, for example, something is wrongly implemented or missing altogether while we're working on one test, it's usually a good idea to write down a short reminder and continue with what we're working on. This let's us focus on one task at a time instead of overloading our brains by jumping back and forth between multiple things (and likely making a mess of our code base in the process).

Now, let's see how we could apply the search-and-replace approach to pass our current failing test.

New and improved details

Back to business. The search-and-replace-based implementation shown in listing 2.11 does indeed get us back to green.

Listing 2.11 Search-and-replace for handling multiple variables

```
import java.util.Map;
import java.util.HashMap;
import static java.util.Map.Entry;

public class Template {

    private Map<String, String> variables;
    private String templateText;

    public Template(String templateText) {
        this.variables = new HashMap<String, String>();
        this.templateText = templateText;
    }

    public void set(String name, String value) {
        this.variables.put(name, value);
    }

    public String evaluate() {
        String result = templateText;
        for (Entry<String, String> entry : variables.entrySet()) {
            String regex = "\\$\\{" + entry.getKey() + "\\}";
            result = result.replaceAll(regex, entry.getValue());
        }
        return result;
    }
}
```

Annotations: "Store variable values in HashMap" (field declaration); "Store variable values in HashMap" (constructor); "Store variable values in HashMap" (set method); "Loop through variables" (for loop); "Replace each variable with its value" (loop body).

The tests are running green again, which is cool. What's next? Refactoring! I still don't see much to refactor, however, so let's skip that step again and move on to the next test.

We've got the following tests still untouched on our list:

- Evaluating template "Hello, ${name}" with no value for variable "name" raises a `MissingValueError`.
- Evaluating template "Hello, ${name}" with values "Hi" and "Reader" for variables "doesnotexist" and "name", respectively, results in the string "Hello, Reader".
- Evaluate template "${one}, ${two}, ${three}" with values "1", "${foo}", and "3", respectively, and verify that the template engine renders the result as "1, ${foo}, 3".

I'm thinking the second of these seems like it should pass already. Let's see whether that's the case.

Testing for a special case

The following snippet introduces a new test with which we assert that if we set variables that don't exist in the template text, the variables are ignored by the `Template` class. I have a theory that our current implementation should pass this test with flying colors without any changes:

```
@Test
public void unknownVariablesAreIgnored() throws Exception {
    Template template = new Template("Hello, ${name}");
    template.set("name", "Reader");
    template.set("doesnotexist", "Hi");
    assertEquals("Hello, Reader", template.evaluate());
}
```

Yep. It passes right away. Or does it?

My IDE runs unit tests so fast that every now and then I'm not 100% sure whether I actually ran the tests or not. This is why you might want to consider insisting on seeing red before green. In other words, fail the test intentionally at first, just to see that our test execution catches the failure—that we're really executing the newly added test—and only then proceed to implement the test and see the bar turn green again.

TIP Most modern IDEs let us customize the code templates used for code generation. I have configured the "test" template in my Eclipse, for example, to include a statement to throw a `RuntimeException` with the message *Not implemented.* This statement gets added into every test method I generate by typing *test* and pressing Ctrl+Space, and it serves not only as a time-saver but also as a reminder for me to run the failing test first.

In this case, the code really does pass the new test with no changes. Wouldn't it be wonderful if all development were this easy? Perhaps not, but it's nice to have a freebie every now and then, isn't it?

Moving on, it's time for the refactoring step again.

2.4 Let's not forget to refactor

We haven't yet refactored anything, even though we've written a lot of code. The reason is that we haven't spotted anything that needs refactoring. Is there still nothing to refactor? Probably not, because we didn't add any code, right? Wrong. Even though we didn't add any production code, we added test code, and that's code just like any other—and we know better than to let our test code rot and get us into serious trouble later on.

Let's see what we could do about our test code by first identifying any potential refactorings we might want to do and then deciding which of them we'll carry out. Listing 2.12 presents our test class so far.

Listing 2.12 Our test code up to this point—can you spot anything to refactor?

```
public class TestTemplate {

    @Test
    public void oneVariable() throws Exception {
        Template template = new Template("Hello, ${name}");
        template.set("name", "Reader");
        assertEquals("Hello, Reader", template.evaluate());
    }

    @Test
    public void differentTemplate() throws Exception {
        template = new Template("Hi, ${name}");
        template.set("name", "someone else");
        assertEquals("Hi, someone else", template.evaluate());
    }

    @Test
    public void multipleVariables() throws Exception {
        Template template = new Template("${one}, ${two}, ${three}");
        template.set("one", "1");
```

```
        template.set("two", "2");
        template.set("three", "3");
        assertEquals("1, 2, 3", template.evaluate());
    }

    @Test
    public void unknownVariablesAreIgnored() throws Exception {
        Template template = new Template("Hello, ${name}");
        template.set("name", "Reader");
        template.set("doesnotexist", "Hi");
        assertEquals("Hello, Reader", template.evaluate());
    }
}
```

Take a moment to think about what we could improve in the test code. Duplication. Semantic redundancy. Anything that jumps out. Anything we perhaps should clean up. We're next going to take a look at a couple of potential refactorings that I've spotted, but I urge you to see what kind of smells you find from the code we have so far. We'll continue when you're ready to compare notes.

2.4.1 Potential refactorings in test code

There are at least a couple of things that come to mind when scanning through the code. First, all of our tests are using a `Template` object, so we probably should extract that into an instance variable rather than declare it over and over again. Second, we're calling the `evaluate` method several times as an argument to `assertEquals`. Third, we're instantiating the `Template` class with the same template text in two places. That's duplication and probably should be removed somehow.

However, one of the tests is using a different template text. Should we use two instance variables, one for each template text? If so, we probably should split the class into two to deal with the two fixtures we clearly have.

NOTE If you're not familiar with the concept of fixtures, they're basically the set of objects—the state—we've initialized for our test to use. With JUnit, the fixture is effectively the set of instance variables and the other configured state of a test class instance. We'll talk more about fixtures in chapter 4, but for now just think of the shared starting state between different test methods of a test class.

There is an alternative, however, to splitting the class with `TestTemplate`. Let's see what that alternative refactoring is.

2.4.2 *Removing a redundant test*

There's a more fundamental type of duplication present in our test code between `oneVariable`, `differentTemplate`, and `multipleVariables`. Thinking about it, the latter test basically covers the first one as well, so we can safely get rid of the single-variable version if we also add a new test to verify that we can set a new value for a variable and re-evaluate the template. Furthermore, we can make `unknownVariablesAreIgnored` use the same template text as `multipleVariables`. And I'm not so sure we need `differentTemplate` either, so maybe that should go, too.

Let's see what the refactored test code shown in listing 2.13 looks like.

Listing 2.13 Test code after removing a redundant test and unifying the fixture

```
import org.junit.Test;
import org.junit.Before;
import static org.junit.Assert.*;

public class TestTemplate {

    private Template template;

    @Before
    public void setUp() throws Exception {
        template = new Template("${one}, ${two}, ${three}");
        template.set("one", "1");
        template.set("two", "2");
        template.set("three", "3");
    }

    @Test
    public void multipleVariables() throws Exception {
        assertTemplateEvaluatesTo("1, 2, 3");
    }

    @Test
    public void unknownVariablesAreIgnored() throws Exception {
        template.set("doesnotexist", "whatever");
        assertTemplateEvaluatesTo("1, 2, 3");
    }

    private void assertTemplateEvaluatesTo(String expected) {
        assertEquals(expected, template.evaluate());
    }
}
```

A common fixture for all tests

Simple, focused test

Simple, focused test

As you can see, we were able to mold our tests toward using a single template text and common setup,[4] leaving the test methods themselves delightfully trivial and focusing only on the essential—the specific aspect of functionality they're testing.

But now, time for more functionality—that is, another test. I'm thinking it might be a good time to look into error handling now that we have the basic functionality for a template engine in place.

2.5 Adding a bit of error handling

It's again time to add a new test. The only one remaining on our list is the one about raising an error when evaluating a template with some variable left without a value. You guessed right, we're going to proceed by first writing a test, then making it pass, and refactoring it to the best design we can think of.

Now, let's see how we'd like the template engine to work in the case of missing values, shall we?

2.5.1 Expecting an exception

How do we write a JUnit test that verifies that an exception is thrown? With the `try-catch` construct, of course, except that this time, the code throwing an exception is a good thing—the expected behavior. The approach shown in listing 2.14 is a common pattern[5] for testing exception-throwing behavior with JUnit.

Listing 2.14 Testing for an exception

```
@Test
public void missingValueRaisesException() throws Exception {
    try {
        new Template("${foo}").evaluate();
        fail("evaluate() should throw an exception if "
                + "a variable was left without a value!");
    } catch (MissingValueException expected) {
    }
}
```

Note the call to the `fail` method right after `evaluate`. With that call to `org.junit.Assert#fail`, we're basically saying, "if we got this far, something went wrong" and the `fail` method fails the test. If, however, the call to `evaluate` throws

[4] The `@Before` annotated method is invoked by JUnit before each `@Test` method.

[5] See Recipe 2.8 in *JUnit Recipes* by J. B. Rainsberger (Manning Publications, 2005).

Testing for exceptions with an annotation

JUnit 4 brought us a handy annotation-based syntax for expressing exception tests such as our `missingValueRaisesException` in listing 2.14. Using the annotation syntax, the same test could be written as follows:

```
@Test(expected=MissingValueException.class)
public void testMissingValueRaisesException() throws Exception {
    new Template("${foo}").evaluate();
}
```

Although this annotation-based version of our test is less verbose than our `try-catch`, with the `try-catch` we can also make further assertions about the exception thrown (for example, that the error message contains a key piece of information). Some folks like to use the annotation syntax where they can, while others prefer always using the same `try-catch` pattern. Personally, I use the annotation shorthand when I'm only interested in the type and use the `try-catch` when I feel like digging deeper.

an exception, we either catch it and ignore it—if it's of the expected type—or let it bubble up to JUnit, which will then mark the test as having had an error.

OK. We've got a test that's failing. Well, at first it's not even compiling, but adding an empty `MissingValueException` class makes that go away:

```
public class MissingValueException extends RuntimeException {
    // this is all we need for now
}
```

We have the red bar again, and we're ready to make the test pass. And that means we have to somehow check for missing variables.

Once again, we're faced with the question of how to get to the green as quickly as possible. How do we know, inside `evaluate`, whether some of the variables specified in the template text are without a value? The simplest solution that springs to my mind right now is to look at the output and figure out whether it still contains pieces that look like variables. This is by no means a robust solution, but it'll do for now and it should be pretty easy to implement.

Sure enough, it was easy—as you can see from listing 2.15.

Listing 2.15 Checking for remaining variables after the search-and-replace

```
public String evaluate() {
    String result = templateText;
    for (Entry<String, String> entry : variables.entrySet()) {
        String regex = "\\$\\{" + entry.getKey() + "\\}";
```

```
            result = result.replaceAll(regex, entry.getValue());
        }
        if (result.matches(".*\\$\\{.+\\}.*")) {        <- Does it look like
            throw new MissingValueException();              we left a variable
        }                                                   in there?
        return result;
    }
```

We're back from red to green again. See anything to refactor this time? Nothing critical, I think, but the evaluate method is starting to become rather big. "Big?" you say. "That tiny piece of code?" I think so. I think it's time to refactor.

2.5.2 Refactoring toward smaller methods

There are differences in what size people prefer for their methods, classes, and so forth. Myself? I'm most comfortable with fewer than 10 lines of Java code per method.[6] Anything beyond that, and I start to wonder if there's something I could throw away or move somewhere else. Also, evaluate is on the verge of doing too many different things—replacing variables with values and checking for missing values. I'm starting to think it's already over the edge.

Let's apply some refactoring magic on evaluate to make it cleaner. I'm thinking we could at least extract the check for missing values into its own method. Listing 2.16 shows the refactored version of our evaluate method.

Listing 2.16 Extracting the check for missing variables into a method

```
public String evaluate() {
    String result = templateText;
    for (Entry<String, String> entry : variables.entrySet()) {
        String regex = "\\$\\{" + entry.getKey() + "\\}";
        result = result.replaceAll(regex, entry.getValue());
    }
    checkForMissingValues(result);        <- Hooray! We got rid
    return result;                           of a whole if-block
}                                            from evaluate()

private void checkForMissingValues(String result) {
    if (result.matches(".*\\$\\{.+\\}.*")) {
        throw new MissingValueException();
    }
}
```

[6] A perhaps better indicator of too big a method would be a complexity metric such as McCabe. Long methods are pretty good indicators of too high complexity as well, however.

Much better already, but there's still more to do. As we extracted the check for missing values from the `evaluate` method, we introduced a mismatch in the level of abstraction present in the `evaluate` method. We made `evaluate` less balanced than we'd like our methods to be. Let's talk about balance for a minute before moving on with our implementation.

2.5.3 Keeping methods in balance

One property of a method that has quite an effect on the readability of our code is the consistency of the abstraction level of the code within that method. Let's take another look at `evaluate` as an example of what we're talking about:

```
public String evaluate() {
    String result = templateText;
    for (Entry<String, String> entry : variables.entrySet()) {
        String regex = "\\$\\{" + entry.getKey() + "\\}";
        result = result.replaceAll(regex, entry.getValue());
    }
    checkForMissingValues(result);
    return result;
}
```

The `evaluate` method is doing two things: replacing variables with values and checking for missing values, which are at a completely different level of abstraction. The `for` loop is clearly more involved than the method call to `checkfor-MissingValues`. It's often easy to add little pieces of functionality by gluing a one-liner to an existing method, but without keeping an eye on inconsistencies in abstraction levels, the code is soon an unintelligible mess.

Fortunately, these kinds of issues usually don't require anything more than a simple application of the *extract method* refactoring, illustrated by listing 2.17.

Listing 2.17 Extracting another method from `evaluate()`

```
public String evaluate() {
    String result = replaceVariables();
    checkForMissingValues(result);
    return result;
}

private String replaceVariables() {
    String result = templateText;
    for (Entry<String, String> entry : variables.entrySet()) {
        String regex = "\\$\\{" + entry.getKey() + "\\}";
        result = result.replaceAll(regex, entry.getValue());
    }
    return result;
}
```

evaluate() method's internals much better balanced

New method is simple and has single, clear purpose

```
private void checkForMissingValues(String result) {
    if (result.matches(".*\\$\\{.+\\}.*")) {
        throw new MissingValueException();
    }
}
```

Running our tests, we realize that we didn't break anything with the refactoring, so we're good to go. Doing these kinds of edits on working code would be a much bigger effort if we didn't have the test battery watching our back. Let's face it: we might not have even carried out the refactoring we just did if we hadn't had those tests.

Our tests are running green again, which is a good thing. We're not done with the exception case yet, however. There's still one piece of functionality that we want to have for handling missing values: a meaningful exception message.

2.5.4 *Expecting details from an exception*

While writing the test for the missing value, we just caught a `MissingValueException` and called it a day. You can't possibly know how many times I've stared at a meaningless exception message[7] and cursed the developer who didn't bother giving even the least bit of information to help in problem solving. In this case, we probably should embed the name of the variable missing a value into the exception message. And, since we're all set, why not do just that (see listing 2.18)?

Listing 2.18 Testing for an expected exception

```
@Test
public void missingValueRaisesException() throws Exception {
    try {
        new Template("${foo}").evaluate();
        fail("evaluate() should throw an exception if "
                + "a variable was left without a value!");
    } catch (MissingValueException expected) {
        assertEquals("No value for ${foo}",
                     expected.getMessage());
    }
}
```

Exception should name missing variable

As usual, the edit needed for making a test pass is a matter of a couple of minutes. This time, we need to use the `java.util.regex` API a bit differently in order to

[7] Does "java.lang.NullPointerException: null" ring a bell...?

dig out the part of the rendered result that matches a variable pattern. Perhaps a snippet of code would explain that better:

```
import java.util.regex.Pattern;
import java.util.regex.Matcher;
private void checkForMissingValues(String result) {
    Matcher m = Pattern.compile("\\$\\{.+\\}").matcher(result);
    if (m.find()) {
        throw new MissingValueException("No value for " + m.group());
    }
}
```

Of course, we'll also need to add a constructor to `MissingValueException`:

```
public class MissingValueException extends RuntimeException  {
    public MissingValueException(String message) {
        super(message);
    }
}
```

That's it. A couple of minutes ago, we thought of a new test and decided to implement it right away. If it would've seemed like a bigger task, we might have just added it as a new test to our test list and come back to it later. Speaking of the test list, I think it's time for an update.

2.6 Loose ends on the test list

We've now implemented all the test cases that we thought of in the beginning. We did, however, spot some issues with our current implementation along the way. For one, it doesn't handle situations where the variable values contain delimiters such as "${" and "}". I've also got some worries with regard to how well our template engine performs. Adding performance to our task list, these are the remaining tests:

- Evaluate template "${one}, ${two}, ${three}" with values "1", "${foo}", and "3", respectively, and verify that the template engine renders the result as "1, ${foo}, 3".
- Verify that a template of 100 words and 20 variables with values of approximately 15 characters each is evaluated in 200 milliseconds or less.

We should add tests to the list as soon as we think of them, just to be sure we don't forget. That doesn't mean, however, that we should immediately drop on all fours and start chasing cars—we don't want to let these new tests interrupt our flow. We write down a simple reminder and continue with what we're currently working with, knowing that we'll come back to that new test later.

In our case, "later" is actually "as soon as I stop babbling," so let's get to it right away. How about going after that performance check first and then returning to the double-rendering issue?

2.6.1 Testing for performance

Wanting to get an idea of whether our template engine is any good performance-wise, let's quickly add a test for the performance of `evaluate` to see whether we're close to a reasonable execution time. Listing 2.19 presents our new test class for such a micro-performance check.

Listing 2.19 Writing a simple performance check to act as an early warning system

```
import org.junit.Test;
import static org.junit.Assert.*;

public class TestTemplatePerformance {

    // Omitted the setUp() for creating a 100-word template
    // with 20 variables and populating it with approximately
    // 15-character values

    @Test
    public void templateWith100WordsAnd20Variables() throws Exception {
        long expected = 200L;
        long time = System.currentTimeMillis();
        template.evaluate();
        time = System.currentTimeMillis() - time;
        assertTrue("Rendering the template took " + time
                + "ms while the target was " + expected + "ms",
                time <= expected);
    }
}
```

It seems that our `Template` implementation does pass this performance check for now, taking approximately 100 milliseconds to render the 100-word template with some 20 variables. Nice to know that we're not already spending over our budget! Besides, now that we've got the test in place, we'll know immediately when we do something that makes the template engine slower than we're expecting it to be.

This is not an approach without any issues, of course. Because our code is not executing in the computer equivalent of a vacuum, the test—which depends on the elapsed system time—is non-deterministic. In other words, the test might pass on one machine but fail on another. It might even alternate between passing and failing on a single machine based on what other software happens to be running at the same time. This is something we'll have to deal with, unless we're willing to accept the fact that some of our test runs might fail seemingly sporadically. Most of the time, it's a good enough solution to tune the test such that it won't fail too often while still alerting us to a performance problem.

With that worry largely behind us, let's see about that other test we added for the double-rendering problem—the one about rendering variables that have values that look like variable placeholders.

2.6.2 A looming design dead-end

Regarding the remaining test for variable values that contain "${" and "}", things are starting to look more difficult. For one thing, we can't just do a search-and-replace over and over again until we've covered all variable values set to the template, because some of the variable values rendered first could be re-rendered with something completely different during later rounds of search-and-replace. In addition, we can't rely on our method of detecting unset variables by looking for "${...}" in the result.

Before we go further, let's stop all this speculation and write a test that proves whether our assumptions about the code's current behavior are correct! Adding the following test into the `TestTemplate` class does just that:

```
@Test
public void variablesGetProcessedJustOnce() throws Exception {
    template.set("one", "${one}");
    template.set("two", "${three}");
    template.set("three", "${two}");
    assertTemplateEvaluatesTo("${one}, ${three}, ${two}");
}
```

Running the test tells us that we certainly have a problem. This test is causing an `IllegalArgumentException` to be thrown from the regular expression code invoked from `evaluate`, saying something about an "illegal group reference," so our code is definitely not handling the scenario well. I'm thinking it's time to back out of that test, pick up the notepad, and sketch a bit. Instead, let's sum up the chapter so far, take a break, and continue with this double-rendering issue in the next chapter.

2.7 Summary

Test-driven development is a powerful technique that helps us write better software faster. It does so by focusing on what is absolutely needed right now, then making that tiny piece work, and finally cleaning up any mess we might've made while making it work, effectively keeping the code base healthy. This cycle of first writing a test, then writing the code to make it pass, and finally refactoring the design makes heavy use of programming by intention—writing the test as if the ideal implementation exists already—as a tool for creating usable and testable designs.

In this chapter, we have seen TDD in action, we've lived through the TDD cycle, and we've realized that our current design for the template engine doesn't quite cut it. We set out to write a template engine based on a short list of tests that specify the expected behavior of the engine, and we followed the test-code-refactor (or red-green-green) cycle all the way.[8] The code already satisfies most of our requirements (we've got tests to prove it!) and would certainly be useful in many contexts as it is. We are able to make progress fast with the tests watching our backs, and we're not afraid to refactor knowing that the safety net will catch us should we fail to retain functionality as it is.

Now, let's flip the page to the next chapter and see how we can overcome the remaining issues and wrap up that template engine into a fully functional, beautifully constructed piece of product!

---

[8] I'll forgive you if you slipped. I do that, too. And it tends to come back to bite me, reminding of the various benefits of TDD. I'm sure you'll also get better and better at doing TDD as time goes by.

3 *Refactoring in small steps*

The most powerful designs are always the result of a continuous process of simplification and refinement.

—Kevin Mullet, *Designing Visual Interfaces: Communication Oriented Techniques*

In the previous chapter, we began implementing a template engine using test-driven development, starting from basically nothing and ending up with a rather useful chunk of code. In fact, we've gotten this far with almost laughably little code. If you look at our `Template` class, it's a lot smaller than I suppose most would've guessed based on years of experience in waterfall-style, big-design-up-front development. Or maybe it's just me. Perhaps others have indeed come up with small and simple solutions while I devised fancy and complex designs.

We did bump into a problem, however, with our use of regular expressions to scan the template text for variables. I like to think of these kinds of obstacles as opportunities to make design decisions. A lot of the time while developing test-first, the steps we take are relatively trivial, obvious even. It's refreshing when the going gets rough for a while and we need to stretch our imagination to figure out how to solve the problem. In this chapter, we'll learn to make a big change in our design in small steps and in a controlled manner.

We'll begin by mapping the territory with something we call *spike solution.* A spike is basically throwaway prototyping with the goal of learning whether and with how much effort a potential solution can be implemented. Once we've learned whether and how Java's regular expression API could help us in parsing our templates, we'll use that knowledge in implementing a parser.

We'll also refactor our existing implementation of the template engine into a design that makes it easy to replace the existing parsing logic with our brand-new parser. Once we've finished introducing a proper template parser into our engine, we'll finish the chapter by further refactoring, promoting some implicit types in our code into explicit, first-class concepts in our design.

All right, it's time to start the spike.

3.1 Exploring a potential solution

Have you already thought about potential approaches to getting our problem of double-rendering solved? If you haven't, do take a few minutes to think about how you would go about solving it.

Ready? Good. What did you *do* just now? Did you sketch something on paper? Did you write code to a temp file to figure out how the Java regular expression API works? Did you reach for Google and the Javadocs? Or did you just try to think your way through to devise an approach completely different than regular expressions? From the point of view of TDD, the exploratory process of figuring out whether a given solution would solve our problem or what might be the best approach to solving a given problem, is what the Extreme Programming vocabulary calls a *spike.*

3.1.1 Prototyping with spikes

Sometimes when facing a stop, breathe, design moment, we decide to dig deeper into a potential solution—be it some fancy new technology, that ancient API nobody has used since the company's infamous Y2K project, or an algorithm that seems to fit the bill better than what we currently have. A spike is a short[1] experiment with the purpose of familiarizing ourselves with the technology, tools, algorithms, and so forth, that we need for solving the problem at hand. A spike is a way to make an unknown known—at least to a point where we know whether it's worth continuing to dig that way or whether we should start looking for another way.

We typically don't do our spikes quite as strictly as regular development with regard to programming test-first. Some do, however, stick to TDD also for spikes—and, since we're getting so many nice benefits out of it for the rest of our work, why not! The important thing is, though, that we don't just take what we hacked together in a spike and glue it on top of our production code. We want to keep our software healthy, so we'll write the test first and only then write the code—not by copying and pasting the whole spike product piece by piece, but rather using our newly acquired knowledge from the spike and keeping the design lean and clean.

Now, let's take a look at an example spike. We start by writing learning tests to increase our understanding and knowledge of what we're trying to learn—the Java regular expression API—and then begin making use of that new knowledge. Let's go.

3.1.2 Learning by writing tests

Where were we? Ah, right. We wrote a test that reveals the deficiency in our `Template` class with regard to handling variable values, which look like variables themselves. Call me persistent, but I'm still thinking regular expressions are a Good Thing™. We probably could keep our code pretty clean and tight by implementing this latest challenge using Java's regular expression API, `java.util.regex`.

The way I tend to do smaller spikes, like getting to know how some particular API works or whether it can do what I'm looking for, is by writing *learning tests*. Learning tests are automated tests whose purpose is to verify assumptions about a piece of code, therefore teaching us—by example—what works. In the case of Java's regular expression API, a learning test or two is a perfect way to map out a

[1] "Short" relatively speaking—most spikes are a matter of 15 minutes to a couple of hours—a lot longer than the TDD cycles we're used to measuring in seconds or minutes rather than hours...

potential solution for our situation in light of the new test our existing implementation doesn't pass.

The solution I'm thinking of is to parse the template at load time into plain-text segments and variable segments and then to evaluate them in sequence, appending to a `StringBuilder` or something similar. For example, given a template "${first} and ${second}", the parsing logic would produce the following sequence: variable named "first", a plain-text segment " and ", and a variable named "second". Evaluating these one by one would definitely prevent the problem of a variable's rendered value getting interpreted as another variable.

Let's write some learning tests to see how this could be done with the regular expression API.

3.1.3 Example spike for learning an API

There's a nice method called `groupCount` in the `java.util.regex.Matcher` class, and I remember that groups in the Java regular expression vocabulary refer to stuff surrounded with parentheses, so let's see if we could use that. I wrote the following test to verify my understanding of an unfamiliar API:

```
public class RegexLearningTest {
    @Test
    public void testHowGroupCountWorks() throws Exception {
        String haystack = "The needle shop sells needles";
        String regex = "(needle)";
        Matcher matcher = Pattern.compile(regex).matcher(haystack);
        assertEquals(2, matcher.groupCount());
    }
}
```

And it fails. It fails because I thought (don't ask why) that the `groupCount` method would give me the number of occurrences of the pattern in the data, not the number of groups identified in the regular expression itself. Well, at least I found that out before writing the whole implementation based on my incorrect assumption about the API.

This time, reading the Javadocs for `java.util.regex.Matcher` a bit more carefully, I find the following sentence: "The find() method scans the input sequence looking for the next subsequence that matches the pattern." That looks promising, especially since the documentation says the following:

> *[The method] attempts to find the next subsequence of the input sequence that matches the pattern. This method starts at the beginning of the input sequence or, if a previous invocation of the method was successful and the matcher has not since been reset, at the first character not matched by the previous match. If the match succeeds then more information can be obtained via the start, end, and group methods.*

Now let's write some more learning tests to see whether we could loop through all matches using the `find` method.

If I understood the documentation correctly, the `find` method should scan up until the first instance of "needle" in the data and return `true` because it finds one. Let's first add an assertion to verify my interpretation:

```
@Test
public void testFindStartAndEnd() throws Exception {
    String haystack = "The needle shop sells needles";
    String regex = "(needle)";
    Matcher matcher = Pattern.compile(regex).matcher(haystack);
    assertTrue(matcher.find());
}
```

That's correct. Next, we should be able to get some relevant character positions with the `start` and `end` methods. Let's write assertions for those as well:

```
@Test
public void testFindStartAndEnd() throws Exception {
    String haystack = "The needle shop sells needles";
    String regex = "(needle)";
    Matcher matcher = Pattern.compile(regex).matcher(haystack);
    assertTrue(matcher.find());
    assertEquals("Wrong start index of 1st match", 4, matcher.start());
    assertEquals("Wrong end index of 1st match", 10, matcher.end());
}
```

Cool. It works. I wonder if the next call to `find` will give us the correct indexes for the second occurrence of "needle"? Listing 3.1 shows the resulting learning test.

Listing 3.1 Making sure we can locate all matches within a given `String`

```
@Test
public void testFindStartAndEnd() throws Exception {
    String haystack = "The needle shop sells needles";
    String regex = "(needle)";
    Matcher matcher = Pattern.compile(regex).matcher(haystack);

    assertTrue(matcher.find());
    assertEquals("Wrong start index of 1st match.", 4, matcher.start());
    assertEquals("Wrong end index of 1st match.", 10, matcher.end());

    assertTrue(matcher.find());
    assertEquals("Wrong start index of 2nd match.", 22, matcher.start());
    assertEquals("Wrong end index of 2nd match.", 28, matcher.end());

    assertFalse("Should not have any more matches", matcher.find());
}
```

Excellent! The test passes. Now we know how to get the indexes for all instances of a regular expression within a given string. From there, I'm pretty confident we can write a relatively simple loop that collects all the variables and plain text segments into a list of some sort. Time to face the challenge! No, wait! One more thing...

Don't ask me why, but something about that regular expression I used in listing 3.1 caught my attention or, should I say, curiosity. For some reason, I used the regular expression "(needle)" in the test. It might be because parentheses are generally used for grouping in regular expressions; however, I'm not so sure whether those parentheses are important in this case. After all, we're looking for matches for the *whole* regular expression, not a specific *match group* within the regular expression.

It turns out that the test runs successfully even after removing the parentheses from the regular expression. The match groups in the regular expression we used have no relevance for finding and iterating through matches. That's another new piece of information I just learned from such a small experiment.

NOTE The outcome of a spike is information and knowledge, not code. Don't get me wrong—it's essential in a spike to write code. It's just that we shouldn't expect the code itself to be of much value. Instead, we're expecting to have *learned about the problem and a potential solution* while doing the spike. And that's what we've accomplished with our learning tests—we now know we can obtain the starting and ending indices of variable placeholders in a string; thus we're able to split the template into plain text and variable segments.

Going forward, our next task is to take this newly acquired knowledge and put it to practice. First of all, we probably should split the two logical phases—parsing the template and rendering the result—into separate methods orchestrated from the public `evaluate` method. Making this change directly to the `evaluate` method might be a little too big a step for our taste, however. It's time to go *depth-first* for a change, first implementing the new parsing logic and then swapping it in to the template engine itself.

3.2 Changing design in a controlled manner

As we discussed earlier in the context of breadth-first and depth-first, there is more than one approach to plotting our way towards a full solution. At that time, we decided to keep faking the template parsing logic, effectively postponing the implementation of that part until it was absolutely required. We could've decided otherwise just as well. There are no hard and fast rules about which approach to adopt—it's very much a case-by-case decision. This time, we've come to realize that it's probably better to take the depth-first route, as our `Template` class is gaining more and more complexity.

To outline a rough plan of how we're going to tackle this refactoring, we're first going to introduce a new class named `TemplateParse`, which will be responsible for taking a template text and splitting it into a sequence of plain-text and variable segments. And we're going to do that by writing tests, of course. Once we have a good enough parser, we'll switch `Template` to using that instead of the old implementation within the `Template` class.

Before we start, let's run the tests once again to make sure we're not working against a broken code base. There. All tests are passing, now that we've temporarily commented out the test that exposes the double-rendering problem.

3.2.1 Creating an alternative implementation

Our depth-first approach now means that we're going to forget everything about the `Template` class for a while and focus solely on adding the necessary functionality into a class named `TemplateParse` to support slicing and dicing a template text appropriately. The `TemplateParse` will essentially represent the result of parsing a template into segments. It's a completely new class with no dependencies to existing code, which means we'll have to start from a clean plate. As mentioned before, an easy way to start fresh is to start with the simplest test we can think of.

Starting with a low-hanging fruit

Feeling unsure about where to start? How about testing for an empty template? Listing 3.2 shows our first stab at the new test class for our new `TemplateParse` class.

Listing 3.2 Parsing an empty template using the `TemplateParse` class

```
public class TestTemplateParse {

    @Test
    public void emptyTemplateRendersAsEmptyString() throws Exception {
        TemplateParse parse = new TemplateParse();
        List<String> segments = parse.parse("");
        assertEquals("Number of segments", 1, segments.size());
        assertEquals("", segments.get(0));
    }
}
```

Adding the missing `TemplateParse` class and stubbing out the `parse` method with a `return null`, we have a failing test to show us the way. Quickly adding a return statement for a `List` containing the template text as is (listing 3.3) is enough to get us back to green, which makes sense because a template without any variables is essentially a single plain text segment for the `TemplateParse` class.

We're moving fast, so let's just see the next test:

```
@Test
public void templateWithOnlyPlainText() throws Exception {
    TemplateParse parse = new TemplateParse();
    List<String> segments = parse.parse("plain text only");
    assertEquals("Number of segments", 1, segments.size());
    assertEquals("plain text only", segments.get(0));
}
```

Making the test pass is still next to trivial. In fact, the test passes with the implementation we wrote for the previous test, as shown in listing 3.3.

Listing 3.3 The simplest implementation that fulfills the plain-text only tests

```
import java.util.List;
import java.util.Collections;

public class TemplateParse {
    public List<String> parse(String template) {
        return Collections.singletonList(template);
    }
}
```

At this point, we're again starting to collect duplication in our test code between `emptyTemplateRendersAsEmptyString` and `templateWithOnlyPlainText`. Before we start driving `TemplateParse` closer to where we want it to be, let's take care of that duplication.

Removing duplication from tests

At this point, both of our tests are creating a `TemplateParse` and giving it a template to be parsed into a `List` of segments. That's clearly duplication, so let's refactor the common part into a nice little helper method that does all of that for us. Listing 3.4 shows how our tests look after getting rid of the duplication.

Listing 3.4 Refactoring away duplication in our test method

```
private List<String> parse(String template) {
    return new TemplateParse().parse(template);
}
```

```
@Test
public void emptyTemplateRendersAsEmptyString() throws Exception {
    List<String> segments = parse("");
    assertEquals("Number of segments", 1, segments.size());
    assertEquals("", segments.get(0));
}

@Test
public void templateWithOnlyPlainText() throws Exception {
    List<String> segments = parse("plain text only");
    assertEquals("Number of segments", 1, segments.size());
    assertEquals("plain text only", segments.get(0));
}
```

There's some further refactoring to do. We're asserting the size of the returned `List` in both tests. We can see a clear pattern in what we really want to assert with the two `assertEquals` calls in each test. Realizing this, we want to make our code communicate that intent better. Let's see if a bit of *varargs* magic, courtesy of Java 5,[2] could help us out.

Listing 3.5 Refactoring the assertions to communicate intent better

```
private void assertSegments(List<? extends Object> actual,
                            Object... expected) {
    assertEquals("Number of segments doesn't match.",
            expected.length, actual.size());
    assertEquals(Arrays.asList(expected), actual);
}

@Test
public void emptyTemplateRendersAsEmptyString() throws Exception {
    List<String> segments = parse("");
    assertSegments(segments, "");
}

@Test
public void templateWithOnlyPlainText() throws Exception {
    List<String> segments = parse("plain text only");
    assertSegments(segments, "plain text only");
}
```

Variable-length argument list simplifies assertions

[2] Java 5 introduced the concept of variable-length argument lists into the language, which has made certain things a lot easier to achieve than before. One good example is custom assertion methods that deal with simple lists.

Tests are still passing after the refactoring—as they should—so let's try to shake it up by adding a variable or two into the mix. And, since we're test-driven, we'll do that by adding another test:

```
@Test
public void parsingMultipleVariables() throws Exception {
    List<String> segments = parse("${a}:${b}:${c}");
    assertSegments(segments, "${a}", ":", "${b}", ":", "${c}");
}
```

Aha! This is starting to get more interesting. It's no longer enough to return a list with the template text as the sole element. Let's see how we can accomplish the actual parsing of the template text.

Applying learnings from the spike

At this point, we pull our spike learnings from our short-term memory and apply them to the actual problem at hand. Here's the first strategy that popped to my mind: a loop that reads plain text from the beginning of the template, then reads the variable placeholder, sets a pointer to where in the template the loop should continue, and so forth. This strategy has been implemented in one big step as listing 3.6, using the features of the Java Regular Expression API we learned earlier in our spike and the existing tests as our safety net.

Listing 3.6 Parsing variables from plain text

```
public class TemplateParse {

    public List<String> parse(String template) {
        List<String> segments = new ArrayList<String>();
        int index = collectSegments(segments, template);
        addTail(segments, template, index);
        addEmptyStringIfTemplateWasEmpty(segments);
        return segments;
    }

    private int collectSegments(List<String> segs, String src) {
        Pattern pattern = Pattern.compile("\\$\\{[^}]*\\}");
        Matcher matcher = pattern.matcher(src);
        int index = 0;
        while (matcher.find()) {
            addPrecedingPlainText(segs, src, matcher, index);
            addVariable(segs, src, matcher);
            index = matcher.end();
        }
       return index;
    }
```

The high-level parsing logic (annotates the body of `parse`)

Collect variables and intermediate plain text (annotates the `while` loop)

```
    private void addTail(List<String> segs, String template, int index) {
        if (index < template.length()) {
            segs.add(template.substring(index));
        }
    }

    private void addVariable(List<String> segs, String src,Matcher m) {
        segs.add(src.substring(m.start(), m.end()));
    }

    private void addPrecedingPlainText(List<String> segs, String src,
                                      Matcher m, int index) {
        if (index != m.start()) {
            segs.add(src.substring(index, m.start()));
        }
    }

    private void addEmptyStringIfTemplateWasEmpty(List<String> segs) {
        if (segs.isEmpty()) {
            segs.add("");
        }
    }
}
```

Add remaining plain text, if any

The structure presented in listing 3.6 is suddenly much more complex than it was before. The public `parse` method is basically an outline describing an algorithm, which first parses the input into segments, then adds the remaining tail of plain text after the last variable placeholder, and, if the list of segments found would otherwise remain empty, adds an empty string to represent a zero-length template.

Looking inside the `collectSegments` method, the segments are gathered into an `ArrayList`. We're basically enumerating through matches for the regular expression of a variable placeholder. For each found variable placeholder, we add any plain text between the previous and the current match into the list. Then we add the variable to the list and update the `index` variable to point to the end of the latest match. The private methods doing the work of extracting the segments from the template text are each relatively simple and easy to understand, largely because they have descriptive names.

We now have a class that knows how to parse a template into a parse tree of plain-text segments and variable segments. Before we proceed to adding our shiny new parser to the template engine, however, let's reflect a bit on what we just did.

Quick reflection before moving on

It's a good thing we decided to split this parsing logic into its own class. We did, however, take too large a leap at once: It took several minutes to get the parsing logic together and the test passing. The `TemplateParse` implementation might also benefit from moving the list of segments being passed around into an instance variable. That would require synchronizing the `parse` method, though, if we'd like to keep our parser thread-safe. Then again, we don't have a need for multithreaded access, so not sharing instances of the parse object should be fine for now. Perhaps we'll not go down that path right now—but feel free to refactor your code further if you're following along.

Having a helper method in our test class that doesn't deal with setting up data or objects' state for the test might be an indicator that the method should be a public method in production code—a static builder method in the `TemplateParse` class.

After adding a short note of this potential refactoring to our test list, deciding to take smaller steps from now on, and keeping an eye on the parser's complexity, let's turn our attention back to the `Template` class. Our next step is to change `Template` by making it use `TemplateParse` for slicing the template.

3.2.2 Switching over safely

Now that we've got the necessary functionality in `TemplateParse` to give us a nicely chewed list of segments in a template, we want to make the leap by adopting `TemplateParse` as a replacement for our existing parsing logic in the `Template` class. We're not changing any functionality here. In fact, that's the last thing we want to happen! Luckily, the tests are all green, so we can refactor safely.

Adopting the new implementation

Without further ado, listing 3.7 presents the current implementation of `evaluate` from the `Template` class, which we want to migrate to by using `TemplateParse`.

Listing 3.7 The current implementation of `evaluate()`

```
public String evaluate() {
    String result = replaceVariables();
    checkForMissingValues(result);
    return result;
}
```

Now, programming by intention, we change the evaluate method into:

```
public String evaluate() {
    TemplateParse parser = new TemplateParse();
    List<String> segments = parser.parse(templateText);
    StringBuilder result = new StringBuilder();
    for (String segment : segments) {
        append(segment, result);
    }
    return result.toString();
}
```

Nice. That should do it. We're basically just getting a `TemplateParse` and letting it do the hard work of parsing the template. Then, we're looping through the list of parsed segments and appending them one by one to a `StringBuilder`. The compiler is whining about not knowing about any `append` method so we add that next, already anxious to see our thorough test suite passing again:

```
private void append(String segment, StringBuilder result) {
    if (segment.startsWith("${") && segment.endsWith("}")) {
        String var = segment.substring(2, segment.length() - 1);
        if (!variables.containsKey(var)) {
            throw new MissingValueException("No value for " + segment);
        }
        result.append(variables.get(var));
    } else {
        result.append(segment);
    }
}
```

The `append` implementation concatenates segments based on their type. For variables—that is, segments that are wrapped in the squiggly brackets after a dollar sign—we append the respective value from our variables map. For plain-text segments, we append the segment itself.

Run the tests, and we get the familiar green bar indicating that our switch worked. That wasn't too hard, was it? But what just happened? We had such nice, clean code, and then we write *this*? Well, at least the tests are passing, so we can safely refactor that chunk toward something more hygienic. Besides, now that we're using `TemplateParse` and appending segments into a `StringBuilder`, we can get rid of the `replaceVariables` and `checkForMissingValues` methods from our previous implementation. Maybe the code is not *that* bad after all. But let's see if we could improve it by refactoring again.

Keeping a uniform level of abstraction

First, let's do something about that `evaluate` method. The current implementation, shown next, is again doing too much on two different levels of abstraction:

```
public String evaluate() {
    TemplateParse parser = new TemplateParse();
    List<String> segments = parser.parse(templateText);
    StringBuilder result = new StringBuilder();
    for (String segment : segments) {
        append(segment, result);
    }
    return result.toString();
}
```

Fortunately, extracting the rendering logic into a separate method is a piece of cake, as illustrated in listing 3.8.

Listing 3.8 Extracting the rendering logic into a separate method

```
public String evaluate() {
    TemplateParse parser = new TemplateParse();
    List<String> segments = parser.parse(templateText);
    return concatenate(segments);
}

private String concatenate(List<String> segments) {
    StringBuilder result = new StringBuilder();
    for (String segment : segments) {
        append(segment, result);
    }
    return result.toString();
}
```

evaluate() is now more balanced...

...and concatenate() is doing just one thing

That's not all we want to refactor, though. There's still that ugly append method we'd like to trim into something we're not ashamed to show to our colleagues.

Cleaning up by extracting methods

What are we going to do with the nasty `if-else` structure in append, shown in the following code snippet?

```
private void append(String segment, StringBuilder result) {
    if (segment.startsWith("${") && segment.endsWith("}")) {
        String var = segment.substring(2, segment.length() - 1);
        if (!variables.containsKey(var)) {
            throw new MissingValueException("No value for " + segment);
        }
        result.append(variables.get(var));
    } else {
        result.append(segment);
    }
}
```

How about, say, extracting a couple of methods? We could take that code block inside the `if`-block and turn it into a method. We should also make the condition for the `if`-block communicate its purpose better. That should leave `append` a bit less eye-straining. Listing 3.9 confirms that this is the case.

Listing 3.9 The `append()` method after a quick diet

```
private void append(String segment, StringBuilder result) {
    if (isVariable(segment)) {
        evaluateVariable(segment, result);
    } else {
        result.append(segment);
    }
}

private boolean isVariable(String segment) {
    return segment.startsWith("${") && segment.endsWith("}");
}

private void evaluateVariable(String segment, StringBuilder result) {
    String var = segment.substring(2, segment.length() - 1);
    if (!variables.containsKey(var)) {
        throw new MissingValueException("No value for " + segment);
    }
    result.append(variables.get(var));
}
```

❶ Branch execution based on segment type

Variables surrounded by "${" and "}"

Render value of variable

Better, and definitely easier on the eyes. But that `if-else` structure in ❶ `append` still has a stench I'd rather get rid of. We're making a decision based on the type of a segment object, which is a clear violation of the Pragmatic Programmers' "Tell, Don't Ask" principle,[3] and using strings to represent something more than text smells a lot like *Primitive Obsession*.[4] If we'd make those segments first-class objects instead of mere `Strings`, we should be able to get rid of both of these code smells. We could hide the `if-else` logic behind polymorphism and simply *tell* the segments to do their thing instead of asking and then doing. Let's see what that would take.

But first, let's run the tests again—just to be sure. Good. All tests are passing, so we're good for another refactoring session. All these important `Strings` we call segments really ought to be first-class objects.

---

[3] http://www.pragmaticprogrammer.com/ppllc/papers/1998_05.html.

[4] The Primitive Obsession code smell is described in Martin Fowler's *Refactoring: Improving the Design of Existing Code* (Addison-Wesley, 1999).

3.3 *Taking the new design further*

So far, we've adopted our alternative implementation for the core of the template engine and refactored the resulting code a bit. There's still more to do, however.

We'd like to be able to ignore the actual type of each segment and treat them all the same, meaning we wouldn't need the smelly `if-else` structure and instead we could delegate the appending to the segments. Why not start, again, programming by intention and designing the way we want the new `Segment` interface to behave? Listing 3.10 shows how I'd like it to work from the perspective of the `Template` class.

Listing 3.10 Treating all segments the same

```
public String evaluate() {
    TemplateParse parser = new TemplateParse();
    List&lt;Segment&gt; segments = parser.parse(templateText);    <-- Use Segments instead of Strings
    return concatenate(segments);
}

private String concatenate(List&lt;Segment&gt; segments) {
    StringBuilder result = new StringBuilder();
    for (Segment segment : segments) {
        segment.appendTo(result, variables);    <-- Let Segment append itself to buffer
    }
    return result.toString();
}
```

The code looks much better again. From listing 3.10, we see that we need to change the `parse` method in `TemplateParse` to return a `List` of `Segment` objects instead of `Strings`. The `Segment` objects need to be able to append themselves on a given `StringBuilder`, possibly acquiring a variable value from a `Map`, which we also pass in as an argument. That shouldn't be a problem.

The question becomes how to proceed with this refactoring. We need to change how `TemplateParse` works, so maybe we should change `TemplateParse`—test first, of course—and only then come back to the `Template` class. We don't like taking big steps, remember? Having learned from our past, let's undo the changes to the `evaluate` method for now until we've implemented the new functionality in `TemplateParse` and come back once we've gotten the other pieces in place.

3.3.1 *Keeping things compatible*

Not wanting to break any tests while introducing the concept of `Segment` objects, we might keep both the `String`-based and a new `Segment` object-based version of the `parse` method around—only temporarily for backward compatibility. In practice, that means that we add a new `parseSegments` method and let existing code call the old `parse` until we get to switching them over.

Our test for driving out this new parsing method could, for instance, look like this:

```
public class TestTemplateParse {
    @Test
    public void parsingTemplateIntoSegmentObjects() throws Exception {
        TemplateParse p = new TemplateParse();
        List&lt;Segment&gt; segments = p.parseSegments("a ${b} c ${d}");
        assertSegments(segments,
                new PlainText("a "), new Variable("b"),
                new PlainText(" c "), new Variable("d"));
    }
}
```

Voilà. We've identified that we need two implementations of a `Segment` interface. Let's quickly satisfy the compiler by creating those so that we get a failing test, as illustrated in listing 3.11.

Listing 3.11 The `Segment` interface and its initial implementations

```
public interface Segment {
}

public class PlainText implements Segment {
    public PlainText(String text) { }
}

public class Variable implements Segment {
    public Variable(String name) { }
}
```

And here's the skeleton for the missing `parseSegments` method in `TemplateParse`:

```
public List&lt;Segment&gt; parseSegments(String template) {
    return null;
}
```

That's all we need to have a red bar to work against. Now, let's see how to get back to green.

Building on existing functionality

We already have the code necessary for parsing a template into segment strings, so let's start by building on that. We can basically just ask for the `List` of `Strings` and then convert each into its respective `Segment` implementations. In fact, we already have some code in the `Template` class that handles this kind of stuff. Let's look at whether we could reuse some parts.

There is already a method for determining from a given `String` whether it represents a variable segment or a plain text segment. It's now a `private` instance method, but we should be able to make it `public` and `static` so that we can use it from `TemplateParse` as well, right? Quickly commenting out the failing test, running the tests to see that they all pass, changing the `isVariable` method into `public` and `static`, and running all tests again to verify that we really can get away with that, we realize that we can now call the static method from `Template`, displayed in listing 3.12, in our `TemplateParse`.

Listing 3.12 Utility method for detecting whether a given segment represents a variable

```
public class Template {
    ...
    public static boolean isVariable(String segment) {
        return segment.startsWith("${") && segment.endsWith("}");
    }
}
```

We can now implement the new `parseSegments` method by calling on the static utility method. Yes, it's a rather questionable dependency, but I'm sure we can figure out a way to clean it up in the refactoring step.

Listing 3.13 presents an initial implementation of the `parseSegments` method built on top of the existing parsing logic.

Listing 3.13 Converting the List of Strings into a List of Segment objects

```
public class TemplateParse {
    ...
    public List&lt;Segment&gt; parseSegments(String template) {
        List&lt;Segment&gt; segments = new ArrayList&lt;Segment&gt;();
        List<String> strings = parse(template);          <-- Parse template into String segments
        for (String s : strings) {
            if (Template.isVariable(s)) {
                String name = s.substring(2, s.length() - 1);
                segments.add(new Variable(name));
            } else {                                      <-- Convert each String into Segment object
                segments.add(new PlainText(s));
            }
        }
        return segments;
    }
}
```

This is enough to make our new test pass once we've added the appropriate `equals` implementations to the `Segment` classes, shown in listing 3.14.

Listing 3.14 Minimal implementations of the two `Segment` classes

```
public class PlainText implements Segment {
    private String text;

    public PlainText(String text) {
        this.text = text;
    }

    public boolean equals(Object other) {
        return text.equals(((PlainText) other).text);
    }
}

public class Variable implements Segment {
    private String name;

    public Variable(String name) {
        this.name = name;
    }

    public boolean equals(Object other) {
        return name.equals(((Variable) other).name);
    }
}
```

On equals() and hashCode()

The astute reader might be worried about not implementing the `hashCode` method to go with `equals` in listing 3.14, which is what the contract for the `hashCode` method would require. Yes, we could've easily implemented the `hashCode` method into the `Segment` implementations. Our current tests do not require such implementations, however, so we would need to write tests to document our intention first. Although we won't do that here, there's a handy utility class called `EqualsTester` available as part of the GSBase JUnit extensions (http://gsbase.sf.net), which helps enormously in verifying that a given class has implemented the delicate contract for `equals` and `hashCode` properly.

Because we're on the green again with all tests happily passing, we are almost ready to take another look at making the `Template` class use this new method instead of the old one. But before we can touch the `Template` class, let's test-drive some functionality into our two newly created `Segment` classes!

Refactoring logic into objects

An essential part of our grand plan of avoiding ugly `if-else` blocks by means of polymorphism is to embed the varying functionality into the different implementations of the polymorphic concept of `Segment` objects. In practice, this functionality realizes itself as a method used for rendering a `Segment` with a `Map` of variable values. We'll add a method `evaluate` to our `Segment` interface:

```
public interface Segment {
    String evaluate(Map<String, String> variables);
}
```

Starting from the plain-text segment implementation, the test for introducing this functionality is trivial, as can be seen from the code snippet in listing 3.15.

Listing 3.15 Test class for the plain-text segment

```
public class TestPlainTextSegment {
    @Test
    public void plainTextEvaluatesAsIs() throws Exception {
        Map<String, String> variables = new HashMap<String, String>();
        String text = "abc def";
        assertEquals(text, new PlainText(text).evaluate(variables));
    }
}
```

And, as is typical for such small and focused, test-driven steps, the implementation isn't much trickier (see listing 3.16).

Listing 3.16 Implementation of the `evaluate()` method for plain-text segments

```
public class PlainText implements Segment {

    private String text;

    public PlainText(String text) {
        this.text = text;
    }

    ...

    public String evaluate(Map<String, String> variables) {
        return text;      <-- I wish programming was always this easy!
    }
}
```

That covers the plain-text stuff. Doing the same for variables, the test in listing 3.17 verifies that `Variable` objects render themselves by appending the matching value for the variable's name from the given `Map`.

Listing 3.17 Test class for variable segments

```
public class TestVariableSegment {
    @Test
    public void variableEvaluatesToItsValue() throws Exception {
        Map<String, String> variables = new HashMap<String, String>();
        String name = "myvar";
        String value = "myvalue";
        variables.put(name, value);
        assertEquals(value, new Variable(name).evaluate(variables));
    }
}
```

The implementation is still rather straightforward, as listing 3.18 succinctly proves.

Listing 3.18 Implementation of evaluate() for variable segments

```
public class Variable implements Segment {

    private String name;

    public Variable(String name) {
        this.name = name;
    }

    ...

    public String evaluate(Map<String, String> variables) {
        return variables.get(name);    <-- Variables aren't that hard to render either.
    }
}
```

Tests are running green, we have different kinds of `Segments` that know how to evaluate themselves given a `Map` of variables, and we're finally ready to make that switchover in the `Template` class.

3.3.2 Making the switchover

With our tests as a safety net, we change the `evaluate` method on `Template` to what we envisioned 10 minutes ago. For your convenience, listing 3.19 reproduces our vision.

Listing 3.19 Making the switchover in `Template`

```
public String evaluate() {
    TemplateParse p = new TemplateParse();
    List&lt;Segment&gt; segments = p.parseSegments(templateText);
    return concatenate(segments);
}

private String concatenate(List&lt;Segment&gt; segments) {
    StringBuilder result = new StringBuilder();
    for (Segment segment : segments) {
        result.append(segment.evaluate(variables));
    }
    return result.toString();
}
```

Parse template into Segment objects

Let Segment objects evaluate themselves

There. An almost trivial change, now that we already have the `TemplateParse` and `Segment` objects that know how to evaluate themselves. What's interesting is that running our tests after this change reveals that we forgot something rather important.

Getting caught by the safety net

The new `evaluate` method on the `Template` class seems to work as expected with one exception—we're not raising an exception anymore upon missing variable values! It's a good thing we have those tests, isn't it?

Let's remedy the situation by adding a test to handle this case and get us back on track. Now, where should we raise the exception for a missing variable value? The first place that comes to mind—a place where we have access to both the variable's name and the whole set of variable values—is the `Variable` class. Listing 3.20 presents our full test class for the `Variable` class.

Listing 3.20 The proper test for missing variable values

```
public class TestVariableSegment {

    private Map<String, String> variables;

    @Before
    public void setUp() {
        variables = new HashMap<String, String>();
    }

    @Test
    public void variableEvaluatesToItsValue() throws Exception {
        String name = "myvar";
        String value = "myvalue";
```

Refactored duplicated code into fixture

```
        variables.put(name, value);
        assertEquals(value, new Variable(name).evaluate(variables));
    }

    @Test
    public void missingVariableRaisesException() throws Exception {
        String name = "myvar";
        try {
            new Variable(name).evaluate(variables);
            fail("Missing variable value should raise an exception");
        } catch (MissingValueException expected) {
            assertEquals("No value for ${" + name + "}",
                    expected.getMessage());
        }
    }
}
```

Added test for missing variable

We almost introduced a significant change to our template engine's behavior by omitting that second test. Thanks to our test suite, we realized our mistake early and got a chance to correct our wrongdoing. Listing 3.21 shows our path to righteousness.

Listing 3.21 Checking for missing values in the `Variable` class at rendering time

```
public class Variable implements Segment {
    ...
    public String evaluate(Map<String,String> variables) {
        if (!variables.containsKey(name)) {
            throw new MissingValueException(
                    "No value for ${" + name + "}");
        }
        return variables.get(name);
    }
}
```

Raise exception for missing value

Running our tests, we're once again greeted with a bright green bar telling us that everything is well in the kingdom of template engines. Except...

Deleting dead code and further cleanup

Glancing over our code after this switchover to using `Segment` objects in the `Template` class, we realize that a bunch of methods are no longer used by anyone. Deleting code is relieving, isn't it? While getting rid of the dead code—including that ugly `if-else` block with the stench—we also notice the `isVariable` method that we blatantly made `public` and `static` in order to be able to call it from the

`TemplateParse`. Because it's no longer used anywhere other than `TemplateParse`, we move it to the `TemplateParse` class and make it `private` again.

Phew. This has been a long and intensive session, but now that we're through it, our code does have a much better shape and a much cleaner division of responsibilities.

There would still be more to do before declaring our template engine a work of art, however. First, `TemplateParse`'s `String`-parsing method is also no longer used outside the `TemplateParse` class, so we should probably make that `private` as well. Furthermore, now that nobody's using the old parsing method, we should streamline the `TemplateParse` class by skipping the string-to-segment object conversion in the first place and add `PlainText` and `Variable` objects to the `List` where we're now adding `Strings`. With a thorough test suite as our bodyguard, that shouldn't be too big a task. Consider that refactoring an exercise for you.

Now, let's wrap up the chapter so we can move on to other topics—there's plenty of stuff about test-driven development that we've yet to see!

3.4 Summary

Yes! We managed to put together a solid template engine using test-driven development, and it took, I speculate, no longer than doing all the design first and then writing the code would have. Besides, now that we've got the extensive test suite covering every branch of our production code, we don't need to worry too much about breaking stuff when we add some new feature into the engine—again, the tests will tell us when we screw up.

Having said that, the template engine was a trivial example—most code we face in the field tends to not be as isolated as what we had the pleasure of writing. Not to worry, though. We'll face some of these real-world challenges in the following chapters, and we'll discuss ways to get past those challenges. Part 2 is chock-full of just such real-world challenges posed by difficult APIs and troublesome technologies.

Regardless of how fascinated we might be right now about TDD, it is not an all-encompassing silver bullet. Although test-driven development helps us produce working software, we still need something extra to help us deliver working functionality—and the right functionality. In part 3, we will take the concepts of test-first and TDD and apply them on a more coarse-grained level of user stories, features, and requirements through a technique called acceptance test-driven development.

That's still to come, though. For now, let's move on to chapter 4, where we will learn some useful tricks of the trade and gain even more insight into the technique of TDD.

4 Concepts and patterns for TDD

I remember growing up with television, from the time it was just a test pattern, with maybe a little bit of programming once in a while.

—Francis Ford Coppola

In chapters 2 and 3, we saw test-driven development being used for developing a template engine. That example was intentionally what many would consider a trivial case—a sort of "ideal" scenario with no tough cookies to crack. In this chapter, we'll study different patterns and techniques that a seasoned test-driven developer can pull out from their toolbox when the going gets tough. These patterns range from design patterns that we can apply to our production code for making it more testable to different ways of organizing and implementing our tests. I'm about to reveal some heavily guarded secrets of the guild. Don't tell anyone.

We'll begin by asking how to write tests and approach the answer by looking at a handful of test-selection strategies and some more general principles we should keep in mind. We'll also discuss three slightly different strategies for making tests pass—just as essential to TDD as writing tests is. Having learned some new techniques for writing tests and making them pass, we'll look at some essential testing concepts, including fixtures, test doubles, and the differing natures of state- versus interaction-based testing. We'll devote additional time and attention to dealing with difficult collaborators by using test doubles; we'll study three different kinds of test doubles: fakes, stubs, and mocks.

After winding up our discussion about testing concepts, we will turn the tables and start looking at design. First, we'll discuss four guidelines for creating testable designs. Then, we'll explore a number of patterns related to unit tests, from different types of assertion techniques to higher-level patterns of structuring our tests.

To finish off, we'll take a look at how to apply TDD with a legacy code base that typically isn't designed with testability in mind and that doesn't have too thorough a test suite in place.

We're going to cover a lot of ground in this chapter, and we'll be moving fast. Not to worry, though. We'll take a break if the pace gets too fast. Now, let's ask ourselves how to write tests.

4.1 How to write tests and make them pass

Like so many other things in life, writing tests and test-driving are often easier said than done. For starters, one of the first decisions we need to make when starting to test-drive code is which test to start with—not necessarily an easy choice. Furthermore, the whole TDD cycle seems to rely heavily on the individual between the chair and the keyboard in terms of what we test for, how we organize our tests, and so forth.

In an attempt to make the first TDD steps easier for the beginning test-driver, we're going to look at a handful of test-selection strategies—simple heuristics—

that we can use for evaluating which test we should write next. We're also going to talk about more general principles of test-driving. You could think of those guidelines as a short list of Very Important Practices you simply must follow—everything else you can ramp up on the side as you start feeling more comfortable with what's going on around you.

First, let's study some interesting test-selection strategies.

4.1.1 Test-selection strategies

Let's say you've been thinking about buying yourself a new digital camera. How do you select one of the dozens and dozens of alternatives? If you're anything like me, you'll spend hours browsing various websites and camera magazines reading reviews, comparing technical specifications, comparing prices, evaluating the aesthetic form of the cameras, and procrastinating between a few different but equally good products. There's no single property of a digital camera that would tell us which one to buy.

Selecting the next test to write from a list isn't that different. We need to rely on our intuition and a variety of heuristics when thinking about the multiple properties of the candidate tests. To start with, we might want to consider the following four strategies to aid our decision of which test to write next:

- Diving first into details versus starting with the big picture
- Exploring uncertain territory versus sticking with the familiar and comfortable
- Going for the highest value versus picking the low-hanging fruit first
- Treading the happy path[1] first versus starting with handling error situations

Let's briefly elaborate on these four strategies for evaluating which test we should write next.

Details vs. big picture

I'm confident we've both learned in a computer science class that there's more than one way to traverse a tree. Just as we can traverse a tree of nodes in a breadth-first or a depth-first order, we can proceed with test-driving through the envisioned design and functionality from different directions.

For example, we can choose to first implement the framework surrounding a faked algorithm and only start worrying about the algorithm once we've proven that the rest of the component works. Another option could be to start with the

---

[1] http://en.wikipedia.org/wiki/Happy_path.

algorithm—the details—and start building the surrounding structures—the big picture—after we've test-driven the building blocks into existence.

I call these two approaches *details first* and *big picture first*. Both approaches have their unique advantages and disadvantages, of course. Details first is a good way of tackling risks such as, "Are we able to recognize a pattern from a user-submitted image?" but solving the pattern recognition problem delays progress (certainty) regarding the big picture. Big-picture first, on the other hand, is a good way of testing out the envisioned design quickly without needing to worry about the details. The downside of big-picture first is that we're delaying progress on the details.

In practice, we identify the risks and uncertainties associated with these alternative foci and usually (but not necessarily—which we'll discuss in the next section) tackle the aspect we're more concerned about. Which leads us directly to our second test-selection strategy—choosing between exploring the uncertain versus sticking with the familiar.

Uncertain vs. familiar

Reducing uncertainty is one factor we might consider when selecting the next test. The alternative for reducing uncertainty would be to stick with the familiar and proceed on a safe, known path for the moment, dealing with the uncertain later. The advantage of exploring the uncertain is simple and straightforward—we're effectively reducing risks by turning the unknown into the known.

So what's the advantage of sticking with the cozy old couch, the familiar area of our design that isn't likely to reveal that much new information? Well, it turns out that not all paths embed an equal amount of value in return for the effort spent. Although there is value in reducing risk, sometimes there's even more value in quickly beating down a known path and picking the low-hanging fruit first, instead of climbing the tree right away to figure out whether we can do it.[2]

Which brings us to our third test-selection strategy—high value versus the low-hanging fruit.

High value vs. low-hanging fruit

Looking at a list of tests we have yet to write, we can usually identify a couple of tests that are clearly more work than others. Similarly, we can usually identify differences in how valuable the behavior represented by the test in question is for the larger whole. Ideally, we should try to identify and select tests that let us make the most progress (yield the most value) with the smallest effort. Most of the time,

[2] After all, we might not be hungry anymore after eating a dozen juicy apples from the low-hanging branch.

however, there's no such clear candidate, and we need to decide among multiple tests with more or less equal benefit-to-effort price tags.

A typical (if somewhat exaggerated) example of a high-value test versus a low-hanging fruit might be testing an object for positive functionality versus testing the same object for handling null input. The positive functionality is likely more laborious to implement but almost by definition yields more value. The defensive functionality, handling null input, is likely far easier to implement but also yields much, much less value in terms of functionality.

The essence of our fourth and last test-selection strategy is the happy path versus error situations.

Happy path vs. error situations

As a rule of thumb, I drive for the happy path first before proceeding to handle exceptional scenarios, such as exceptions thrown by third-party APIs, malformed input, and so forth. The reason for doing so is mostly about value. Even the most robust system capable of handling any conceivable error situation is practically useless when it isn't able to perform its basic function. On the other hand, even a system that, for example, is prone to crash if the network is temporarily down still provides value as long as the network isn't down.

Having said that, every once in a while we might face a situation where it makes sense to test-drive by leaving the happy path for last, first going through all error situations. These situations are typically such that proceeding through error scenarios one by one provides a natural, intuitive progression—and we know that all of those error scenarios will need to be handled before the system really is valuable. An example of such a situation might be one where we need to implement state machine-like functionality or some kind of a well-defined workflow where an error situation effectively short-circuits the process, bypassing the remainder of logic in the workflow. Having said that, the happy path should still be your first choice over an error situation!

We're now aware of a handful of different strategies for selecting the next test to write. Don't think too much about which test is the "right" one to write next. There's no right sequence in the first place, and these test-selection strategies will become second nature over time. As a rule of thumb, though, it's probably a good idea to start with an easy test—something you feel can be made to pass very quickly. Once you've got that first test nailed down, it's much easier to start thinking about what the next test should be.

Before we can select the next test, though, we need to make the first one pass. Let's see how we can do that.

4.1.2 Implementation strategies

Just like there are many ways to select and write a test, there are many ways to make those tests pass. In his excellent introductory text on TDD, *Test-Driven Development by Example*, (Addison-Wesley, 2002), Kent Beck lists three ways to make progress: faking it, triangulation, and obvious implementation. In this section, we'll familiarize ourselves with these three strategies.

Let's begin with the most straightforward—faking it.

Faking it

Sometimes after writing a failing test, we don't have an idea how to correctly implement the code that makes the test pass. In such cases, we might want to resort to faking the particular functionality so that we get back to green. This might be because we've taken too big a step, or it might be because we've reached some virtual boundary within our system. Whatever the reason, our primary goal is to get to a solid state by making the tests pass, and faking it is better than staying in the red for a long time. As it happens, the easiest way to fake something is often to return hard-coded results—you might remember us doing just that back in chapter 2 with our first tests for the template engine.

After we've faked something, it's easy to switch into *triangulation* mode, mainly because we know there's that one tiny snippet of clearly non-production-quality code in our code base that we need to somehow smoke out and replace with a real implementation. We do so—by writing a new failing test, of course.

Triangulation

We already saw triangulation in effect in chapter 3 when we wanted to squeeze out a hard-coded string from our production code. Triangulation is a useful technique for evolving toward a correct implementation when we don't yet have a clear concept of how to generalize a given piece of hard-coded logic.

We call the technique triangulation because it's a lot like how the cops on TV track down bad guys based on their cell-phone signals. The cops' triangulation involves observing the direction of the subject's signal from multiple locations. Knowing the locations of the observation stations, the cops can draw two lines on a map and see where the lines intercept.

In the triangulation technique we TDD folks use, we don't observe signals and we don't draw lines on maps. Instead, each of the tests we write constrains the available solution space to one dimension. When we have enough tests, as illustrated in figure 4.1, the tests effectively narrow down—triangulate—the exact solution we were looking for.

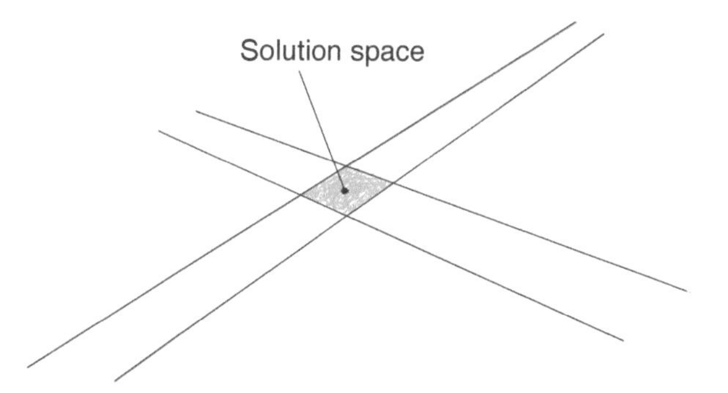

Figure 4.1
Triangulation is about narrowing down the solution space until it matches our exact needs.

For example, in developing a credit-card validation component, we might not know how to structure our class hierarchy for supporting multiple credit cards with their slightly differing number lengths and validation rules.[3] Using triangulation, we might first write tests and implement the code for validating just one brand of cards, say, MasterCard. These tests would be easy to write, and the code to satisfy those tests would be just as straightforward.

Next, we'd pick another card vendor, say, Visa, and we'd write tests to verify that our component handles Visa as well as MasterCard, distinguishing between them where necessary. These new tests would slowly start pushing our code toward a state where the suitable places for generalization become obvious. By the time we're adding a test for Diners Club, it's likely that we'll see where the code wants us to generalize.

Obvious implementation

Luckily, most of the time the necessary step to make a test pass is an obvious one. We don't mean obvious as in hard coding something, but rather as the "correct" implementation being obvious. In such situations, we can simply proceed with what we consider an obvious implementation, taking a slightly bigger step than we usually take when triangulating or faking our way towards the ultimate goal.

An example of an obvious implementation could be a regularly occurring pattern, such as collecting a subset of items from a collection based on a given predicate. When going for an obvious implementation, we type in the solution and see if it worked—if the test passes. If it doesn't, we back it out. All of it! No second chances with this one.

---

[3] Major credit-card vendors currently use the Luhn formula for calculating a checksum and a set of assigned prefixes to distinguish the various brands from each other. Google "credit card validation" and "luhn formula" for more details.

In the next section, we're going to look at an extremely simple set of guidelines for test-driving that you can start with. Over time, as you become more familiar with TDD, you can start giving more attention to the various test selection strategies, but these first guidelines for test-driving should be enough to keep you on the right track while you're learning.

4.1.3 Prime guidelines for test-driving

I've been running classroom trainings on test-driven development with my friend Bas for some time. Along the way, we've seen many aspiring developers struggle with the variety of practices involved in writing good tests, test-driving effectively, and gotchas to look out for.

One day, we were sitting on a train on our way to run another training session and started talking about the kind of short list of principles we could come up with to help people stay on track without the presence of a more experienced TDD'er. We wanted the list to be extremely short so that it's easy to remember. As well as helping people get started, the list would also need to act as a lighthouse, guiding a test-driven developer safely toward the port of productivity.

We ended up with the following list of guidelines:

- Do. Not. Skip. Refactoring.
- Get to green fast.
- Slow down after a mistake.

Let's go through these guidelines one by one, examining what makes them so important that they made it to our short list.

Do. Not. Skip. Refactoring.

If you haven't yet considered tattooing the word *refactor* on the back of both your hands, now would be a good time to do that. And I'm only half joking. The single biggest problem I've witnessed after watching dozens of teams take their first steps in test-driven development is insufficient refactoring.

Not refactoring mercilessly and leaving duplication in the code base is about the closest thing to attaching a time bomb to your chair. Unfortunately, we are good at remembering the "test" and "code" steps of the TDD cycle and extremely proficient at neglecting a code smell that screams for the missing step.

Thus, I urge you to pay attention to not skipping refactoring. If you have someone to pair with, do so. Crosscheck with your programming buddy to spot any duplication you may have missed. Bring Fowler's *Refactoring* book with you to the toilet.[4] Learn to use your IDE's automated refactorings. It's good for you—the doctor said so!

I apologize if I'm being too patronizing, but following the TDD cycle all the way is important. Now that we've got that in check, there are two more guidelines for us to go through. The first of them relates to the code step of the TDD cycle—get to green fast. Let's talk about that.

Get to green fast

As we test-drive, we're basically aiming for the simplest design we can think of for the problem at hand. We don't, however, go for the simplest design right off the bat in the code step. Instead, we should strive to get back to green fast. The code step is where we get to that green bar with as few edits as possible. The refactoring step is where we perfect our design.

You might want to read the previous paragraph out loud. Don't worry about others looking at you like you're a freak. You're just pointing out facts.

Speaking of facts, it's more than likely that you will make one or two mistakes in your career even after adopting TDD. Our third guideline tells us to slow down once the proverbial smelly substance hits the fan.

Slow down after a mistake

It is common for developers practicing TDD to start taking slightly bigger and bigger steps as time goes by. At some point, however, we'll take too big a bite off our test list and end up reverting our changes. At these points, we should realize that the steps we're taking are too big compared to our ability to understand the needed changes to our implementation. We need to realize that we must tighten our play. Small steps. Merciless refactoring. It's that simple. Walking to the water cooler might not be a bad idea either.

These guidelines are certainly not a complete reference to successful test-driving. Practices and guidelines don't create success. People do. Having said that, I hope they will help you find your way to working more productively and to avoiding some of the pitfalls I've seen many people stumble into as beginning TDD'ers.

We'll soon talk about similar guidelines and strategies for creating testable designs; but before that, we should establish some basic concepts that we have encountered and will continue to encounter as we're working with automated tests and test-driven development.

---

[4] I'm sure Martin won't mind. After all, you're just being passionate about your profession.

4.2 Essential testing concepts

French political scientist Alexis de Tocqueville has said that the "last thing a [political] party abandons is its vocabulary."[5] You could say the same thing about software engineers. Vocabulary is not just words, though. A shared vocabulary helps us communicate with our fellow engineers about our work, and a good vocabulary helps us understand the purpose and intent of the concepts it describes.

There are a few basic concepts related to the unit tests that we write as part of test-driven development that I feel deserve more of our attention than we've given them so far. Next, we're going to fix the situation by discussing the meaning of terms such as fixtures and test doubles. We'll also highlight two different approaches of verification that we can make use of in our tests. Finally, before taking a closer look into test doubles in section 4.3, we'll discuss when to use which approach—or whether we can use both.

And now, back to our regularly scheduled programming. Fixtures.

4.2.1 Fixtures are the context for tests

In chapter 2, we quickly defined a fixture as being the shared state from which all the different test methods of a test class begin their execution. Let's explore that definition further and clarify why we want to have fixtures in the first place. Let's begin by discussing the components of the shared starting state and then continue to answer the good ol' "why" question.

Holistic view of state

So far we've seen a fixture being built by creating objects and object graphs in some kind of a setup method that prepares the context—the fixture—for each individual test method. Fixtures are more than just what we create in the setup method.

If you remember, in chapter 2 we said that (assuming JUnit is the unit-testing framework being used) the fixture is formed by the instance variables of a test case class that are populated in the class's setup method *and other configured state*. What is this "other configured state"?

In practice, the other configured state refers to the state of the runtime (for example, the Java Virtual Machine instance that's running our unit tests) when JUnit invokes the setup method. A typical example of such a state is static variables and objects created at class-loading time through static initializer blocks. This includes static variables both in our test code and our production code.

[5] Alexis de Tocqueville, *The Old Regime and the French Revolution*, ed. J. P. Mayer and A. P. Kerr (Doubleday, 1955).

For example, we might have some kind of a platform class that assigns an implementation of itself to a static variable based on the system properties available at class-loading time. When running a single unit test, the system's state is effectively configured to something that becomes part of the fixture for that unit test—the state from which the test begins its execution.

To summarize the essence of fixtures, they're the whole shebang—the state of the whole runtime environment—rather than just the instance variables of a test class instance and the internal state of those objects.

So what about the "why" question? Why should we care about fixtures? What makes them worth worrying about? The answer is this: because we want to avoid duplication and because we want our tests to be clear and focused.

Fixtures remove duplication

The first half of our answer to why we should care about our fixtures is because fixtures are all about good design. In fact, we can evaluate our fixtures with the same principles of good design that we apply to our production code. Perhaps the most essential one of those principles is the lack of duplication. Fixtures move the shared state for multiple tests into one place, effectively removing duplication.

Just as with design principles in general, there's no absolute best. For example, it might not always be better to literally get rid of every single bit of duplication. Although removing all duplication is definitely a good rule of thumb, sometimes it's better to leave some duplication in our test code for the sake of readability.

The opposite, however, is rarely true. That is, having test code with what we call a *clean slate fixture*—a fixture that's built by each test method from scratch with zero commonalities in setup—is definitely an anti-pattern and should be remedied. Either there's too much duplication between the tests or there's no cohesion between them, the latter of which is a clear indicator that the test class should be split into two or more classes.

Although the removal of duplication in our test code should be enough to make us care about fixtures, there's another benefit that is worth mentioning. Paying attention to having proper fixtures for our tests facilitates more focused tests.

Fixtures allow for focused tests

Experienced TDD'ers are often good at creating focused tests. A key to being able to have a focused test is to have a suitable fixture that brings the system and the objects involved to a state in which the test doesn't need to do much more than a single assertion call, possibly after first invoking a one-liner on the object being tested.

The benefit of letting each test method focus on exactly what it's testing and nothing else is clear—we can immediately see the forest for the trees. That is, we don't waste any of our precious time wading through code, trying to figure out where "it" happens. When our fixture is built well, the fixture tells us the context and the test goes straight to the point.

And as if that wasn't reason enough, being aware of what our fixtures look like in terms of cohesion and complexity pushes our tests toward being good, focused tests that communicate intent effectively, rather than complex tests that are so unfathomable that a week later we can't tell whether the test is correct or not. So keep an eye on your fixtures. Doctor's orders.

From fixtures, let's hop topics again and turn our attention to another essential testing concept that hasn't gotten much face time in the earlier chapters—test doubles.

4.2.2 Test doubles stand in for dependencies

Many, if not most, of our difficulties in testing a given class or object have to do with their collaborators and other kinds of dependencies. For example, we might have a class that takes an instance of `java.sql.ResultSet` as argument for the sole constructor. The `java.sql.*` interfaces are notoriously difficult to instantiate because there's no standard, standalone implementation for those interfaces—it's the JDBC driver vendor which provides the implementations, and that implementation is typically tightly coupled to creating a live connection to a database. This makes such dependencies difficult to deal with.

These are the kind of issues that we need to contend with at times if we want to do test-driven development and write automated unit tests. Difficult objects. Luckily, most of the time there is a workaround to make our job easier without sacrificing quality, speed, or effort, and that workaround is called *test doubles.*

Test doubles are objects that stand in for the real thing. They pretend to be something they're not, but they do it in a way that the client has no idea, and they typically do it faster than the real thing—often in terms of both execution time and time spent writing and maintaining the test. A typical use of test doubles in our unit tests is to first create the test double (or multiple, depending on your needs), then configure state and/or behavior and/or expectations for the test double, pass the test double to the code you're testing, and verify the results.

We now have a general idea of what test doubles are. Before taking a closer look at different *kinds* of test doubles, let's talk a bit about two different styles of testing we can do.

4.2.3 State and interaction-based testing

On the highest level, the use of test doubles can be divided into two general groups based on their approach to verifying the expected behavior. Those approaches are called *state-based* and *interaction-based* testing, respectively.[6] Let's take a closer look at each.

State-based testing

State-based testing refers to the use of the fixture objects' (the objects that make up the test fixture) internal state after invoking the class under test in order to verify the correct behavior. We verify the correctness by comparing the primary (class under test) and the collaborator objects' state to what we expect them to be.

To better understand what that means, let's look at the following snippet, which presents one example of a state-based test:

```
@Test
public void listShouldNotBeEmptyAfterAddingSomethingToIt()
        throws Exception {
    List<String> list = new ArrayList<String>();
    assertTrue(list.isEmpty());
    list.add("something");
    assertFalse(list.isEmpty());
}
```

The previous snippet is state-based testing in its simplest form—using the real production classes throughout. The same approach can be applied with test doubles, too. We might, for example, replace the real `System.out` in our tests with an alternative `PrintStream` implementation that appends its output into an in-memory buffer. The benefit of doing this is that the tests would then be able to assert that the buffer's content matches what we expected the code under test to write into `System.out`.

In some cases, when the fixture is small and doesn't need much setup, state-based testing is a good way to use test doubles, especially if we can use a readily available stub implementation for the required interface instead of writing our own. In some cases, however, we might want to test for interactions rather than changes in the objects' states.

Testing for interactions

Interaction-based testing takes a vastly different approach to verifying correct behavior. Instead of asserting that the ending states of the object under test and its collaborators match what we expect, interaction-based tests verify that the object under test interacted with its collaborators as we expected. In other words, we are not interested in the internal state of the collaborators, but we are inter-

---

[6] For more discussion on state-based and interaction-based testing, refer to Martin Fowler's article "Mocks Aren't Stubs" at http://www.martinfowler.com/articles/mocksArentStubs.html.

ested in whether the object being tested made the expected method calls with the expected parameters and, if applicable, in the expected sequence.

Interaction-based tests are made possible by what we call *dynamic mock object* libraries. Examples of such libraries for Java include EasyMock,[7] jMock,[8] and rMock,[9] which are all open source and have fairly large user bases.

What these libraries do is let us point to an interface (or a class) and specify the expected collaborations (method calls); the library then gives us a test double that implements that interface. We can then pass on the test double, which we generally refer to as a *mock object*, to our code under test. After executing the class under test, we can ask the mock object to verify that its expectations were indeed met. Look at appendix C for an example of an interaction-based test using the EasyMock API.

Homegrown interaction-based mock objects

It is certainly possible to write homegrown mock objects that count the number of function calls received and their arguments. Having said that, using a full-blown mock object framework is usually less work than a static stub with some added smarts. Frameworks also support more complex features such as mocking concrete classes with byte code manipulation, which isn't exactly a walk in the park to implement yourself.

There's one important thing to watch when testing for interactions: when the interactions become long and complex, it's time to refactor. Not doing so tends to lead to brittle tests—ones that fail because of some irrelevant change in the way two objects interact. This is often a sign of either an interface being too big or there being interactions among objects at different levels of abstraction.[10]

When to use which approach?

As you can see, the dynamic mock object or interaction-based version of our test is more complex and more verbose than the earlier state-based version. That is typical for simple test fixtures like ours in this example. The benefits of not having to write or populate a state-based test double implementation start showing when dealing with more complex tests focusing on collaboration between multiple

---

[7] http://www.easymock.org.

[8] http://www.jmock.org.

[9] http://rmock.sf.net.

[10] Thanks to J. B. Rainsberger for offering the eloquent description of this code smell in a private email exchange.

objects instead of simple calculations or state modifications. Not to worry, we'll have plenty of time in part 2 to see interaction-based testing in action.

Both state- and interaction-based tests are useful, and both are often necessary to cover all bases. To paraphrase J. B. Rainsberger, author of *JUnit Recipes* (Manning Publications, 2005), "We lean on interaction-based testing to verify how an object talks to its collaborators; and we lean on state-based testing to verify how well the object listens." In other words, we're using these two types of testing techniques to answer the questions, "Am I using the objects around me correctly?" and, "Am I responding correctly to the input I get and to the responses I get from others?"

We can test for the expected state, or we can test for expected interactions between objects; each of these approaches has its relative pros and cons. Next, we're going to take a closer look at the diverse world of test doubles and a classification scheme of *stubs*, *fakes*, and *mocks*.

4.3 Closer look into test doubles

As we just learned, test doubles are substitutable, alternative implementations of an interface or class that we don't want to use in a test—the reason often being that the real thing has one of these issues:

- It's too slow.
- It's not available (or doesn't exist).
- It depends on something that's not available (or doesn't exist).
- It's too difficult to instantiate and configure for a test.

Let's try to make this more concrete with an example.

4.3.1 Example of a test double

Say there is a method that needs an instance of `com.acme.PricingService` in order to fulfill its responsibility of calculating the total price for an order. Creating an instance of the `PricingService` could well be trivial, but what if it takes a full second to execute its `calculateDiscountedPrice(Order)` method? Surely we wouldn't want too many of our tests to use the real thing if that would mean each test takes at least a second to execute. One second might not sound like much, but if one of your tests takes a full second, it's likely that many of them do—and it all adds up.

There might be other issues with using the real thing. For example, what if we needed to create a huge amount of test data for the `PricingService` to work on? What if the `PricingService` required a live connection to a database? What if we haven't yet implemented the `PricingService` in the first place? Further examples of issues with regard to testability of objects could include nondeterministic behavior, such as primary-key generation or time-dependent functionality. Additionally, it is often difficult to cause exceptions when using real objects in tests (for example, try to think of a way to unplug and plug the network cable from your unit test in order to cause a temporary network error).

Listing 4.1 illustrates how we might use a test double in the previous scenario to stand in for the real `PricingService` implementation.

Listing 4.1 Typical usage pattern for a test double

```
public class PricingServiceTestDouble extends PricingService {
    private float discount;

    public PricingServiceTestDouble(float discount) {
        this.discount = discount;
    }

    public float getDiscountPercentage(Customer c, Product p) {
        return discount;
    }
}

public class OrderProcessorTest {
    @Test
    public void testOrderProcessorWithMockObject() throws Exception {
        float initialBalance = 100.0f;
        float listPrice = 30.0f;
        float discount = 10.0f;
        float expectedBalance =
                (initialBalance - (listPrice * (1 - discount/100)));

        Customer customer = new Customer(initialBalance);
        Product product = new Product("TDD in Action", listPrice);
        OrderProcessor processor = new OrderProcessor();
        PricingService service =
            new PricingServiceTestDouble(discount);
        processor.setPricingService(service);

        processor.process(new Order(customer, product));

        assertEquals(expectedBalance,
            customer.getBalance(), 0.001f);
    }
}
```

1. Test double fakes behavior
2. ARRANGE test data and fake collaborator
3. ACT out operation
4. ASSERT that result is as expected

In short, the example in listing 4.1 shows how we can transparently hand out a ❶ fake implementation of the `PricingService` interface to the class under test, `OrderProcessor`, and thus bypass the costly step of connecting to the database and doing all sorts of customer behavior calculations and adjustments—which we don't care about right now for this test's purpose and which would take forever to execute compared to a blazing fast fake implementation. Instead, we ❷ configure our object under test to use the test double, ❸ invoke the object under test, and ❹ verify that the expected stuff happened.

We just saw one example of a test double. There are, however, more than one type of test double that we can differentiate using the simple classification scheme of stubs, fakes, and mocks. Let's talk about those next.

4.3.2 Stubs, fakes, and mocks

The French poet Victor Hugo wrote, "The future has many names: For the weak, it means the unattainable. For the fearful, it means the unknown. For the courageous, it means opportunity." Test doubles are a bit like that. We have different names to use for referring to test doubles, but there's also a slightly different substance behind those names. I will try to present a reasonably global definition in table 4.1, although there are other (sometimes conflicting) taxonomies out there.

Table 4.1 Categorization of different types of mock objects

Type of mock	Description
Stubs	Stubs are essentially the simplest possible implementation of a given interface you can think of. For example, stubs' methods typically return hardcoded, meaningless values.
Fakes	Fakes are a degree more sophisticated than stubs in that they can be considered an alternative implementation of the interface. In other words, a fake looks like a duck and walks like a duck even though it isn't a real duck. In contrast, a stub only looks like a duck.
Mocks	Mocks can be considered even more sophisticated in terms of their implementation, because they incorporate assertions for verifying expected collaboration with other objects during a test. Depending on the implementation of a mock, it can be set up either to return hardcoded values or to provide a fake implementation of the logic. Mocks are typically generated dynamically with frameworks and libraries, such as EasyMock, but they can also be implemented by hand.

As mentioned, this is just one way to define the terms *stub*, *fake*, and *mock*, and I'm sure you will encounter other, partly conflicting definitions. One source for such definitions is Gerard Meszaros' website, xunitpatterns.com (see "Test Double Patterns"). From here on, however, I will be using the terms *mock* and *test double* rather liberally to refer to using any of the three types of test doubles described previously, unless it the type is significant in the particular context I am talking about.

The definitions of stubs and fakes are straightforward, really—they're just alternative implementations for a given interface or class. The third category of test doubles, however, requires more elaboration. Maybe we should take a look at mock objects in action to understand what that gibberish in table 4.1 means in practice.

4.3.3 Mock objects in action

Do you recall listing 4.1 in which we passed in a fake `PricingService` implementation to an `OrderProcessor` because using the real implementation would've required a network connection, be slow, and all that nasty stuff? The test double we used in listing 4.1 was a *fake* because it employed a simplified algorithm for pricing products—the test double was hard coded to always give a discount of $10.

To illustrate the dynamic and self-verifying nature of the most sophisticated type of test double—a *mock object*—let's rewrite our test from listing 4.1 to use interaction-based testing, passing in a mock object as the `PricingService` implementation. Listing 4.2 shows how we could implement the `OrderProcessorTest` from listing 4.1 using a dynamic mock object created with the EasyMock library.[11]

Listing 4.2 (Re)implementing `OrderProcessorTest` with dynamic mock

```
import static org.easymock.classextension.EasyMock.*;
import static org.junit.Assert.*;
import org.junit.*;

public class OrderProcessorEasymockTest {

    @Test
    public void testOrderProcessorWithEasyMock() throws Exception {
        // arrange
        float initialBalance = 100.0f;
        float listPrice = 30.0f;
        float discount = 10.0f;
        float expectedBalance =
                initialBalance - (listPrice * (1 - discount / 100));
        Customer customer = new Customer(initialBalance);
        Product product = new Product("TDD in Action", listPrice);
```

Set up regular objects and data for test

[11] Technically, we're using EasyMock along with its class extension, which gives EasyMock the ability to mock concrete classes in addition to plain interfaces.

```
        // record expected collaboration with mock PricingService
        PricingService mock = createMock(PricingService.class);
        expect(mock.getDiscountPercentage(customer, product))
               .andReturn(discount);
        replay(mock);                                    Create dynamic mock
                                                         for PricingService

        // act
        OrderProcessor processor = new OrderProcessor();
        processor.setPricingService(mock);           <--  Pass mock
        processor.process(new Order(customer, product));  to code
                                                          under test
        // assert
        assertEquals(expectedBalance, customer.getBalance(),
            0.001f);
        verify(mock);     <-- Ask mock to verify
    }                         expectations
}
```

The example test in listing 4.2 first creates a bunch of regular objects to be used in the test and then proceeds to create a mock object for the difficult collaborator, `PricingService`. EasyMock is based on a concept where each mock object is born in *recording mode*. In the recording mode, we record the expected interactions and the mock object's behavior by calling methods on the mock object itself and telling EasyMock how the mock object should react—for example, what return value it should return or what exception it should throw. In listing 4.2, this is exactly what the following lines accomplish:

```
PricingService mock = createMock(PricingService.class);
expect(mock.getDiscountPercentage(customer, product)).
➥andReturn(discount);
```

When we're done recording the expected collaboration and behavior of the mock object, we tell EasyMock to move our mock to *replay mode* by passing it to the `replay` method. At that point, the mock object begins capturing events. As we hand our mock object to the code under test, the code under test invokes its collaborators—including our mock object—and the mock object automatically fails the test if a given collaboration was not expected (that is, recorded before moving to replay mode).

Finally, after we've exercised the code under test by using mock objects as collaborators, and assuming that the mock objects hadn't already blown the whistle on an unexpected method call, we ask the mock object to verify that all expected collaboration has taken place.

That's enough about test doubles for now. Before moving on to discussing about the application of TDD in the context of legacy code, I'd like to spend a moment talking about design and how certain guidelines can help us produce more testable designs.[12]

4.4 Guidelines for testable designs

It's all fine and dandy to know about the different kinds of test doubles we might employ in improving the maintainability and execution speed of test code, but that's only one aspect to consider when talking about testability. The low-level techniques like stubs, fakes, and mocks or state- versus interaction-based tests are what we might consider tools for solving technical challenges in testing our code. Although it's good to have an array of tools at hand, it would be much better if we didn't have to resort to working around a design in the first place, wouldn't it?

When we test-drive code, we're making design decisions, and those decisions have a direct effect on how easy it is for us to work with that code in the future. Writing the tests before the code does indeed enforce a certain level of testability, but it helps if we're aware of what kinds of designs promote testability and what kinds of designs might work now but will likely blow up soon after. For example, when we know that the Singleton pattern[13] often becomes a testability problem, we know not to write a test that drives the production code to use the Singleton pattern.

Aiming at helping you avoid creating testability challenges for yourself, here are a few simple design guidelines that we should pay attention to:

- Choose composition over inheritance.
- Avoid static and the Singleton.
- Isolate dependencies.
- Inject dependencies.

This is certainly not a comprehensive list for design principles that lead to more testable design, but these four simple items take us a long way. How about a closer look at each of these?

[12] After all, we don't want to leave a bad *legacy* to our fellow engineers, do we?

[13] http://en.wikipedia.org/wiki/Singleton_pattern.

4.4.1 Choose composition over inheritance

One particular aspect of how to structure your code in order to make it more testable is the way we build complex objects out of smaller islands of functionality. In object-oriented programming languages, the main candidates for doing that are *inheritance* and *composition*.

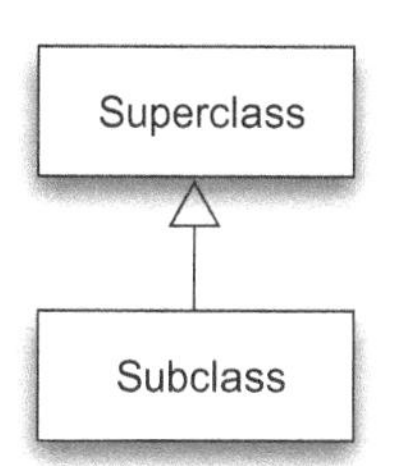

Figure 4.2 Inheriting from a superclass lets the subclass inherit all the functionality of the superclass. It does, however, also introduce inconvenient constraints related to instantiating the subclass in a test harness.

Inheritance, having a class inherit functionality from a superclass as shown in figure 4.2, has traditionally been used to enable reuse of functionality within a class hierarchy. Although it's a nice feature for a programming language, inheritance does have its downside when it comes to testability, maintainability, and overall flexibility of design.

Specifically, having to deal with an inheritance hierarchy can sometimes make it unnecessarily difficult to instantiate our objects in a test harness. In Java, for example, we might have to provide valid input only needed by the superclass constructor even though we're just interested in an aspect of the child class. This can be a real pain if the input itself is a complex object graph and, thus, difficult or laborious to instantiate.

Furthermore, even the smallest of changes could potentially cause a ripple effect throughout the class hierarchy, which is obviously not an ideal situation. Inheritance is often too restrictive to be an easily testable construct. This leads us to the alternative—composition—shown in figure 4.3.

Composition is a way to build objects that provide complex functionality by combining a set of less complex component objects. The top-level composite object delegates work to its components instead of invoking methods from its superclass.[14] In essence, composition is based on object-level division of responsibility instead of

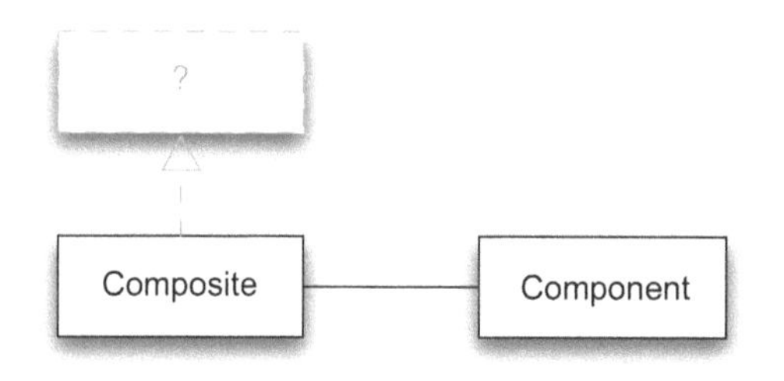

Figure 4.3
Composition allows for a more flexible design solution for reusing functionality from another class. For example, we can instantiate the composite object with alternative implementations of its components if they are difficult to obtain in a test harness.

[14] ...or its superclass's superclass's superclass's superclass.

static, class-level division. Composition tends to be slightly more verbose than inheritance, measured in lines of code, but its improved characteristics in terms of testability, flexibility, and maintainability often more than outweigh the cost of those extra lines of code.

4.4.2 Avoid static and the Singleton

Another potential obstacle in terms of testability of your code is the use of static method calls and the Singleton pattern. Depending on how intertwined your particular static/Singleton is in the code base you're testing, it might be surprisingly difficult or awkward to replace the implementation behind the static method with a test double for your test. Perhaps most of the time we don't need to fake the Singleton or a static method, but when we do (for example, if the static method or Singleton instance would try to connect to a remote server during a test run), it sure isn't as easy as it could be.

Figure 4.4 depicts a situation of the class under test (`ClassUnderTest`) calling a static method or using a Singleton.

In fact, it's not the Singleton pattern itself that causes trouble—it's the default implementation of the Singleton. In any case, we need a way for test code to configure a fake implementation for the static method or Singleton for the duration of the test. In practice, that means providing a static method somewhere for replacing the default implementation with a fake implementation and one for reverting back to the default implementation when the test has executed.

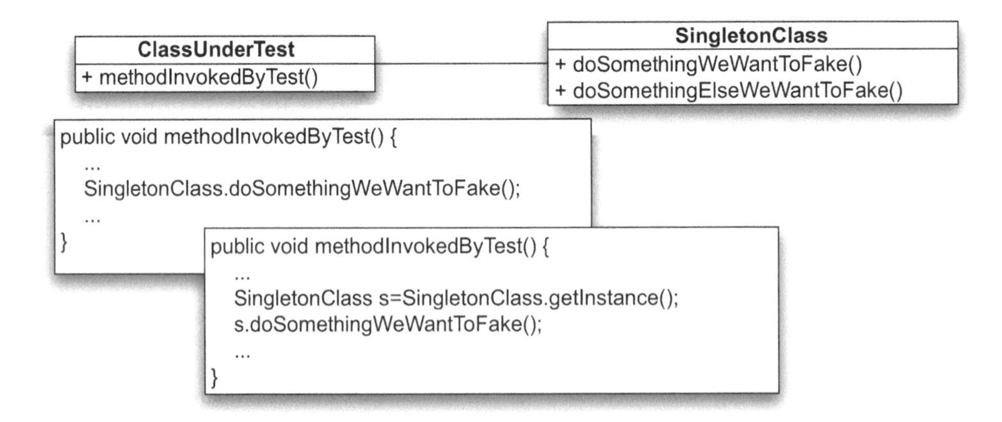

Figure 4.4 Static method calls are difficult to fake because the target class for the call is hardcoded. Similarly, it is difficult to substitute a fake implementation for a Singleton class obtained through the usual (static...) `getInstance()` method call.

In most cases, however, I'd recommend first looking at ways to get rid of the static methods by converting them into instance methods. In many cases, and with object instantiation being dirt cheap with modern virtual machines, that's a question of simply removing the `static` keyword and replacing static references with instance method calls.

To showcase the problem static variables and methods present for testability, refer to listing 4.3, which illustrates a situation where it's technically not possible to fake a method by simply subclassing and overriding it.

Listing 4.3 The problem with static methods and testability

```
public class Database {
    public static Object findById(String id) {
        // fetch an object from the database,
        // returning a null if the id is not found
    }

    public static boolean objectExists(String id) {
        return (findById(id) != null);
    }
}

public class TestDatabase {
    @Test
    public void testObjectExists() throws Exception {
        // How can I fake findById() to return
        // "true" or "false" as I wish?
        assertTrue(Database.objectExists("123"));
    }
}
```

In the code shown in listing 4.3, there's just no way to fake `findById` without altering the compiled byte code because the code under tests references the specific implementation class explicitly. We can't subclass and override it because it's all static.[15]

A common trend in how people use Singleton classes revolves around the pattern's characteristic of providing a single point of access. Although it's good to have that single point of access, it can become problematic if the access to that single point of access is sprinkled throughout the rest of your code base. For example, consider the example in listing 4.4 of a method making use of a static method to obtain a dependency.

[15] We could alter byte code, but that's quite an investment that we're not ready to make right now.

Listing 4.4 Code smell: methods obtaining dependencies through static method calls

```
public class OrderProcessor {
    public void process(Order order) {
        PricingService service = PricingService.getInstance();
        // use the PricingService object for processing the order
    }
}
```

This is bad form. We're mixing the acquisition of the dependencies with the logic that makes use of those dependencies. In short, we need to…

4.4.3 Isolate dependencies

In order to facilitate replacement of dependencies with test doubles, it is essential to first isolate the dependencies in a way that lets us perform the replacement as easily as possible. One delightfully trivial way to do that is to wrap access to static methods like the one in listing 4.4 into instance methods. This makes for more code, yes, but it also lets us override the method in question, thereby eliminating the tightly coupled dependency caused by a static method call. Listing 4.5 presents the same example with this isolation.

Listing 4.5 Code smell relieved: static method call wrapped into an instance method

```
public class OrderProcessor {
    public void process(Order order) {
        PricingService service = getPricingService();      <-- Obtain dependency through getter
        // use the PricingService object for processing the order
    }

    protected PricingService getPricingService() {         | Can be overridden to
        return PricingService.getInstance();               | return test double
    }
}
```

In *Working Effectively with Legacy Code,*[16] Michael Feathers defines the concept of *seams*: "a place where you can alter behavior in your program without editing in that place." In other words, seams are places where we can replace a piece of code with other code for the duration of a test run, for example, without touching the

[16] Michael Feathers, *Working Effectively with Legacy Code* (Addison-Wesley, 2004). I can't possibly recommend it enough. If you're working with software that needs to survive the test of time, you practically owe yourself reading that book.

code under test. In listing 4.5, the call to the `getPricingService` method is a seam from the point of view of a test case exercising the `process` method. A seam is by definition accompanied by one or more *enabling points*, that is, ways to exploit the seam. In listing 4.5, the enabling point is the `getPricingService` method itself, which we can exploit by overriding it as illustrated by listing 4.6.

Listing 4.6 Exploiting a seam

```
public class OrderProcessor {
    public void process(Order order) {
        PricingService service = getPricingService();      <-- That's a seam!
        // use the PricingService object for processing the order
    }

    protected PricingService getPricingService() {     <-- Enabling point
        return PricingService.getInstance();
    }
}

public class OrderProcessorTest {
    @Test
    public void testOrderProcessorByExploitingTheSeam()
            throws exception {
        OrderProcessor p = new OrderProcessor() {
            protected PricingService getPricingService() {
                return new FakePricingService();      <-- Exploit seam through enabling point
            }
        };
        ...
    }
}
```

The seam we just saw is an example of what Feathers calls an *object seam*, referring to the use of the object-oriented feature of being able to override the method transparently to the code that calls it. There are other kinds of seams as well (and differences between programming languages), namely *preprocessing seams* and *link seams*. For example, C/C++ developers can take advantage of preprocessing seams represented by `ifdefs` and macros. Similarly, a Java developer might decide to treat configuration items such as property files, XDoclet tags, and so on. as seams to be exploited with a smart Ant script or two. Examples of link seams could be replacing a dynamic library with a fake version or swapping a JAR file with a fake one using an environment variable such as `LD_LIBRARY_PATH` or `CLASSPATH`.

Isolating dependencies is critical for testability and maintainability. We'll encounter plenty more examples of isolating dependencies in part 2 of this book. Also, Michael Feathers' *Working Effectively with Legacy Code* offers a thorough coverage of the topic, but I cannot proceed without highlighting one especially helpful pattern. An especially helpful way this isolation improves testability is by letting us turn around the dependencies and, instead of having the production code obtain its dependencies, having someone external *inject* those dependencies in our production code.

4.4.4 Inject dependencies

Dependency injection (DI)[17] is one of the recent buzzwords in software circles. It is an approach to structuring code in a way that reduces direct dependencies to indirect dependencies or, to put it another way, replaces the getter with a setter. Before I manage to confuse you any further, let's use our earlier example, reproduced in listing 4.7, to explain what the name of the game is.

Listing 4.7 A getter dependency

```
public class OrderProcessor {
    public void process(Order order) {
        PricingService service = getPricingService();
        // use the PricingService object for processing the order
    }

    protected PricingService getPricingService() {
        return PricingService.getInstance();
    }
}
```

Production code actively "gets" its dependency

What we have here is an isolated dependency—a dependency we isolated with the intention of making it possible to swap in an alternative implementation for `PricingService`. My reference to the getter is that the default implementation of `getPricingService` *actively* obtains a `PricingService` implementation from the `PricingService` class using a static get method. The `OrderProcessor` class is tightly coupled to the `PricingService` class and its `getInstance` method. Although this sort of coupling is no longer a problem in terms of testability because we can override the `getPricingService` method in our tests, we could make it a notch easier still.

[17] Inversion of Control is reported as the original name for the concept of reversing the direction of dependencies. Martin Fowler from ThoughtWorks soon coined the term Dependency Injection in order to better express what many—if not most—people valued IoC for the most: injecting dependencies on objects instead of having them ask for the same.

OrderProcessor having a dependency on the PricingService means that it needs access to an implementation of the PricingService, not that it needs to know where to get that implementation. The dependency injection pattern presents an alternative way to organize things such that the true need of the OrderProcessor is fulfilled while still avoiding the tight coupling of OrderProcessor being too friendly with the PricingService class. Figure 4.5 illustrates this reversing of dependency acquisition.

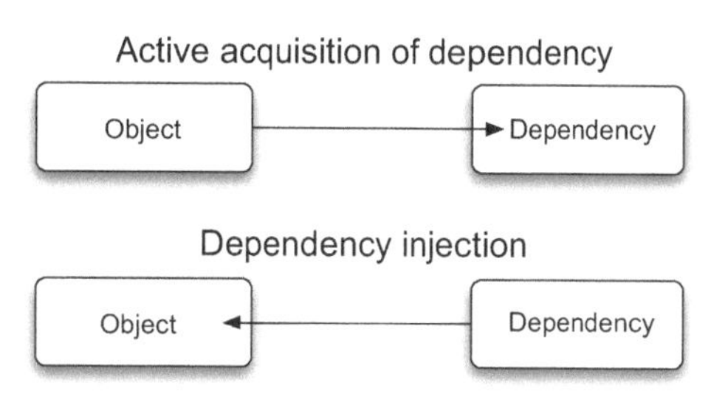

Figure 4.5 Dependency Injection reverses the fulfillment of dependencies.

In all of its simplicity, dependency injection means that we make OrderProcessor say, "I need a PricingService. Please give me one before using my services." Listing 4.8 shows how this looks in practice.

Listing 4.8 Dissolving tight coupling with dependency injection

```
public class OrderProcessor {

    private PricingService pricingService;        <-- Store dependencies as instance variables

    /**
     * Hand me my dependency by calling this method.
     */
    public void setPricingService(PricingService pricingService) {
        this.pricingService = pricingService;       <-- Let someone else give dependencies
    }

    /**
     * Please call setPricingService() before invoking me. Thanks.
     */
    public void process(Order order) {
        float price = pricingService.getDiscountedPrice(order)     <-- Use dependency directly
    }
}
```

That's it. The getPricingService method magically changed into a setPricingService method, and we introduced an instance variable to hold the dependency. Also, the process method no longer needs to ask for the dependency—it already has it readily available through the instance variable!

In case you were wondering how this change would affect our test code, listing 4.9 shows that the moderately awkward overriding of `getPricingService` is no longer necessary, and configuring the object under test is much more straightforward.

Listing 4.9 Test code made more readable thanks to Dependency Injection

```
public class OrderProcessorTest {
    @Test
    public void testOrderProcessorWithDependencyInjection()
            throws Exception {
        OrderProcessor p = new OrderProcessor();
        p.setPricingService(new FakePricingService());
        ...
    }
}
```

Cool beans! Where do I sign?

Although dependency injection does wonders for our code's general testability, it does have its cost. Test code immediately becomes much cleaner than before, now that our tests are free to configure the fixture objects as they wish; but the cost of dependency injection rears its head when we start to think about how things are handled when executing in production mode—someone (or something) needs to hand out all those dependencies to our components.

Different types of dependency injection

Listings 4.8 and 4.9 illustrate what is known as setter-based dependency injection, due to the dependency getting injected through a method invocation. This is not the only type of approach at our disposal, however. The other two types commonly in use are *field-based* and *constructor-based* dependency injection.

Field-based injection is fundamentally the same as setter-based injection, except that the implementation is populated directly into an instance variable and the receiving object does not have a chance to perform any computation upon receiving the dependency. In part due to this fact, the primary use case for field-based injection is in framework code, using the Reflection API to inject dependencies to arbitrary objects without requiring the application developer to write boilerplate code for dumb setter methods.

Constructor-based dependency injection simply means that the object receives its dependencies as constructor arguments. This can be considered a better approach than setter-based injection because with setter-based injection, the programmer is expected to take responsibility for knowing the order in which the dependencies should be injected. In other words, setter-based injection leaves the possibility of having half-configured objects in the wild.

Different types of dependency injection *(continued)*

The downsides of constructor-based dependency are that there is no way of defining an interface through which framework code could inject dependencies to an existing object and that long lists of dependencies might clutter the constructor's usage (which, on the other hand, might be a welcome warning sign of a design flaw).

In theory, we could do the necessary wiring with some bootstrap code, by creating some abstract factories, or by scattering factory methods all over the code base. In practice, we need an *inversion of control (IoC) container* to do that for us. Such containers will effectively take care of the bootstrapping of dependencies to implementations, generally using some centralized method of configuration (typically XML or property files of some sort). Examples of popular IoC containers include the `BeanFactory` of the Spring Framework,[18] PicoContainer,[19] and its big brother NanoContainer.[20]

We'll see DI and IoC in action in part 2 as well, but there are a few more topics I'd like to spend some time with before we go there. The first one is common patterns related to unit tests, followed by a discussion of different ways to tackle the dreaded source of headache and work-related stress we sometimes call *legacy code.* A lot of stuff still ahead, so we better keep moving!

4.5 Unit-testing patterns

Unit tests are an integral part of TDD. Thus, it's good for us to be aware of common patterns of writing unit tests. In this section, we will get to know a handful of common patterns, including the following:

- Patterns for writing assertions
- Patterns for structuring and building fixtures
- Patterns for test-case classes in general

---

[18] Spring Framework (www.springframework.org) is a popular open source project providing a collection of frameworks for things like Aspect-Oriented Programming, MVC in web applications, and dependency injection.

[19] PicoContainer (www.picocontainer.org) was one of the first open source DI/IoC frameworks and containers to reach a wider audience. It is an extremely primitive container, supporting only programmatic configuration, and it has limitations such as only supporting a single implementation of a given interface at one time.

[20] NanoContainer (www.nanocontainer.org), also open source, extends PicoContainer with a host of useful features its little brother is missing.

We'll run these through quickly because they're straightforward patterns—so straightforward, in fact, that we won't need UML diagrams to understand them! Let's get started with five different patterns for assertions.

4.5.1 Assertion patterns

Assertions are the essence of our tests—after all, a test is not worth much if it doesn't assert anything. We've seen a number of tests and assertions in part 1, and we'll see plenty of more in part 2. Having had some exposure to unit tests and assertions, I think now is a good time to highlight some of the common patterns we've seen and give them a name. The patterns we're describing here are based on Gerard Meszaros' excellent work at xunitpatterns.com. Refer to Gerard's website for some additional variations and more elaborate descriptions of these assertion patterns.

Now, let's look at the first of our assertion patterns—the Resulting State Assertion.

Resulting State Assertion

The Resulting State Assertion pattern is the single most common way to perform assertions in a unit test. The fundamental idea is to exercise some functionality on the fixture objects and afterward assert that the internal state of the fixture objects match our expectations. The following snippet demonstrates this pattern in code:

```
@Test
public void sizeOfListReflectsItemsAddedToIt() throws Exception {
    List<String> list = new ArrayList<String>();
    list.add("something");
    assertEquals(1, list.size());   // state verification
}
```

Notice how our assertion tests that the list object is not empty after invoking the add method? Technically, this test doesn't enforce the desired behavior. In other words, the previous test would pass with an implementation of `size` that always returns 1. In this case, the test is simple enough for anyone to deduce the intent of the test author. In some cases, however, it's worth it to not just assert the after state but also the before state, which is where the Guard Assertion pattern comes into play.

Guard Assertion

The Guard Assertion pattern is about making explicit the assumptions made about the fixture right before invoking the functionality we want to test. Here's a simple example that features a Guard Assertion:

```
@Test
public void listIsNoLongerEmptyAfterAddingAnItemToIt()
        throws Exception {
    List<String> list = new ArrayList<String>();
    assertTrue(list.isEmpty());    // guard assertion
    list.add("something");
    assertFalse(list.isEmpty());  // state verification
}
```

Notice how the Guard Assertion ensures that the list's `isEmpty` method correctly returns `true` for an empty list before we invoke the `add` method—which we're really testing with this test.

The Guard Assertion pattern is a common accomplice of the Resulting State Assertion pattern. That is, the two are often combined into a sequence where the test first asserts that the before state matches the test author's expectations and only then proceeds to invoke the functionality and assert against the resulting state—exactly what's happening in the previous example.

Sometimes, however, the purpose of adding a Guard Assertion is to make sure that an assumption about the fixture's starting state is correct. In these cases, it may make sense to move the Guard Assertion(s) into the end of the setup method. After all, the setup method is what those assertions are testing.

Delta Assertion

Sometimes we may need to work with code that we don't have full control over in our tests. Specifically, our tests may have a fixture we're not in control of. This yields the problem of how to write reliable, robust, self-checking tests when we cannot hard code the fixture's state. The solution is to not assert against the absolute state after invoking the code under test, but rather to test that the difference—or *delta*—between the initial and after states is what we expect.

Listing 4.10 illustrates the basic logic of this pattern we call the Delta Assertion.

Listing 4.10 Example of the Delta Assertion pattern

```
public class TestAddingToArrayList {

    private ArrayList<String> list;

    // setup method omitted for brevity

    @Test
    public void sizeOfListReflectsItemsAddedToIt() throws Exception {
        int sizeBefore = list.size();    // record the "before" state
        list.add("something");
        assertEquals(sizeBefore + 1, list.size());
        // delta verification
    }
}
```

This example is ridiculously trivial but highlights nicely the key aspects of the pattern: recording the state before exercising the code under test in order to be able to express the final assertion relative to the before state.

While admittedly somewhat more complex to write, Delta Assertions also have the advantage over regular Resulting State Assertions in that the test is more focused on the essence of what it's testing rather than throwing seemingly arbitrary values at the poor co-worker trying to make sense of why our test expects the list to contain some magic number of items. Making tests communicate better is always a good idea. Indeed, that's exactly what our next assertion pattern is geared at.

Custom Assertion

Sometimes the amount of code verifying our expectations vastly exceeds the amount of code required to invoke the code under test. When that happens (and especially if it happens more than once), it's often a good idea to extract a Custom Assertion method from the test in order to encapsulate complex verification logic behind a nice little method we can call from the test. Listing 4.11 illustrates this pattern with a simple example.

Listing 4.11 Example of a Custom Assertion method

```
public class TestMeetingCalendar {

    @Test
    public void timeslotsAreOnWeekdays() throws Exception {
        MeetingCalendar calendar = new MeetingCalendar();
        // omitted: add appointments to calendar until
        //          end of office hours next Friday
        Date time = calendar.nextAvailableStartingTime();
        assertIsDuringOfficeHoursOnWeekday(time);
        // encapsulate logic
    }

    private void assertIsDuringOfficeHoursOnWeekday(Date time) {
        // actual assertion logic omitted for brevity
    }
}
```

A common reason for using a Custom Assertion is the ability to perform different types of fuzzy matching. For example, we might want to compare two objects based only on a subset of their properties. Another common reason is a situation where the objects in question don't implement the `equals` method in a suitable way and we cannot modify those classes to fix their `equals` methods. Furthermore, creating a Custom Assertion allows us to provide more meaningful error messages[21] in case of test failure.

Next in our pattern catalog is a slightly bigger deviation from the assertion patterns we've seen so far. It's called the Interaction Assertion and is the integral vehicle for interaction-based tests.

Interaction Assertion

The last of our assertion patterns is called the Interaction Assertion. Interaction Assertions are funny things, in that they don't verify that our code produces the correct results. Instead, they verify that our code interacts with its collaborator objects as we expect it to. Let's clarify this with a small example, shown in listing 4.12.

Listing 4.12 Example of Interaction Assertions

```
public class TestExpectedInteractions {

    private List<Customer> delivered;

    @Before
    public void setup() {
        delivered = new ArrayList<Customer>();
    }

    private class MockCustomer extends Customer {
        @Override
        public void onPaperDelivery(DailyPaper paper) {
            delivered.add(this);
        }
    }

    @Test
    public void paperBoyShouldDeliverPapers() throws Exception {
        Customer david = new MockCustomer();
        Customer esther = new MockCustomer();
        PaperBoy paperboy = new PaperBoy();
        paperboy.addToRoute(david);
        paperboy.addToRoute(esther);

        paperboy.deliver(new DailyPaper());
        assertTrue(delivered.contains(david));
        assertTrue(delivered.contains(esther));
    }
}
```

❶ Have test double record interactions

❷ Check for expected interactions

[21] A meaningful error message is a highly useful aid, especially if your tests tend to be bigger than they perhaps should be.

The test class in listing 4.12 is simple. We ❶ create an empty list object for every new test and have a test double record the interactions to the list. This means that we are able to invoke the production code—ask the paperboy to deliver the daily paper—and then ❷ perform a couple of Interaction Assertions to check that both customers on the paper boy's route received their paper.

The implementation of the test double in listing 4.12 is similar to how dynamic mock object libraries like EasyMock work internally. They record actual and expected method calls into list-like data structures and eventually compare the expected list against the actual. It's worth noting, though, that our test in listing 4.12 doesn't verify that a paper was delivered—only that the paperboy cycled past both customers' houses—because we never assert *what* was delivered!

In this example, our whole fixture consisted of hand-made, interaction-based test doubles—mock objects. In practice, we can mix and match the state-based and interaction-based styles of testing into a single test as we see fit. For example, in our paperboy test in listing 4.12, we could use Interaction Assertions to check that the paperboy delivered the papers correctly (as we did in listing 4.12) and a Resulting State Assertion to verify that the paperboy has no papers left after completing his route.

Enough assertions for now. Let's take a step back and look at some patterns related to setting up and tearing down fixtures.

4.5.2 Fixture patterns

The fixture is an important part of a test. It's also not always a trivial construct, and I've seen plenty of massive fixtures, creating hordes of objects in a massive setup method I can't fit on one screen. Complex, massive code is a problem whether it's in production code or test code. Luckily, we have found a number of patterns over the years that help keep our fixtures in check.

We're going to look at three such patterns. The first two of them are directly related to creating objects in a fixture, and the third ties this object creation to getting rid of the fixture at the end of a test. Ready?

Parameterized Creation Method

A lot of the objects in a typical fixture are so-called *entity objects* in that they represent something that exists in the business domain either as a concrete thing or as a virtual concept. These types of objects generally have a lot of attributes, and most of the code in the bad fixtures I see is about populating those attributes—even though the vast majority of them are of no importance to the test at hand.

The following snippet shows an example of a setup method that populates a lot of attributes for fixture objects—most of which aren't likely to be of importance to the actual tests:

```
@Before
public void setUp() throws Exception {
    alice = new Person();
    alice.setId(1L);
    alice.setFirstname("Alice");
    alice.setLastname("Adams");
    alice.setSsn("111111");

    billy = new Person();
    billy.setId(2L);
    billy.setFirstname("Billy");
    billy.setLastname("Burke");
    billy.setSsn("222222");

    clark = new Person();
    clark.setId(3L);
    clark.setFirstname("Clark");
    clark.setLastname("Cable");
    clark.setSsn("333333");

    alice.isInLoveWith(billy);
}
```

The Parameterized Creation Method attacks this situation by hiding the non-important attributes from the setup by extracting the object creation into a separate creation method, which takes the variable attributes as arguments and populates the non-important ones with constant or random values. Furthermore, the Parameterized Creation Method can take care of populating attributes that aren't essential for the test but that have, for example, uniqueness requirements.

Listing 4.13 shows the Parameterized Creation Method in action, hiding the non-important attributes from the setup (for the sake of example, let's assume that the first and last name of each person are meaningful regarding the behavior we're testing).

Listing 4.13 Example of a Parameterized Creation Method

```
public class ParameterizedCreationMethodExample {

    private Person alice, billy, clark;

    @Before
    public void setUp() throws Exception {
        clark = createPerson("Clark", "Cable");
        billy = createPerson("Billy", "Burke");     ❶ Important attributes
        alice = createPerson("Alice", "Adams");        visible in setup
```

```
        alice.isInLoveWith(billy);
    }

    private Person createPerson(String firstName, String lastName) {
        Person person = new Person();
        person.setFirstname(firstName);
        person.setLastname(lastName);
        person.setId(UniqueNumber.next());
        person.setSsn(String.valueOf(UniqueNumber.next()));
        return person;
    }

    @Test
    public void aliceShouldAcceptWhenProposedToByBilly()
            throws Exception {
        billy.proposeTo(alice);
        assertTrue(alice.isEngagedWith(billy));
    }
}
```

Populate non-important attributes in creation method ❷

In listing 4.13 we can see how the Parameterized Creation Method leaves only the ❶ important attributes visible in the setup method and ❷ hides the non-important ones behind the creation method. The result is that we have no duplication in how we instantiate and populate the `Person` objects for our fixture, and we can immediately see what's happening in the setup because we don't have to wade through three times as much code. Our fixture setup is focused on the essential.

A special case of the Parameterized Creation Method is one where we're not concerned about any specific parameters as long as they fulfill all uniqueness and format requirements, such as every person having a Social Security number that is unique, numeric, and *n* digits long. It's also a common scenario to use multiple different creation methods for different objects in our fixture. That's where our next pattern, *Object Mother*, comes in handy.

Object Mother

At first, we can do a lot of good by refactoring our test classes to use local creation methods instead of duplicating code. Soon, we're likely to find ourselves duplicating the creation methods between different test classes. The next natural step in removing that duplication is to move the creation methods into a separate helper class. The Object Mother pattern describes just such an aggregate of creation methods.

In essence, the Object Mother, as described in the original paper[22] by Peter Schuh and Stephanie Punke, is an object or a set of objects that does the following:

- Provides a fully-formed business object along with all of its required attribute objects
- Returns the requested object at any point in its lifecycle
- Facilitates customization of the delivered object
- Allows for updating of the object during the testing process
- When required, terminates the object and all its related objects at the end of the test process

To summarize, the Object Mother pattern might be realized as a sophisticated object factory that provides access to a complete object graph of valid domain objects, including instances in different states. In addition to this, the Object Mother might provide methods for modifying the given domain objects by, for example, attaching objects to each other, removing relationships, or moving the given objects to a desired state.

In addition to reducing duplication in our test code, the Object Mother pattern makes it easy for programmers new to unit-testing to access the objects they need, thus encouraging them to write more tests where they might otherwise grind to a halt.

The Object Mother pattern can be especially powerful when integrated with personas[23] used by the development team in the real world. For example, if the team has developed personas such as Alice, Billy, and Clark—each presenting a different user role of a trading system—the Object Mother can and should use those same personas in its API. Such a mental connection again makes it easier to create tests when we don't need to scan through the API and perhaps even look inside the creation methods to figure out which object we should use for the test. Instead, we simply say, "OK. I need a purchase order that Clark wants to submit but Jim needs to approve."

Although it's a powerful tool and catalyst to motivate test writing, Object Mothers take time to build. As such, I would recommend taking small steps refactoring your current test code base toward having cohesive creation methods and eventually refactor the creation methods and their canned test data into one or more Object Mothers.

---

[22] http://www.agilealliance.org/system/article/file/910/file.pdf.

[23] Alan Cooper, *The Inmates are Running the Asylum* (SAMS, 1999).

Still recall the Parameterized Creation Method pattern a couple of pages back? There's one reason to use a creation method, whether parameterized or not, that we didn't mention yet; it has to do with automated teardown.

Automated Teardown

The point of testing frameworks such as JUnit having a teardown method is to be able to perform any necessary cleanup after executing a test method. Examples of such necessary cleanup might be integration tests cleaning up created objects from a database or wiping generated files from a file system. When the teardown logic is complex or there are simply a lot of objects to tear down, our tests become cluttered and we can easily skip cleaning up something accidentally. And that can create problems down the road that are extremely hard to debug and trace back to the source.

The Automated Teardown pattern tackles this problem by encapsulating the teardown logic into a separate class and bringing the responsibility for triggering that logic right next to where the objects are created in the first place, as shown in figure 4.6.

As we can see, in the Automated Teardown pattern the fixture setup not only creates the fixture objects but also[24] registers them with a *test object registry*. The registry is a simple collection of references to the registered objects and is responsible for performing cleanup for each individual registered fixture object when the fixture teardown pokes the registry, triggering a wholesale teardown.

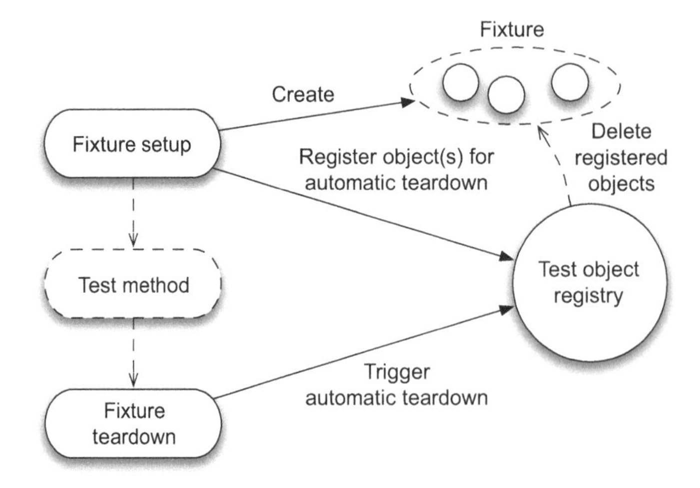

Figure 4.6 Registering fixture objects to a registry allows us to trigger a wholesale teardown easily for all registered objects during fixture teardown.

[24] These two steps are often encapsulated inside creation methods.

Although most of the use cases for the Automated Teardown pattern tend to revolve around integration tests, there's one specific variation that can be extremely useful for pure unit tests: creating self-checking mock objects through a creation method that registers the mock objects for some kind of a wholesale operation. In other words, instead of having to call, say, `replay` and `verify` for all of our mock objects individually (potentially forgetting to call one or two), we can now call a `replayAll` or `verifyAll` and be sure that every mock object receives the call.

Now that we've seen some patterns related to low-level assertions and patterns for setting up and tearing down fixtures, it's time to look at some patterns, tips, and tricks for writing tests in general.

4.5.3 Test patterns

We've already seen a number of testing-related patterns from the Guard Assertion to the Object Mother. Before we jump in to discuss the chapter's final topic of working with legacy code, we're going to look at a number of more generic test patterns. These patterns are a miscellaneous bunch of workarounds to make the untestable testable and handy tricks for using Java syntax to create compact, nicely structured tests.

Our first test pattern, the Parameterized Test, is geared toward creating data-driven tests that reuse the same test logic run against different inputs.

Parameterized Test

Every now and then, we find ourselves writing almost identical tests—tests where only a few input values are different but the logic is essentially the same. In those situations, we might want to consider turning our test class into a Parameterized Test.

The fundamental idea is that there's one and only one test method, which encapsulates the test logic to be applied to the parameterized data. There obviously also needs to be a method that provides the parameterized data, and there needs to be some code to bind the provided data to invocations to the test method.

Fortunately, the necessary plumbing is already built into JUnit 4, so adopting the Parameterized Test pattern is simply a matter of annotating our test class properly. Listing 4.14 presents an example test class that realizes the Parameterized Test pattern with JUnit 4.

Listing 4.14 Example of the Parameterized Test pattern using JUnit 4

```
import org.junit.runner.RunWith;
import org.junit.runners.Parameterized;
import org.junit.runners.Parameterized.Parameters;
```

```
@RunWith(Parameterized.class)
public class ParameterizedTest {

    @Parameters
    public static Collection<Object[]> parameters() {
        Object[][] data = new Object[][] {
                { 0, 0, 0 }, { 1, 1, 0 },
                { 2, 1, 1 }, { 3, 2, 1 },
                { 4, 3, 1 }, { 5, 5, 0 },
                { 6, 8, -2 } };
        return Arrays.asList(data);
    }

    public int expected, input1, input2;

    public ParameterizedTest(int expected, int input1,
        int input2) {
        this.expected = expected;
        this.input1 = input1;
        this.input2 = input2;
    }

    @Test
    public void executeParameterizedTest() throws Exception {
        assertEquals(expected, new Calculator().add(input1,
            input2));
    }
}
```

❶ Provide parameterized data

❷ Data is bound through constructor

❸ Test method invoked once for each data set

The Parameterized Test in listing 4.14 builds up from three parts. First of all, ❶ we provide JUnit with the parameterized data through a static method annotated with `@Parameters`. The method returns a `Collection` of object arrays where each array represents a single data set or a test instance. In other words, JUnit instantiates our test class once for each object array. The instantiation happens by JUnit ❷ passing the object array's contents to the constructor, which typically stores the values to fields for later access. Finally, JUnit invokes the ❸ test method, identified by the usual `@Test` annotation. And that's it.

The Parameterized Test pattern is a good way of supporting some degree of data-driven testing. Once we've written a skeleton like that in listing 4.14, it's extremely fast to start adding new test cases by adding a new object array into the data.

Adding stuff to an object array in Java code isn't exactly the user-friendliest way to create new test cases, however. The example in listing 4.14 would also be much more readable with each of its test cases implemented as separate one-line assertions. Indeed, perhaps the most compelling use case for the Parameterized Test pattern is where the amount of test data is huge and comes from an external data source such as an XML document or an ASCII text file, parsed by the `@Parameters` annotated method. This way, the test class becomes again slightly more complex, but it has the benefit of being able to describe the test data in a more suitable syntax and file format.

Tests that deal with a lot of data are the minority, however, so let's move on to discuss something that's closer to everyday business. Because many objects need to collaborate with dependencies, I'm thinking the Self-Shunt might be an excellent test pattern to cover next.

Self-Shunt

Earlier in section 4.3, we talked about different kinds of test doubles. What we didn't talk about there was the Self-Shunt, which is kind of a test double-except that it's our test class. Yes, you got that right. The Self-Shunt pattern, first documented by Michael Feathers,[25] is one where the test class instance acts as a test double in its own tests. Listing 4.15 illustrates this concept with a concrete example.

Listing 4.15 Example of the Self-Shunt pattern in action

```
public class SelfShuntExample implements PricingService {

    @Override
    public float getDiscountPercentage(Customer c, Product p) {
        return 10.0f;
    }

    @Test
    public void testOrderProcessorWithMockObject() throws Exception {
        // some setup omitted for brevity...
        OrderProcessor processor = new OrderProcessor();
        processor.setPricingService(this);
        processor.process(new Order(customer, product));
        assertEquals(expectedBalance, customer.getBalance(),
            0.001f);
    }
}
```

❶ Implement PricingService interface

❷ Pass "this" to object under test

In listing 4.15, we can see how the test class ❶ implements the `PricingService` interface, which means we can then ❷ pass `this` to the object under test as its collaborator instead of having to create a separate test double class or clutter our test code with an anonymous implementation. An anonymous class isn't a bad idea for

[25] http://objectmentor.com/resources/articles/SelfShunPtrn.pdf.

this kind of simple alternative implementation; but as the fake grows in size, so does the degree of cluttering, driving us toward having a Self-Shunt or an actual, named test-double class.

In other words, the Self-Shunt pattern is an excellent tool for implementing simple test-double logic near the tests that use it. As the logic grows more complex, however, it is often a good idea to move toward a full-blown test double. Having said that, we do have to remember that full-blown test doubles have their own disadvantages, too. If we'd like to share objects and states between our test methods and the test double, an Intimate Inner Class might be a better option.

Intimate Inner Class

There are occasions when we'd like to share some objects between the test class and a test double. This kind of a need can be fulfilled in a number of ways (adding a get method being one of them), but the Intimate Inner Class pattern is perhaps one of the less obvious solutions. That does not mean that it wouldn't be an elegant solution, however. In fact, the ability of a non-static inner class to access and assign to the test class's fields can yield nice, compact test code compared to, for example, exposing the internals of a test double through getter methods.

Let's clarify the role of the Intimate Inner Class through a code example. Listing 4.16 presents an example scenario where we'd like to test that a `Server` object obtains a `Thread` from its configured `ThreadFactory` upon startup and suspends it when stopped. The solution is to use an Intimate Inner Class, which assigns the newly created `Thread` instance to the `thread` field on the surrounding test class.

Listing 4.16 Example of an Intimate Inner Class

```
public class IntimateAnonymousInnerClassExample {

    private StartStopSynchronizedThread thread;        // 1 Shared between test class and test double

    @Test
    public void
        testStartingAndStoppingThreadsThroughAnExecutorService()
            throws Exception {
        Server server = new Server();
        server.setThreadFactory(new ThreadFactory() {
            public Thread newThread(Runnable task) {
                thread = new StartStopSynchronizedThread(task);
                return thread;
            }
        });                                            // 2 Intimate Inner Class
```

```
            server.start();
            thread.shouldBeStartedWithin(1, TimeUnit.SECONDS);
            server.stop();
            thread.shouldBeStoppedWithin(1, TimeUnit.SECONDS);
        }
    }
```

❸ **Test can access shared field**

Notice how ❷ the Intimate Inner Class is ❶ sharing the `thread` field with the test class, allowing the test to ❸ access the underlying `Thread` instance for its assertions.

Technically, the Intimate Inner Class can be implemented as an anonymous or nested inner class. An anonymous inner class, like the one in listing 4.16, can become unwieldy but can access `final` variables from the method it's created from. A nested inner class, on the other hand, is somewhat cleaner but also more restricted in its access. Both alternatives have the benefit of being able to access the test class's fields.

Speaking of accessing fields, our next pattern is all about accessing fields we're not supposed to.

Privileged Access

You may have been in a situation where you needed to change that one bit of legacy code in order to test your stuff—but there was some reason you couldn't touch the legacy code. In such situations, it may be a reasonable workaround to invade the legacy code's privacy and directly tweak its internals through the Reflection API in order to make it possible for us to write tests—Privileged Access, if you will.

In doing so, the `PrivilegedAccessor` class available from the files section of the JUnit mailing list[26] is a useful aid. A similar utility called `PrivateAccessor` is available as part of the JUnit-Addons open source library;[27] and the Laughing Panda community has developed BeanInject,[28] which knows the same tricks. For example, with the BeanInject project's `Inject` class, we can forcibly substitute a test double into a private field of a legacy class with one line of code:

```
Inject.staticField("foo").of(LegacyCode.class).with(ourTestDouble);
```

The ability to inject or read private fields of classes or objects isn't too useful for projects that have been using TDD from the get-go, but for those working with mounds of legacy code not designed with testability in mind, these kinds of tricks

[26] http://groups.yahoo.com/group/junit/files/src/PrivilegedAccessor.java (you need to join the group to gain access).

[27] http://junit-addons.sourceforge.net/junitx/util/PrivateAccessor.html.

[28] http://www.laughingpanda.org/mediawiki/index.php/Bean_Inject.

and utilities can save the day. However, if we *can* change the legacy code we should prefer doing that instead of falling back to some Reflection trickery. In fact, our next test pattern is just such a change—one that makes code testable.

Extra Constructor

The world of computing is full of monolithic code bases that look like a spaghetti monster. When working in these code bases, it's not uncommon to have a headache because we can't seem to instantiate some class without pulling in a dozen other classes along the way. The problem, of course, is that the dependencies of the class we'd like to use haven't been properly isolated. The proper solution would be to isolate the dependencies, perhaps by driving the architecture toward dependency injection, but that might take time. The Extra Constructor pattern, however, provides us with a nice temporary solution.

The basic idea is that because we cannot substitute the dependencies from the outside, we need to do it from the inside. Thus, we add a new constructor to the class we want to test—one that takes as arguments the dependencies we'd like to substitute. This new constructor can then first delegate to the real constructor and subsequently store the passed-in test-double implementations in place of the real dependencies.

If the original constructor is the place where the real dependencies are instantiated (or if we move them there), we can turn the situation around and make the original constructor delegate to the new constructor, as shown in listing 4.17.

Listing 4.17 Example of Extra Constructor exposing dependencies

```
public class LogFileMerge {

    private URL logFileA, logFileB;

    public LogFileMerge() {
        this(new URL("http://server1/system.log"),
             new URL("http://server2/system.log"));
    }

    LogFileMerge(URL a, URL b) {
        this.logFileA = a;
        this.logFileB = b;
    }

    ...
}
```

❶ Original delegates to Extra Constructor

❷ Dependencies exposed to tests

Listing 4.17 is a trivial example but serves well in highlighting the Extra Constructor pattern. In the class under test, `LogFileMerge`, the ❶ original constructor creates two URL objects with hard-coded network addresses to server1 and server2. First, we don't want our unit tests to access the network. Second, making sure that the log files on those two servers contain what we expect them to contain is hardly an easy thing to do.

Thus, instead of assigning the URL objects to the private fields directly in the original constructor, we ❷ introduce an Extra Constructor and make the original delegate to the new constructor. This way, leaving the Extra Constructor's visibility to package private, protected, or public, our tests can instantiate the LogFile-Merge class using the Extra Constructor, passing in URL objects that point to, for example, local files instead of network addresses.

Again, this pattern is mostly used for working around the bad design of code that hasn't been test-driven. Our next and last pattern is also an instrument for facilitating test-driven development in the midst of such legacy code.

Test-Specific Subclass

Another common anti-pattern I've seen a lot during my programming career is the violation of the Single Responsibility Principle.[29] Imagine we're test-driving some billing functionality that needs to use a complex credit-card processing facility. That facility combines in one class everything related to credit-card transactions and is developed by another team within our company.

Now, let's say the class is built such that there's no way to validate a credit-card number without contacting a merchant service provider, because the number validation logic is hidden behind a protected method, as shown in the following snippet:

```
public class CreditCardProcessing {

    public boolean isValid(String cardnumber) {
        return validationCodeMatches(cardnumber)
                && cardIsActive(cardnumber);
    }

    protected boolean validationCodeMatches(String cardnumber) {
        // validation logic omitted for brevity...
    }

    protected boolean cardIsActive(String cardnumber) {
        // access to merchant system's web service
        // omitted for brevity...
    }
}
```

[29] http://www.objectmentor.com/resources/articles/srp.pdf.

Also, for the sake of the example, let's assume that modifying the class is out of the question due to corporate politics and code ownership. What can we do? Is there a way to handle this situation other than to copy-paste the validation code somewhere else, creating loads and loads of duplication?

The Test-Specific Subclass pattern lets us expose or modify internal state or behavior in scenarios like the one we just described. In our credit-card processing example, we might create a behavior-modifying subclass of the `CreditCardProcessing` class and override the `cardIsActive` method to always return `true`. We'd effectively be testing our code with a partially stubbed version of the credit-card processing facility—which is OK as long as our functionality does not need to make a difference between *why* a given card is considered invalid.

Other common variations of the Test-Specific Subclass pattern include behavior and/or state-exposing subclasses where we don't need to change the way a class works, but rather need information about its internal state or information about what the class is doing internally when its public API is invoked. Once again, the pattern is mostly useful where not all code we write is TDD'd and beautiful but rather ugly legacy code.

Speaking of ugly legacy code, we are going to finish off this chapter in the next section with a foray into the grim world of legacy code—and how to be test-driven when you're surrounded by code without tests and code that exhibits bad design.

4.6 Working with legacy code

Legacy code is traditionally considered to mean code written by someone else somewhere at some point in time. Old code, that is. Old code with a bad stench! The source for that bad stench is not the fact that the code is old but that it's difficult to read and possibly buggy, and there's no way of telling whether changing one thing here will break stuff elsewhere. Based on this thinking, Michael Feathers, in the preface of his book *Working Effectively with Legacy Code*, coined a new definition for legacy code: "code without tests."[30]

NOTE If we define *legacy code* as "code without tests," then writing code not test-first would basically be like writing *instant legacy code*.

[30] Michael first introduced this definition in an article with the same title (http://www.objectmentor.com/resources/articles/WorkingEffectivelyWithLegacyCode.pdf), but it didn't seem to catch on until the book came out. In any case, the definition itself is a remarkably good one, in my opinion.

Probably the vast majority of us are not working on green-field projects but rather maintaining, developing further, and integrating with systems that have been and will be running in production for an arbitrary number of months, years, or even decades. This means that we must be able to use TDD in the context of an existing code base that wasn't developed test-first from the beginning.

How do we test-drive on top of a legacy code base? While you're putting in an order for Michael's book, which is the bible for working with legacy code, I'll try to summarize the process of test-driving changes into legacy code.

4.6.1 Test-driven legacy development

The way to develop test-first in the context of legacy code is similar to what we need to do when others on our team or project don't write tests first or at all. We begin by writing tests around the code we want to change. That might require first breaking some dependencies without having tests to watch our back, which means proceeding more slowly than usual. That shouldn't discourage you, however, because breaking those dependencies and getting in those tests will pay back the investment sooner than you think.

In his book, Michael also describes a process for working with legacy code, illustrated in figure 4.7, which aims to make changing legacy code a disciplined act of software development rather than a cross-fingers-and-press-Enter type of marathon of trial, error, and debugging.

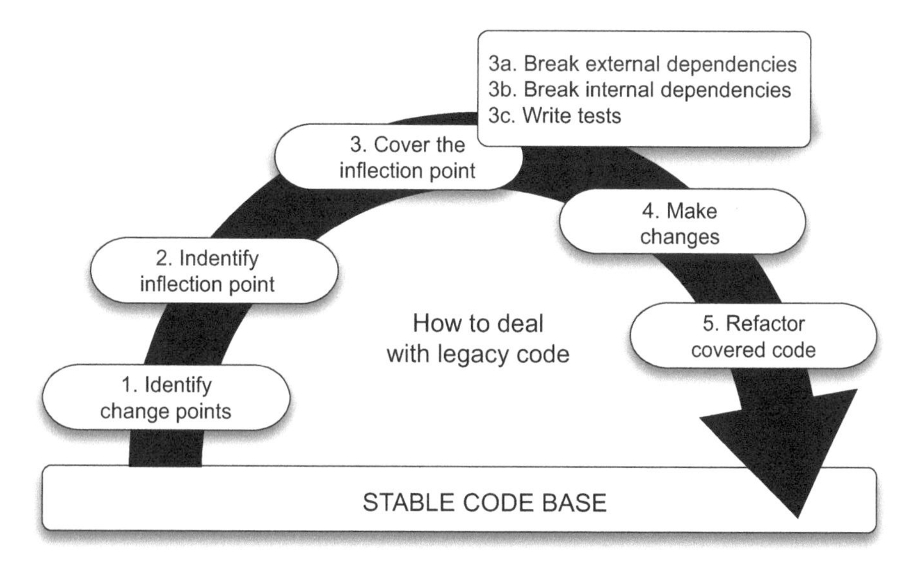

Figure 4.7 The process of working with legacy code

The process described in figure 4.7 could be split into three main phases:

- Analyzing the change
- Preparing for the change
- Test-driving the change

The process begins from a (we hope) stable code base and a need to change the system in some way. For example, we might need to add a new configuration parameter that switches between two alternative behaviors. From this state, we go through the three phases of first analyzing the change, then preparing for making the change in a safe and controlled manner, and finally test-driving the change. Eventually, we have created a new stable code base, including our change.

Next, let's look at each of these phases in more detail and explore what the five detailed steps shown in figure 4.7 mean in practice.

4.6.2 Analyzing the change

When we start analyzing the change we want to make, we first identify the *change points*. Change points are the places in the code base where we need to edit code in order to implement the desired change. This is fundamentally no different from the analysis we carry out with any kind of code base, legacy or not. The main difference is that a legacy code base is generally more difficult to learn and understand than one with thorough unit tests documenting the intent and purpose of individual classes and methods.

When we know where the change should take place, we identify the *inflection point*. The inflection point (or *test point*) is the point "downstream" in our code where we can detect any relevant change in the system's behavior after touching the code in the change points. Typical inflection points are close-proximity seams such as method invocations after or around the change points. Figure 4.8 attempts to illustrate a situation where we have opted for a close-proximity inflection point—that is, testing close to the actual change.

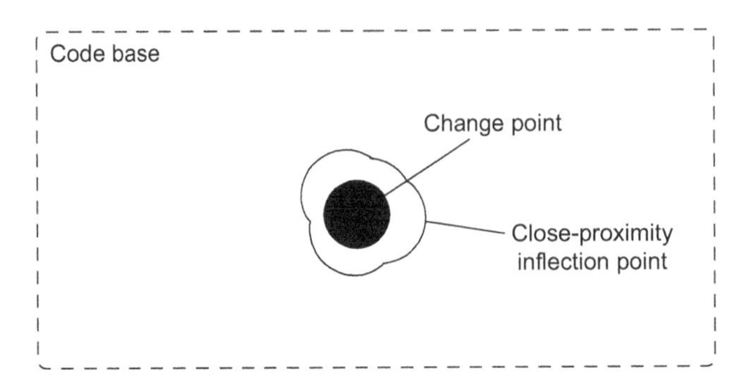

Figure 4.8 Close-proximity inflection points typically cover the change point tightly, making it easy to test for the current behavior in detail.

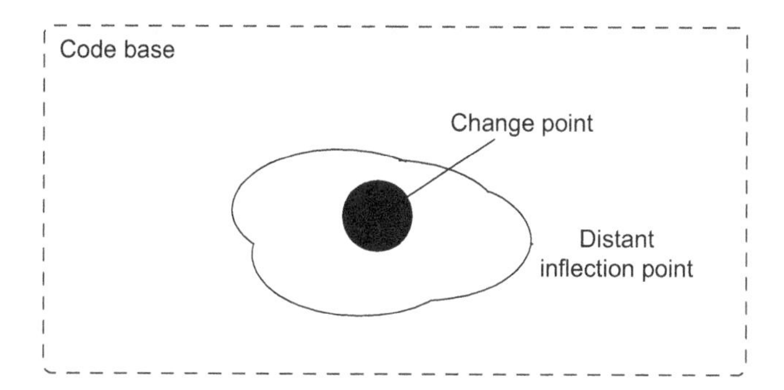

Figure 4.9 More distant inflection points by definition cover more ground and, thus, may protect us from side effects of the change that our analysis had missed.

Sometimes, however, it might make sense to find the inflection point farther away from the change point, as shown in figure 4.9. Examples of such distant inflection points might be network connections to external systems and log output produced by the code in and around the change point. In some cases, it might even be sufficient to treat the system's persistent data source as the inflection point. The trade-off to make is basically between the ease of writing tests at the chosen inflection point and the certainty provided by those tests.

Close-proximity inflection points tend to provide a more localized checkpoint without too much noise around the signal. Distant inflection points, on the other hand, are more likely to catch side effects our analysis hadn't found—but in exchange for potentially more effort in writing the tests because we often don't have access to the kind of detailed information we usually have when testing close to the change point.

After having analyzed the code base looking for the change and inflection points, we know what we need to change and where we can test for the expected behavior. In the next phase, we prepare to make the change in a safe, test-driven manner.

4.6.3 Preparing for the change

Once we've spotted the change and inflection points, we proceed to cover the inflection point with tests that nail down the current behavior before we make our change. This might involve breaking dependencies with careful edits that expose the dependency through a seam we can manipulate in our tests.

The tests we write to cover the inflection point are typically what we call *characterization tests,* meaning that they nail down the current functionality as is, without worrying about whether that behavior is correct. Characterization tests are often also learning tests in the sense that we use them to verify assumptions we've made while identifying the change points.

With sufficient characterization tests in place, we're ready to move on to the third phase of our test-driven legacy development process—making the change.

4.6.4 Test-driving the change

After we've written tests around the change and inflection points to the degree that we're comfortable with our test coverage, we make the change by adding a test for the desired new functionality. As we proceed with implementing the change, our characterization tests tell us if we broke anything while editing the legacy code, and the newly added tests tell us when we have managed to implement the desired change correctly. Finally, once we've successfully made the change and all tests are passing, we refactor the code as usual, enjoying the cover of our automated tests.

That's all there is to working with legacy code in general. The main differences between the regular test-driven development cycle and the process described are that we need to write tests for the existing behavior before adding a test for the new behavior and that we often need to make small dependency-breaking edits without our safety net in order to be able to start writing those tests. It just requires a bit more care and thought.

4.7 Summary

In this last chapter of part 1, we've taken a peek at some of the heavily (or not so heavily) guarded secrets of test-driven developers. These are not silver bullets;[31] they are just techniques. They go into our personal toolbox, and we grab them when we consider them useful.

We started by asking ourselves how to write tests, and we answered the question with a set of test-selection strategies with which we can decide on the next test to write. From test writing, we then moved over to discussing the most fundamental techniques of making tests pass: faking the functionality, triangulating toward the correct functionality, and the occasional obvious implementation. Then, we formulated a set of three prime guidelines for starting our test-driving journey: refactoring mercilessly, getting to green fast, and slowing down when we stumble.

Next, we took some space to discuss a number of essential testing concepts. We defined fixtures as the state and context upon which our tests operate and begin their execution. We studied the fascinating world of test doubles and learned about the categorization of test doubles into fakes, stubs, and mocks. Then, we

[31] Fred Brooks got it wrong. There *are* silver bullets—it's the werewolves that don't exist.

contrasted the state-based style of testing with the more sophisticated, interaction-based testing.

After elaborating and furthering our understanding of the taxonomy of test doubles through a closer look at fakes, stubs, and especially mock objects, we turned our attention to higher-level guidelines for enabling testability by discussing the relative merits of composition versus inheritance and the lurking trouble of static methods and the Singleton pattern. After talking about isolating the troublemakers behind seams, we ventured further into reversing the dependency with dependency injection.

Having an understanding of the key testing concepts and principles that drive testable designs, it was time to put our patterns hat on, inspired by the great work of Gerard Meszaros at xunitpatterns.com. We explored a vast number of different patterns related to unit testing, from the itsy bitsy differences between various kinds of assertions to the more grandiose patterns of setting up and tearing down fixtures.

Our journey in the land of patterns concluded with six more generic test patterns, many of which were especially targeted at surviving in the presence of legacy code—the topic of the last section of this chapter, where we got a brief introduction into working effectively with legacy code, drawing from Michael Feathers' excellent work.

These tips and tricks are something we make use of almost daily when test-driving, regardless of the technology involved. In part 2, we'll focus on tackling specific problems with applying test-driven development on the tough cookies of Java Enterprise Edition technology. Java Enterprise Edition is a platform that gives us much power but also makes our lives that much harder when it comes to verifying that the code we've crunched out works as we expect. Or maybe that's just a myth. I guess we'll know soon enough!

Hang on tight. It's going to be a bit of a wild ride, but I assure you we'll do just fine.

Part 2

Applying TDD to specific technologies

In part 1, you learned to test-drive plain old Java code and put a selection of handy tricks and techniques up your sleeve. Unfortunately, most of the time we won't be lucky enough to get to work with plain old Java code for a living. Instead, we get all that enterprise stuff that they say is "impossible to test-drive." Obviously, that's not true; and in part 2, we'll bust that myth, one technology at a time.

In chapter 5, we learn to test-drive Java EE web applications—not just pure Java like Java servlets and Spring controllers, but also the view templates we use for generating markup. In chapter 6, we step behind the face of our applications and learn to test and test-drive data-access code: code that operates on and manipulates data using not just raw JDBC but also Spring Framework's JdbcTemplate and the popular Hibernate object-relational mapping framework. In chapter 7, we tread farther outside our comfort zone and sort out how to test for concurrent and otherwise unpredictable code. We finish part 2 with a full treatment of test-driving Java Swing applications, including a number of design patterns that simplify that task.

5 Test-driving web components

Test-driving Java EE web components is hard.

—A myth

In this chapter, we'll tackle some of the most common headaches of the modern day Java Platform Enterprise Edition (Java EE) developer trying to apply test-driven development in their everyday job—web components. So far, we've mostly seen the kind of stuff that a typical TDD classroom training would present as introductory material. That's the kind of material that helps us understand the concepts behind the technique and see progress. It's not that easy to do the same when you have to deal with not just plain old Java objects but with the sometimes heinous Java EE interfaces that allow for great flexibility on paper, but at the cost of non-trivial effort on the part of the developer. After finishing this chapter, we will have ideas and ammunition to take on developing Java EE web components test-first.

Speaking of great flexibility and Java EE, there's only so much we can cover in one chapter. Within these limits, we want to cover both the C and the V of the Model-View-Controller (MVC) design pattern so prevalent in today's Java EE architectures for web applications. If you aren't familiar with the MVC pattern, I warmly recommend doing a quick web search or picking up a patterns book such as *Core J2EE Patterns* (Prentice-Hall, 2003). Again, there's a horde of different frameworks out there to help us implement our controllers and views. In an attempt to cover as much ground with as little effort as we can, we'll cherry-pick two technologies from each camp for a closer look.

We'll look at implementing our controllers as raw Java Servlets to get an idea of how to proceed when there is no framework to help us, and we'll look at implementing our controllers using the Spring Framework to get an idea of how this task is simplified when using a testing-friendly framework such as Spring.

On the view side, we'll investigate how to test-drive views based on JavaServer Pages without running them inside a web container to cover the worst-case scenario. Again, we'll glance at an alternative technology, Apache Velocity, to get a picture of how easy test-driving our views can be when the technologies involved are amenable for testing outside the container.

Finally, we'll talk a little bit about component-based frameworks and how test-driving components and pages with those frameworks differs (or doesn't differ!) from request-response technologies. We'll also get our hands dirty with components using Wicket, an open source component-based web framework.

As I've said before, it's going to be a rough ride these following chapters, but I promise we'll come out that much wiser in the end.

5.1 MVC in web applications in 60 seconds

Before jumping head first into test-driving these controller things, let's remind ourselves what the MVC pattern is all about.

MVC stands for Model-View-Controller and is a software architecture or design pattern that splits an application's user-facing components into separate pieces responsible for the domain logic and data (model), the presentation (view), and the application control logic (controller). In principle, the model is only responsible for business logic (and data), the view is only responsible for rendering the model for user interaction, and the controller is only responsible for handling user interaction by invoking changes on the model and selecting which view to render next.

In the Java EE web application context, MVC is most often implemented with the model/view separation being perhaps not as strict as the original pattern intended (originating from the Smalltalk community and desktop graphical user interface [GUI] domain). What this means is that the controller typically passes a specialized (view-oriented) model to the view instead of having the view access the real model.

For example, when asked for a list of cars built in the United States, the controller would ask for the list from the model and pass that list to the view for rendering instead of letting the view perform the query against the model. This way, if we have to do anything special to display the data, such as format numbers or currency, there is a place to do so (the controller) that doesn't depend on details of how the data is displayed (by the view). Figure 5.1 is an attempt at illustrating this concept with boxes and arrows.

Did we exceed 60 seconds? Sorry about that. I just wanted to make sure that we're on the same page when talking about controllers, models, and views. Now, let's get

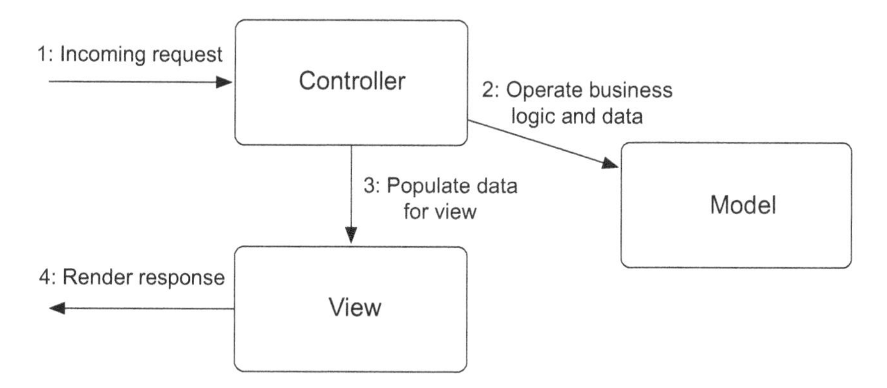

Figure 5.1 The division of responsibilities in the MVC architecture is straightforward. The lifecycle of a request begins with the controller component receiving an incoming HTTP request. The controller then delegates any business logic and data manipulation to the model components and obtains the necessary data from the model. In the third step, the controller populates the necessary data and domain objects for the response, finally delegating the rendering of the response to a view component.

back to our regularly scheduled test-first programming, shall we? Because the code that belongs to the model in MVC is pretty much regular Java code for which we already know how to write tests first, we'll focus on test-driving the stuff that goes into controllers and views, and only discuss the role of the model where necessary.

Let's start by taming the controller logic and continue to the view once we've got our controllers in check.

5.2 Taming the controller

Controllers in the web application MVC architecture are the plumbing between the application and the HTTP traffic coming from the browser. As such, their role is essential in the overall functionality of the web application even though they don't (or at least should not!) contain core business logic. In other words, we'd very much benefit from having our controllers covered under automated unit tests just like we have our model code.

The main difficulties related to test-driving controller code, or writing automated tests for it in general, originate from dependencies to awkward or difficult APIs to mock. The awkwardness of such APIs typically springs from the need to mock up an entire hierarchy of interfaces rather than just one because your application code needs information or functionality provided not by the direct dependency but by an indirect dependency—an object you get access to only by asking another object to give you one. This is what the Pragmatic Programmers Andy Hunt and Dave Thomas refer to with their infamous design principles "Tell, Don't Ask" and the "Law of Demeter."[1]

The mother of all controller-layer technologies in the Java EE world is Java Servlets, so let's start from there and move on to more advanced controller frameworks using the already ubiquitous Spring Framework as our guinea pig.

5.2.1 Test-driving Java Servlets

Servlets are the fundamental building block of Java web applications. Even as fewer and fewer web applications are built directly on top of the Servlet API—with most green-field projects favoring frameworks like Spring, WebWork, Struts, Tapestry, Wicket, or JavaServer Faces (JSF)—many of us will continue to face legacy code bases full of Servlets.[2]

Before we start test-driving Servlets, however, let's first go through some basics.

---

[1] http://www.pragmaticprogrammer.com/ppllc/papers/1998_05.html.

[2] Besides, it might be better for more web applications to start with a plain Servlet, adopting a more complicated framework only when facing a real need. Who knows, that real need might never come…

Servlet API basics

To make sure we're on the same page, let's look at a trivial example Servlet. Listing 5.1 shows a Servlet class responsible for echoing the request parameters it receives back to the requester in plain text, one parameter value per line.

Listing 5.1 Example Servlet echoing request parameters

```
import javax.servlet.*;
import javax.servlet.http.*;
import java.io.*;
import java.util.Enumeration;

public class EchoServlet extends HttpServlet {

    protected void doGet(HttpServletRequest request,
                         HttpServletResponse response)
            throws ServletException, IOException {
        response.setHeader("Content-Type", "text/plain");
        PrintWriter writer = response.getWriter();
        Enumeration e = request.getParameterNames();
        while (e.hasMoreElements()) {
            String parameter = String.valueOf(e.nextElement());
            String[] values = request.getParameterValues(parameter);
            for (int i = 0; i < values.length; i++) {
                writer.write(parameter + "=" + values[i]);
                writer.write("\n");
            }
        }
        writer.close();
    }
}
```

Response object generates response

Request object encapsulates request parameters

Response object generates response

Servlets usually have just one or two public methods like the `doGet` method in listing 5.1, each handling a specific type of HTTP request (GET, POST, HEAD, PUT, and so forth, and each mapping to a method named `do`*XXX*). GET and POST are the usual suspects, although sometimes the developer might want the Servlet to also handle HTTP HEAD or other more exotic types of requests. The common base class for all Servlets—`javax.servlet.http.HttpServlet`—carries out this mapping of HTTP request types to the `do`*XXX* methods, as illustrated in figure 5.2.

The `EchoServlet` class in listing 5.1 only handles GET requests with its `doGet` method. A request of any other type directed at the `EchoServlet` would result in an error response being sent, which is kind of natural because the `EchoServlet`'s author wasn't prepared to handle any other kinds of requests.

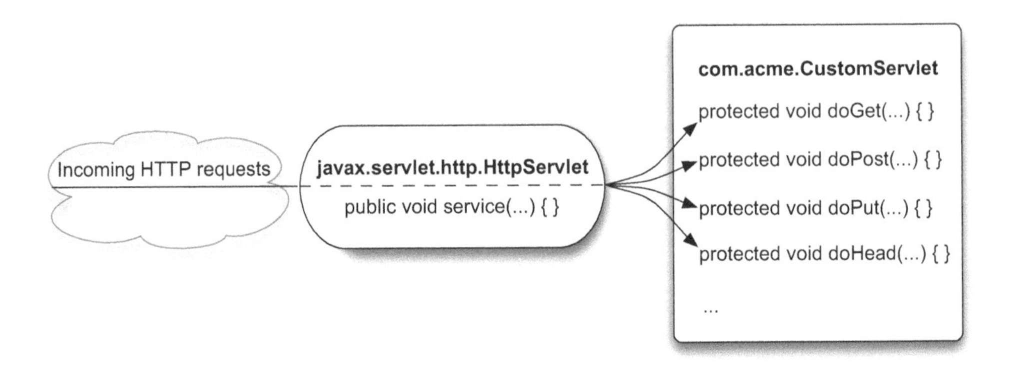

Figure 5.2 Incoming HTTP requests are handled by the `service()` method of the `HttpServlet` base class from which our custom Servlets inherit. The `service()` method looks at the type of the HTTP request and subsequently dispatches the request to the matching `do`*`XXX`*`()` method.

Now let's take a closer look at what all those weird interfaces and classes represent.

The first method argument, `HttpServletRequest`, represents the incoming HTTP request and encapsulates the associated request parameters, HTTP headers, and so forth. The request object also acts as a medium for passing data from one request-handling component to another in the form of request attributes. For example, a Servlet might need to do some pre-processing for a given request, store the intermediate results as objects in the request's attributes, and then forward the request to another Servlet for further processing. In listing 5.1, the `doGet` method interrogates the request object for the names of all request parameters present and then loops through each of them, obtaining the values for those.

The second argument, the `HttpServletResponse` object, is the gateway to generating a response to the client. Any HTTP headers you want to send back to the web browser are set on the response object. Any output you want to write goes through the `PrintWriter` and `ServletOutputStream` objects acquired from the response object. In listing 5.1, for example, the Servlet is writing the received request parameters back into the response object's `PrintWriter`.

That's it. It's definitely not a complicated API. How about looking at how we test these things? In short, we fake the request and the response.

Faking the request and response

Now, if we'd like to write a test for the previous Servlet, verifying that it does indeed generate the expected response, we'll have to provide instances of the `HttpServletRequest` and `HttpServletResponse` interfaces that the Servlet can invoke. Listing 5.2 shows us what a unit test for the `EchoServlet` might look like.

Listing 5.2 Example unit test for the `EchoServlet`

```
import org.springframework.mock.web.MockHttpServletRequest;
import org.springframework.mock.web.MockHttpServletResponse;

public class TestEchoServlet {
    @Test
    public void testEchoingParametersWithMultipleValues()
            throws Exception {
        MockHttpServletRequest request =
            new MockHttpServletRequest();
        MockHttpServletResponse response =
            new MockHttpServletResponse();
        request.addParameter("param1", "param1value1");
        request.addParameter("param2", "param2value1");
        request.addParameter("param2", "param2value2");

        new EchoServlet().doGet(request, response);

        String[] lines = response.getContentAsString().split("\n");
        assertEquals(
                "Expected as many lines as we have parameter values",
                3, lines.length);
        assertEquals("param1=param1value1", lines[0]);
        assertEquals("param2=param2value1", lines[1]);
        assertEquals("param2=param2value2", lines[2]);
    }
}
```

❶ Create and populate mock objects
❷ Execute production code with mocks
❸ Make assertions against response

Looking at listing 5.2, it's not as bad as I painted it to be, is it? I guess it isn't, especially if we already have the `MockHttpServletRequest` and `MockHttpServletResponse` classes at our disposal.[3] We create two test doubles in ❶ and populate them with suitable request parameters, headers, requested URIs, and so forth to simulate a request coming from a web browser. After invoking our Servlet with our fake request and response objects in ❷, all we need to do is ❸ ask the response object for the generated response and perform some assertions just like in any other JUnit test.

So that's how we can test Servlets—by faking the request and response objects with readily available third-party test doubles (although writing our own wouldn't be that hard either). Then again, the previous test is exercising a trivial Servlet. What if we need to test something more real life and complex? We need something

[3] The mock-object implementations used in listing 5.2 have been imported from the Spring Framework. There are also a bunch of other freely available mock object libraries floating around on the Internet.

more realistic than an EchoServlet, because we're about to start implementing our first Servlet test-first!

Testing for redirections

Let's see, what could be an example of a real-world Servlet that would be interesting to test-drive? How about a Servlet that handles logins? Let's make it a tad bit more interesting still and say that the Servlet is responsible for first authenticating login requests and then redirecting the user to the front page or the "change password" page, depending on whether it's been 90 days since the last password change. Sounds like a plan? Great!

What should we test first? I'm tempted to start with a failing login because rejecting a login sounds like an easy thing to do. We could test that the LoginServlet doesn't let a wrong password through but forwards the request to an error page of some kind. Let's see how that might look like in Java code:

```
MockHttpServletRequest request = new MockHttpServletRequest();
MockHttpServletResponse response = new MockHttpServletResponse();
HttpServlet servlet = new LoginServlet();
servlet.service(request, response);
assertEquals("/invalidlogin", response.getRedirectedUrl());
```

We'll want to simulate a request, and we'll want to check that the request was redirected to the error page. The fake implementation of HttpServletResponse lets us do that elegantly.

Oh, and obviously we'll need to fake the user's login credentials somehow. Because we're doing Java EE stuff, how about using request parameters named j_username and j_password for the credentials? Also, we need some kind of fake implementations of the request and response objects so that we can fake the parameters and assert that the redirection takes place.

We could use a dynamic mock-object framework like EasyMock for this, or we could grab a library of static fake implementations. The Spring Framework project comes with a handy set of just such mock implementations for a bunch of javax interfaces—including HttpServletRequest and HttpServletResponse. Let's use those in our tests for now, even though we're not using Spring in our production code.

Listing 5.3 shows our first test for the LoginServlet.

Listing 5.3 First test for the LoginServlet

```
import javax.servlet.http.HttpServlet;
import org.junit.Test;
import static org.junit.Assert.assertEquals;
import org.springframework.mock.web.MockHttpServletRequest;
import org.springframework.mock.web.MockHttpServletResponse;
```

```
public class TestLoginServlet {

    @Test
    public void wrongPasswordShouldRedirectToErrorPage()
            throws Exception {
        HttpServlet servlet = new LoginServlet();
        MockHttpServletRequest request =
            new MockHttpServletRequest("GET", "/login");
        request.addParameter("j_username", "nosuchuser");
        request.addParameter("j_password", "wrongpassword");
        MockHttpServletResponse response =
          new MockHttpServletResponse();
        servlet.service(request, response);
        assertEquals("/invalidlogin", response.getRedirectedUrl());
    }
}
```

Create fake request object ...

... and fake response object

Assert expected outcome

That was easy. We added two request parameters for the username and password to be used in the login request, invoked an instance of the forthcoming `LoginServlet` class (the code doesn't exist yet, remember?), and finally asked the fake response object to verify that it was told to redirect to the URL /invalidlogin as expected. At this time, we're not interested in what happens when the browser requests the /invalidlogin URL. We're specifying that failed login attempts be redirected there.

Now, it's time to make our first cut at bringing the `LoginServlet` into being. We create the `LoginServlet` class, as instructed by our compiler, and run the test to assure ourselves that we're running the right test—and that it's failing as expected. Then, we proceed to writing an implementation for the `service` method. The simplest code that can make our test pass *always* redirects the user to /invalidlogin, regardless of the request parameters, as we've done in listing 5.4.

Listing 5.4 Our first cut at the `LoginServlet` (rejects any login attempt)

```
public class LoginServlet extends HttpServlet {
    @Override
    protected void service(HttpServletRequest request,
                            HttpServletResponse response)
            throws ServletException, IOException {
        response.sendRedirect("/invalidlogin");
    }
}
```

Always reject login

Running our test against this tiny snippet does indeed prove that we pass with flying colors. Obviously we're still far from being finished with our functionality, and things start getting more interesting when we write a test for a login with valid credentials.

Working with parameters and the session

Hmm. How will we know whether the login has been successful? At least we need to redirect the user to the front page. Also, we need to somehow remember that the user has logged in. At some point, we might end up using a more sophisticated authentication framework, but for now it should suffice if we store the user's login name into the user's session.

Confident that this is the way to go, we write our second test, shown in listing 5.5.

Listing 5.5 Sketch of our next test, verifying that a valid login attempt succeeds

```
@Test
public void validLoginForwardsToFrontPageAndStoresUsername()
        throws Exception {
    HttpServlet servlet = new LoginServlet();
    MockHttpServletRequest request =
        new MockHttpServletRequest("GET", "/login");
    request.addParameter("j_username", "validuser");
    request.addParameter("j_password", "correctpassword");
    MockHttpServletResponse response =
        new MockHttpServletResponse();
    servlet.service(request, response);
    assertEquals("/frontpage", response.getRedirectedUrl());
    assertEquals("validuser",
                request.getSession().getAttribute("username"));
}
```

There's little difference in this test compared to our first test, except that this test will force us to implement some logic into the `LoginServlet` rather than always rejecting any and all login attempts. We're also checking for the addition of a session attribute named "username" as a means of verifying that the user has been logged in. This was a design decision made on the spot and a decision that we might change later on. For now, storing the username in the session shall indicate a logged-in user.

As I switch back to the `LoginServlet` implementation in my IDE, the need for another design decision dawns on me. How does our `LoginServlet` know that "validuser" is a valid user and that "correctpassword" happens to be that specific user's password? Or, let's put it the other way around. How are we going to tell the `LoginServlet` which users exist in the system? Let's put our designer hats on and think about it for a while.

Evolving towards a better design

The introduction of the additional login test is essentially forcing us to treat valid and invalid credentials differently. Not wanting to dip ourselves into the authentication implementation yet—whether it's based on a file system, a relational database, or an LDAP server—we're naturally driven toward a modular design. In short, we want our Servlet to delegate the authentication decision to someone else and only worry about what the Servlet is responsible for as an MVC controller.

Following our intuition, we might end up with an interface like that shown in listing 5.6 for the authentication service.

Listing 5.6 The `AuthenticationService` interface

```
public interface AuthenticationService {
    boolean isValidLogin(String username, String password);
}
```

Because we don't have a real user database or other authentication service to use, we'll also sketch up a simple fake implementation for the `AuthenticationService` interface, shown as listing 5.7.

Listing 5.7 Fake implementation of the `AuthenticationService` interface

```
public class FakeAuthenticationService implements
    AuthenticationService {

    private Map<String, String> users = new HashMap<String, String>();

    public void addUser(String user, String pass) {
        users.put(user, pass);
    }

    public boolean isValidLogin(String user, String pass) {
        return users.containsKey(user)
                && pass.equals(users.get(user));
    }
}
```

Our fake authentication service uses a simple `Map` containing usernames and passwords. We also included a method for adding valid users into the `Map` so that we can control the "user database" from our test code.

Now, the next question is, how will the `LoginServlet` get hold of the `AuthenticationService` implementation? Knowing that the Servlet container will instantiate our Servlet classes, we can't use constructor injection for dependencies.[4] We could make `AuthenticationService` into an abstract class with a static getter for the currently configured implementation and a matching setter we could use from our test code. That doesn't sound good, though—proper dependency injection would be cleaner.

Instead of pondering for too long about this architectural issue, let's postpone it for now and specify that the `LoginServlet` should obtain its `AuthenticationService` through a protected getter method—something we can override in our test code to return our fake `AuthenticationService` implementation.

Listing 5.8 shows our test from listing 5.5 rewritten to use the `AuthenticationService` interface.

Listing 5.8 Valid login test rewritten to specify use of `AuthenticationService`

```
@Test
public void validLoginForwardsToFrontPageAndStoresUsername()
        throws Exception {
    final String validUsername = "validuser";
    final String validPassword = "validpassword";

    final FakeAuthenticationService authenticator =
            new FakeAuthenticationService();
    authenticator.addUser(validUsername, validPassword);

    LoginServlet servlet = new LoginServlet() {
        @Override
        protected AuthenticationService getAuthenticationService() {
            return authenticator;
        }
    };

    MockHttpServletRequest request = new MockHttpServletRequest();
    request.addParameter("j_username", validUsername);
    request.addParameter("j_password", validPassword);
    MockHttpServletResponse response =
        new MockHttpServletResponse();

    servlet.service(request, response);
    assertEquals("/frontpage", response.getRedirectedUrl());
    assertEquals("validuser",
                 request.getSession().getAttribute("username"));
}
```

Configure fake Authentication-Service

Use fake instead of real thing

[4] Not without overloading the constructor for testing purposes, that is.

Wow. That's a big test method. We'll have to do some serious refactoring as soon as we get back to green. In fact, the code is not even compiling right now, so let's fix that first by giving `LoginServlet` the missing getter method our IDE is complaining about:

```
public class LoginServlet extends HttpServlet {

    protected AuthenticationService getAuthenticationService() {
        return null;
    }

    @Override
    protected void service(HttpServletRequest request,
                           HttpServletResponse response)
            throws ServletException, IOException {
        response.sendRedirect("/invalidlogin");
    }
}
```

That gets us through the compiler error, and our test is failing—as expected—because we're getting redirected to the wrong place. Time to add functionality.

Although the introduction of an `AuthenticationService` interface is significant for our design, the implementation step in order to get our currently failing test back to green shouldn't be complicated. The implementation in listing 5.9 should pass our tests with flying colors.

Listing 5.9 `LoginServlet` delegating authentication to a separate service interface

```
public class LoginServlet extends HttpServlet {

    protected AuthenticationService getAuthenticationService() {
        return null;     <-- No need to implement this method yet
    }

    @Override
    protected void doGet(HttpServletRequest request,
                         HttpServletResponse response)
            throws ServletException, IOException {
        String user = request.getParameter("j_username");
        String pass = request.getParameter("j_password");
        if (getAuthenticationService().isValidLogin(user, pass)) {   <-- Branch execution based on AuthenticationService's ruling
            response.sendRedirect("/frontpage");
            request.getSession().setAttribute("username", user);
        } else {
            response.sendRedirect("/invalidlogin");
        }
    }
}
```

Oops. Our test is passing, but we broke our previous test because we're not configuring an `AuthenticationService` implementation for the `LoginServlet` instance in the first test. Let's remedy that situation by pulling out some common setup code from our second test.

Let's see—we can convert the anonymously subclassed `LoginServlet` instance into a field as well as the `FakeAuthenticationService` instance. Also, we're using the fake request and response objects in both tests, so let's move those into fields as well. And how about turning some of those duplicated strings into constants. That should clean up the mess. The resulting test class structure is shown in listing 5.10.

Listing 5.10 Configuring a `LoginServlet` with an `AuthenticationService`

```
public class TestLoginServlet {

    private static final String CORRECT_PASSWORD = "correctpassword";
    private static final String VALID_USERNAME = "validuser";

    private LoginServlet servlet;
    private FakeAuthenticationService authenticator;
    private MockHttpServletRequest request;
    private MockHttpServletResponse response;

    @Before
    public void setUp() {
        authenticator = new FakeAuthenticationService();
        authenticator.addUser(VALID_USERNAME, CORRECT_PASSWORD);

        servlet = new LoginServlet() {
            @Override
            protected AuthenticationService
                getAuthenticationService() {
                return authenticator;
            }
        };

        request = new MockHttpServletRequest();
        response = new MockHttpServletResponse();
    }

    @Test
    public void wrongPasswordShouldRedirectToErrorPage()
            throws Exception {
        request.addParameter("j_username", VALID_USERNAME);
        request.addParameter("j_password", "wrongpassword");
        servlet.service(request, response);
        assertEquals("/invalidlogin", response.getRedirectedUrl());
    }
```

By moving common objects into fields...

...our test methods are much, much more concise and to the point

```
    @Test
    public void validLoginForwardsToFrontPageAndStoresUsername()
            throws Exception {
        request.addParameter("j_username", VALID_USERNAME);
        request.addParameter("j_password", CORRECT_PASSWORD);
        servlet.service(request, response);
        assertEquals("/frontpage", response.getRedirectedUrl());
        assertEquals(VALID_USERNAME, request.getSession()
                .getAttribute("username"));
    }
}
```

...test methods are much more concise and to the point

After using the same setup for the `LoginServlet` and the `FakeAuthentication-Service` for both of our tests, they run successfully, giving us a green bar. There's some duplication in the form of the literal strings "j_username" and "j_password", which we possibly should refactor into constants. Sometimes, readability overrides the "no duplication" rule, but in this case, I'm strongly leaning toward refactoring. The duplication involves not just our test code but is shared between the tests and the production code. One possibility would be to define public constants for the two request parameters in our production code and reference them from both places. Consider that an exercise for you.

We could easily go on for another 10 pages or so; but to leave time to discuss other technologies, let's wrap up this Servlet example. Now we can move on to test-driving a controller on top of a slightly different technology than the bare Servlet API.

Reflecting on test-driving Servlets

Now, let's see what we did here with the `AuthenticationService` interface. We introduced the `AuthenticationService` interface to prevent the `LoginServlet` from knowing how to authenticate login attempts. We decided to postpone the decision of how to inject the `AuthenticationService` for now, using a getter method we override in our tests. We only have a fake implementation of the `AuthenticationService` interface, and we can implement the real thing later.

The key to keeping our Java Servlets clean and testable is to divide and conquer. Programming by intention, aiming to get our tests passing in the smallest steps we dare, we approach a fully test-driven Servlet component piece by piece. As we witnessed first-hand with our `LoginServlet` example, if we don't try to cut corners, we find that Servlets aren't any more of a pain to test-drive than a regular Java class.

Now that we've cleared the topic of test-driving Servlets, the mother of all controllers in the Java EE web application scene, let's see whether things are any different if we used a modern MVC framework instead of building our application directly on top of Java Servlets. With the recent strong growth in popularity of the Spring Framework, we'll use the Spring MVC module as our guinea pig.

5.2.2 Test-driving Spring controllers

The Spring Framework realizes the C in MVC through different types of `Controller` classes. They're similar to Servlets but somewhat more abstract. For one, Spring controllers are not responsible for dispatching the request to the view directly. Instead, they indicate to the surrounding framework what the framework should do by returning a `ModelAndView` object. To clarify this a bit, let's look at some code.

Listing 5.11 Example of a Spring controller

```
public class SampleController implements Controller {

    protected ModelAndView handleRequest(HttpServletRequest request,
                                         HttpServletResponse response)
            throws Exception {
        return new ModelAndView("viewname");
    }
}
```

The example `SampleController` class in listing 5.11 illustrates how, to satisfy Spring MVC's `Controller` interface, we need to implement one simple method that handles an incoming request and is responsible for returning a `ModelAndView` for further processing. This is as simple as it can get. The `SampleController` will be mapped to handle specific URLs using an external configuration file so there's no need to dispatch between several logical actions. The incoming request object is our gateway to all the data we need for doing whatever our `SampleController` needs to do, and the `ModelAndView` object we return tells Spring MVC which view to render for the response.

That was Spring MVC in a bit over 150 words. Now, let's start test-driving some Spring MVC controller code!

Writing the first test

Let's see what kind of a test we might write if we were to implement the same functionality as with our `LoginServlet`, only this time using a Spring MVC `Controller` class. Again, when someone attempts to log in with an incorrect password, we want our controller to send us to the "wrong password" page. To do this with Spring MVC, it means having the controller's `handleRequest` method return a `ModelAndView` object for a view named "wrongpassword". Listing 5.12 presents a test that verifies that.

Listing 5.12 Sample unit test for the `LoginController`

```
public class TestLoginController {
    @Test
    public void wrongPasswordShouldRedirectToErrorPage()
            throws Exception {
        MockHttpServletRequest request =
            new MockHttpServletRequest();
        request.addParameter("j_username", "nosuchusername");
        request.addParameter("j_password", "nosuchpassword");
        MockHttpServletResponse response =
            new MockHttpServletResponse();

        Controller c = new LoginController();
        ModelAndView v = c.handleRequest(request, response);

        assertEquals("wrongpassword", v.getViewName());
    }
}
```

❶ Populate mock objects

❷ Invoke Controller's handleRequest() method

❸ User should land on "wrong password" page

As you can see, there isn't much of a difference between the "failed login" test case for the Spring controller versus the Servlet-based implementation. We ❶ create test doubles for the standard request and response interfaces, then ❷ invoke the controller's request-handling method with our test doubles, and finally ❸ perform assertions to verify expected behavior.

The small difference in asserting the outcome of a Spring controller's execution compared to that of a Servlet's is that Spring has the `ModelAndView` concept as an abstraction between the controller and the view implementation. The controller only needs to return a `ModelAndView` object, which carries all the data the view should need for rendering itself plus the name of the view. The remainder of the Spring MVC framework then takes care of mapping and rendering the named view—whatever technology it is implemented with—using the data received within the `ModelAndView` object.

So, where are we now? We've got a test, and once we've created the missing `LoginController` class, we can run it and see the familiar red bar telling us we've got work to do.

Faking it the easy way

The test in listing 5.12 happens to pass with almost the same one-liner implementation we saw for the `SampleController` in listing 5.11—we just need a different hard-coded view name, as illustrated in listing 5.13.

Listing 5.13 Faking rejected authentication

```
import javax.servlet.http.*;
import org.springframework.web.servlet.ModelAndView;
import org.springframework.web.servlet.mvc.Controller;

public class LoginController implements Controller {

    public ModelAndView handleRequest(HttpServletRequest request,
                                      HttpServletResponse response)
            throws Exception {
        return new ModelAndView("wrongpassword");
    }
}
```

That wasn't much of a task (not that it would've been with the `LoginServlet` either). Run tests. Green. Great, what's next?

Bringing in dependencies

Perhaps the biggest advantage of Spring's controllers over plain Servlets from testability's point of view is how we manage the dependencies for controllers. To demonstrate this, let's write a test for a successful login.

Suppose we use the same `AuthenticationService` interface from the `LoginServlet` example for delegating the authentication from the controller. We need a way to pass the controller a suitable `AuthenticationService` implementation for testing purposes. Thanks to Spring Framework's dependency-injection features, all we need to do to have our `LoginController` injected with the proper `AuthenticationService` implementation in a deployment environment is to declare a setter method, `setAuthenticationService`, and wire an implementation *bean* (Spring nomenclature for objects managed by the framework) to the `LoginController` in a separate configuration file. Figure 5.3 illustrates this.

In the test, we pass a test double for the real `AuthenticationService` to the `LoginController`. In production, Spring will inject a real implementation based on the previous configuration file.

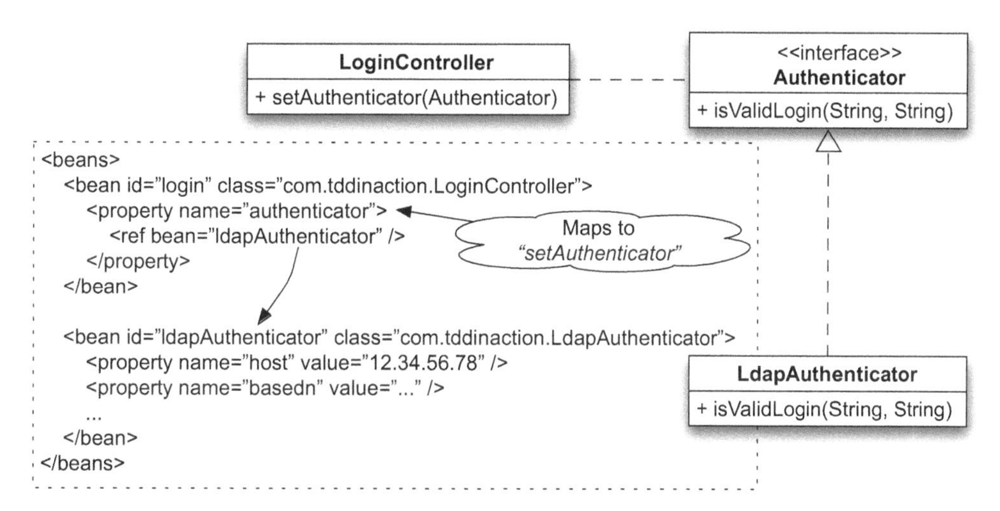

Figure 5.3 Mapping between `LoginController` and its dependency to an `AuthenticationService` implementation

Listing 5.14 demonstrates how our test for the valid login looks much like the one we wrote for the `LoginServlet`.

Listing 5.14 Testing a valid login

```
private static final String CORRECT_PASSWORD = "correctpassword";
private static final String VALID_USERNAME = "validuser";
...

@Test
public void validLoginForwardsToFrontPage() throws Exception {
    MockHttpServletRequest request = new MockHttpServletRequest();
    request.setMethod("GET");
    request.addParameter("j_username", VALID_USERNAME);
    request.addParameter("j_password", CORRECT_PASSWORD);
    MockHttpServletResponse response =
        new MockHttpServletResponse();

    FakeAuthenticationService mock =
        new FakeAuthenticationService();
    mock.addUser(VALID_USERNAME, CORRECT_PASSWORD);

    LoginController c = new LoginController();
    c.setAuthenticationService(mock);            <-- Simulate dependency injection
    ModelAndView v = c.handleRequest(request, response);

    assertEquals("frontpage", v.getViewName());
}
```

The only differences between our `LoginServlet` tests and `LoginController` tests seem to be that we're invoking a different handler method (`service` for a Servlet versus `handleRequest` for a Spring controller) and that with Spring MVC, we don't need to worry about designing a dependency-injection architecture because Spring gives us one out of the box—we can add a setter, and we know that the rest is configuration.

Before wrapping up this topic, let's quickly see how we could make the tests pass again. Listing 5.15 shows the full controller implementation.

Listing 5.15 `LoginController` implementation, complete with dependency injection

```
public class LoginController implements Controller {

    private AuthenticationService authenticator;

    public void
       setAuthenticationService(AuthenticationService authService) {
        this.authenticator = authService;
    }

    public ModelAndView handleRequest(HttpServletRequest request,
            HttpServletResponse response) throws Exception {
        String user = request.getParameter("j_username");
        String pass = request.getParameter("j_password");
        if (authenticator.isValidLogin(user, pass)) {
            return new ModelAndView("frontpage");
        }
        return new ModelAndView("wrongpassword");
    }
}
```

Nothing fancy there. Running our tests, we again realize that the valid login test passes but that our first test now fails because the test didn't inject an `AuthenticationService` implementation for it. The test is broken, so we need to fix it by moving the common setup into instance variables being set up in a `@Before` method. Although we're not going to look at the result of that cleanup, if you're following along, by all means try it and see how it works out and how much cleaner your code becomes.

In the light of these examples, there's hardly a valid argument to claim that test-driving controller classes in modern MVC frameworks is somehow difficult or laborious. It's all plain Java—the interfaces just tend to be slightly larger than our application-specific ones typically are.

Now that we have seen how test-driving MVC controllers is possible without bending over backward, let's move on to tackling the "V" next.

5.3 Creating the view test-first

Perhaps the biggest obstacle, as usual, to testing the view layer automatically is lack of faith: lack of faith that it can be done or that it makes sense in the first place. Speaking of web applications, there are certain things that must always be verified visually, such as the overall aesthetics

and that the pixels line up as intended on all supported browsers. This is not something we'll likely want to automate, because the effort of creating such tests would be unreasonably high considering the information value provided by such tests (can we trust a computer to tell whether a web page looks alright?) and considering such tests' tendency towards brittleness. Figure 5.4 illustrates this division between things we need to verify visually and things for which we can automate the tests.

There are, however, aspects of the view layer that it makes sense to verify automatically. Let's call those aspects the *view logic*. By view logic, we mean stuff like "given a list of items, the details of the first item are rendered in full and only the name is rendered for the rest of the list." Not only that, but it's something we want to test-drive into our view!

From a technology perspective, the view layer sometimes poses some extra hurdles we'll need to jump over if we want to employ an extremely short TDD cycle.

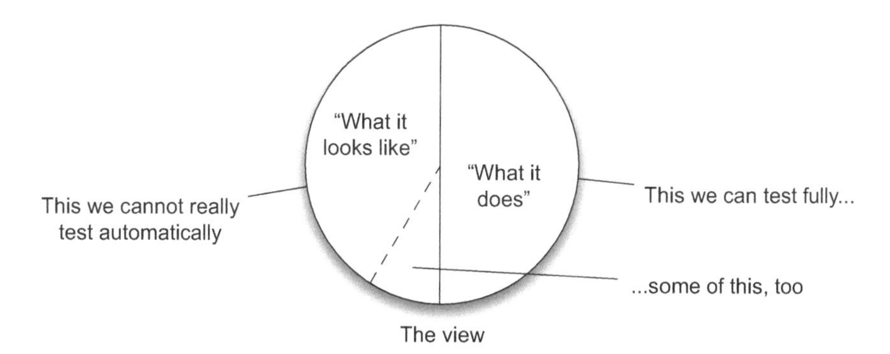

Figure 5.4 Although it's not practical to write tests for what the view *looks* like, it is most certainly possible to test the *view logic*. That is, it's possible to test what the view *does*. In addition, although it's typically not feasible to fully test the left side of the pie with automated tests, there are often some small aspects of the view that can be tested. For instance, we might want to have an automated test for checking that our web pages comply with the accessibility requirements of Section 508 (that is, those parts of Section 508 that don't require human judgment—such as every image tag having a text equivalent defined with the `alt` attribute).

The prime example of such hurdles must be JavaServer Pages (JSP), which require a JSP engine in order to render into HTML (or whatever markup language or other form of content your specific JSP components are supposed to generate).

All hope is not lost, however, because there is a way to embed a lightweight JSP engine into our unit tests. Being lightweight, such a JSP engine doesn't take long to initialize and lets our unit tests run reasonably quickly compared to the alternative of deploying the view components under test on a full-blown application server.

Let's first see how to test-drive the classic login page using JavaServer Pages as the view technology. Once we've got that covered, we'll take a quick look at how an alternative template technology, Velocity, would mold in our test-driven hands. Finally, we'll venture into the world of component-based web frameworks and figure out whether there's anything special about test-driving views using such technology.

5.3.1 Test-driving JSPs with JspTest

As we already discussed, test-driving JavaServer Pages requires infrastructure in the form of a JSP engine. We'll use a little open source library named JspTest.[5] JspTest is essentially the smallest slice of infrastructure necessary for compiling JavaServer Pages into Servlet classes and then invoking the compiled Servlet. Internally, JspTest uses Jasper, the JSP engine used by Apache Tomcat, Jetty, Glassfish, and a bunch of other web containers and application servers. It's not the most mature Java library around, but it is already usable and faster than test-driving JSP development against a full-blown web container.

But now, let's get back to work!

Building just enough plumbing

Let's start building up our infrastructure in a piecemeal fashion so we know what's going on under the hood when running the tests.

Our interface toward JspTest is the abstract `HtmlTestCase` class, which our tests need to extend. The `HtmlTestCase` class provides us with methods for rendering a given JSP file with a simulated HTTP request as well as a bunch of HTML-oriented assertion methods we can use for verifying the expected output.

Let's say we have our JSP source files in a directory named websrc/jsp. By default, JspTest will look for the given JSP path starting from the current working directory, which means that we'll need to always spell out the full path, including websrc/jsp. Obviously we don't want to do that every time, so we override the `getWebRoot` method in our own custom, abstract base class for all of our JSP tests:

---

[5] http://jsptest.sf.net.

```
import net.sf.jsptest.HtmlTestCase;

public abstract class MyJspTestCase extends HtmlTestCase {
    @Override
    protected String getWebRoot() {
        return "./websrc/jsp";
    }
}
```

There. Now we can render websrc/jsp/foo.jsp by saying /foo.jsp. Perhaps not a big difference now, but it all adds up—especially when we're told to move our JSP sources into some other directory.

Actually, that's about the entire infrastructure we're going to need for now (other than putting the JspTest dependencies into our class path), so let's start writing some real tests.

Testing for rendered content

We're on our way to developing a simple login page using JavaServer Pages as our technology and test-driven development as our method. One easy choice for the first test could be to test that the necessary form elements are present on the rendered page when a user arrives on the page. Stretching our programming by intention skills, we come up with the test shown in listing 5.16.

Listing 5.16 Making use of our abstract `JspTest` base class

```
public class TestLoginPage extends MyJspTestCase {

    public void testFormFieldsArePresent() throws Exception {
        get("/login.jsp");
        form().shouldHaveField("j_username");
        form().shouldHaveField("j_password");
        form().shouldHaveSubmitButton("login");
    }
}
```

In all of its simplicity, this test expresses our intention of rendering login.jsp using an HTTP GET request and asserting that the page includes form fields named "j_username" and "j_password" as well as a submit button named "login". Hey, I think we're done with the test—let's run it!

Red bar due to JspTest not being able to find login.jsp from our web root—and it shouldn't, because we're test-driving! Now, let's go and write some JSP code to get back to green.

> **Why aren't we using the JUnit 4 annotations?**
>
> Even though we're lucky enough to be able to use the latest and greatest, the JspTest project needs to support those who are still stuck with Java 1.4 or (shrug) older. Thus, we rely on JUnit 4's backward compatibility for running our JspTest tests alongside our other, annotation-laden test code.

Creating just enough JSP

In order to quickly see if we're adding the JSP to the right place in the file system, we start with the simplest JavaServer Page we can think of, shown in listing 5.17.

Listing 5.17 Our first cut at login.jsp

```

```

An empty page. It can't get any simpler than that. That's enough to make sure we're not plowing ahead full-speed only to find out that our test isn't even executing the file we're editing. Later on, we'll probably speed up a bit, but it's often good to go slow in the beginning.

Running our test again, we learn that JspTest finds our JSP from the file system. We now see our test failing because there's no form field named "j_username" on the page. No surprise, really, because all we have is an empty JSP file. That is, we did until we now add a rudimentary form along with the HTML skeleton. The failure point moves to the next assertion, "j_password", and then to complaining about the missing submit button, and eventually we get the familiar green bar as we add all the missing pieces, as shown in listing 5.18.

Listing 5.18 The JSP that passes our first test

```
<%@ page language="Java" %>
<html>
  <body>
    <form>
      <input type="text" name="j_username" />
      <input type="password" name="j_password" />
      <input type="submit" name="login" />
    </form>
  </body>
</html>
```

There. Our first test is running and we've test-driven a concrete piece of our user interface. We had to do some plumbing to get here, and we're likely to add more plumbing as we encounter the need for more elaborate assertions and so forth, but it wasn't a big hurdle to jump to get started, was it? Now, we can continue by adding more tests, each nudging our JSP template an inch closer to being complete.

Driving behavior into our page

Let's continue developing our login page for a moment. We're curious as to how we could test-drive a bit of dynamic behavior into our page, so let's write a test for verifying that the login page auto-populates the user's login name into the "j_username" field upon a failed login attempt. Listing 5.19 shows our test.

Listing 5.19 Test for retaining the username but not the password upon a failed login

```
public void testPreviousUsernameIsRetained() throws Exception {
    setRequestAttribute("j_username", "bob");
    get("/login.jsp");
    form().field("j_username").shouldHaveValue("bob");
}
```

Our test is saying that the JSP should know to render the value of a request parameter named "j_username" into one of the input fields upon rendering. Running the test, the assertion indeed fails because the input field's value is not set at all. The scriptlet shown in listing 5.20 remedies the situation, and we're soon on green again.

Listing 5.20 Adding a scriptlet to pre-populate the username field upon failed login

```
<%@ page language="Java" %>
<html>
  <body>
    <form>
      <%
        String username =
            (String) request.getAttribute("j_username");
        if (username == null) username = "";
      %>
      <input type="text" name="j_username" value="<%= username %>"/>
      <input type="password" name="j_password" />
      <input type="submit" name="login" />
    </form>
  </body>
</html>
```

Wasn't that easy? Who said that you can't unit-test JavaServer Pages? I'm sure we're both confident by now that test-driving JavaServer Pages is feasible and well within our reach—and without much ramp-up time needed.

Alternatives to JspTest

The JspTest project is an extremely suitable approach to testing what's probably the majority of JavaServer Pages. It is a young project, however, and thus it does have its shortcomings. For example, the available set of HTML-oriented and other content assertions is still somewhat limited. Furthermore, not all aspects of the built-in objects (`request`, `response`, `session`, `pageContext`, and so on) can be fully controlled, which might mean that another approach is needed to accompany our JspTest tests.

Beyond JspTest, the best alternative approach for unit-testing JavaServer Pages at the time of writing this book is probably the ServletRunner (part of the HttpUnit project), which is a lightweight web container purpose-built for testing Servlets and, by means of forwarding, JavaServer Pages. You can refer to Recipe 12.3 in J. B. Rainsberger's excellent *JUnit Recipes* (Manning Publications, 2005) for details on using the ServletRunner. Figure 5.5 shows the architecture of this approach of using a special forwarding Servlet for accessing and testing JSP output.

Other alternatives include embedding an Java EE web container in our tests. Jetty[6] is just such a lightweight, standards-compliant web container that we can run in embedded mode. Jetty does, however, require a valid web application context and, thus, requires more infrastructure than JspTest (mostly because JspTest hides all that complexity under its hood).

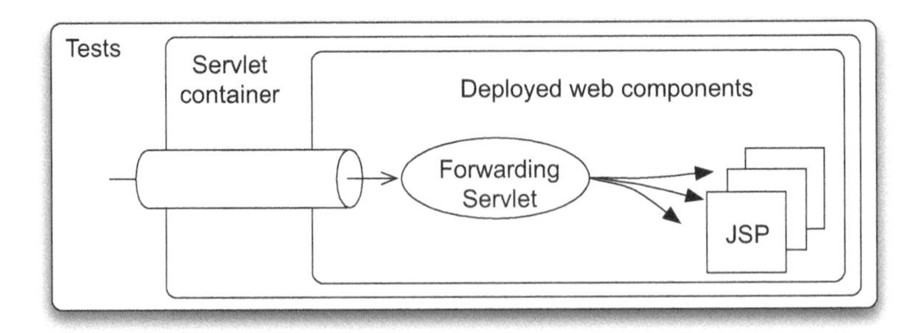

Figure 5.5 One possibility for test-driving JavaServer Pages is to deploy them into a lightweight, embeddable Servlet container and access them either using HTTP requests or through the container's internal API.

[6] http://jetty.mortbay.org.

Deploying our JSP code on a separate, standalone container instance is also an option but is again much slower compared to the embedded alternatives. If you feel like going for this kind of in-container (integration) testing, look at Jakarta Cactus, which is the leading open source framework in that domain. Be warned, though, it's not nearly as suitable for blazing-fast feedback as JspTest and friends!

I think that's about enough of JavaServer Pages for now. Let's take a peek at how green the grass is on the open source side of the Java view template fence.

5.3.2 Test-driving Velocity templates

Velocity[7] is a general-purpose template engine without any ties to the Java EE platform. Although this might sound like a handicap from the perspective of a Java EE web application developer, it is a strong advantage over other, more complex and fully featured technologies like JavaServer Pages.

We already mentioned in passing that Velocity is a lightweight view technology. What does that mean? Well, if we look at the plumbing inside frameworks like JspTest, it's not exactly a small chunk of code. Rendering a JSP requires a lot of plumbing. Yes, someone else has already done most of the work for us, but my gut tells me that rendering a view template should not be such a difficult thing to do.

Velocity is designed to be embedded into tools and applications of all kinds and doesn't have any dependencies to the Java EE stack. This is the key in making it a lightweight alternative for our purposes. We still need some plumbing to support a smooth test-driven development experience, but a lot less than for JavaServer Pages. Namely, we don't need a container in front of the template engine, and the template engine itself (Velocity) is also smaller than, say, Apache Tomcat's Jasper.

Before we dive deeper, let's familiarize ourselves with the basics of Velocity templates and the Velocity API.

Velocity basics

Velocity's concept is simple: We take a template, we take a mapping of variables and their values, and we shove those two through Velocity, evaluating the mixture of plain text, variables, and basic conditional and looping constructs in the template in the context of the given variable values. Figure 5.6 illustrates this with boxes and arrows.

Velocity's API isn't much more complicated. You create a `VelocityContext` object and populate it with a bunch of named attributes (key-value pairs), and then you create a `VelocityEngine` and ask the engine to evaluate the template, rendering the output to a given output stream (a `java.io.Writer`, to be more

[7] http://velocity.apache.org.

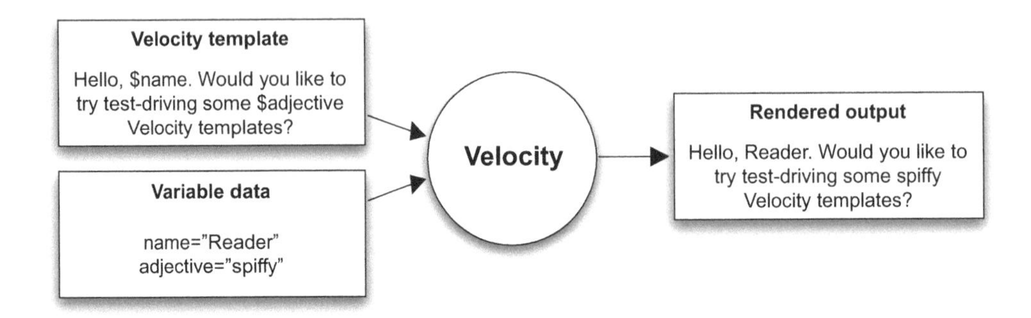

Figure 5.6 Velocity's basic concept is extremely simple. Velocity eats template text consisting of specialized markup for variable data and basic programming constructs, drinks some variable values on top, and spits out the rendered output.

specific). In other words, what we need to do in our tests to render a Velocity template is more or less the following:

```
String template = "Hello $user";
StringWriter writer = new StringWriter();
VelocityContext context = new VelocityContext();
context.put("user", "Reader");
VelocityEngine engine = new VelocityEngine();
engine.init();
engine.evaluate(context, writer, "test", template);
```

After executing the previous sequence of statements, the `StringWriter` instance contains the rendered output from the template—we hope it's something that resembles "Hello Reader" because we populated a value "Reader" for the variable "user" in the `VelocityContext` we used for rendering the template.

Let's now move on to seeing what kind of plumbing we might need in order to write compact, expressive tests for driving our Velocity template into the login page we're after.

Building the plumbing

As we just saw, the pieces of information required for rendering a Velocity template include a `VelocityContext` (encapsulating the equivalent to request attributes in the JSP and the Servlets domain), a `Writer` to render the output to, a name for the template (for logging purposes), and the template text. As such, and considering that we'd like to read the Velocity template from the file system, the kind of tests we'd like to write would look something like listing 5.21.

Listing 5.21 Beginnings of a `VelocityTestCase`

```
public class TestLoginTemplate extends VelocityTestCase {

    @Override
    protected String getWebRoot() {
        return "./websrc/velocity";
    }

    @Test
    public void previousUsernameIsRetained() throws Exception {
        String previousUsername = "Bob";
        setAttribute("username", previousUsername);
        render("/login.vtl");
        assertFormFieldValue("j_username", previousUsername);
    }
}
```

Override "web root" to shorten template paths in tests

Render "./websrc/velocity/login.vtl" here

What we have here is a test class that extends an abstract base class, which provides the plumbing and exposes a set of rendering methods (`setAttribute`, `render`) as well as assertions for verifying the rendered output, HTML in our case. Let's start by looking at how we can implement the plumbing up to rendering the template. We'll figure out how to parse the resulting HTML and provide the assertions once we've got the Velocity stuff sorted out.

Listing 5.22 illustrates the necessary pipe works for loading and rendering a template with the attributes populated from concrete test methods.

Listing 5.22 Abstract base class provides plumbing to render Velocity templates

```
import java.io.*;
import javax.xml.parsers.*;
import javax.xml.xpath.*;
import org.apache.velocity.*;
import org.apache.velocity.app.*;
import org.w3c.dom.*;
import org.junit.*;

public abstract class VelocityTestCase {

    private VelocityContext context;
    protected Document document;

    @Before
    public void setUp() throws Exception {
        context = new VelocityContext();
    }
```

❶ Fresh context for each test

```
    protected String getWebRoot() {
        return ".";                              Tests need to
    }                                            populate attributes
                                                 to VelocityContext ❷
    protected void setAttribute(String name, Object value) {
        context.put(name, value);
    }

    protected void render(String templatePath) throws Exception {
        File templateFile = new File(getWebRoot(), templatePath);
        String template = readFileContent(templateFile);
        String renderedHtml = renderTemplate(template);
        this.document = parseAsXml(renderedHtml);
    }                          Parse rendered HTML into DOM tree ❹

    private String renderTemplate(String template) throws Exception {
        VelocityEngine engine = new VelocityEngine();
        engine.init();
        StringWriter writer = new StringWriter();
        engine.evaluate(context, writer, "test", template);
        return writer.toString();
    }                                            Render template
                                                   in memory ❸
    private Document parseAsXml(String html) throws Exception {
        // omitted for brevity...
    }

    private String readFileContent(File file) throws Exception {
        // omitted for brevity...
    }
}
```

In listing 5.22, we ❶ create a fresh `VelocityContext` for each new test so that subsequent tests are safe from random data that prior tests have ❷ populated into the context. In the `render` method, we basically create a new `VelocityEngine` and ❸ `evaluate` the specified template in memory using a `StringWriter`. Finally, when the template has been rendered, we ❹ parse the resulting HTML into a DOM tree, which we can later perform assertions against.

In fact, those couple of assertions are the only things still keeping us from seeing the red bar. Let's add those so that we can finally get our code base back to a known state.

Adding assertions

We should now have a `Document` object—a DOM tree—for the rendered template. And our compiler is telling us that we need to implement the assertion, `assertFormFieldValue`. Because we already have a DOM tree, and Java 5 finally introduced

XPath into the standard libraries, how about using XPath queries for verifying that our template renders the appropriate HTML elements?

Listing 5.23 illustrates the implementation of the missing assertions, using the standard DOM and XPath APIs.

Listing 5.23 Parsing the generated HTML file with HttpUnit

```
import static org.junit.Assert.*;
import javax.xml.parsers.*;
import javax.xml.xpath.*;
import org.w3c.dom.*;
...

public abstract class VelocityTestCase {
    ...
    protected void assertFormFieldValue(String name,
            String expectedValue) throws Exception {
        String xpath = xpathForField(name);
        assertNodeExists(xpath);
        String actual = getString(xpath + "/@value");
        assertEquals(expectedValue, actual);
    }

    private String xpathForField(String name) {
        return "//form//input[@name='" + name + "']";
    }

    private void assertNodeExists(String xpath) throws Exception {
        assertNotNull("Node doesn't exist: " + xpath,
            getNode(xpath));
    }

    private Node getNode(String xpath) throws Exception {
        return (Node) evaluate(xpath, XPathConstants.NODE);
    }

    private String getString(String xpath) throws Exception {
        return (String) evaluate(xpath, XPathConstants.STRING);
    }

    private Object evaluate(String xpath, QName type)
            throws Exception {
        XPath engine = XPathFactory.newInstance().newXPath();
        return engine.evaluate(xpath, getResponse(), type);
    }
}
```

Finally! A red bar, saying that the login.vtl template we're trying to render doesn't exist. From here on out, it's back to our stress-free short cycles of test-code-refactor. In the name of completeness, listing 5.24 presents the little Velocity template that we save as login.vtl to get our green bar.

Listing 5.24 Velocity template for our login page

```
<html>
  <body>
    <form>
      <input type="text" name="j_username" />
      <input type="password" name="j_password" />
      <input type="submit" name="login" />
    </form>
  </body>
</html>
```

I think we've already gotten the idea of how we could test-drive Velocity templates from here. We basically need two things: a way to render our templates and a way to assert the rendered output. Velocity is so simple a technology that we could write the rendering facility from scratch in a matter of minutes rather than hours. Furthermore, the problem of asserting an HTML document is the same as with any other view template technology, so we should be able to reuse existing libraries as well; pointing a tool such as HttpUnit at a locally stored file containing the rendered output might not be such a bad idea either.

But now, let's wrap up our templates and turn our attention to test-driving yet more exciting web components and technologies. Earlier, we talked about how easy it is to test-drive both controllers and the view part of request-response-style MVC frameworks. We'll finish this chapter on test-driving web components by looking at the situation over at component-based frameworks' side of the fence.

5.4 TDD with component-based web frameworks

We could argue that one of the biggest influences on the relative ease with which we test-drive web components like Servlets and Spring's controllers is the availability of freely available tools and test-double libraries for faking the key interfaces and objects, whether they're from standard Java EE APIs or from an open source framework such as the Spring Framework. Effectively, the maturity of the involved technologies gives us a head start that we might not have with brand-new technologies.[8]

[8] Although it has to be said that many open source projects these days deliver proper support for automated testing as the norm rather than the exception.

But what about component-based frameworks, such as Apache Tapestry, Wicket, or the Java EE standards' representative, JavaServer Faces (JSF)?

The request-response design embodied in technologies such as the Servlet API and Spring MVC is by far the dominant genre in the Java EE web-development arena. It is not, however, the only viable option for developing web applications. We are seeing the rise of a number of component-based frameworks that offer better reuse throughout the applications' code bases and a higher level of abstraction. These attributes let us developers focus on the gist of what we're supposed to do rather than always thinking in terms of request parameters, parsing strings into date objects, and so forth.

Let's begin this last leg of our journey in the world of web components by dissecting the term *component-based framework* and what it really means. Then let's move on to test-driving components with the latest and greatest that the open source community has to offer for component-based web development.

5.4.1 Anatomy of a typical framework

Looking at component-based frameworks, we can identify certain patterns emerging from their respective architectures. And looking at these patterns, we can already say a lot about how receptive these frameworks are for unit-testing and, specifically, test-driven development.

Components provide the behavior

First of all, the word *component* in *component-based* refers to the existence of *UI components*. These are widgets implemented as regular Java classes, often extending the selected framework's built-in base classes or implementing specific interfaces. The framework itself takes the responsibility of handling all interaction between the component instances and the requests coming from the web browser according to some kind of a *component life cycle*. This approach makes test-driving the components themselves often simple because what we're dealing with is not much different from other regular Java code. And, as we know by now, we can test-drive pretty much any piece of regular Java code.

Templates encapsulate the visuals

The components are usually[9] laid out in HTML pages using a template language. These components and templates are sometimes accompanied by additional

[9] JSF templates are pretty much markup agnostic in the sense that pages consisting of components can often be rendered not just to HTML but also to alternative markup languages without changes to the template.

configuration files (usually XML), which provide mapping information for the framework so that the framework knows which component to bind to which placeholder in the template, which other resources the component needs to be hooked up with upon initialization, and which client-generated events should be routed to which method on which component instance. Some frameworks make heavy use of Java 5 annotations for centralizing this additional configuration into the same source files where the developer implements the component. Wicket goes as far as representing pages in the web application as Java classes, making the HTML templates the only non-Java artifacts to deal with, except for our good old friend, `web.xml`, of course.

Differences in testability

While test-driving the components is usually not an issue, as we mentioned earlier, testing the page templates in a meaningful way outside a real container is not a lost battle either. The Apache Shale project, building an open source JSF-based web framework, provides a handy library of test-double implementations for faking the `javax.faces` interfaces and simple base classes for your own JUnit tests to extend. These base classes provide access to pre-configured fake implementations for the key JSF interfaces, which is a vital asset to have when trying to get JSF components under test.

Neither Tapestry nor JSF is particularly supportive of unit testing, however, which shows in the amount of work involved in writing tests for various artifacts under these frameworks. In fact, the majority of developers seem to have opted for in-container and functional testing for their JSF and Tapestry applications.

For this reason, my personal bias is strongly toward Wicket, which has been developed with testability in mind from the beginning. Let's take a journey into the Wicket world of pages and components for a while and see how this test-driven thing operates in this context.

5.4.2 Fleshing out Wicket pages test-first

Wicket[10] is an open source framework for component-based web development. Although that doesn't make it unique, its implementation most certainly is rather unique at the moment. Let's begin by sorting out what's what in Wicket and what kind of artifacts Wicket applications consist of.

---

[10] We're using the 1.3.0 release of Wicket in our examples.

Simplicity without a configuration jungle

First of all, everything in Wicket is either Java or HTML (or JavaScript, or CSS). What this means is that there's no scripting language involved in defining view templates—the HTML is just HTML without a single scriptlet mixed in. All logic, including view logic, is embedded into Java classes that build up the application. In fact, a Wicket-based web application is represented by a Java class that extends `org.apache.wicket.protocol.http.WebApplication`. The same goes for the web pages that are part of the application—they're Java classes extending from `org.apache.wicket.markup.html.WebPage`.

The only configuration that's required for a Wicket application is an entry in the standard web.xml registering a `WicketFilter`, telling it the name of your application class, and the `filter-mapping` for binding the `WicketFilter` to your application's URLs. Listing 5.25 shows an example of this configuration.

Listing 5.25 Example web.xml for a Wicket application

```
<?xml version="1.0" encoding="UTF-8"?>
<!DOCTYPE web-app PUBLIC
 "-//Sun Microsystems, Inc.//DTD Web Application 2.3//EN"

 "http://java.sun.com/dtd/web-app_2_3.dtd">
<web-app>

  <filter>
    <filter-name>MyWicketApplication</filter-name>
    <filter-class>org.apache.wicket.protocol.http.WicketFilter
➥</filter-class>
    <init-param>
      <param-name>applicationClassName</param-name>
      <param-value>com.tddinaction.wicket.MyWicketApp</param-value>
    </init-param>
  </filter>

  <filter-mapping>
    <filter-name>MyWicketApplication</filter-name>
    <url-pattern>/*</url-pattern>
  </filter-mapping>
</web-app>
```

Wicket needs application class from us

WicketFilter handles all HTTP traffic

This is the entire configuration that is required for a simple Wicket application. Wicket can be configured further in the application class or by passing an "applicationFactoryClassName" `init-param` element to the `WicketFilter` in web.xml rather than the "applicationClassName," as seen in listing 5.25.

Starting from the home page

The first thing to do when ramping up a Wicket project—right after downloading the associated JAR files and setting up the necessary directory structures—is to create your application class. Because we're into test-driving our way toward a healthy code base that will stay that way, let's write the standard first test, shown in listing 5.26.

Listing 5.26 Nailing down our application class and home page

```
import org.apache.wicket.protocol.http.WebApplication;
import org.junit.*;

public class TestApplicationClass {
    @Test
    public void homePageHasBeenDefined() throws Exception {
        WebApplication app = new MyWicketApp();
        assertEquals(MyHomePage.class, app.getHomePage());
    }
}
```

This test is basically telling us two things. First, `MyWicketApp` should extend Wicket's `WebApplication` class. Second, its `getHomePage` method should return the class we're about to use as our home page. This is also a good example of how Wicket treats pages as classes—just pass the page class, and Wicket takes care of the rest.

The implementation in listing 5.27 that turns our red bar into a green one isn't any closer to space technology either, as you might have guessed.

Listing 5.27 Application class implemented

```
import org.apache.wicket.protocol.http.WebApplication;
import org.apache.wicket.Page;

public class MyWicketApp extends WebApplication {

    public Class<? extends Page> getHomePage() {
        return MyHomePage.class;
    }
}
```

The `getHomePage` method in our application class is our way of telling Wicket which page should be displayed first when a user points their web browser at our application. In order to get our code compiling, we obviously needed to create the `MyHomePage` class, so while we're here let's take a peek at its contents:

```
import org.apache.wicket.markup.html.WebPage;

public class MyHomePage extends WebPage {
}
```

That's it. What we just saw is a blank web page, Wicket style. Well, a not functional blank web page. In order for Wicket to know what to render for the web browser, we also need to create an HTML template to go with the page class before Wicket can render our page. Let's not create that one yet, however. After all, we don't yet have a failing test and thus no permission to add functionality!

Testing with the WicketTester

One way in which the attention given to testability within the Wicket project is showing is the existence of tools such as the `WicketTester` class that's part of the Wicket distribution. `WicketTester` is essentially a testing tool for running our Wicket pages and components outside of a web container. In order to see `WicketTester` in action, let's write a little test for our home page. Listing 5.28 shows a regular JUnit test class making use of the `WicketTester`.

Listing 5.28 Our first `WicketTester` test

```
import org.junit.*;
import org.apache.wicket.util.tester.WicketTester;

public class TestMyHomePage {
    @Test
    public void homePageHasWelcomeText() throws Exception {
        WicketTester tester = new WicketTester();
        tester.startPage(MyHomePage.class);              ❶ Create Wicket-Tester for page

        tester.assertRenderedPage(MyHomePage.class);
        tester.assertNoErrorMessage();                   ❷ Check for rendering errors

        tester.assertContains("Welcome to the home page!");   ❸ Assert page contents
    }
}
```

In listing 5.28, we first ❶ create an instance of the `WicketTester` and point it to the page we want to test. Then, we ❷ assert that the given page was rendered without errors or redirects, and finally we ❸ assert that the rendered HTML contains the phrase "Welcome to the home page!" This test finally forces us to add MyHomePage.html into our source tree, as shown in listing 5.29.

Listing 5.29 Humble beginnings of a home page

```
<?xml version="1.0" encoding="UTF-8" ?>
<!DOCTYPE html PUBLIC "-//W3C//DTD XHTML 1.0 Strict//EN"
 "http://www.w3.org/TR/xhtml1/DTD/xhtml1-strict.dtd">
<html xmlns:wicket="http://wicket.sourceforge.net/">
  <body>
    <p>Welcome to the home page!</p>
  </body>
</html>
```

The standard convention in Wicket is to place the view templates—the HTML files—into the same directory where the Java class for that page resides. This might seem odd at first but is helpful because we don't have to go out of our way to locate the view template when it's right next to the Java code we're working on. There are other options as well, but those require additional configuration. In practice, this means either telling Wicket the location of the directory structure holding our HTML or, alternatively, implementing a custom resource locator. The latter is obviously more laborious but also gives us more flexibility and power in determining where we want to keep (and deploy) our view templates.

We've now seen how we can test-drive a simple Wicket page using nothing but good ol' JUnit and the `WicketTester`. Most applications are not just static web pages, however, so it would be nice to see how Wicket lets us test-drive functionality into our pages. Let's spend a few minutes linking our newly created home page to another page using Wicket components.

Adding components to the picture

As mentioned before, almost everything in Wicket is represented by Java classes, and that is the case for components as well. When we're talking about Wicket, the word *component* refers to any dynamic element on our web pages. For example, a link from one Wicket page to another is a component, a label with dynamically resolved content is a component, and a form—and the associated form elements—are all components.

It's simple, really, but before we get ahead of ourselves, let's add a test that pushes us toward having some components on our home page. Evolving from listing 5.28, listing 5.30 again makes use of the `WicketTester`.

Listing 5.30 Testing for the presence of components

```
import org.junit.*;
import org.apache.wicket.util.tester.WicketTester;

public class TestMyHomePage {
    @Test
    public void homePageHasLinkToLoginPage() throws Exception {
        WicketTester tester = new WicketTester();
        tester.startPage(MyHomePage.class);
        tester.assertRenderedPage(MyHomePage.class);
        tester.assertNoErrorMessage();

        tester.assertLabel("welcomeMessage",
                           "Welcome to the home page!");
        tester.assertPageLink("linkToLoginPage", LoginPage.class);
    }
}
```

❶ Expect to find label named "welcomeMessage"...

❷ ... and link to login page

The enhanced test in listing 5.30 tells us that ❶ our page should contain a `Label` component by the name "welcomeMessage" and that its contents should be "Welcome to the home page!" Our test also says that ❷ we should have a `PageLink` component named "loginPage" which should link to a `LoginPage`, which we also need to create before getting our code to compile:

```
public class LoginPage extends org.apache.wicket.markup.html.WebPage {
}
```

Running our test now results in complaints about no such components being found on the page, so let's get to work.

Adding components on a page in Wicket involves two tasks. First, we need to add the component in the page class, and then we need to add a bit of markup into our HTML template so Wicket knows where to render the component. Listing 5.31 shows how we add the `Label` and `PageLink` components to the `MyHomePage` class.

Listing 5.31 Adding components to our home page

```
import org.apache.wicket.markup.html.WebPage;
import org.apache.wicket.markup.html.basic.Label;
import org.apache.wicket.markup.html.link.PageLink;

public class MyHomePage extends WebPage {
```

```
    public MyHomePage() {
        add(new Label("welcomeMessage",
            "Welcome to the home page!"));
        add(new PageLink("linkToLoginPage", LoginPage.class));
    }
}
```

That's it. Not exactly what I'd call a laborious step! What we've done here in listing 5.31 is construct the component tree for Wicket by instantiating a `Label` component and a `PageLink` component passing the `LoginPage` object to their constructor (effectively telling them, "you belong to this container"). The tree for `MyHomePage` now contains two child components named "welcome- Message" and "linkToLoginPage". At this point, if we run our unit test from listing 5.30, we get a rather descriptive error message indicating what we need to do next:

```
org.apache.wicket.WicketRuntimeException: The component(s) below failed to
   render. A common problem is that you have added a component in code but
   forgot to reference it in the markup (thus the component will never be
   rendered).
```

Yes, that is our problem—we have added the components into the component tree but we haven't referenced them in our HTML markup. Listing 5.32 fixes that.

Listing 5.32 Laying out our components in the HTML

```
<?xml version="1.0" encoding="UTF-8" ?>
<!DOCTYPE html PUBLIC "-//W3C//DTD XHTML 1.0 Strict//EN"
 "http://www.w3.org/TR/xhtml1/DTD/xhtml1-strict.dtd">
<html xmlns:wicket="http://wicket.sourceforge.net/">
  <body>
    <span wicket:id="welcomeMessage">welcome message goes here</span>
    Please, <a href="#" wicket:id="linkToLoginPage">log in</a>.
  </body>
</html>
```

You can probably figure out from the previous snippet what Wicket is doing when it renders this view template. When it encounters an HTML element with the attribute "wicket:id", Wicket looks up a component with that specific name from the component tree and asks the component to render itself. In other words, what gets rendered to the web browser would not be "welcome message goes here" but rather "Welcome to the home page!" (or whatever value was given for the label in the Java code).

Now that we have components on our pages, how about seeing how we can interact with them in our tests? After all, some of our components might have state, and just seeing a button on a page does not mean that the button does what we expect it to do!

Interacting with components

It's trivial to verify the presence of components on a page with the `WicketTester`. How about testing for the behavior of those components when we try to interact with them? We'll do one better than just answering that question—let's see some concrete tests that demonstrate the answer in action.

We have a home page with a link to the login page. Let's quickly write a test that verifies we can click that link and get to the login page:

```
@Test
public void interactingWithComponents() throws Exception {
    WicketTester tester = new WicketTester();
    tester.startPage(MyHomePage.class);
    tester.assertRenderedPage(MyHomePage.class);
    tester.clickLink("linkToLoginPage");
    tester.assertRenderedPage(LoginPage.class);
}
```

Can't get much simpler than that, can it? The `WicketTester` provides a handy `clickLink` method for simulating clicks on link components. After clicking a link, we can use the `assertRenderedPage` method for asserting that we landed on the expected page as a result.

This has only been a quick scratch on the surface of the Wicket framework, but we now have a better idea of how test-driving works in general with component-based frameworks. For a more thorough introduction to the technology, refer to titles such as *JavaServer Faces in Action* (Kito Mann; Manning, 2004) for JSF, *Tapestry in Action* (Howard M. Lewis Ship; Manning, 2004) for Apache Tapestry, and *Wicket in Action* (Martijn Dashorst and Eelco Hillenius; Manning, 2008) for Wicket. The latter book includes a whole chapter dedicated to testing Wicket components.

5.5 Summary

We've just seen that test-driving web components is far from mission impossible and, indeed, a feasible approach that gives us all the quality-improving benefits of TDD while keeping our code from suffering unnecessary bloat.

So, in addition to the model (which we didn't discuss in this chapter because it's basically regular Java code that we already know we can test-drive), the controller and the view portions of the MVC triplet also can be effectively developed test-first.

It's not quite like working with plain Java code, but it's close. With a bit of plumbing tucked away into a base class for our unit tests, we're in a good position to follow our tight loop of test-code-refactor without having to think too much about things we're not interested in for a given test.

When developing controller components, our attention is not tied to dealing with awkward APIs; instead we're focused on the behavior desired from our components. While doing that, we're facing a lot of the obstacles we discussed in part 1—and the solutions presented in part 1 work here, too.

Although view components such as JavaServer Pages and Velocity templates aren't, perhaps, as trivial to test as controller components, there are ways of test-driving these without resorting to the slow alternative of deploying to an external web container. The JspTest framework gives us the means to render JavaServer Pages in our unit tests quickly; using an embedded Jetty web container isn't a bad option either. For test-driving Velocity templates, we hardly need any plumbing at all, because the Velocity API makes it easy to render templates without any dependencies on any kind of containers whatsoever.

Component-based web frameworks have been rearing their heads recently along with the release of JavaServer Faces and the success of open source projects such as Apache Tapestry and the Wicket framework. These technologies are generally slightly more complex to embed into a test harness than their request-response-style counterparts, which makes test-driving that much harder. The Wicket framework, however, leads the pack as a prime example of awareness for testability, making test-driven web development with Wicket seem like a walk in the park.

In the next chapter, having already tamed the Java EE web development scene, we'll move from the web tier to the so-called data access layer and, of course, to an explanation of how to deploy our test-driven way of working in that context.

6 *Test-driving data access*

Information is the currency of democracy.
—Thomas Jefferson

Data is everywhere. Think about it. How many systems have you worked with in your professional career where the business logic you implemented did not operate on persistent data? Exceptions do exist, of course, but the majority of systems in today's enterprises deal with persistent data—and with lots of it. As such, data has a central role in the development of these systems and in the day-to-day lives of software developers. Furthermore, if you'd have to pick one component of an enterprise system as the single most important, it'd have to be the data. Yet software developers have a long tradition of relying on manual, visual inspection for testing their data-access code. Visual inspection is slow and error-prone—not how we as professional craftsmen want to work.

So far, we've ignored data as an element in our tests by faking where it's coming from. In other words, although we have seen how we can implement business logic that needs persistence services using test-driven development and test doubles, we haven't seen how to implement the persistence layer itself. In this chapter, we'll pick up the slack and give the data layer our full attention.

After finishing this chapter, we'll have all the tools necessary for using test-driven development on code that accesses and manipulates data, be it on the file system or in a relational database. We will focus on facilitating our test-driven process with testability-aware design and with technology that helps us get the job done. Along the way, we will also discuss the relative advantages and disadvantages of test-driving with unit tests and integration tests and of different strategies for managing our test data.

Ready. Set. Go.

6.1 Exploring the problem domain

Let's begin by exploring the problem space before getting grease on our hands. First of all, we need to establish what supposedly makes test-driving data access code somehow different from test-driving "regular" code (for whatever definition of "regular").

The main difference in data-access code compared to most other code is that its behavior typically spans multiple layers of a system's architecture. Another common difference is that data-access code tends to make use of third-party APIs that are, nicely put, sometimes not as testing-friendly as they could be. In order to be able to test without all of the third-party stuff constantly hitting the disk or a database server, we need to be able to separate these issues.

Let's continue our journey by identifying what kinds of boundaries data-access code typically crosses in Java and Java EE applications. Then let's briefly study a design pattern that helps us implement our data access code using a testable design.

6.1.1 Data access crosses boundaries

Data-access code almost by definition crosses boundaries in a system. Our application logic talks to our persistence logic, and the persistence logic talks to a persistence framework such as Hibernate or the EJB 3.0 `EntityManager` interface, or directly to the JDBC API, which in turn is implemented by a JDBC driver, which in turn connects to a relational database. Figure 6.1 illustrates this stack of layers on top of layers.

> **TIP** Test-driving EJB 3.0 code is covered in the bonus chapter, available online.

Ideally, we'd want to test-drive the code we're working on without involving the layer below. We want our tests to be independent and running fast. Including too much from the layers below into our unit test increases the coupling in our tests and inevitably makes our tests run slower—and setting up the other layers would most definitely be more work we'd rather not do. Furthermore, the layer below might not exist yet.

With this in mind, let's look at our options of test-driving the code inside the layers in figure 6.1. Working on the application logic layer, it's easy to stub out the persistence logic. We verify that the chunk of business logic we're testing invokes the appropriate methods on a persistence logic layer interface with the appropriate parameters. But looking at how to test-drive the persistence logic layer, we face a slightly more difficult decision—should we stub or mock the JDBC API (or the selected persistence framework's interfaces, if applicable), or should we hit a database? Furthermore, should we hit a real database or a lightweight, in-memory database that is faster but not exactly identical to the real thing?

Later in this chapter, we will look at each of these different strategies one at a time, always implementing the same example scenario so that we can do a subjective comparison between them. First, though, let's familiarize ourselves with a design pattern that helps us separate our code base into appropriate layers.

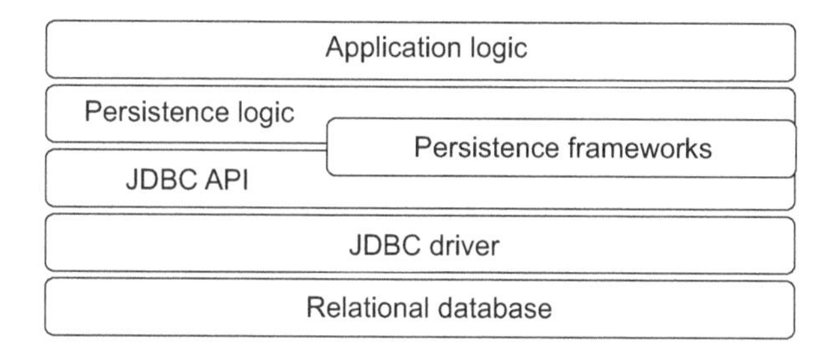

Figure 6.1
A pile of logical layers of a system. If we want to test-drive the persistence logic layer, which of the underlying layers should our tests exercise?

6.1.2 Separating layers with the DAO pattern

It might have something to do with the Java EE community's long-time affection for design patterns and architecture blueprints (or it might be just that this stuff makes sense), but for one reason or another, most of the Java EE systems I've seen during the past five years have applied some kind of a variation of the Data Access Object (DAO) pattern, described in *Core J2EE Patterns: Best Practices and Design Strategies* (Deepak Alur, Dan Malks, and John Crupi; Addison-Wesley, 2003).

The core of the pattern is that for each persistent domain object, there is a Data Access Object interface (and implementation) for persisting the said type of object to a database, be it a relational database, an object database, or a bunch of XML files on the file system. The point is that the object itself doesn't know and whoever is using the DAO doesn't know where (and whether) the object was persisted or where it came from. As a result, we can swap the actual persistence technology without the application noticing. Figure 6.2 illustrates this with boxes and lines.

In the following sections, we'll reuse this pattern to illustrate the process of test-driving data-access-related code using different technologies. To give you a better idea of what a DAO interface might look like and to give us a basis for later examples, listing 6.1 shows a simple `PersonDao` interface for persisting `Person` objects.

Listing 6.1 `PersonDao` interface hiding the implementation from application code

```
public interface PersonDao {
    Person find(Integer id);
    void save(Person person);
    void update(Person person);
    void delete(Person person);
    List<Person> findAll();
    List<Person> findByLastname(String lastname);
}
```

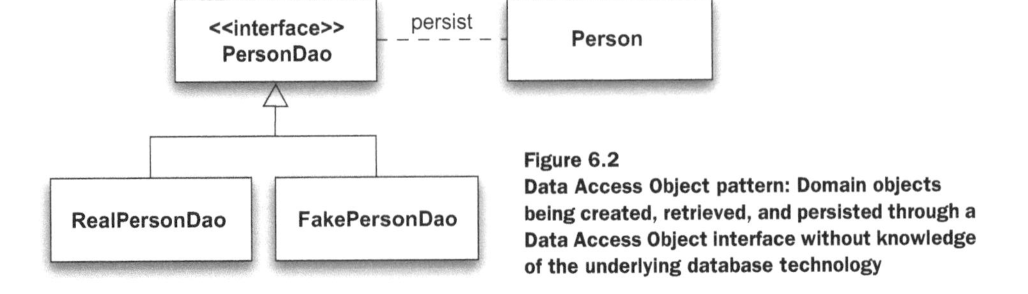

Figure 6.2
Data Access Object pattern: Domain objects being created, retrieved, and persisted through a Data Access Object interface without knowledge of the underlying database technology

The DAO pattern is enormously helpful compared to scattering data access all around the business logic. Also, although the DAO pattern typically reduces the absolute volume of data access code we need to write, adopting freely available open source persistence frameworks like Hibernate or more trivial support libraries like the `JdbcTemplate` facility from the Spring Framework can radically reduce this work. Essentially, a good framework can do most of the plumbing work for you and leave you to worry about the persistence logic rather than the gritty details of the persistence technology.

> **TIP** The implementation for the `Person` class referenced by the `PersonDao` interface is available as part of the source code download at the book's website.

Without further ado, let's roll up our sleeves again and start test-driving code that needs data and, therefore, needs to use a DAO to get at that data. We'll start from a plain JDBC implementation of the `PersonDao` interface in listing 6.1, acknowledge its main problems, and then introduce Spring Framework's `JdbcTemplate` and Hibernate as alternative solutions that simplify our work quite a bit.

6.2 Driving data access with unit tests

Traditionally, Java developers have written raw JDBC code for accessing data in relational databases. Especially during the late nineties when the IT bubble was at its peak and everyone became a Java programmer, we could see JDBC calls scattered throughout a code base—with the result of having to change things all over when renaming a column in the database, for example. This was obviously a bad thing, and developers today are much more aware of the need to avoid such mistakes.

In this section, we'll look at two frameworks that simplify our data-access code and the way we can test-drive such code with our unit tests. Those two frameworks are the Spring Framework and its `JdbcTemplate` and the Hibernate persistence framework. We'll start, however, by looking at the foundation of all Java database access—the JDBC API—and how to test-drive JDBC-based data-access code.

Before we begin, perhaps we should clarify what we mean by unit tests in this context. I've seen people utter the words *unit test* when talking about a wide variety of things, including JUnit test classes running external system commands that fork JVM instances to run Java classes' main methods. Those might be called developer tests, but they're most certainly not unit tests according to my definition. I personally subscribe to Michael Feathers' definition for unit tests,[1] which says that a test is not a unit test if:

---

[1] *Working Effectively With Legacy Code* (Addison-Wesley, 2005)

- It talks to the database.
- It communicates across the network.
- It touches the file system.
- It can't run at the same time as any of your other unit tests.
- You have to do special things to your environment to run it.

These things are costly to do and make our tests run slower than necessary—sometimes up to several magnitudes slower than they would using a test double. With this in mind, we don't want to hit a database repeatedly in our unit tests but rather want to fake it somehow. This section will show us how to test-drive our data access objects effectively by using test doubles in the context of the aforementioned persistence frameworks and APIs.

6.2.1 Witnessing the tyranny of the JDBC API

JDBC could be considered one of the most important factors in the adoption of Java—accessing relational databases in a standard way is important, after all—but the API could've been made slightly easier to use. We say this because JDBC requires the developer to write a lot of plumbing code to catch checked exceptions and make sure to close various resources. Furthermore, the depth of the JDBC API makes it somewhat cumbersome to test. Let's see this by test-driving a piece of a pure JDBC-based implementation of the `PersonDao` interface from listing 6.1.

Let's say we've decided to start by implementing a `findByLastname` method from the `PersonDao` interface. Because we're implementing a pure JDBC DAO, we're going to fake the JDBC connection and return hard-coded data when the DAO performs a query. The way we want our DAO to work is by passing it a `DataSource` from which to obtain JDBC connections. In our test, we're obviously going to pass a test double as the `DataSource`. In production mode, we'll use dependency injection to obtain a real `DataSource`. In code, what we want is this:

```
JdbcPersonDao dao = new JdbcPersonDao();
dao.setDatasource(datasource);
List<Person> people = dao.findByLastname("Smith");
```

The problem is, of course, that we don't yet have a `DataSource` object, and we don't want to connect to a real database from our unit tests.

Creating test doubles

Because we don't have a `DataSource` object yet, we'll need to create one prior to proceeding to the previous block of code invoking our production code. We've decided to use EasyMock for creating a mock implementation for the `DataSource`. Not counting the static import statement, creating the test double with EasyMock is a one-liner:

```
import static org.easymock.EasyMock.*;
...
DataSource datasource = createMock(DataSource.class);
```

Now, when we execute `findByLastName`, we expect the DAO implementation to ask the `DataSource` for a `Connection`. That means we need a test double for the `Connection` interface. Then, we expect the DAO to ask the connection object to prepare a statement with an SQL template string and to populate the statement with the last name given as argument. So, we also need a test double for the `PreparedStatement` interface. Let's look at what we've got so far for creating all of these mock objects and expectations:

```
DataSource datasource = createMock(DataSource.class);
Connection connection = createMock(Connection.class);
expect(datasource.getConnection()).andReturn(connection);
String sql = "SELECT * FROM people WHERE last_name = ?";
PreparedStatement stmt = createMock(PreparedStatement.class);
expect(connection.prepareStatement(sql)).andReturn(stmt);

stmt.setString(1, "Smith");
```

That's a lot of mock objects already, and there are more to come. Next, we'd like the DAO to execute the statement object. The `executeQuery` method returns a `java.sql.ResultSet` interface for which we still need one more test double.

Faking the ResultSet with a static mock

This time, we'll decide to not use EasyMock but rather a fake implementation provided by the MockObjects.com library. This is because (especially for large result sets) setting expectations for each and every method call would quickly explode the volume of our test code, and we're not interested in how the DAO pulls out the pieces of data from the `ResultSet`—we're interested in knowing that it builds and returns the right kind of list of people from the result set.

The following snippet shows how we configure a `MockMultiRowResultSet` object and make our mock `PreparedStatement` object return it when `executeQuery` is called:

```
MockMultiRowResultSet resultset = new MockMultiRowResultSet();
String[] columns = new String[] { "first_name", "last_name" };
resultset.setupColumnNames(columns);
List<Person> smiths = createListOfPeopleWithLastname("Smith");
resultset.setupRows(convertIntoResultSetArray(smiths));
expect(stmt.executeQuery()).andReturn(resultset);
```

The MockMultiRowResultSet object expects the data to be given to it as a two-dimensional array. In the end, we'd like to be able to compare the List of Person objects returned by the DAO's findByLastname method with something. In order to minimize duplication of data, we want to create the list of people just once, convert the list into a two-dimensional object array for the MockMultiRowResultSet, and use the same list in comparing the DAO's output.

After everything else, we still want our DAO implementation to do something—release (close) all of the JDBC resources:

```
resultset.setExpectedCloseCalls(1);
stmt.close();
connection.close();
```

Writing a test for JDBC code

Listing 6.2 shows our test in its final form, specifying the wanted behavior for our DAO implementation—that is, when everything goes according to plan and the database contains three matching people.

Listing 6.2 Test for a pure JDBC DAO implementation

```
import static org.junit.Assert.*;
import static org.easymock.EasyMock.*;
import com.mockobjects.sql.*;
import org.junit.*;
import java.sql.*;
import javax.sql.*;
import java.util.*;

public class JdbcPersonDaoTest {

    @Test
    public void testFindByLastname() throws Exception {
        DataSource datasource = createMock(DataSource.class);
        Connection connection = createMock(Connection.class);
        expect(datasource.getConnection()).andReturn(connection);
        String sql = "SELECT * FROM people WHERE last_name = ?";
        PreparedStatement stmt =
            createMock(PreparedStatement.class);
        expect(connection.prepareStatement(sql)).andReturn(stmt);
        stmt.setString(1, "Smith");

        MockMultiRowResultSet resultset =
            new MockMultiRowResultSet();
        String[] columns = new String[]
            { "first_name", "last_name" };
        resultset.setupColumnNames(columns);
        List<Person> smiths =
```

Mock database connection ❶

❷ Fake query result

```
            createListOfPeopleWithLastname("Smith");
        resultset.setupRows(asResultSetArray(smiths));
        expect(stmt.executeQuery()).andReturn(resultset);

        resultset.setExpectedCloseCalls(1);
        stmt.close();
        connection.close();

        replay(datasource, connection, stmt);

        JdbcPersonDao dao = new JdbcPersonDao();
        dao.setDatasource(datasource);
        List<Person> people = dao.findByLastname("Smith");
        assertEquals(smiths, people);
        verify(datasource, connection, stmt);
        resultset.verify();
    }

    private List<Person>
            createListOfPeopleWithLastname(String lastName) {
        List<Person> expected = new ArrayList<Person>();
        expected.add(new Person("Alice", lastName));
        expected.add(new Person("Billy", lastName));
        expected.add(new Person("Clark", lastName));
        return expected;
    }

    private Object[][] asResultSetArray(List<Person> people) {
        Object[][] array = new Object[people.size()][2];
        for (int i = 0; i < array.length; i++) {
            Person person = people.get(i);
            array[i] = new Object[] {
                    person.getFirstName(),
                    person.getLastName() };
        }
        return array;
    }
}
```

❷ **Fake query result**

❸ **We want resources released**

❹ **Act and verify**

That's what I call a big test. First, we ❶ create and configure mock implementations for the `DataSource`, `Connection`, and `PreparedStatement` JDBC interfaces by using EasyMock. Then, we ❷ populate a test double for the `ResultSet` JDBC interface using a static mock object from the MockObjects.com library. Finally, after ❸ recording the expected release of all JDBC resources, we ❹ inject our mock `DataSource` into a `JdbcPersonDao` instance, invoke the finder method, and compare the returned list of `Person` objects to the one with which we populated the mock `ResultSet`. Not the most compact test method we've seen (although I have seen worse), but this is to be expected when working with the JDBC interfaces.

Writing code to pass the test

For the sake of completeness, listing 6.3 shows an implementation of the `findByLastname` method that passes the previous test with flying colors.

Listing 6.3 Pure JDBC DAO implementation

```
import javax.sql.*;
import java.sql.*;
import java.util.*;

public class JdbcPersonDao implements PersonDao {

    private DataSource datasource;

    public void setDatasource(DataSource datasource) {
        this.datasource = datasource;
    }

    public List<Person> findByLastname(String lastname) {
        try {
            Connection conn = datasource.getConnection();
            String sql = "SELECT * FROM people WHERE last_name = ?";
            PreparedStatement stmt = conn.prepareStatement(sql);
            stmt.setString(1, lastname);
            ResultSet rset = stmt.executeQuery();
            List<Person> people = new ArrayList<Person>();
            while (rset.next()) {
                String firstName = rset.getString("first_name");
                String lastName = rset.getString("last_name");
                people.add(new Person(firstName, lastName));
            }
            rset.close();
            stmt.close();
            conn.close();
            return people;
        } catch (SQLException e) {
            throw new RuntimeException(e);
        }
    }
    // Other PersonDao methods not shown
}
```

Note that our implementation is only closing the JDBC connection, for example, if everything goes fine and none of the prior method invocations to the JDBC API throw exceptions. In other words, we'd still need to write a couple of tests to verify that the proper close calls take place even though a query throws an exception, for example.

Instead of doing that, let's look at how the use of a good framework can alleviate the pain of test-driving JDBC code. There are plenty of open source frameworks that attempt to simplify data-access code in Java and Java EE applications, but we'll look at only two of those: the JDBC support provided by the almost ubiquitous Spring Framework, and the Hibernate persistence framework that has led object-relational mapping in Java to the mainstream.

Let's begin with a tour of how Spring's `JdbcTemplate` can significantly reduce the pain of working with the JDBC API.

6.2.2 Reducing pain with Spring's JdbcTemplate

The Spring Framework includes a facility named `JdbcTemplate`, which purports to simplify data-access code to only the essential. The fundamental idea behind the implementation is that most raw JDBC code follows the same pattern with certain boilerplate code always present: nested `try-catch` structures with conditional close calls for making sure all resources are released is a prime example. In practice, `JdbcTemplate` employs something similar to the well-known Template Method design pattern[2] and achieves a structure where the developer only needs to worry about the varying part; the boilerplate is taken care of by the framework. Figure 6.3 illustrates the structure with boxes and lines.

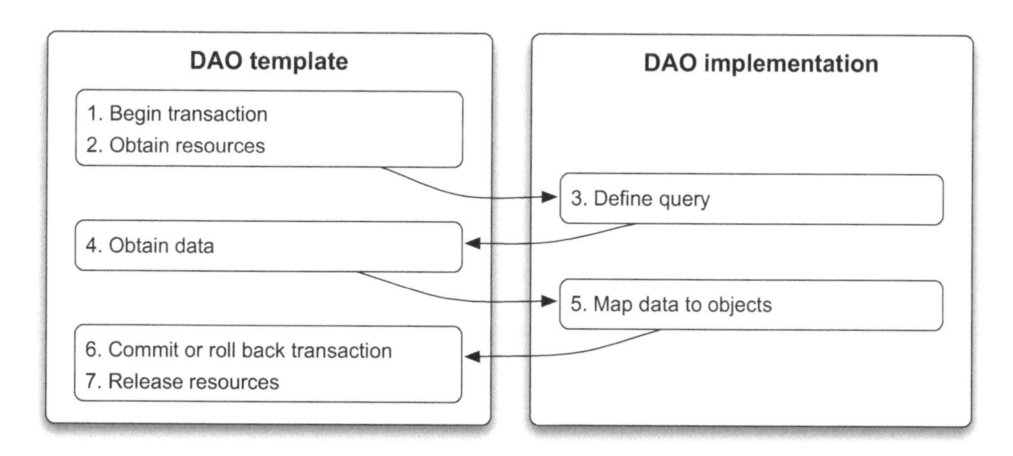

Figure 6.3 Collaboration between the template code provided by the Spring Framework and the DAO implementation provided by the developer

[2] See *Design Patterns: Elements of Reusable Object-Oriented Software* (Addison-Wesley, 1994).

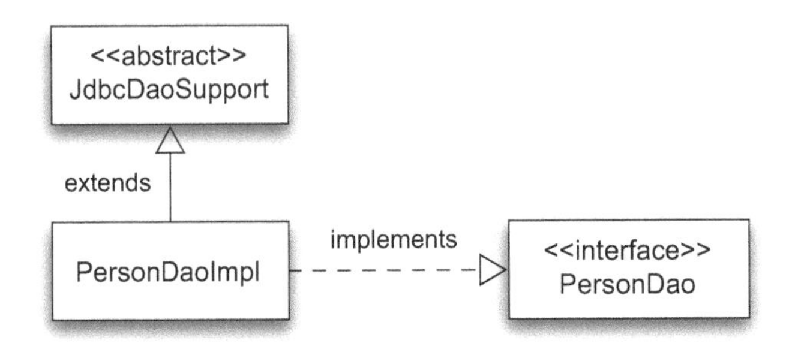

Figure 6.4 DAO implementation extends from Spring's `JdbcDaoSupport` class that provides `JdbcTemplate` functionality

Spring implements this division of responsibilities through an abstract base class named `JdbcDaoSupport`, which our specific data-access object implementations can extend. Figure 6.4 depicts this structure.

What the abstract base class in figure 6.4—`JdbcDaoSupport`—provides is essentially one getter method for obtaining an instance of the `JdbcTemplate` class. The `JdbcTemplate` class encapsulates the gritty details of raw JDBC interfaces, offering instead higher-level methods to the DAO implementor's disposal. The signature of one of these higher-level methods is shown here as an example:

```
List query(String sql, Object[] args, RowMapper rowMapper)
```

Notice how there's no reference to a `Connection`, a `PreparedStatement`, or anything else JDBC. We pass in a SQL statement, the argument values with which to populate any parameter placeholders, and something named `RowMapper`. The `RowMapper` is an interface provided by Spring and basically represents an object that knows how to convert a row in a database table into an object. The `RowMapper` interface is presented here in full:

```
public interface RowMapper {
    Object mapRow(ResultSet rs, int rowNumber)
}
```

The `RowMapper` interface has a dependency to the JDBC `ResultSet` interface, but this single dependency doesn't pose a problem when testing DAO implementations because it's hidden inside a `RowMapper` implementation—which can be test-driven separately. Furthermore, the same `RowMapper` implementation can be reused for practically all queries dealing with the table in question.

Although the `JdbcTemplate` class provides a horde of other methods in addition to the `query` method we just saw, we'll ignore those others for now and get our hands dirty again, implementing a `JdbcTemplate`-based DAO class test-first. We'll again implement the `findByLastname` method from the `PersonDao` interface introduced in listing 6.1. For that purpose, we're going to need a

RowMapper implementation that converts rows into Person objects, so why not start from there?

Implementing a RowMapper

Let's assume for the sake of this example that a Person object consists of only two properties—first name and last name—and that these properties map to columns first_name and last_name in the database. With these assumptions, we could write the test in listing 6.4.

Listing 6.4 Test for the RowMapper implementation for Person objects

```
import org.springframework.jdbc.core.RowMapper;
import com.mockobjects.sql.MockSingleRowResultSet;
import java.util.*;
import org.junit.*;
import static org.junit.Assert.*;

public class PersonRowMapperTest {

    @Test
    public void testMappingRow() throws Exception {
        Person expected = new Person("John", "Doe");

        Map<String, Object> data = new HashMap<String, Object>();
        data.put("first_name", expected.getFirstName());
        data.put("last_name", expected.getLastName());
        MockSingleRowResultSet rs = new MockSingleRowResultSet();
        rs.addExpectedNamedValues(data);
                                                  Populate mock
        assertEquals(expected,                    ResultSet object ❶
            new PersonRowMapper().mapRow(rs, 1));
    }
}                                     Perform mapping
                                      and compare result ❷
```

In listing 6.4, we're ❶ creating a mock ResultSet object representing a single row and then ❷ comparing the return value from the RowMapper implementation to a Person instance populated with the expected values. The matching implementation is shown in listing 6.5.

Listing 6.5 Trivial PersonRowMapper implementation

```
import java.sql.*;
import org.springframework.jdbc.core.RowMapper;

public class PersonRowMapper implements RowMapper {
```

```
        public Object mapRow(ResultSet rs, int rowNum)
            throws SQLException {
            return new Person(rs.getString("first_name"),
                              rs.getString("last_name"));
        }
    }
```

This is the basic scenario—straightforward mapping of a row to an object—but there can be other kinds of scenarios as well. For example, we might want the `PersonRowMapper` to populate several fields of the `Person` object based on a single column value. Null values, conversions between `Booleans` and numeric values, and so forth are other scenarios where a more elaborate implementation—and the associated tests—would be necessary.

But now that we have a `PersonRowMapper` implementation, let's move on and test some functionality in the `JdbcTemplate` DAO implementation.

Test-driving the DAO using JdbcTemplate

In addition to implementing the `PersonDao` interface, our `JdbcTemplate`-based DAO implementation should also extend `JdbcDaoSupport` from the Spring Framework. The `JdbcDaoSupport` provides all the plumbing for our DAO class and exposes access to `JdbcTemplate` through a simple getter method, `getJdbcTemplate`. The DAO can then invoke `JdbcTemplate`'s methods and the framework takes care of cleaning up resources afterwards.

In our case, we want to test-drive an implementation for the `findByLastname` method and decide that the DAO should use the `query` method that takes the SQL template, an array of query parameters, and a `RowMapper` implementation as arguments. We also need to stub the `JdbcTemplate` class itself in our test and make it return our hard-coded list of `Person` objects when the `query` method is invoked.

Listing 6.6 shows our test in its full glory.

Listing 6.6 Full test for the `JdbcTemplate`-based `PersonDao` implementation

```
import static org.easymock.classextension.EasyMock.*;
import static org.junit.Assert.*;
import java.util.*;
import org.junit.Test;
import org.springframework.jdbc.core.JdbcTemplate;

public class JdbcTemplatePersonDaoTest {

    @Test
    public void testFindByLastname() throws Exception {
        final String lastName = "Smith";
```

```
        final List<Person> smiths =
            createListOfPeopleNamed(lastName);

        JdbcTemplate template = createMock(JdbcTemplate.class);
        template.query(
                eq("SELECT * FROM employee WHERE last_name = ?"),
                aryEq(new Object[] { lastName }),
                isA(PersonRowMapper.class));
        expectLastCall().andReturn(smiths);

        replay(template);

        JdbcTemplatePersonDao dao = new JdbcTemplatePersonDao();
        dao.setJdbcTemplate(template);
        assertEquals(smiths, dao.findByLastname(lastName));

        verify(template);
    }

    private List<Person> createListOfPeopleNamed(String lastName) {
        List<Person> expectedList = new ArrayList<Person>();
        expectedList.add(new Person("Alice", lastName));
        expectedList.add(new Person("Billy", lastName));
        expectedList.add(new Person("Clark", lastName));
        return expectedList;
    }
}
```

❶ Return hard-coded list of people from query()

❷ Populate DAO with mock JdbcTemplate

❸ DAO should return list as is

Our test in listing 6.6 creates a mock implementation of the `JdbcTemplate` class and ❶ configures it to return a hard-coded list of `Person` objects for the `SELECT * FROM employee WHERE last_name = ?` query. Then we ❷ inject our mock `JdbcTemplate` into the DAO and ❸ invoke the finder method, verifying that it returns the list received from the `query` method.

Listing 6.6 also uses EasyMock's custom argument-matching functionality because we need to make our test double expect a method call that involves arrays, and the default matching logic doesn't work with arrays. As you might not be familiar with custom matchers just yet, perhaps a word about them is called for. Let's take a closer look at what we instructed EasyMock to do regarding the `query` call.

EasyMock and custom matchers

The common case with recording expectations with EasyMock is to invoke the method and specify a return value with `andReturn` or by asking EasyMock for an interface to tell the return value for the previous method call. In replay mode, EasyMock then records the method calls as they take place. Finally, when we ask EasyMock to `verify` that our mock objects' expected collaboration did take place,

EasyMock takes the list of recorded method calls and the list of method calls and performs a simple comparison, using the objects' `equals` method to compare argument values.

In some cases, the `equals` method is not a valid strategy for comparing the expected with the actual. Arrays are a good example—two array objects claim they're not equal even though they contain objects that are equal between the two arrays. Furthermore, in some cases we're not interested in the exact arguments being passed. For example, we might only be interested to know that a `String` starting with certain characters is passed or that the argument is an instance of a certain class. For these cases, EasyMock gives us a way to override the default behavior of using `equals` for argument matching.

In listing 6.6 we executed the following statement:

```
template.query(
        eq("SELECT * FROM employee WHERE last_name = ?"),
        aryEq(new Object[] { lastName }),
        isA(PersonRowMapper.class));
```

The `eq`, `aryEq`, and `isA` methods were statically imported from the `EasyMock` class. The implementations of these methods do exactly one thing: register an implementation of the `IArgumentMatcher` interface with the current execution context. The `eq` method registers an implementation that uses the `equals` method. The `aryEq` method registers an implementation that first compares the lengths of the expected and actual array and then (if the array lengths match) loops through the arrays, comparing each entry with its `equals` method. The `isA` method registers an implementation that only checks that the actual argument is an instance of the expected class.

Because of Java's language semantics, the `eq`, `aryEq`, and `isA` methods are executed before the `query` method. As a result, when the mock object receives the `query` invocation, EasyMock notices it has custom argument-matchers registered and knows to use those matcher implementations when the method is later called when the mock is in replay mode.

You can learn more about the advanced features of the EasyMock framework from the project's website. Now, let's get back to the `PersonDao` implementation.

Implementing the DAO with JdbcDaoSupport

In our test, we injected a `JdbcTemplate` into the DAO, expecting the template object's `query` method to be called with certain arguments. In fact, that's pretty much all we need to do in our DAO because `JdbcTemplate` takes full care of handling the JDBC resources. Listing 6.7 shows the complete DAO implementation.

Listing 6.7 `JdbcTemplate`-based `PersonDao` implementation

```
import java.util.List;
import org.springframework.jdbc.core.RowMapper;
import org.springframework.jdbc.core.support.JdbcDaoSupport;

public class JdbcTemplatePersonDao extends JdbcDaoSupport
                                implements PersonDao {

    public List<Person> findByLastname(String lastname) {
        String sql = "SELECT * FROM employee WHERE last_name = ?";
        String[] args = new String[] { lastname };
        RowMapper mapper = new PersonRowMapper();          <-- Use PersonRowMapper to convert rows to objects
        return getJdbcTemplate().query(sql, args, mapper);  <-- Delegate hard work to JdbcTemplate
    }
}
```

As we can see, `JdbcTemplate` takes away all the boilerplate from our data-access objects and leaves us to worry about the query logic alone—making our tests more compact and maintainable in the process.

As much as I appreciate the band-aid `JdbcTemplate` brings to both writing and testing data-access code, I personally like our next subject—the Hibernate framework—even more. Enough that the section's title includes the word *nirvana*!

6.2.3 Closer to test-driven nirvana with Hibernate

Although Spring's `JdbcTemplate` and the `RowMapper` interface make JDBC code less of a pain to work with, the code we write for mapping our domain objects into database columns is still boilerplate we'd rather not write (and maintain). After all, because we're going to add a new field and accessor methods to our domain object anyway, why should we need to tell our `RowMapper` implementation about the new field? Wouldn't it be nice if our persistence infrastructure would pick up the new field automatically?

This is what modern object-relational mapping (ORM) frameworks like Hibernate do for us. Hibernate lets us define our persistent fields in exactly one place—in the code with simple annotations. The framework takes care of mapping annotated fields on a domain object into a database table and columns. The key is having smart defaults. Most of the time, we can add a field, and it is by default considered persistent. On those occasions when this default doesn't suit our purposes, we can declare the field as being transient either by adding the `@javax.persistence.Transient` annotation on the field or by using Java's `transient` keyword.

These advantages have made Hibernate one of the most popular Java persistence frameworks. Considering how Hibernate has spread all over the place, we'd better know how to work with it and, especially, how to test and test-drive the data-access objects of a Hibernate-based application. Before looking at how Hibernate changes the way we write our unit tests and how it simplifies our data-access code, let's take a brief tour of some of the main concepts in the Hibernate API.

Essentials of the Hibernate API

The Hibernate API has been designed to give its users complete independence of the JDBC API—if that's what they want—while still leaving enough hooks in place to bypass Hibernate's abstractions when necessary, exposing access to the underlying JDBC connections. Furthermore, Hibernate gives us a specialized query language named Hibernate Query Language (HQL) while also supporting SQL-based queries for situations where proprietary database features are required.

For the majority of users, the Hibernate API's most important abstractions are the `SessionFactory`, `Session`, and `Query` interfaces; their collaboration is described on a high level in figure 6.5.

The `SessionFactory` acts as the starting point for everything related to Hibernate. The `SessionFactory` is configured to wrap the `DataSource` and is responsible for keeping up a façade, handing out `Session` objects when asked. We could consider sessions the rough equivalent of connections in the JDBC API, except that they're responsible for some serious persistence and optimization magic that leaves the JDBC API spinning its wheels. With the `Session` object, we perform basic CRUD operations directly by using methods defined in the `Session` interface, or more elaborate queries by asking the `Session` object to create a `Query`. The `Query` interface gives us ways to build dynamic queries at runtime.

These three interfaces are—most of the time—all we need to worry about when developing data access objects using Hibernate. So, if they're all interfaces and the `SessionFactory` is our access point to the triad, where does the `SessionFactory`

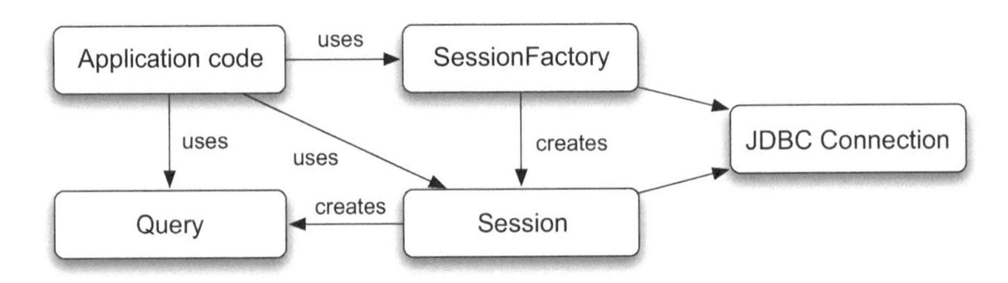

Figure 6.5 The `SessionFactory`, `Session`, and `Query` interfaces represent the main concepts of the Hibernate API.

come from? You might've guessed already that we typically pass the SessionFactory to our data-access objects using dependency injection, but we haven't yet discussed how to get an instance to inject in the first place. There are two answers to this question—both involving the Configuration class.

The first and more common way to obtain a SessionFactory instance is to define an external configuration file as either a properties file or an XML document (named hibernate.properties or hibernate.cfg.xml, respectively) in our class path and let the Configuration class load the configuration from there, constructing an implementation of the SessionFactory on top of the configured database, using the configured connection details, pooling, caching strategy, and so on.

The other, less frequently encountered means of obtaining a SessionFactory instance is to tweak a Configuration object programmatically in Java and thus get a dynamically configured SessionFactory object. The programmatic configuration can come extremely handy in building a suite of automated integration tests with a framework like JUnit. On the other hand, an external file representing a test configuration might be easier to keep in sync with the production configuration.

Because this is a chapter about test-driven development and not Hibernate, this is as far as we'll go with regard to Hibernate details. What we know about the responsibilities of the SessionFactory, Session, and Query interfaces is enough for us to be able to start test-driving Hibernate DAOs. In fact, because we don't want our unit tests to touch the database, we're going to mock everything! Let's redo the PersonDao one more time, Hibernate-style.

Writing a test for expected interaction

Let's build up our first test for a Hibernate-based DAO in small steps—the API is pretty simple and the patterns are easy to pick up, leading to a somewhat routine process (which is good news because it means we can move the little plumbing we need into a common setup shared between tests and test classes).

Say we want to start again by implementing the findByLastname method into our DAO. We know we're going to need a SessionFactory as well as a Session. We also know that we're going to use the Query interface for implementing this specific finder, so we'll need one of those as well. Our first step in writing a test is thus creating dynamic mock objects for these three interfaces using EasyMock, as shown in listing 6.8.

Listing 6.8 Basic plumbing for test-driving a Hibernate-based DAO

```
import static org.easymock.EasyMock.*;
import org.junit.*;
import org.hibernate.*;
import org.hibernate.classic.Session;
```

```
public class HibernatePersonDaoTest {

    private SessionFactory factory;
    private Session session;
    private Query query;

    @Before
    public void setUp() {
        factory = createMock(SessionFactory.class);
        session = createMock(Session.class);
        query = createMock(Query.class);
    }
}
```

With the plumbing in place, we are ready to proceed to defining our test. I've developed a habit of defining the expected HQL statement and any parameters for the query in the beginning of the test method. In the case of looking up people by their last name, we might type something like this:

```
@Test
public void testFindByLastname() throws Exception {
    String hql = "from Person p where p.lastname = :lastname";
    String lastname = "Smith";
    ...
}
```

We also need to make our mock objects return a bunch of `Person` objects when asked for people named Smith, so let's quickly create a list of Smiths:

```
...
String name = "Smith";
List<Person> theSmiths = new ArrayList<Person>();
theSmiths.add(new Person("Alice", name));
theSmiths.add(new Person("Billy", name));
theSmiths.add(new Person("Clark", name));
...
```

That should do it. Now, what remains is the meat of our test—that is, defining the way we expect our DAO to interact with the Hibernate API.

Let's assume for a while that we're using an architecture where the opening and closing of sessions is performed in a crosscutting way using something like a Servlet filter—a component that executes around the Servlet itself, freeing the Servlet from worrying about the session getting closed.

In other words, all of our DAO classes should use the current session rather than ask the `SessionFactory` to create a new one. Next, having a reference to a `Session` object, we want our DAO to ask the `Session` for a `Query`, passing the HQL statement as an argument. Finally, after populating any query parameters in the `Query` object, we expect our DAO to ask the `Query` to `list` all matching `Person` objects (and to return that list). Listing 6.9 shows how these expectations translate to the EasyMock syntax.

Listing 6.9 Setting up expectations for a Hibernate DAO

```
...
expect( factory.getCurrentSession() ).andReturn(session);
expect( session.createQuery(hql) ).andReturn(query);
expect( query.setParameter("lastname", name) ).andReturn(query);
expect( query.list() ).andReturn(people);
...
```

Having configured the `SessionFactory`'s `getCurrentSession` method to return our mock `Session`, which in turn is configured to return our mock `Query`, we're all set for switching our mocks into replay mode and invoking the production code. Listing 6.10 shows our complete test for the `findByLastname` method.

Listing 6.10 Full test for finding people by their last name

```
import static org.easymock.EasyMock.*;
import static org.junit.Assert.*;
import org.junit.*;
import java.util.*;
import org.hibernate.*;
import org.hibernate.classic.Session;

public class HibernatePersonDaoTest {

    private SessionFactory factory;
    private Session session;
    private Query query;

    @Before
    public void setUp() {
        factory = createMock(SessionFactory.class);
        session = createMock(Session.class);
        query = createMock(Query.class);
    }

    @Test
    public void testFindByLastname() throws Exception {
        String hql = "from Person p where p.lastname = :lastname";
        String name = "Smith";

        List<Person> theSmiths = new ArrayList<Person>();
```

```
        theSmiths.add(new Person("Alice", name));
        theSmiths.add(new Person("Billy", name));
        theSmiths.add(new Person("Clark", name));

        expect(factory.getCurrentSession()).andReturn(session);
        expect(session.createQuery(hql)).andReturn(query);
        expect(query.setParameter("lastname",
            name)).andReturn(query);
        expect(query.list()).andReturn(theSmiths);

        replay(factory, session, query);

        HibernatePersonDao dao = new HibernatePersonDao();
        dao.setSessionFactory(factory);
        assertEquals(theSmiths, dao.findByLastname(name));

        verify(factory, session, query);
    }
}
```

Record expected API calls ❶

Inject SessionFactory with setter

Expect finder method to return hard-coded list

❶ Recording the expected interaction with the Hibernate API using EasyMock is easy compared to a similar test for a JDBC-based implementation. This is both because there are not many method calls to make to the Hibernate interfaces in the first place and, especially with more complex queries, because the `Query` API happens to have almost no void methods, thus making it possible to use the compact `expect(...).andReturn(...)` syntax. With a dependency injection-based design, it's also straightforward to wire our DAO implementation with our small graph of test doubles.

Enough praise for the Hibernate API; let's look at what kind of implementation would satisfy our test in listing 6.10.

Making the interaction happen

The implementations for most finder methods in Hibernate-based DAO classes are almost trivial, and this is certainly the case with our `findByLastname` method, shown in listing 6.11. We ❶ store the injected `SessionFactory` into a private field, ❷ ask for the current session when a method call comes in, ❸ create and ❹ populate a query object, and return the resulting `List` directly. This is all listing 6.11 does.

Listing 6.11 Hibernate-based implementation of the `PersonDao`

```
import java.util.*;
import org.hibernate.*;
```

```
public class HibernatePersonDao implements PersonDao {

    private SessionFactory sessionFactory;                    Store injected    ❶
                                                              SessionFactory
    public void setSessionFactory(SessionFactory sessionFactory) {
        this.sessionFactory = sessionFactory;              <-
    }

    public List<Person> findByLastname(String lastname) {         ❷ Get
        Session session = sessionFactory.getCurrentSession();  <-  Session
        String hql = "from Person p where p.lastname = :lastname";
        Query query = session.createQuery(hql);     <-
        query.setParameter("lastname", lastname);   <-
        return query.list();                             ❸ Create Query
    }                               Populate Query ❹
}
```

The implementation is straightforward—too straightforward, actually. Our test hasn't pushed our implementation to handle exceptions properly yet. Before it becomes a habit to skip the exception cases, let's look at how such a variation might look like for our Hibernate-based DAO.

Testing for exceptions

Let's say we'd like our DAO to throw an unchecked exception from the `findByLastname` method when there's an exception thrown from the Hibernate API. Further, let's say we want the original exception to be chained as the cause for the unchecked exception. For that behavior, we might write a test like that in listing 6.12.

Listing 6.12 Testing that the session is closed even after an exception

```
@Test
public void testFindByLastnameReturnsEmptyListUponException()
        throws Exception {
    String hql = "from Person p where p.lastname = :lastname";
    String name = "Smith";
    HibernateException hibernateError = new HibernateException("");

    expect(factory.getCurrentSession()).andReturn(session);
    expect(session.createQuery(hql)).andReturn(query);
    expect(query.setParameter("lastname", name)).andReturn(query);
    expect(query.list()).andThrow(hibernateError);      <-
                                                    ❶ Make list() throw
    replay(factory, session, query);                   exception

    HibernatePersonDao dao = new HibernatePersonDao();
```

```
        dao.setSessionFactory(factory);
        try {
            dao.findByLastname(name);
            fail("should've thrown an exception");
        } catch (RuntimeException expected) {
            assertSame(hibernateError, expected.getCause());
        }

        verify(factory, session, query);
    }
```

findByLastname() wraps HibernateException into RuntimeException

Instead of configuring our mock `Query` to return a list of people from the `list` method, we now ❶ make it throw a `HibernateException`. Also, instead of expecting a `List` to be returned, we expect to see a `RuntimeException` that wraps the original `HibernateException` we've configured our mock to raise.

Now, let's see what kind of changes this test implies for our production code. Our tests are expecting a `RuntimeException` when the `Query` object's `list` method fails. Although we could be sneaky with our implementation and only wrap the `list` call with a `try-finally` block, forcing us to write further tests that throw the exception from, say, `SessionFactory#getCurrentSession`, we won't do that. Instead, we'll go for the correct, obvious implementation directly. The final implementation is shown in listing 6.13.

Listing 6.13 Implementation with rudimentary exception handling

```
public List<Person> findByLastname(String name) {
    try {
        Session session = sessionFactory.getCurrentSession();
        String hql = "from Person p where p.lastname = :lastname";
        Query query = session.createQuery(hql);
        query.setParameter("lastname", name);
        return query.list();
    } catch (HibernateException e) {
        throw new RuntimeException(e);
    }
}
```

Our production code got a bit more verbose, but it's also a lot more robust because we're now explicitly dealing with situations where, for example, the database connection dies suddenly in the middle of a transaction. Similarly, if we had wanted our DAO methods to ask the `SessionFactory` for a brand-new `Session`, our test would've probably wanted to check that the `Session` object also gets closed if there's an exception, not leaving the sessions and their associated database connections hanging open indefinitely.

> **Reducing duplication with fuzzy matching and named queries**
>
> By configuring the expected query string in our test, we are effectively duplicating data between our test and production code. We could make our test reference a constant defined in our production code but that's not the cleanest of solutions either, at least if you share my taste for code aesthetics.
>
> One way of reducing this duplication is to use *fuzzy matching* in our tests, leaving the specific query string unverified. In other words, we would be relying on integration tests to verify that the query does work. EasyMock, for example, allows custom argument matching, which makes the use of regular expressions and similar techniques almost trivial. Following this approach, our mock objects would be only checking that the production code passes the right arguments to the persistence API.
>
> Another useful technique for reducing duplication is the concept of *named queries*. Hibernate, among other modern ORM tools, supports externally configured, named queries in its API, which makes it possible to write unit tests using test doubles without dictating the query syntax. Again, the correctness of the queries would need to be verified with integration tests.

Speaking of database connections, let's pull away from test-driving data-access objects with test doubles for a moment and think about the big picture. So far, we've executed our code only against test doubles, and we've configured them to expect certain queries with certain parameters, making them return hard-coded data. How do we know that the query we expected would work against the real database schema?

The answer is, we don't. Knowing our tools well does make for a good probability that we've gotten a simple parameterized query correct, but we don't *really* know until we've tested that it does work with the real thing. And this leads us to our next topic—driving our data-access code with integration tests rather than unit tests.

6.3 Writing integration tests before the code

So far, we've written unit tests for our data-access objects that have led to an implementation that works correctly against our test doubles—mock objects we've configured expectations for based on our understanding of what the underlying database schema is (or will be) or what kind of a query the data-access code should use. Mock objects are a powerful tool for testing exception situations and avoiding the burden of having to maintain a test database. On the other hand, as already noted, we can't be sure that we got our expectations correct until we execute our data-access code and our selected persistence framework against a real database.

Thus, we might also want to consider test-driving our data-access code with *integration tests.*

6.3.1 What is an integration test?

Integration tests for data-access code are tests that connect the code under test into a database. In other words, looking back at figure 6.1, on page 198, we're testing everything from the persistence logic layer down to the relational database. Or, at least, down to the JDBC driver. What exactly do we mean by "at least"? Let me explain.

In other words, we're testing the end-to-end integration of our data-access components, the persistence framework employed, and the relational database. Having said that, we might stretch the definition of "end to end" a bit by swapping a different relational database product for our tests than we have in production. This is where we need to make informed decisions about what are acceptable differences between the environment used for integration testing and the production environment.

Differences between production and testing

Our production environment might be composed of a cluster of application servers, connecting to a cluster of database servers running Oracle, for example, and we might have configured our application server with a cluster-aware `DataSource`. In production, our persistence logic would connect to our persistence framework, which would talk to a JDBC connection, which would talk to a cluster-aware JDBC driver, which would talk to a whole bunch of other stuff before our request would hit the database node. All of this might be awesome for the system's high availability or scalability, but it's also probably at least a couple of magnitudes slower than a test double returning hard-coded data. And speed of test execution is crucial for test-driven development.

Not all systems require a heavy, clustered, load-balanced infrastructure for persistence. Some systems are perfectly suitable for a standalone relational database product running locally to the application server. Furthermore, some systems might deploy an embedded relational database. Even with all this variance between different systems, we can be reasonably confident about our persistence logic by using *some* kind of a relational database.

With that in mind, let's think about what we're interested in testing when it comes to data-access code. That is, what problems might've we missed with our unit tests?

What might've we missed with our unit tests?

We want fast tests. Blazing fast. If we can't get that, we want almost blazing fast. What we don't need is the absolute best, identical representation of the production environment for our integration tests. Thinking about the kinds of assumptions we make while writing pure unit tests for data-access code, we can identify three aspects that are more or less the biggest risks:

- Assumptions about the database schema or domain model
- Assumptions about the query statements used
- Assumptions about the object-relational mappings, if applicable

We have already eliminated things like correct use of the persistence API, because that's what our unit tests are verifying. We have also eliminated the JDBC driver as a risk (as well as the underlying database), because we should be able to expect third-party code to function properly.[3] Let's take a closer look at the three risks that remain on our list.

The assumptions we make about the database schema or domain model are largely about the existence of and the naming of fields and columns. This is a risk because the references to fields or columns in our data-access code are often literal, expressed as strings rather than as part of our programming language syntax, which our compiler would be able to verify for us.

Similarly, to the compiler, our query statements are just strings and nothing more. Our ability to get them right is solely dependent on our knowledge of the query language syntax. In some cases, it's also dependent on the support for the syntax features used by the underlying database engine. In other words, we need to know our tools and, believe it or not, sometimes we make mistakes anyway.

The assumptions about our object-relational mappings are effectively an extension of the first class of assumptions. For example, when we wrote unit tests for our Hibernate-backed DAO, we configured our mock objects to expect a certain kind of query statement and to return data upon that query. In doing that, we made assumptions about the mapping of the fields used in the query. Naming conventions do help, but still we inevitably sometimes leave a typo in, only to be discovered later when someone happens to use the functionality in a real deployment environment—finding out that *lastName* should've been *lastname*.

So the question becomes, how do we respond to the risks that are built in to these assumptions?

---

[3] There are valid reasons for having tests for third-party software, including learning tests, but none directly related to test-driving data-access code.

How do we make up for what we've missed?

These are all things that we might go wrong even though we've built up a thorough suite of unit tests as part of our test-driven development. The good news is that these are all things that we can verify well enough with any standards-compliant relational database, even if it wouldn't be the exact same product with which we're going to deploy to production. After all, what we need is to execute our JDBC code against a database schema on pretty much any database that supports the SQL features we're using; or, if we're using an ORM framework like Hibernate, we need to execute our persistence logic and the framework code against any database supported by the framework.

Saying "any database" sounds perhaps a bit too grandiose to be accurate, though. Let's talk a bit more about our options and their relative pros and cons in order to help us grasp the limits of this flexibility and what properties to consider when selecting the database for use in our integration tests.

6.3.2 Selecting the database

When it comes to deciding which database to use in our integration tests, there are a few factors to consider:

- How closely the setup matches our production environment
- How easy it is to share and manage the configuration within the team
- How easy it is to access and control the database

Starting from the first...

Close enough to the production setup

Even though the JDBC API is a standard and seemingly common denominator among any databases we connect to from a Java application, there are differences that matter. These differences can make our system incompatible with the production database, somewhat dysfunctional, or behave seemingly erratically in production, even though all of our integration tests are passing against the test database.

The most obvious differences are in support for identity and uniqueness-related database features. For example, the concept of database sequences is a feature commonly used in high-end commercial databases such as Oracle and DB2 but not too widespread among popular open source databases.[4] This can cause some gray hairs for developers, for example, when the production database is MySQL, which doesn't support `SEQUENCE` objects but rather uses its own `AUTO_INCREMENT` column type, which practically no other database supports. Furthermore, although two

---

[4] I'm certainly hoping this will change, because the SQL:2003 standard introduced sequence generators.

database products might have support for the same concept, the syntax for using the concept might be different. Sequence or identity generators and stored procedures are prime examples.

Because we need the same SQL syntax to work for both the production database and for whatever database product we use in our integration tests, a common solution is to pull the responsibility for generating unique identifiers from the database and inside the application's persistence layer. Such an approach also tackles another related problem—how to figure out the assigned identifier for the newly persisted object/row—which also requires the use of proprietary database features. Generating identifiers in the application is not necessarily a mere workaround, however, because it does give our code base full control of the identity information for our domain objects.

Effectively, we're talking about a trade-off between architectural complexity (having a portion of our application logic reside in the database) and code complexity (having to implement a sequence generator). Luckily, many persistence frameworks (including Hibernate) provide such functionality out of the box. Hibernate supports primary-key generators based on standalone algorithms as well as database concepts like sequences and identity columns, for example.

Another common problem with compatibility between two database products is the use of reserved words. For example, we might have a legacy system running on MySQL for which we'd like to start writing automated integration tests using a more lightweight database, HSQLDB.[5] Now, there's a table that stores items that belong to ordered lists. For each row, there's one column referring to the list it belongs to and another column indicating the absolute position of that item in the list. I'd wager that there's a fifty-fifty chance that the developers have named the positional column "position" rather than something like "indx" or "ordinal." The bad news is that although "position" is a perfect name for that column, it's also a reserved word in HSQLDB. The good news is that columns and tables are easy to rename, so this is mostly a small annoyance rather than a showstopper for using a lighter-weight database.

There can also be more subtle differences between databases, such as the semantics of `UNIQUE` constraints for multiple columns. Although in most databases a multi-column `UNIQUE` constraint allows duplicates if at least one of the constituent values is `NULL`, this might not be the case with the database you're planning to use for production or testing.

Even after all of these gotchas, it still makes sense to see if there's a way to use a substitute for the real database in our integration tests. After all, we're interested

---

[5] http://www.hsqldb.org/.

in improving our productivity, and getting to use a database in our integration tests that's easier and faster to set up can be a huge improvement—huge enough that it might well be worth the trouble of changing our code base to accommodate for differences between the database products.

And speaking of ease of use, it's not just about one developer, but a whole team. In other words, our setup needs to be easily shared and maintainable.

Easily shared configuration

Another important aspect to consider when deciding which database to run our integration tests against is the amount of work involved in getting a fresh development environment set up and the tests running. Ideally, everything should work out of the box with no software to install manually. In practice, it's often acceptable to be required to install software such as a database server as long as the installation doesn't require too much configuration.

The problem with non-default configurations is that it suddenly becomes necessary to have developers maintain a custom configuration file somewhere specifying, for example, which port the database server is listening to and what are the username and password for connecting to it. A much better setup is one where all configuration information is maintained in the configuration management system, versioned along with revisions of the software itself and not requiring a new developer to perform any manual work in order to get going.

The ultimate ease of maintenance is reached when the database server is downloaded from version control and installed by automated build scripts, if necessary. Such a scenario is possible with many embedded or otherwise extremely lightweight database servers such as HSQLDB or McKoi.[6] We'll soon see how HSQLDB can be embedded into our test suite, but before we go there let's talk about the third factor that might affect our selection of the database for our integration tests.

Access and control over the server

Having a database server for our integration tests to successfully run against is one thing. It's another thing to find out what went wrong when a test fails. Depending on the database server, the JDBC driver, and our persistence framework, the reason for a given failure might be blatantly obvious from the error message or it might require an elaborate debugging session. In some situations, it's not that simple—especially when there's no exception telling us that we've tried to use invalid syntax or that there's "no such column" in the table we attempted to query. Analyzing our

---

[6] http://mckoi.com/database/.

way down to the root cause of a discrepancy between what a query returns and what we expected it to return can be extremely tasking unless we can easily browse the contents of the database.

Having a local installation of a standalone database server listening for incoming connections on a network interface is probably the easiest of our options when it comes to access. This is because we can choose to use pretty much any graphical or command-line tool for browsing the database, executing SQL statements against it, and so forth. Embedded databases fare worse in this regard, because we typically need to access them through the Java API in-process rather than be able to connect remotely with our favorite graphical database browser. Then there's the middle ground of an embedded database to which the application still connects over a network connection.

My personal preference is toward using a pure embedded database like HSQLDB because of its ease of integration with the test suite and zero installation. There are some downsides to using HSQLDB in embedded mode as we've just learned, of course, but these can be mitigated to a large degree by building simple tools for dumping the contents of the database to an external file, for example. Furthermore, there's hardly anything faster than HSQLDB for integration-testing data-access objects written in Java.

We're now going to look more closely at integrating HSQLDB into our integration test suite and test-drive a bit of data-access code. It's still not rocket science, though, and we'll proceed in small steps as usual.

6.4 Integration tests in action

In this section, we'll add more functionality into the Hibernate-based `PersonDao` implementation we started developing earlier in this chapter. The ultimate purpose in this is to see first-hand what kind of infrastructure we might have for integration testing and what kind of obstacles we need to overcome. Even though we're using Hibernate here as our persistence framework, after we're through with our examples, you'll be well-equipped to establish a similar setup for your specific technology stack.

We'll begin by writing a simple integration test for persisting a transient object into the database. Once we've sketched an outline for the test, we'll look into using an in-memory database and learn how to create the database schema for a test database built from scratch. After we've gotten that test implemented and running green, we'll move on to discuss how we can keep our test data intact from one test to another using transactional fixtures.

That's a lot to cover, so let's get started!

6.4.1 Writing our first Hibernate integration test

We're about to write our first integration test for a DAO dealing with Person objects. Our persistence architecture is Hibernate, but the whole HibernatePersonDao class we now want to test-drive doesn't exist yet. The first thing we want the DAO to be able to do is persist a Person object. Persisting an object takes us straight into the beef with integration tests because it's a simple piece of functionality and because it's a write operation. Write operations are generally trickier than read operations and, thus, bring up interesting issues regarding how our tests maintain the database in a known state.

> **Don't overdo it**
>
> Integration tests that hit a database (or a web service, for example) are a must-have. With that said, it's worth noting that it is generally not necessary to test *all* persistence-related operations end-to-end with a database if most of them are similar. In other words, try to write integration tests against a database only for a representative subset of all read and write operations (or for learning purposes). The rest of the cases can then be covered with unit tests using test doubles, which generally cuts down the overall test run times significantly.

This is our starting point. What do we do first? How about programming by intention a little and writing a little test that verifies that a Person object we persist using the DAO can be found from the database afterward? Sounds good to me, of course, so let's do it.

Sketching an outline for a test

Wanting our DAO to be able to persist Person objects, we proceed to writing the outline of a test, shown in listing 6.14.

Listing 6.14 Skeleton for our first integration test class

```
public class HibernatePersonDaoIntegrationTest {

    @Test
    public void persistedObjectExistsInDatabase() throws Exception {
        SessionFactory sf = getSessionFactory();           <-- 1 Create SessionFactory that knows about Person class
        HibernatePersonDao dao = new HibernatePersonDao();
        dao.setSessionFactory(sf);

        Person person = new Person("John", "Doe");
        dao.save(person);
        assertNotNull(person.getId());      <-- 2 Persisted object receives ID
```

```
        Session s = sf.openSession();
        Object copy = s.get(Person.class, person.getId());
        assertEquals(person, copy);
    }
}
```

❸ **John Doe now in database**

We first create an instance of the `HibernatePersonDao` class and ❶ configure it with a Hibernate `SessionFactory` that knows of the `Person` class. We've omitted the implementation of the `getSessionFactory` method so far—we're just programming by intention for now.

Next we proceed to the "act" portion of our test in listing 6.14. We create a new, transient `Person` object and ask the `HibernatePersonDao` to save it. We then ❷ verify that the object received an ID and that ❸ an identical `Person` object can be found from the database with that specific ID.

Beware of reusing a Session in tests

Notice how in listing 6.14 we obtain a new `Session` for verifying that the given `Person` object was indeed persisted. We could've just asked the `SessionFactory` for the current `Session` instead of creating a new one, but using an entirely separate `Session` is a more reliable technique. Using the same `Session` can sometimes hide a nasty bug when there is transactional behavior involved because all changes are visible within a given `Session`, regardless of whether or not those changes have been committed as part of the transaction.

That seems like a sufficient test for verifying that the DAO successfully persists the object through the Hibernate API into the database. Now, let's look at how we could implement the missing `getSessionFactory` method.

Configuring Hibernate for testing

The problem we're facing is that we need to have two different Hibernate configurations—one for production and one for integration testing. And we need to be able to swap in the testing configuration transparently and, preferably, without duplicating data unnecessarily between the two configurations.

One solution that I've been using is to maintain the production configuration in the standard hibernate.properties file in the class path and the differing properties in a testing-only configuration file named hibernate.test.properties. The trick is to have the testing configuration override the production configuration where there is overlap. This helps us minimize the risk of finding a configuration issue only after deploying the application to a testing environment—we'll catch most of our Hibernate-related integration problems with data access already in the developer's workspace.

Now, let's look at listing 6.15 to see how we can implement the missing `getSessionFactory` method from listing 6.14 and realize the approach I've described.

Listing 6.15 Configuring a `SessionFactory` for tests

```
public class HibernatePersonDaoIntegrationTest {

    ...

    private SessionFactory getSessionFactory() throws Exception {
        return createConfiguration().buildSessionFactory();
    }

    private Configuration createConfiguration() throws Exception {
        Configuration cfg = loadProductionConfiguration();
        loadTestConfigInto(cfg, "/hibernate.test.properties");
        return cfg;
    }

    private Configuration loadProductionConfiguration() {
        return new Configuration().configure();
    }

    private void loadTestConfigInto(Configuration cfg, String path)
            throws Exception {
        Properties properties = loadPropertiesFrom(path);
        Enumeration keys = properties.keys();
        while (keys.hasMoreElements()) {
            String key = (String) keys.nextElement();
            String value = properties.getProperty(key);
            cfg.setProperty(key, value);
        }
    }

    private Properties loadPropertiesFrom(String path)
            throws Exception {
        InputStream stream = getClass().getResourceAsStream(path);
        assertNotNull("Resource not found: " + path, stream);
        Properties props = new Properties();
        props.load(stream);
        stream.close();
        return props;
    }
}
```

1 Load production config from classpath

1 Load production config from classpath

2 Load test config from file

3 Override individual properties

In order to obtain a `SessionFactory`, we need a `Configuration` object that knows how to create one. In listing 6.15, we first ❶ load a `Configuration` object based on the default production configuration from the hibernate.properties file sitting somewhere in our class path. We then pass on the production configuration object to another method that ❷ loads the test configuration on top of the production configuration, ❸ overriding any preexisting properties.

That's quite a bit of code just to get Hibernate to connect to our test database, but the good news is that we'll only need to write this code once. Speaking of connecting to the database, we should probably specify the test configuration for Hibernate at this point so that we're not letting our integration tests hit a slow remote database or (gasp) the production database.

Configuring an in-memory HSQLDB database

The next question is, if our test configuration file should override database connection-related properties, what exactly are those properties? In our case, we want the integration tests to run against an in-memory HSQLDB database. Assuming that HSQLDB isn't also our production database, that means we need to override at least the SQL dialect and a number of properties prefixed with `hibernate.connection`. Listing 6.16 lists a sample properties file that does the trick.

Listing 6.16 Hibernate configuration file for an in-memory HSQLDB

```
hibernate.dialect=org.hibernate.dialect.HSQLDialect
hibernate.connection.driver_class=org.hsqldb.jdbcDriver
hibernate.connection.url=jdbc:hsqldb:mem:testdb
hibernate.connection.username=sa
hibernate.connection.password=
hibernate.show_sql=true
hibernate.hbm2ddl.auto=create-drop
```

The configurations in listing 6.16 aren't much different than for a production setup—we just need to tell Hibernate which product-specific dialect of SQL to generate, where the database is located (the JDBC URL), which JDBC driver to use for connecting to the database, and what user account to use. The last configuration, `hibernate.show_sql`, isn't required but is useful for testing purposes. By enabling the `show_sql` feature, Hibernate will print out the generated SQL statements as it executes them, which can be extremely helpful in figuring out why things don't work the way we expect.

The `hibernate.connection.url` property's value, `jdbc:hsqldb:mem:testdb`, is basically saying that we want to connect to an in-memory HSQLDB database named "testdb." If such a database doesn't exist already in the running JVM,

HSQLDB creates one. Using an in-memory database also means that, because we're creating the database from scratch, there are no tables to begin with. Somehow, we need to initialize our database schema when the database is created.

Finally, with the `hibernate.hbm2ddl.auto` value of `create-drop`, we're instructing Hibernate to automatically create and drop the database schema when the `SessionFactory` is created and closed, respectively. That's not the only way to go about creating the database schema, though. Let's see what our options are.

6.4.2 Creating the database schema

The database schema is part of the code base. With this in mind, and considering that the database schema should be versioned along with the rest of the system, we quickly come to the conclusion that we need to have a single representation of the schema in a file (or files) that's under version control.

The universal SQL script

The traditional solution has been to maintain the DDL (data definition language) statements used for creating the schema in an SQL script file (or a set of SQL scripts). This has many benefits: it's easy to put under version control, and it uses the familiar SQL statements that the database administrator and the developers are already familiar with.

The downside with external SQL scripts is two-fold. First, we need some way to execute such scripts from Java code in order to set up the schema for our integration tests. Second, if we'd like to use a different database for integration tests than in production, the DDL statements must also be compatible between the two products. Otherwise, we'll have to maintain two schema-definition files, and that's just asking for trouble.

The first of these issues can be tackled easily by hacking together a utility that can parse SQL statements from a file and feed them to the JDBC API. The second, however, is trickier. Unless you happen to be using Hibernate, that is.

Letting Hibernate take care of everything

Fortunate for those of us who are using Hibernate, Hibernate offers a way to automatically export the schema into the configured database when the `SessionFactory` is created. Hibernate accomplishes this based on the mapping documents. The good news is that the only thing required from the developer is to add the `hibernate.hbm2ddl.auto=create-drop` property to our integration test configuration. The not-so-good thing about it is that the schema derived from mapping files is typically not identical to what we'd create by hand.

For example, Hibernate by default might create a `VARCHAR(255)` column for a field of type `java.lang.String`, whereas we might prefer an arbitrary long data type instead of one limited to 255 characters. This has caused more than a few gray hairs in the past: Some database products silently crop the incoming data when it doesn't fit into the allocated column length. The defaults can be overridden in the mapping documents by defining the `sql-type` attribute for each column for which we want to explicitly declare its type. This may or may not be a problem for you, depending on whether your production database and your test database both support the same data type.

Before we continue with our integration test cycle by implementing the missing production code, there's one more thing about the SQL scripts I feel you should know. I call it *incremental DDL scripts.*

Incremental DDL scripts

If you've ever been elbow-deep in grease on a production deployment gone wrong, you've probably witnessed a database rollback. It's relatively simple to roll back application code—just take the current stuff out and put something else back in. It's not that simple with the database, however, because the database is not just the schema. It's also the data stored in that schema, and it's that data that makes things more difficult—we can't just throw away all of the data and create the schema again from scratch. This is where incremental DDL scripts come into play.

The fundamental idea of incremental DDL scripts is that every big schema can be created in small steps, adding one column or one table at a time—and that these little steps are often reversible! If we define the database schema as an ordered sequence of small DDL scripts "patching" the current version of the schema in a database, we can easily re-create an arbitrary version of the schema, and we can revert from a newer version back to an older version of the schema without losing all of our data.

Probably the first public incremental DDL script implementation I've seen is *migrations* in the Ruby on Rails web framework.[7] This is a Java-oriented book, however, so let's not talk about Rails migrations. The closest thing to the incremental DDL scripts idea I've seen in the Java world is an open source project named *dbdeploy*.[8]

The dbdeploy tool is a database change-management tool that generates an SQL script from a set of smaller SQL scripts. The small patch files are sorted by their numerical prefix that identifies the patch file's version. For instance, we might have a directory structure of delta scripts such as that shown in figure 6.6.

[7] http://wiki.rubyonrails.com/rails/pages/UnderstandingMigrations.

[8] http://dbdeploy.com/.

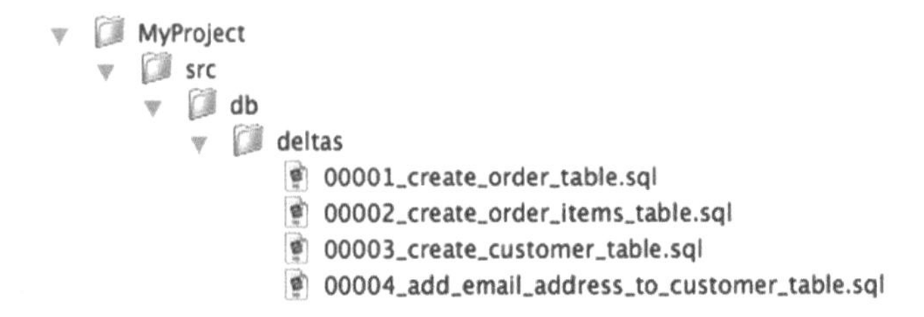

Figure 6.6 Example directory structure with a set of delta change scripts for creating the database schema incrementally. The four scripts in the directory src/db/deltas will be applied in order according to the numerical prefix.

In our example in figure 6.6, we have four delta scripts that dbdeploy will apply in the order specified by the numerical prefix. Each of the four delta files would then contain plain ol' SQL statements and, optionally, an undo block that dbdeploy applies when rolling back to an older version of the schema. For instance, the delta file named 00002_create_order_items_table.sql might look like listing 6.17.

Listing 6.17 Example delta script with an @UNDO-block for rollback

```
CREATE TABLE ORDER_ITEMS (
  ID INTEGER NOT NULL,
  ORDER_ID INTEGER NOT NULL,
  ITEM_DESCRIPTION VARCHAR(100)
)
;
ALTER TABLE ORDER_ITEMS
  ADD (CONSTRAINT PK_ORDER_ITEMS)
  PRIMARY KEY (ID)
;
ALTER TABLE ORDER_ITEMS
  ADD (CONSTRAINT FK_ORDER_ITEMS_ORDER)
  FOREIGN KEY (ORDER_ID) REFERENCES ORDER(ID)
;

--//@UNDO                         <-- (1) Everything after this line is rollback
ALTER TABLE ORDER_ITEMS
  DROP CONSTRAINT FK_ORDERS_ORDER_ITEMS
;
DROP TABLE ORDER_ITEMS
;
```

The dbdeploy tool would read the SQL statements in listing 6.17 until it encounters a row containing the ❶ magic string `--//@UNDO`, which effectively says, "that's all there is for updating the schema—the rest of the file is rollback statements."

Now, dbdeploy can be pointed to a database and a set of delta scripts, and it will generate migration scripts for that specific database. But how does dbdeploy know which delta files have already been applied? For that purpose, we need to maintain a dedicated table in the database that contains information about the deltas applied to that specific database. We need to create the table manually; but the dbdeploy distribution contains the necessary SQL scripts for doing that, so we just need to execute it once when creating a database.

An incremental DDL-script solution such as dbdeploy is definitely worth considering. It is yet another tool to learn, but it also gives a number of benefits that are hard to argue. For this chapter's purposes, however (and especially for our integration test example, which we still haven't finished!), we'll go with the Hibernate solution, letting it drop and create our database schema behind the scenes. Now, let's pick up our integration test again and finally make it pass.

6.4.3 Implementing the production code

Let's recap what our test back in listing 6.14 was expecting of us. We wanted the `HibernatePersonDao` class, configured with a proper `SessionFactory` object, to save the given `Person` object so that it is indeed persisted into the underlying database behind the `SessionFactory`. Listing 6.18 presents a sufficient implementation in all of its glory.

Listing 6.18 Skeleton for our first integration test class

```
public class HibernatePersonDao {

    private SessionFactory sessionFactory;              // (1) Hang on to SessionFactory

    public void setSessionFactory(SessionFactory sessionFactory) {
        this.sessionFactory = sessionFactory;           // (1)
    }

    public void save(Person person) {
        Session session = sessionFactory.getCurrentSession();   // (2) Obtain existing session, if applicable
        Transaction tx = session.beginTransaction();    // (3) Persist Person within transaction
        session.save(person);
        tx.commit();
    }
}
```

All that our DAO implementation needs to do to make the test pass is to (1) store the `SessionFactory` that was passed in into a `private` field and in the `save` method use it for the persistence operation. In the `save` method, we (2) obtain an existing `Session` from the `SessionFactory` (or let it create a new one if there's no existing session), (3) begin a transaction, invoke `save(person)` on the `Session` object, and commit the transaction.

Speaking of transactions, let's look at a concept called *transactional fixtures* and why we should consider using such things.

6.4.4 Staying clean with transactional fixtures

It's a piece of cake to test read operations. They're straightforward: We have some data in the database, and the read operation returns objects that represent that data (or a subset of that data). Write operations change the state of the database, so we need to check that the expected change happened. They're also difficult because the state of the database is not the same anymore for the next test. If we don't make sure that the database's state is retained from one test to another, the read operations quickly become part of this non-trivial problem as well. So, how do we keep the state of the database from changing?

We could, of course, implement a set of undo operations into our teardown methods for each test, essentially undoing all changes made to the integration test database during the execution of the previous test method. The complexity of such undo-logic would soon explode in our faces, however, so we need another solution. Possibly our best option is something we call a transactional fixture.

A transactional fixture is a fixture—the state upon which our test methods operate—that gets rolled back into its original state automatically at teardown. As the name implies, we use the persistence framework's and the database's transactional capabilities for implementing this. In other words, we literally begin a database transaction in our setup method and perform a rollback in our teardown method. Listing 6.19 shows how this can be done with our Hibernate example.

Listing 6.19 Integration test rolls back changes using a transactional fixture

```
public class HibernatePersonDaoIntegrationTest extends
        HibernateIntegrationTestCase {

    private SessionFactory sf;
    private Transaction tx;
    ...

    @Before
    public void setUp() throws Exception {
        sf = getSessionFactory();
        ...
        tx = sf.getCurrentSession().beginTransaction();
        tx.begin();
    }
```

❶ Begin transaction in setup

```
    @After
    public void tearDown() {
        tx.rollback();    <-- 2 Rollback in teardown
    }

    ...
}
```

We begin each test execution by ❶ starting a `Transaction` for the `Session` inside the `setUp` method. From this point onward, all database operations through the associated `Session` object are part of the database transaction and will be rolled back when we later ❷ invoke `rollback` on the `Transaction` object in our `tearDown` method.

The fundamental advantage of using transactional fixtures over having our test suite constantly populate the database into a known state before each and every test is speed. Importing data from an external file can take a lot of time, and even with small data sets, the number of tests accumulates the problem with slower test execution. With transactional fixtures, we can choose to populate our test database just once before running our tests, knowing that our tests will always leave the database exactly as they found it.

The only significant disadvantage of transactional fixtures is that they cannot be used for testing transactional behavior. That is, if our test is supposed to test that a certain piece of code commits the ongoing transaction, it's too late for us to cry for a rollback in teardown.

If transactional fixtures help us retain the state of the database throughout our test run, how can we populate the known state into the database in the first place? Let's talk about populating test data into a database for our integration tests.

6.5 Populating data for integration tests

Let's say we're writing an integration test for a read operation such as `findByLastname`. Because we're no longer faking the results coming from the persistence framework, we need some data in the database. A somewhat classic but brutal way of accomplishing this has been to execute SQL scripts with a bunch of `INSERT` statements. Although technically a feasible solution, SQL scripts are hardly the most user-friendly and far from the most portable way of populating our test database.

We'd very much like some alternatives, and, luckily, we have at least a couple: Hibernate, if applicable, and an open source framework named DbUnit. Let's take a closer look at these two.

6.5.1 Populating objects with Hibernate

If we happen to be using an object-relational mapping framework like Hibernate, why not take advantage of the capability of creating object graphs in plain Java and of having them automatically persisted into the database? In many aspects, representing the state of the database in the same language—and same location—as the rest of our test assets makes perfect sense. Let's look at an example in listing 6.20.

Listing 6.20 Integration test populating data using the Hibernate API

```
@Test
public void testFindingAllSmiths() throws Exception {
    List<Person> theSmiths = new ArrayList<Person>();
    theSmiths.add(new Person("Alice", "Smith"));
    theSmiths.add(new Person("Billy", "Smith"));

    List<Person> allPeople = new ArrayList<Person>();
    allPeople.addAll(theSmiths);
    allPeople.add(new Person("John", "Doe"));

    persist(allPeople);
    assertEquals(theSmiths, dao.findByLastname("Smith"));
}

private void persist(List<? extends Object> objects) {
    Session s = sf.getCurrentSession();
    for (Object object : objects) {
        s.save(object);
    }
    s.flush();
}
```

❶ Create objects

❷ Persist objects with Hibernate API

The test for the `findByLastname` method on our familiar `HibernatePersonDao` class starts by ❶ creating a bunch of `Person` objects and then ❷ using the Hibernate API for persisting them into the database, flushing the session to make sure the objects are saved right away. Then, it uses the DAO to find the subset of those `Person` objects—now records in a database table—that have the last name Smith.

Notice how the test data in this test is right next to the production code we're invoking. Contrast this to a situation when our test would call the finder method and expect a list containing Alice and Billy Smith. Why is that so? Because the external SQL file that's associated with this particular test class has inserted exactly those two Smiths into the database before this test runs. When the test data and test logic are separated, it's much harder to figure out what's going on when a test fails.

NOTE Although we're populating the database inside a test method in listing 6.20, it is possible to use the same Hibernate API for populating the database just once in a suite or class-level setup.

Having said all that, there are also some downsides to using the API of an object-relational mapping tool to populate our test data. For instance, by relying solely on the object-relational mappings and the persistence framework, we might be missing problems that would become blatantly obvious if we had populated the data using raw SQL or some other lower-level format. Also, not all projects use ORM frameworks like Hibernate, so another alternative for plain SQL scripts is still warmly welcomed. Yet another potential downside is that it's harder to test-drive when we might not yet have a suitable data-access object to use for populating the data we need!

For a couple of years, and for many projects, that other alternative has been a tool named DbUnit.[9]

6.5.2 Populating data with DbUnit

DbUnit is an all-around workhorse for testing database code with externally defined test data. It can be used for populating the contents of a database from data files in various formats—most notably two alternative forms of XML—as well as for exporting the contents of a database into a data file. Furthermore, DbUnit lets us perform comparisons between two *data sets*, typically an external data file and the current contents of a database. We're not going too deep into using DbUnit (the project's website offers sufficient documentation and examples for getting started), but let's take a brief glance at how populating test data from external files works.

Getting to a known state

DbUnit provides a base class named `DatabaseTestCase` for us to extend. This base class makes sure to populate the appointed database with the appointed data set in the setup method. The developer's responsibility is to provide the base class with the database connection and the data set through a pair of abstract methods.

In practice, though, it makes sense to create an abstract base class of our own for our DbUnit tests, isolating the database connection and data-loading details into a single place rather than dealing with them everywhere. With that in mind, listing 6.21 illustrates what such a class might look like.

[9] http://dbunit.sf.net.

Listing 6.21 Abstract base class for DbUnit-based integration tests

```
import java.io.InputStream;
import java.sql.*;
import org.dbunit.database.*;
import org.dbunit.DatabaseTestCase;
import org.dbunit.dataset.IDataSet;
import org.dbunit.dataset.xml.FlatXmlDataSet;
import org.junit.Before;

/**
 * Abstract base class for integration tests using DbUnit for
 * populating the database to a known state before each test run.
 */
public abstract class DbUnitIntegrationTestCase extends
    DatabaseTestCase {

    protected Connection getJdbcConnection() throws SQLException {
        // obtain a JDBC connection to the database
    }                                          Create JDBC connection ❶

    @Override
    protected IDatabaseConnection getConnection() throws
        Exception {                                   ❷ Wrap connection for DbUnit
        return new DatabaseConnection(getJdbcConnection());
    }

    @Override
    protected IDataSet getDataSet() throws Exception {
        String resource = getClass().getSimpleName() +
            ".initial.xml";                          ❸ Load data set from disk
        InputStream stream =
            getClass().getResourceAsStream(resource);
        assertNotNull("Resource " + resource + " not found.",
            stream);
        return new FlatXmlDataSet(stream);   ❹ Feed data to DbUnit
    }
}
```

The two responsibilities of the developer have been fulfilled by overriding two abstract methods from `DatabaseTestCase`. In listing 6.21, we first ❶ create a JDBC connection using whatever means necessary (using `java.sql.DriverManager`, for example) and ❷ wrap the connection object with a DbUnit-specific `DatabaseConnection` object. The second responsibility, appointing the initial data set for DbUnit to populate to our database, is implemented by ❸ loading an XML file from the class path based on the test class's name and ❹ parsing the file as a flat XML data set.

With this base class, we can extend from `DbUnitIntegrationTestCase`, create an XML file to describe the data set our tests should begin with, and start writing the Java code for executing our data-access code against the same database connection that we gave to DbUnit. Listing 6.22 shows an example of a concrete test class that extends our abstract base class.

Listing 6.22 Concrete test class extending the base class from listing 6.21

```
import java.sql.*
import java.util.*;
import org.apache.commons.dbcp.BasicDataSource;
import org.junit.*;

public class PersonDaoDbunitIntegrationTest
        extends DbUnitIntegrationTestCase {

    private List<Person> expectedList;

    @Before
    @Override
    public void setUp() throws Exception {
        super.setUp();
        expectedList = new ArrayList<Person>();
        expectedList.add(new Person("Al", "Freeman"));
        expectedList.add(new Person("Bill", "Brewster"));
        expectedList.add(new Person("Juan", "Alvarez"));
    }

    @Test
    public void testFindAll() throws Exception {
        JdbcTemplatePersonDao dao = new JdbcTemplatePersonDao();
        dao.setDataSource(new BasicDataSource() {
            @Override
            public Connection getConnection() throws SQLException {
                return getJdbcConnection();
            }
        });
        assertEquals(expectedList, dao.findAll());
    }
}
```

❶ Invoke superclass, populating database
❷ Set up expected result
❸ Configure code under test
❹ Match expected with actual

After ❶ letting DbUnit populate the database from an XML file named after the test class, we ❷ create a `List` of `Person` objects named `expectedList`, then ❸ configure our data-access code to connect to the same database our base class appointed to DbUnit, and ❹ assert that the `List` returned by the `findAll` method matches our expectations. We're basically assuming (correctly) that

DbUnit will have populated "Al Freeman", "Bill Brewster", and "Juan Alvarez" into the database before our test method runs. The assumption is correct as long as we've placed a file named PersonDaoDbUnitIntegrationTest.initial.xml somewhere in our class path where the class loader can find it. How about peeking at exactly what the data file should contain?

Defining a data set

Listing 6.23 illustrates how we would tell DbUnit to populate Al, Bill, and Juan into a table named "employees" and their salaries into a table named "salaries" using DbUnit's so-called "flat" XML format.

Listing 6.23 Sample data set in the flat XML format

```
<?xml version='1.0' encoding='UTF-8'?>
<dataset>
    <employees employee_uid="1" start_date="2005-01-01"
               ssn="000-29-2030"
               first_name="Al" last_name="Freeman" />
    <employees employee_uid='2' start_date="2005-04-04"
               ssn="000-90-0000"
               first_name="Bill" last_name="Brewster" />
    <employees employee_uid='3' start_date="2006-06-03"
               ssn="000-67-0000"
               first_name="Juan" last_name="Alvarez" />
    <salaries employee_uid="1" salary="45000" />
    <salaries employee_uid="2" salary="50000" />
    <salaries employee_uid="3" salary="47000" />
</dataset>
```

The flat XML format works by encoding each row to be populated into a single XML element under the `dataset` root element. The element's name identifies the name of the table into which DbUnit should insert the record, and each attribute for the element represents a column name-value pair. DbUnit is smart enough to figure out basic type conversions based on the data type information provided by the JDBC connection. For example, the attribute values for the `start_date` column are nicely parsed into `java.sql.Date` objects if the column's data type has been defined as `DATE`.

Defining our test data in an XML format such as that shown in listing 6.23 translates to easier maintenance, as we don't need to change our test data when switching our test database, for example. Furthermore, the XML format is easier to read than SQL statements. The main downside to this approach of defining our test data in external files the way we've seen in listings 6.22 and 6.23 is that we've duplicated our test data in two places. One way to get rid of this kind of annoyance when testing write operations is to use DbUnit's provided data set assertions, which we'll look at next.

Comparing data sets with DbUnit

We can make effective use of DbUnit's ability to export the contents of a database as an `IDataSet` object in the context of comparing two data sets with each other. Compared to going back and forth between an XML document and Java source code, it is somewhat more natural to express the expected contents of the database in the same format we use to define the initial data.

There are three steps to accomplishing this—the first of which is to export the current contents of the database. That's as simple as taking the same connection object we've given DbUnit for populating initial data and asking it to create an `IDataSet` for us:

```
IDataSet fullDatabase = getConnection().createDataSet();
String[] tables = { "apples", "oranges" };
IDataSet justSomeTables = getConnection().createDataSet(tables);
```

Next, we need to get another `IDataSet` to compare the data set with. We can employ the same code we added earlier to our base class, after a small refactoring:

```
@Override
protected IDataSet getDataSet() throws Exception {
    return getDataSet("initial");
}

protected IDataSet getDataSet(String name) throws Exception {
    String resource = getClass().getSimpleName() + "." +
        name + ".xml";
    InputStream stream = getClass().getResourceAsStream(resource);
    assertNotNull("Resource " + resource + " not found.", stream);
    return new FlatXmlDataSet(stream);
}
```

By extracting the logical name of the data-set file into a method parameter, we can use the overloaded `getDataSet(String)` method in our test methods for reading an arbitrary data file from the disk and parse it into an `IDataSet`.

Now that we know how to get two data set objects to compare—the actual and the expected—we just need to compare them somehow. DbUnit offers a helping hand in the form of the `Assertion` class, which defines two overloaded assertion methods:

```
void assertEquals(IDataSet expected, IDataSet actual);
void assertEquals(ITable expected, ITable actual);
```

The former compares two data sets, whereas the latter compares two individual tables. The latter is useful when we're only interested in the contents of a specific table. By comparing one table, we can maintain just the specific part of the full database contents in our "expected" data-set file that we're interested in. Perhaps a more common approach to narrowing the comparison to what's relevant is, though, to ask DbUnit to export only certain tables rather than every table in the database.

With these two assertion methods at our disposal, and with the code snippets for exporting the current contents of the database and for reading a data set from the file system, we could now proceed to write a test such as that shown in listing 6.24.

Listing 6.24 Using DbUnit for comparing data sets

```
@Test
public void testSavePerson() throws Exception {
    JdbcTemplatePersonDao dao = new JdbcTemplatePersonDao();
    dao.setDataSource(new BasicDataSource() {
        @Override
        public Connection getConnection() throws SQLException {
            return getJdbcConnection();
        }
    });
    Person person = new Person("John", "Doe");
    dao.save(person);

    IDataSet expectedData = getDataSet("afterSavePerson");
    String[] tables = new String[] { "employee", "salary" };
    IDataSet actualData = getConnection().createDataSet(tables);
    Assertion.assertEquals(expectedData, actualData);
}
```

❶ Read expected "after" state from disk

❷ Read state from database

❸ Ask DbUnit to do hard work

After configuring and invoking some data access code, we ❶ read the expected contents of tables "employee" and "salary" from a file, ❷ ask DbUnit to extract the current contents of tables "employee" and "salary" from the database, and ❸ compare the two data sets to find out any discrepancies. Pretty simple, eh?

That's about all we need to know about DbUnit to get started. It's a simple tool that can make our lives a lot easier. It is, of course, up to you to decide whether to use DbUnit or not. In fact, we've now seen a lot of unit-testing and integration-testing techniques for data-access code, but we haven't yet discussed how exactly these two mix in our development process. The main question is whether we should drive the development of our data-access code with unit or integration tests.

6.6 Should I drive with unit or integration tests?

In a traditional development process, we proceed through stages of testing from unit-level tests to integration tests to system-level tests. But test-driven development is not a traditional development process. To start with, we don't have anything to test until after we've written our first test. From the perspective of getting production code implemented, there's little difference between driving with unit tests using test doubles and driving with integration tests that hit a database. Having said that, there are differences in what we can do with each type of test and what kind of a rhythm our development follows.

Let's first see at what our TDD cycle would look like if we were to use integration tests to drive development; then, we'll discuss how integration tests and unit tests mesh in our overall process.

6.6.1 TDD cycle with integration tests

Perhaps you've noticed that integration tests require some plumbing before we can get down to business. Building enough plumbing to get the first test written can take time—especially when using a specific tool or technology for the first time—but once the basic plumbing is in place, its evolution follows the same path as the rest of our test code through small refactorings and removing duplication by moving shared functionality toward utility classes or higher up in the inheritance tree.

Integration tests with plain Java don't differ from regular unit test–based TDD, except that the tests are somewhat slower to run. Integration tests making use of DbUnit, however, are more interesting. What happens once we have the necessary plumbing in place for DbUnit is akin to the following sequence:

1. Write a test method.
2. Run the test, getting a complaint about missing data file(s).
3. Edit the data file(s).
4. Run the test, getting a complaint about missing table, column, and so on (if applicable).
5. Implement a change to the database schema (if applicable).
6. Run the test, getting the expected complaint about missing functionality.
7. Implement functionality.
8. Run the test, getting a green bar.

This isn't radically different from regular unit test–based TDD, but it includes steps that imply a longer round-trip between two green states. In other words, our cycle becomes longer. Also worth noting is that, because we might need to make changes to the database schema, we might need to do some code as well as database refactorings[10] before getting to a form where it's straightforward to introduce the new functionality.

In my experience, integration tests can be used to test-drive data-access code effectively as long as the toolset is in place—a persistence framework that does most of the plumbing, a test harness that facilitates adding new tests easily, and a database that's fast to work with. That's not to say that we should start running around with just one hammer in hand, though.

6.6.2 *Best of both worlds*

As you know, integration tests can yield valuable information about our data-access code working properly with a database—something that we verify in unit tests only indirectly, relying on our knowledge of how the persistence framework's query language works, how we should use the API, and so forth.

One of the biggest downsides with integration tests is that the tests are slower to execute. The slowness starts to show with only a handful of tests; and with the full integration test suite taking up to 10 minutes to execute, the temptation to commit changes before knowing their full effect on the health of the code base increases.

Another downside of integration tests as a driver for development is that they're incapable of simulating certain situations, and writing a unit test using test doubles is often easier than setting up the test data for an integration test. For instance, it's pretty darn difficult to make a database connection fail temporarily just at the right time, although it's trivial to simulate the symptoms (an exception) with test doubles. Further, it's generally easier to wire a test double to return a set of domain objects than it is to populate a database with equivalent data.

With these trade-offs in mind, we don't want to make an either-or decision; instead, we want to find some kind of golden middle ground that mixes the best of both worlds. Although it makes sense to have a degree of consistency with regard to the kinds of tests our team writes for data-access code, it also makes sense to keep both tools in our bag and be able to pick the one most suitable for the task at hand.

---

[10] Scott Ambler's and Pramodkumar Sadalage's *Refactoring Databases* (Addison-Wesley, 2006) is the prime resource on the topic of evolving a database schema in a disciplined manner.

Before summing up what we've gone through in this chapter so far, let's take a quick look at a domain of data access we haven't yet touched—the good ol' file system.

6.7 File-system access

Remember Michael Feathers' definition of a unit test, which we saw earlier in section 6.2? Among other things, the definition says that a unit test does not touch the file system; a unit test can run in parallel with other unit tests; and a unit test doesn't require you to do special things to your environment to run it. The main reasons for having these rules for unit tests are speed and maintainability. Now, keeping the goal of fast test execution and maintainable test code in mind, what should we do with file-system access?

In short, we should avoid file system access as far as possible, instead abstracting files with Java's streams or the `java.io.Writer` and `java.io.Reader` interfaces. After all, most of the time we're interested in the data inside the file, not the file itself, and streams are well-suited for feeding data to our classes.

The question remains, then, how should we test that thin slice of our code base responsible for adapting the File API to our application's needs? We're going to answer that exact question in this section. Let's start with a little story from a past project of mine.

6.7.1 A tale from the trenches

I recently faced a requirement for downloading content updates in the background over the network from another server. The background download component was supposed to first download the new packages into a temporary file, apply some integrity checks, and then copy the downloaded package over the previous version of the package. This led to the introduction of a `ContentStorage` interface, which the `ContentDownload` class used for writing files and moving them around inside the system's content directory structure.

By faking the `ContentStorage` interface in unit tests, we avoided file access and the trouble of configuring file paths for the real storage implementation and cleaning up afterward. Furthermore, we only needed to deal with the file system in a handful of focused tests for the real, disk-based `ContentStorage` implementation, which limited the number of slow tests performing file I/O and the need to clean up the file system after each test.

Realizing that file access can be made to support testing is the first step toward improved testability. In the next section, before wrapping up this chapter, we'll look at a handful of practical tips for improving our file-access code's testability.

6.7.2 Practices for testable file access

Following good design principles generally leads to testable designs. There's something about file access, however, that somehow seems to make us drop our design awareness when it comes to reading from or writing to the file system. For some reason, we Java developers have traditionally not given a second thought to, for example, using the `java.io.File*` API directly from pretty much everywhere in our code base. OK, maybe it's just what I used to do, but I'd like to think that I wasn't alone. In any case, what follows is a handful of design tips for simplifying our life with file access and, specifically, making the test-driving of file access-related functionality as easy as possible.

Isolate file access behind an interface

Java's File API is good for the most part, but that's no reason to scatter file access all around the code base. The problem is perhaps most visible when we need to add or change functionality in legacy code, which does direct file access. If you're as lucky as me, you might need to create a whole directory structure in your test in order to successfully invoke the code you want to change. By encapsulating file access behind a custom interface and having the rest of the code base use that interface, we can usually get away with less setup code in our tests.

Pass around streams instead of files

When we have a piece of code that needs to, say, perform a *diff* operation on two files, the code easily ends up taking in two `java.io.File` objects. It makes perfect sense because we're supposed to be comparing two files. However, as it turns out, it doesn't make perfect sense. The problem is that the diff operation, for example, doesn't care about the file as such—it cares about the file's *contents*. In other words, the code needs to open a `FileInputStream` in order to read the files' contents, which in turn means that the `File` objects must refer to an actual, existing file in the file system. And this tends to require more code to accomplish compared to a situation where we could feed the file contents directly from Java code. Passing around stream objects rather than file handles removes this problem nicely for the majority of cases.

Use custom File objects

We're better off passing around stream objects than file handles in the majority of—but not all—cases. The exception is situations where the code needs more than just the contents of the file: for example, information about the file's location, size, and so forth. Even in these situations, however, we shouldn't blindly fall back on passing around `java.io.File` objects, because the testability hindrances are still there.

Instead, it might make sense to introduce a custom file interface, which would be a façade for the `java.io.File` API, offering access both to metadata such as the file's path as well as to the file's contents. With this kind of an interface, code dealing with files becomes easier to test, because we can truly simulate files without messing around with temporary files and directories.

A good candidate for implementing a custom API for the file system is the Jakarta Commons VFS project.[11] The VFS stands for virtual file system and does just that—allows us to swap in a purely virtual, in-memory file system for use in our tests while running with the regular, disk-based file system in production.

Use a dedicated temp directory

If we are facing a situation where we need to generate actual, physical files on the file system, it makes sense to use a dedicated temporary directory for all of our output files as well as for dynamically generated input files. By isolating all test files under a single directory, we simplify our test cleanup procedures into wiping a single directory.

Clean up before, not after

Speaking of cleaning up, sometimes it might make sense to perform cleanup only before each test and not clean up generated files afterward. The reason for this is that sometimes the generated data might be non-trivial in size. With large data sets, it's useful to be able to study discrepancies between the expected and actual data manually by using our chosen tools (a diff tool, for example) rather than have the failing test wipe out all of our evidence.

These are simple practices—not silver bullets—but they can make our lives a lot easier when we need to work with file-access-related functionality. But now, let's sum up the chapter and move on to yet other interesting and challenging topics.

6.8 Summary

In this chapter, we took a dive into the world of test-driving data-access code. And we came out alive and well! It turns out that test-driving data-access code isn't all that complicated after all. We tackled this on two fronts—using both unit tests and integration tests to drive our production code.

We started off by discussing how data-access code differs from general application or business logic and how data access spans several layers. From there, we moved on to refresh our knowledge of the DAO pattern and how it can make testing our code a far less taxing task than it could be.

---

[11] http://jakarta.apache.org/commons/vfs/.

Next, we rolled up our sleeves and went on to test-drive a simple DAO class using three different persistence technologies: the plain JDBC API, `JdbcTemplate` from the Spring Framework, and the Hibernate API. With each of these technologies, we saw the same piece of functionality build up and watched how the technologies facilitated test-driven development through their respective flavors of testability.

After learning how to test-drive data-access code with unit tests, we switched gears and grabbed a larger piece of the puzzle: writing integration tests for a DAO class against an in-memory HSQLDB database. We discussed issues to consider when picking a lightweight database for integration tests, including the importance of being able to put the full configuration under version control.

We learned to build the necessary plumbing for making integration tests a breeze to write, discussed ways of creating the database schema with SQL scripts as well as using the Hibernate API, and touched on the use of transactional fixtures for cleaning up after our tests. To complete our discussion of integration tests, we introduced DbUnit as a tool for populating a database and performing comparisons based on externally defined XML data files.

After seeing two different strategies for test-driving data access code, we concluded that they both have their sweet spots and should both be kept in our toolbox. We should use the best tool for the job.

To finish the chapter, we briefly discussed the nuances with file access and how to design our code to simplify dealing with the file system.

In the next chapter, we'll move a notch closer to the underlying platform and set out to conquer more unpredictable genres of programming tasks with our test-driven method: time-dependent functionality and concurrent programming.

7 Test-driving the unpredictable

Horses are predictably unpredictable.

—Loretta Gage, the oldest student at Colorado State University's College of Veterinary Medicine

So far, we've dealt with data-access code, web components, and regular business logic. The common denominator for what we've seen so far is that this type of code executes somewhat detached from the underlying platform and, most notably, executes in a predictable manner. Not all code is like that. In this chapter, we'll drop the gloves and go knuckle-to-knuckle against specific domains of programming in Java, which involve unpredictable functionality and are typically somewhat more complex to work with in a test-first manner:

- Time-dependent functionality
- Multithreaded programming

We'll start from time-dependent functionality because it's the least troublesome of the bunch, and then we'll move on to discuss the kinds of problems multithreading and concurrent programming represent to testing and, thus, to test-driven development. To finish off the chapter, we'll arm ourselves with knowledge of the basic synchronization objects provided by the `java.util.concurrent` package.

7.1 Test-driving time-based functionality

Many developers have at least once been faced with the problem of writing a test for a piece of code whose output or behavior depends on the current time. The problem with time is that we can't control it. That is, unless we make it so. Let us concretize the problem and the solution with an example.

7.1.1 Example: logs and timestamps

Say we want to implement a logging component for our home-grown Java EE application server[1] that takes an `HttpServletRequest` object and produces a matching log entry in the common log format,[2] which looks like this

```
1.2.3.4 - bob [09/Jun/2006:20:55:59 +0300]
    "GET /page.html HTTP/1.1" 200 5678
```

or this:

```
host - user [timestamp] "request line" status bytes
```

[1] You'd probably win pretty much any bragging contest among a bunch of Java geeks by revealing that you didn't feel the quality of available application server offerings was in line with your standards and that you decided to implement one yourself.

[2] http://www.w3.org/Daemon/User/Config/Logging.html#common_logfile_format.

Most of this information can be requested from the HttpServletRequest object. The only exceptions are the HTTP status code and content length—the two numbers at the end of the log entry. In other words, our logging component should accept an HttpServletRequest and the two numeric values as arguments to its formatting method.

Listing 7.1 shows what a simplistic first implementation of a unit test for our logging component might look like.

Listing 7.1 Naïve test for the log output

```
import static org.easymock.EasyMock.*;
import static org.junit.Assert.*;
import javax.servlet.http.HttpServletRequest;
import org.junit.Test;

public class TestHttpRequestLogFormatter {
    @Test
    public void testCommonLogFormat() throws Exception {
        String expected =
            "1.2.3.4 - bob [09/Jun/2006:20:55:59 +0300] "
                + "\"GET /ctx/resource HTTP/1.1\" 200 2326";
        HttpServletRequest request =
            createMock(HttpServletRequest.class);
        expect(request.getRemoteAddr()).andReturn("1.2.3.4");
        expect(request.getRemoteUser()).andReturn("bob");
        expect(request.getMethod()).andReturn("GET");
        expect(request.getRequestURI()).andReturn("/ctx/resource");
        expect(request.getProtocol()).andReturn("HTTP/1.1");
        replay(request);

        HttpRequestLogFormatter formatter =
            new HttpRequestLogFormatter();
        assertEquals(expected, formatter.format(request, 200,
            2326));
    }
}
```

Why is this a naïve test? The issue is with the log format including a timestamp, which is information that's not passed into the component within the request object or otherwise. In other words, the component is expected to query the system clock for the current time and produce the timestamp based on that information. Unfortunately, our test in listing 7.1 has pretty much a zero chance of ever passing if we're hard-coding the expected timestamp. We need to do something to work around this dependency on the current system time.

A quick hack would be to externalize the current time into an additional method parameter for the formatter. That, however, would postpone the need to deal with the time issue for only so long. At some point, we need to obtain the real system time from somewhere. Besides, passing the current time all around the code base would likely trigger all the code police within 50 miles. So, how about skipping that option and looking for something better?

Another, less ugly solution would be to extract the time-dependent part of our code under test into a method we can override in our tests. This would be a relatively clean solution for the logging component alone. Let's think a bit further, though.

Logging components aren't the only kinds of components in enterprise systems that care about time. Overall, we'd rather have a generic solution than fumble our way through each instance of system-time access with an overridden method—even if it would be just a simple one-liner delegating to `System#currentTimeMillis`.

Let's think about how to abstract system time so that we can fake it as transparently as possible.

7.1.2 Abstracting system time

There are a couple of ways a Java application obtains the current time and date. One is to invoke the static method `System#currentTimeMillis`; another way is to create a new `java.util.Date` object; and a third way is to ask the `java.util.Calendar` class for an instance.[3] What if we—instead of instantiating these classes or calling the `System` class directly—obtain our time objects through our own `SystemTime` class?[4]

Perhaps the least intrusive way of refactoring our code base toward a system-time abstraction is to replace the existing static method calls (`System#currentTimeMillis` and `Calendar#getInstance`) and direct construction (`new Date()`) with a set of static method calls to a different class, which by default delegates to the usual suspects:

```
long time = SystemTime.asMillis();
Calendar calendar = SystemTime.asCalendar();
Date date = SystemTime.asDate();
```

In order to fake the system time, we'd then reconfigure the way our `SystemTime` class obtains its time. Because we'd like to have multiple sources for the time, we might introduce an interface named `TimeSource`, shown here:

---

[3] If you haven't already, do look at the excellent Joda-Time library that simplifies working with dates in Java (http://joda-time.sourceforge.net).

[4] The idea of an abstract system clock comes from a paper by Paolo Perrotta, originally published in the extremeprogramming Yahoo! group in 2003. http://www.nusco.org/docs/virtual_clock.pdf.

```
public interface TimeSource {
    long millis();
}
```

By default, our `SystemTime` class would use a `TimeSource` that delegates to `System#currentTimeMillis`. In our unit tests, we could swap in our own fake `TimeSource` implementation. Let's see how that would work out—with the appropriate tests, of course.

Listing 7.2 presents a simple test, which verifies that `SystemTime` by default returns whatever time the `System#currentTimeMillis` method returns.

Listing 7.2 Test for verifying that `SystemTime` obtains real time

```
import static org.junit.Assert.*;
import org.junit.*;

public class TestSystemTimeAbstraction {

    @Test
    public void clockReturnsValidTimeInMilliseconds() throws
            Exception {
        long before = System.currentTimeMillis();
        long clock = SystemTime.asMillis();
        long after = System.currentTimeMillis();
        assertBetween(before, clock, after);
    }

    private void assertBetween(long before, long actual,
        long after) {
        assertTrue("Should've returned something between " + before
                + " and " + after + " (instead of " + actual + ")",
                before <= actual && actual <= after);
    }
}
```

Triangulate SystemTime's correctness with System.currentTimeMillis()

Listing 7.2 tells our `SystemTime` class to delegate directly to the `System` class, which is exactly what our implementation in listing 7.3 does.

Listing 7.3 Trivial solution delegating directly to `System.currentTimeMillis()`

```
public class SystemTime {
    public static long asMillis() {
        return System.currentTimeMillis();
    }
}
```

This was just the first step, though. We'd like to be able to configure an alternative `TimeSource` for the `SystemTime` class. Time for another test, shown as listing 7.4.

Listing 7.4 Test for verifying that `SystemTime` uses the configured `TimeSource`

```
import static org.junit.Assert.*;
import org.junit.*;

public class TestSystemTimeAbstraction {

    @After
    public void resetTimeSource() {
        SystemTime.reset();
    }

    ...

    @Test
    public void clockReturnsFakedTimeInMilliseconds()
        throws Exception {
        final long fakeTime = 123456790L;
        SystemTime.setTimeSource(new TimeSource() {
            public long millis() {
                return fakeTime;
            }
        });
        long clock = SystemTime.asMillis();
        assertEquals("Should return fake time",
            fakeTime, clock);
    }
}
```

❶ Reset default TimeSource after each test

❷ Swap in fixed time source

❸ SystemTime should use our TimeSource

In listing 7.4, we've ❶ introduced a teardown method for resetting the `SystemTime` class to use the default `TimeSource`. Not doing this might lead to a nasty debugging session when the remainder of our test suite would run against a different `TimeSource` implementation than we expect. All we need to do in order to drive in the configurability we're looking for is to ❷ inject a custom `TimeSource` implementation that returns an arbitrary, fixed time. Once we've done that, ❸ `SystemTime` should return our arbitrary time instead of the real system time.[5]

Now, let's see what the implementation might look like; see listing 7.5.

[5] As soon as we're doing this more than twice, we'll obviously extract the anonymous implementation into a top-level class named, for example, `FixedTimeSource`.

Listing 7.5 The configurable `SystemTime` implementation

```
import java.util.Date;

public class SystemTime {

    private static final TimeSource defaultSrc =
        new TimeSource() {
        public long millis() {
            return System.currentTimeMillis();
        }
    };

    private static TimeSource source = null;

    public static long asMillis() {
        return getTimeSource().millis();
    }

    public static Date asDate() {
        return new Date(asMillis());
    }

    public static void reset() {
        setTimeSource(null);
    }

    public static void setTimeSource(TimeSource source) {
        SystemTime.source = source;
    }

    private static TimeSource getTimeSource() {
        return (source != null ? source : defaultSrc);
    }
}
```

❶ Default TimeSource delegates to system clock

❷ SystemTime asks for active TimeSource implementation

❸ Use configured TimeSource, if present

The `SystemTime` class keeps its ❶ default `TimeSource` implementation stashed in a `final static` field. When ❷ asked for the time, the `System- Time` ❸ checks whether there's an explicitly configured `TimeSource` implementation available or uses the default `TimeSource`.

This is a simple facility implementing the Strategy design pattern that yields a lot of power when all of our production code obtains its time through the `SystemTime` class rather than directly from the standard API. The use of a `TimeSource` interface rather than setting a fixed time for the `SystemTime` class to return and returning a hard-coded time, also enables more sophisticated schemes. For example, we could effectively turn the hands of time from a unit test by providing a configurable `TimeSource` implementation.

Let's see how we could apply our newfangled `SystemTime` class to test-drive the request logging component—the one that got us into all this time-faking stuff.

7.1.3 Testing log output with faked system time

We need to change two things about our existing code: the way we obtain the current time in the production code and the way we define the expected output in our test. Neither of these changes is too big, so let's go ahead and see what our test looks like after adopting the `SystemTime` class. The rewrite of our log-formatter test is shown in listing 7.6.

Listing 7.6 HTTP request log-formatter test using faked system time

```
public class TestHttpRequestLogFormatter {

    @After
    public void tearDown() {                              ❶ Don't leave
        SystemTime.reset();                                  residue
    }

    @Test
    public void testCommonLogFormat() throws Exception {
        final long time = SystemTime.asMillis();
        SystemTime.setTimeSource(new TimeSource() {
            public long millis() {                        ❷ Configure
                return time;                                 fixed time
            }
        });

        DateFormat dateFormat =
            HttpRequestLogFormatter.dateFormat;      Build expected ❸
        String timestamp =                           output based on
            dateFormat.format(SystemTime.asDate());       fixed time
        String expected = "1.2.3.4 - bob [" + timestamp
                + "] \"GET /ctx/resource HTTP/1.1\" 200 2326";

        HttpServletRequest request =
            createMock(HttpServletRequest.class);
        expect(request.getRemoteAddr()).andReturn("1.2.3.4");
        expect(request.getRemoteUser()).andReturn("bob");
        expect(request.getMethod()).andReturn("GET");
        expect(request.getRequestURI()).andReturn("/ctx/resource");
        expect(request.getProtocol()).andReturn("HTTP/1.1");
```

```
        replay(request);

        HttpRequestLogFormatter formatter =
            new HttpRequestLogFormatter();
        assertEquals(expected, formatter.format(request, 200,
            2326));
    }
}
```

Again, the first thing to do is to ❶ make sure that after its execution, our test doesn't leave any residue in the form of a fake `TimeSource`, because the remaining tests might assume the real system time and we don't like surprises. Not that much, at least. Inside our test method, we ❷ fix the time to a known value by injecting a custom `TimeSource` into `SystemTime`. Having done this, we can safely proceed to ❸ generate the expected timestamp based on the fixed point in time.

With this relatively small change, we have suddenly made our test robust against time.

Adopting the abstract system time API

Using the `SystemTime` class in production code is simple, as you can see in listing 7.7.

Listing 7.7 HTTP request log formatter implementation using `SystemTime`

```
import java.text.*;
import javax.servlet.http.HttpServletRequest;

public class HttpRequestLogFormatter {

    public static DateFormat dateFormat =
            new SimpleDateFormat("dd/MMM/yyyy:HH:mm:ss Z");

    public String format(HttpServletRequest request,
                         int httpStatusCode,
                         int contentLength) {
        StringBuffer line = new StringBuffer();
        line.append(request.getRemoteAddr());
        line.append(" - ");
        line.append(request.getRemoteUser());
        line.append(" [");

        line.append(dateFormat.format(SystemTime.asDate()));

        line.append("] \"").append(request.getMethod());
        line.append(" ").append(request.getRequestURI());
        line.append(" ").append(request.getProtocol());
```

❶ Obtain current date and time from SystemTime

```
            line.append("\" ").append(httpStatusCode);
            line.append(" ").append(contentLength);
            return line.toString();
        }
    }
```

All we need to do in our production code is to ❶ call `SystemTime#asDate` instead of `System#currentTimeMillis` and use that time for creating the timestamp. This is good news, of course, especially considering that we might have a legacy code base that we'd like to migrate to using the `SystemTime` abstraction.

Before moving on, there's one thing about our log-formatter test that might warrant a bit of discussion: Our test used a static reference to the public `DateFormat` instance on the production code.

Testing for timestamp format

In listing 7.6, our test code used a `DateFormat` object defined on the class under test for building up the expected timestamp string. Isn't this a bit odd? Technically, the `DateFormat` could be anything but the common log format we want, and our test would still pass.

We could've specified the exact expected format for the timestamp separately in our test code. That way, our test would've enforced the correct implementation the first time. It would also introduce duplication between production code and test code. We could accept the duplication or refactor it away into a constant, or add a separate test that verifies the exact format of the timestamp (see listing 7.8).

Listing 7.8 Nailing down the exact date format

```
public class TestHttpRequestLogFormatter {
    ...

    @Test
    public void testTimestampFormat() throws Exception {
        String date = "\\d{2}/\\w{3}/\\d{4}";
        String time = "\\d{2}:\\d{2}:\\d{2}";
        String timezone = "(-|\\+)\\d{4}";
        String regex = date + ":" + time + " " + timezone;

        DateFormat dateFormat = HttpRequestLogFormatter.dateFormat;
        String timestamp = dateFormat.format(new Date());
        assertTrue("DateFormat should be
➥\"dd/mon/yyyy:HH:mm:ss Z\"",
                timestamp.matches(regex));
    }
}
```

Listing 7.8 effectively nails down the exact format for the timestamp by matching it against a regular expression. Although not an exact comparison, the regular expression combined with our previous test is sufficient for keeping the implementation in check.

Note that we could've used a regular expression to compare the full log-formatter output. That approach would've, however, effectively ignored the exact timestamp as long as it was in the right format. In other words, another test would've been necessary for checking that the formatter uses the current system time. We could've also made our first test more elaborate by defining the fixed time as a string that is parsed into a numeric representation by using the `DateFormat` object, thus enforcing the correct format as well as keeping the test relatively simple. That change, however, is left as an exercise for you.

We'll now move on to another inherently unpredictable domain of programming, where the unpredictability manifests itself in the form of not knowing exactly what gets executed at what time.

7.2 Test-driving multithreaded code

The idea in concurrent programming is that things appear to happen simultaneously. In Java, this concurrency is mostly virtual, which means that things happen serially but it all looks like it's happening in parallel because the thread scheduler interweaves tiny bits of the multiple threads' execution within the process to the CPU. What happens within each thread, however, is largely the same stuff that we do in sequential programs. After all, if we're only looking at a single thread, it looks entirely sequential.

This is also why many ideas and techniques we've learned for testing and test-driving sequential programs are perfectly valid for concurrent programs as well, although sometimes we may need to derive more elaborate techniques to take care of the intricacies of the concurrent implementation.

As a rule of thumb, it makes sense to start test-driving the functionality first in a sequential manner and then move on to putting in place tests that verify correct concurrent behavior. Isolating the sequential logic into a class or behind an interface makes it easier to test the logic in isolation and can simplify the tests we need to write for verifying the concurrent behavior as well. It is important to remember, however, that any synchronization activities within the isolated logic can have an effect on the concurrent behavior of the surrounding thread.

We'll soon go into more depth regarding how we can test for desired concurrent behavior. Before doing so, however, let's talk about the differences between the predictable domain of sequential programs and the unpredictable domain of concurrent programs.

7.2.1 What are we testing for?

With plain ol' sequential code, we're talking about simple program flows with clear rules and deterministic execution of the program logic. Concurrent, multi-threaded code is different. The execution isn't as deterministic anymore, with multiple threads interacting with each other and competing for access to the same objects.

Likewise, there's a difference between sequential and concurrent code in how we test for the desired behavior of our code. When test-driving code for concurrent systems, we are interested in writing tests not just for the sequential behavior but also for the concurrent behavior and, subsequently, a larger error-situation space.

Let's take a closer look at these two aspects.

Wider error-situation space

In concurrent programming, there are more ways things can go wrong, and the scenarios are more difficult to simulate. In other words, concurrent programs have a much larger error-situation space than their sequential counterparts. Furthermore, the test code might inadvertently affect the concurrency of the code under test, causing the phenomenon referred to as *Heisenbugs*—bugs that disappear when adding test or debugging code.

This difference in the number of potential errors is significant enough for it to be impractical for us to exhaust every possible error situation with our tests. Instead, we'll have to resort to simulating a select few explicitly, using our knowledge of Java's concurrency features and the driving design principles of the system we're developing.

Although such a manual analysis can weed out the most obvious—and perhaps the majority of—errors, we should also consider increasing our confidence in the system's concurrent behavior using repeated, long test runs to identify errors that seem to occur at random.

Speaking of different types of errors, what is it exactly that we want to test for when developing concurrent programs that isn't present in sequential programs? Well, the concurrent behavior, of course. But what is that?

Variety of concurrent behavior

There are two major categories of behavior that we typically target with our concurrency-oriented unit tests:

- Good stuff
- Bad stuff

In other words, there's some concurrent behavior that we want our system to exhibit, and there's some that we definitely don't want happening. We might define the good stuff as being desired functionality, such as a service being carried out asynchronously after a delay rather than synchronously upon request. The bad stuff typically consists of different situations or states we don't want our system to enter. The computer science literature on concurrent programming documents a number of such common problems with multithreaded code. Perhaps the two most important are *deadlocks* and *starvation*.[6]

A deadlock is a situation where two or more threads enter a state where each is waiting for an action on the other thread's part (which will never happen because both threads are waiting). Starvation, on the other hand, is a situation where a thread doesn't get a chance to execute, because the thread scheduler for one reason or another doesn't schedule CPU cycles for the starving thread. Deadlocks and starvation basically take away the program's liveness—that is, the system's threads' ability to eventually finish execution.

If these are things that we don't want to happen, what kind of things *do* we want to happen? Things we want to ensure happen correctly include these:

- Sharing objects or resources between threads (thread-safety)
- Method blocking behavior
- Starting and stopping of threads
- Asynchronous execution of requested service
- Synchronization between threads

The previous behavior is something we can, to a certain degree, test-drive into our system, and that's exactly what we're going to do next.

Let's tackle these one at a time, getting our hands dirty again, starting with object thread-safety.

7.2.2 Thread-safety

Code being thread-safe means that its semantics are preserved even when multiple threads execute the code concurrently or use a shared resource. Even though we as programmers think in terms of source-code statements being executed sequentially, the reality is that the compiler crunches our pretty lines of code into one or more tiny byte-code instructions. Instructions whose execution might get interwoven with that of other threads!

---

[6] With names like these, it doesn't take a degree in computer science to figure out that they should be avoided.

Java gives us programmatic control over multithreaded access to our code; but, unfortunately, our facilities aren't good enough for testing that our supposedly thread-safe code really is thread-safe. We do have some means of increasing our confidence, however.

Facing the limitations

The fundamental problem is that we don't want our test code to affect the concurrency of the code under test, which means that hooks through which our tests can control the execution of production code shouldn't be used because they often involve synchronization and thus can affect the behavior we're testing. Basically, we're looking for properties and invariants in our code that we can assert without any synchronization.

As primitive it sounds, a typical approach to testing for thread-safety in the absence of safely accessible invariants is an intelligent brute-force test. By intelligent, we mean a test that is engineered to maximize the chances of error situations taking place during the execution. Typically, this kind of test launches multiple threads to access a given piece of code under test, aiming at as high a concurrency as possible with the use of synchronization objects like barriers and latches. Without the use of rendezvous points like barriers and latches, the overhead of starting threads might even result in entirely sequential execution—with each thread executing to the end before the next one is started.

Let's look at a contrived example to illustrate a typical mix of brute force mixed with Java 5's synchronization objects.

Example of testing for thread-safety

Let's say we need a thread-safe counter, which knows how to increment a number and doesn't get messed up even when there are multiple threads incrementing the same counter.

To start with the basic functionality, we might write the following test to enforce the correct behavior in the case of normal, single-threaded access:

```
@Test
public void testBasicFunctionality() throws Exception {
    Counter counter = new Counter();
    assertEquals(0, counter.value());
    counter.increment();
    assertEquals(1, counter.value());
    counter.increment();
    assertEquals(2, counter.value());
}
```

This would lead us to the implementation shown in listing 7.9.

Listing 7.9 Sufficient implementation for single-threaded access

```
public class Counter {
    private int counter;

    public void increment() {
        counter++;
    }

    public int value() {
        return counter;
    }
}
```

Now, how do we ensure that our `Counter` class also functions properly when accessed by multiple threads simultaneously? By testing, of course. We need to somehow make multiple threads access the same `Counter` instance and verify that no increment was lost because of the concurrent access.

Listing 7.10 illustrates one possible way to accomplish this.

Listing 7.10 Starting multiple threads to increment the counter

```
@Test
public void testForThreadSafety() throws Exception {
    final Counter codeUnderTest = new Counter();
    final int numberOfThreads = 20;
    final int incrementsPerThread = 100;

    Runnable runnable = new Runnable() {
        public void run() {
            for (int i = 0; i < incrementsPerThread; i++) {
                codeUnderTest.increment();
            }
        }
    };

    for (int i = 0; i < numberOfThreads; i++) {      // 1 Start threads
        new Thread(runnable).start();
    }

    Thread.sleep(500);                                 // 2 Wait for threads to finish and assert counter's value
    assertEquals(numberOfThreads * incrementsPerThread,
                 codeUnderTest.value());
}
```

Our test in listing 7.10 essentially ❶ starts multiple threads to invoke a `Counter` object simultaneously and ❷ verify that the `Counter`'s resulting value matches the number of calls to its `increment` method.

The problem with the test that it fails only roughly half the time even though our implementation is clearly not thread-safe (the ++ operation is not atomic, and we're not synchronizing the execution of that piece of code in any way—`Thread#sleep` is about as reliable as the town drunk when it comes to synchronization). There are a couple of ways in which we can improve our test.

Maximizing concurrency in the test

The reason why our test in listing 7.10 passes every now and then is that the threads happen to execute sequentially, not in parallel. We can increase the concurrency of this setup by prolonging the activity so that the other threads get started before the first one finishes. In our contrived example, this might mean increasing the number of increments each thread will perform on the `Counter`.

Another solution, which also helps us get rid of the annoying `Thread#sleep` call (which slows down our test unnecessarily and still doesn't guarantee that all threads have finished their execution after the hard-coded sleep time), is to use a synchronization object such as a barrier to make sure that all threads have been started before letting them proceed to the incrementing loop.

Listing 7.11 shows an improved version of our test with the number of increments per thread raised 10-fold and using a `CyclicBarrier` to minimize the effect of thread startup overhead on the wanted concurrency. (We'll talk more about the `CyclicBarrier` and its friends later in this chapter.)

Listing 7.11 Improved version of our thread-safety test

```
@Test
public void
    testForThreadSafetyUsingCyclicBarrierToMaximizeConcurrency()
        throws Exception {
    final Counter codeUnderTest = new Counter();
    final int numberOfThreads = 20;
    final int incrementsPerThread = 1000;

    CyclicBarrier entryBarrier =
        new CyclicBarrier(numberOfThreads + 1);
    CyclicBarrier exitBarrier =
        new CyclicBarrier(numberOfThreads + 1);

    Runnable runnable = new Runnable() {
        public void run() {
            for (int i = 0; i < incrementsPerThread; i++) {
                codeUnderTest.increment();
```

❶ Create barrier for all created threads plus current one

```
            }
        }
    };

    for (int i = 0; i < numberOfThreads; i++) {
        new SynchedThread(runnable, entryBarrier,
            exitBarrier).start();
    }

    assertEquals(0, codeUnderTest.value());
    entryBarrier.await();
    exitBarrier.await();
    assertEquals(numThreads * incrementsPerThread,
                        codeUnderTest.value());
}
```

❷ Custom Thread implementation waits on barrier

❸ Threads begin executing logic

❹ Wait for all threads to finish

Listing 7.11 ❶ introduces two synchronizing objects of type `CyclicBarrier`. A `CyclicBarrier` acts as a kind of a flood gate: It only lets awaiting threads pass the barrier when the expected number of threads have arrived at the barrier and invoked `await` on it. We make use of these synchronizing objects inside a ❷ custom `Thread` class, shown in listing 7.12, which waits on the given entry barrier before executing its logic and waits on the exit barrier after executing its logic in order to rendezvous with other threads.

Because our incrementing threads are all waiting on the entry barrier, we can ❸ invoke the entry barrier from our test method in order to let the threads proceed only when all of them have been started—essentially not letting the thread startup overhead to affect our concurrency—and to ❹ invoke the exit barrier to block our test method execution until all threads have finished their increments.

Listing 7.12 The custom `Thread` class for synchronized execution

```
import java.util.concurrent.CyclicBarrier;

public class SynchedThread extends Thread {

    private CyclicBarrier entryBarrier;
    private CyclicBarrier exitBarrier;

    public SynchedThread(Runnable runnable,
                         CyclicBarrier entryBarrier,
                         CyclicBarrier exitBarrier) {
        super(runnable);
        this.entryBarrier = entryBarrier;
        this.exitBarrier = exitBarrier;
    }

    @Override
```

```
    public void run() {
        try {
            entryBarrier.await();      <-- Wait for others
            super.run();             <-- Execute logic
            exitBarrier.await();       <-- Indicate completion
        } catch (Exception e) {
            throw new RuntimeException(e);
        }
    }
}
```

The improved test in listing 7.12 already fails more reliably, indicating that some increments seem to get ignored due to the `Counter` class's implementation being non-thread-safe; and finally pushes us to add the `synchronized` modifier to the `increment` method's signature.

Although testing for thread-safety is certainly more complex than testing for basic application logic, it can be done, as we've learned. There's always an element of uncertainty in the form of tests passing accidentally due to thread scheduling being out of our control, but we can minimize the risk of these false negatives by understanding the problem space we're trying to simulate and improving the chances of the thread scheduler creating a potentially critical execution sequence.

In addition to testing for thread-safety, another interesting domain in testing concurrent behavior is that of blocking operations.

7.2.3 Blocking operations

Sometimes, we want a method to block until it has performed whatever function it is responsible for. For instance, we might want a transaction interface's `commit` method to block until the transaction really has been committed before letting the invoking code proceed with its execution. In general terms, we might want a method to block until some specific event or events have occurred.

This poses a couple of problems from the perspective of testing: How do we know that the method is blocking, and how do we unblock the method once we've made sure that it is, indeed, blocking? Let's look at an example and figure it out from there.

Buying tickets from the black market

Let's say you had forgotten that today is your spouse's birthday and that she's anticipating the Knicks game[7] you promised to take her to. The problem is, you don't have the tickets, and the game is sold out. As a last resort, you go to the

[7] We can dream, right?

black market for tickets, but you can't come find one. What you've got is a case of a blocking method: `BlackMarket#buyTicket`.

Because the method we want to test should block, we need to invoke it in another thread. Also, we need to know in our test method's thread whether the method succeeded or whether it did, in fact, block. Once the method has (we hope) blocked, we also need to unblock it by interrupting the thread in question and by verifying that the thread did interrupt and finish its execution.

Listing 7.13 shows an example test that does all of this.

Listing 7.13 Testing for a method blocking and interrupting properly

```
@Test
public void testBlockingBehavior() throws Exception {
    final AtomicBoolean blocked = new AtomicBoolean(true);

    Thread buyer = new Thread() {
        @Override
        public void run() {
            try {
                new BlackMarket().buyTicket();
                blocked.set(false);
            } catch (InterruptedException expected) {
            }
        }
    };

    buyer.start();
    Thread.sleep(1000);
    buyer.interrupt();
    buyer.join(1000);

    assertFalse("Thread didn't interrupt!", buyer.isAlive());
    assertTrue("Method didn't block!", blocked.get());
}
```

❶ Invoke blocking method in another thread

❷ Set flag if method succeeded

❸ Start thread, wait, and interrupt

❹ Assert expected behavior

In listing 7.13, we start a new thread for ❶ invoking the `buyTicket` method on the `BlackMarket`. The method should block because nobody has yet called `sellTicket`. If the method call does not block for some reason, we ❷ set a flag so our test can fail as a result of `buyTicket` not blocking. We're catching an `InterruptedException` around the call to `buyTicket` because, later on, we're going to interrupt the thread and let it exit normally.

Once we've created this kind of a thread, we ❸ start it and sleep for a second, letting the thread's execution reach the blocking method;[8] then, we interrupt the thread and wait for the thread's execution to finish. Finally, we ❹ assert that the thread did finish its execution and that the method call really blocked.

Again, perhaps a verbose test, considering that we're only testing for a method blocking as expected (and interrupting properly). Yet it can be done, and with a little refactoring we could easily extract all the plumbing into a reusable base class for testing blocking methods. Consider that an exercise for you.

Before we move on, however, there's one thing worth noting about the Thread API.

Don't rely on Thread states

If you've been working with Java's Thread API, you may have noticed that the `Thread` class has a method named `getState`, which might sound like the perfect fit for testing whether a thread is blocking. Unfortunately, `Thread#getState` cannot be trusted for testing for blocking behavior. The reason is that there's nothing in the JVM specification that requires a thread to ever enter a waiting (blocking) state. Furthermore, because spurious wakeups from `Object#wait` are also possible, a blocking thread might even temporarily enter the running state as well.

In other words, let's forget about `Thread#getState` and go look at other stuff.

7.2.4 Starting and stopping threads

One of the things multithreaded systems do is start and stop threads. Some systems start and stop a lot of them, and some less. Some software architectures hide the threads from the application developer, and some expose all the gritty details. Just in case we need to write code that starts and stops threads, let's look at a small example using some of the new APIs introduced as part of the `java.util.concurrent` package in Java 5.

Starting threads in a factory

Before Java 5, our only option for launching threads was to directly create a new `Thread` instance and start it. Java 5 introduced the `ThreadFactory`,[9] an interface shown in listing 7.14, which is exactly that—a factory class that creates a `Thread` object when asked for one.

---

[8] We're using `Thread#sleep` instead of a synchronization object for the purpose of simplicity of the example.

[9] If you're not using Java 5, you can still create a similar interface of your own. After all, it's just an interface!

Listing 7.14 The `java.util.concurrent.ThreadFactory` interface

```
public interface ThreadFactory {

    public Thread newThread(Runnable runnable);
}
```

In practice, the `ThreadFactory` interface acts as a handy indirection between code that needs to launch threads and the actual `Thread` implementations. By employing an interface like the `ThreadFactory` and adding a bit of dependency injection into the mix, we can make testing for proper starting and stopping of threads much like stealing candy from a child (albeit less morally suspicious).

Let's explore this with a little example.

Using ThreadFactory and custom threads

Let's say we are developing some kind of a `Server` class, which we want to be able to start and stop. When the `Server` is started, it starts a thread in the background to listen for (for example—we don't care) incoming network connections. When the `Server` is stopped, the background thread is also stopped.

We're going to give the `Server` a custom `ThreadFactory`, which creates a `Thread` object we can observe from our test. First, we need a custom `Thread` class that provides the necessary information. Listing 7.15 shows one such `Thread` class.

Listing 7.15 Custom `Thread` class offering synchronization points

```
import java.util.concurrent.*;
import static junit.framework.Assert.*;

public class StartStopSynchronizedThread extends Thread {

    private CountDownLatch threadStarted;
    private CountDownLatch threadStopped;

    public StartStopSynchronizedThread(Runnable task) {
        super(task);
        threadStarted = new CountDownLatch(1);
        threadStopped = new CountDownLatch(1);
    }

    @Override
    public void run() {
        threadStarted.countDown();     <-- (1)
        super.run();
        threadStopped.countDown();     <-- (1)
    }
```

(1) Trigger latches when thread starts and stops

```
    public void waitForStarted(long timeout, TimeUnit unit)
            throws InterruptedException {
        assertTrue("Thread not started within timeout.",
                threadStarted.await(timeout, unit));
    }

    public void waitForStopped(int timeout, TimeUnit unit)
            throws InterruptedException {
        assertTrue("Thread not stopped within timeout.",
                threadStopped.await(timeout, unit));
    }
}
```

❷ Provide methods that block until thread starts/stops

What we have in listing 7.15 is a simple class that ❶ wraps the regular `Thread` implementation's `run` method with two synchronization objects we call *latches*. These latches are used for waiting until the thread has started and until it is stopping—that is, exiting its `run` method. The ❷ `waitForStarted` and `waitForStopped` methods can be used by other threads to block until this thread has been started or until it has completed its execution.

Now, let's see how we could make use of this nifty utility in test-driving the `start` and `stop` methods into our `Server` class. Listing 7.16 shows one example of how this could be done.

Listing 7.16 Test to verify that a thread is started and stopped

```
import java.util.concurrent.ThreadFactory;
import org.junit.*;

public class TestServerStartsAndStopsThread {

    private StartStopSynchronizedThread thread;

    @Test
    public void testStartingAndStoppingServerThread() throws
        Exception {
        ThreadFactory threadFactory = new ThreadFactory() {
            public Thread newThread(Runnable task) {
                thread = new StartStopSynchronizedThread(task);
                return thread;
            }
        };

        Server server = new Server();
        server.setThreadFactory(threadFactory);

        server.start();
```

❶ Create custom thread and store for later reference

❷ Configure Server with custom ThreadFactory

```
        thread.waitForStarted(1, TimeUnit.SECONDS);

        server.stop();
        thread.waitForStopped(1, TimeUnit.SECONDS);
    }
}
```

❸ Use custom thread's latches to verify that thread is started/stopped

Our test in listing 7.16 boils down to creating a custom `ThreadFactory`, which ❶ returns an instance of our custom thread class and stores the object to a field for later reference. After creating the `ThreadFactory`, we ❷ pass the `ThreadFactory` to the `Server` instance under test with the intention of the `Server` class using the given `ThreadFactory` instead of the default `ThreadFactory` available through the `java.util.concurrent.Executors` class.

The remainder of the test starts the `Server` and starts ❸ waiting on the custom thread class's latch for the thread to start (or a timeout, in which case the test fails). When the start latch is triggered, we then stop the `Server` and wait on the stop latch, expecting the `stop` call to cause the background thread to finish execution.

7.2.5 Asynchronous execution

We've just seen how we can test for the starting of a thread and that a thread eventually finishes its execution after a specific event has occurred. What our tests in the previous section did not verify, however, is what happens within the launched thread. There's (we hope) a reason for our allocating a thread, so we're probably also interested in what happens in that thread. But how can we know?

Isolating the problem with typed Runnables

One possibility is to use typed `Runnable` implementations, verifying in our custom `ThreadFactory` that the code under test passed in a `Runnable` of the expected type (with certain expected properties, if applicable). Then we could separately test an instance of that type of `Runnable` with the same properties. In essence, we'd be splitting one problem into two—both of which are easy to solve in isolation and which together give us reasonable certainty of our code's correct behavior.

This would arguably be a rather odd way to program, however, and certainly is not an established idiom in Java concurrent programming, so let's consider a more typical (not necessarily better, mind you) alternative: waiting for results.

Waiting for results

Probably every programmer I've seen facing the problem of how to verify results from asynchronous service has solved it by waiting. Waiting long enough. Listing 7.17 illustrates this pattern with an imaginary test case.

Listing 7.17 Test waiting for results from an asynchronous service

```
LongLastingCalculation calc = new LongLastingCalculation();
calc.start();
Thread.sleep(2000);                       <-- Calculation takes 1 second;
assertEquals(42, calc.getResult());           wait 2, to be sure
```

How long "enough" is obviously depends on the service in question, and the necessary wait time between two test runs can vary a lot. Because we don't like our tests to fail randomly, we have to bump up our wait time so that we know the asynchronous service has had time to complete its processing. In this example, we make our test thread sleep before asserting for the calculation's results, assuming that two seconds is long enough. If the calculation typically takes one second, we're wasting (on average) an extra second every time we run this test.

Ideally, we'd register some kind of a callback for when the results are available, but sometimes this is not possible for one reason or another (for example, when we're working with an external API). Even when a callback is out of the question, however, we might be able to optimize a little by polling for the results being available. Listing 7.18 shows a handy utility class named `RetriedAssert`, adapted for JUnit 4 from code originally written by Kevin Bourrillion and freely available from the file area of the JUnit Yahoo! Group.[10] The `RetriedAssert` lets us perform an arbitrary assertion in a loop until the assertion succeeds or when we reach the timeout.

Listing 7.18 Retrying an assertion until it succeeds or a timeout is reached

```
/**
 * This class allows you to assert a condition that may not be
 * true right at the moment, but should become true within a
 * specified time frame. To use it, simply replace calls like:
 *
 * assert(someCondition);
 *
 * With:
 *
 * new RetriedAssert(5000, 250) { // timeout, interval
 *   public void run() throws Exception {
 *     assert(someCondition);
 *   }
 * }.start();
```

[10] http://groups.yahoo.com/group/junit/files/src/ (free group membership is required for access).

```
 *
 * The start() and run() methods were named after those in
 * java.lang.Thread, whose function they mimic.
 *
 * This class was written by Model N, Inc. You may use it and
 * modify it any way you wish--but please leave this message intact.
 *
 * @author Kevin Bourrillion (kevinb@modeln.com)
 */
public abstract class RetriedAssert {

    private int _timeOutMs;
    private int _intervalMs;

    protected RetriedAssert(int timeOutMs, int intervalMs) {
        _timeOutMs = timeOutMs;
        _intervalMs = intervalMs;
    }

    public final void start() throws Exception {
        long stopAt = System.currentTimeMillis() + _timeOutMs;
        while (System.currentTimeMillis() < stopAt) {
            try {
                run();
                return;
            } catch (AssertionError ignoreAndRetry) { }
            try {
                Thread.sleep(_intervalMs);
            } catch (InterruptedException ie) {}
        }
        // All tries have failed so far. Try one last time,
        // now letting any failure pass out to the caller.
        run();
    }

    public abstract void run() throws Exception;
}
```

❶ Loop until we reach configured timeout

❷ Attempt assertion and return if it passes

❸ Sleep before retrying assertion

The idea behind the `RetriedAssert` is that we can ❶ execute a loop until we reach the configured timeout, with the loop ❷ attempting to perform our assertion over and over again, and ❸ sleeping for the specified interval in between attempts until either the assertion passes or we reach the specified timeout—in which case the last assertion failure is propagated back to the caller.

Listing 7.19 shows an example of how we might make use of this utility class to test a long-lasting, asynchronous service without excessive unnecessary waiting.

Listing 7.19 Example usage of `RetriedAssert`

```
@Test
public void testByRetryingTheAssertOften() throws Exception {
    final LongLastingCalculation calc =
        new LongLastingCalculation();
    calc.start();
    new RetriedAssert(2000, 100) {          <-- 1 Specify suitable timeout
        @Override                                and retry interval
        public void run() {
            assertEquals(42, calc.getResult());   2 Override
        }                                           abstract run()
    }.start();                                      method
}
```

As we can see, using the `RetriedAssert` class is not exactly rocket science;[11] all we need to do is to ❶ specify a timeout and the frequency or interval with which the `RetriedAssert` will retry our assertion and then ❷ specify the assertion itself. Assuming that the `LongLastingCalculation` in listing 7.19 typically completes its calculation in one second, this test will typically complete successfully in less than 1100 milliseconds. If the calculation takes longer than two seconds to complete, the assertion will time out and alert us at around two seconds.

Note that in the case of a wrong result (say, 13 instead of 42 as we're expecting), we'll not fail fast but instead wait for the `RetriedAssert`'s timeout. Still, better than nothing.

So far, we've learned tricks and seen helpful utilities for testing code that involves launching threads in the background for producing some results (or wanted side effects) asynchronously. What we haven't discussed yet is scenarios where multiple threads collaborate in order to produce an expected outcome. That is, we don't know how to test for collaborative synchronization between threads. Or do we?

7.2.6 Synchronization between threads

Accomplishing big things often requires collaboration between multiple autonomously behaving parties. For example, constructing a summer cabin involves craftspeople of many domains ranging from woodwork to plumbing to insulation to painting. The painter, for example, can only paint a surface once the surface exists, so they have to occasionally wait for other workers to finish some tasks. In

[11] That is, unless you happen to be getting your monthly paycheck from NASA.

terms of software, there are synchronization needs between (worker) threads. How do we test for this synchronization happening?

In many situations, we can let the threads run until completion and assert that the expected invariants hold during and after the execution. This approach, combined with a pinch of divide-and-conquer, is often a good enough harness for ensuring correct behavior. After all, the whole point in having multiple threads is that they execute independently from other threads until they reach a synchronization point of some kind. With a little bit of effort and possibly test doubles, we can ensure the proper behavior of each individual thread, exercising our code for the major error situations.

Essentially, the problem of multithread collaboration breaks down to a series of simple synchronization problems—each of which can be tested for rather easily as long as we know our tools. Before we sum up the chapter, let's take a brief tour through the standard synchronization objects available in Java 5.

7.3 Standard synchronization objects

Although shared-nothing is the ideal when it comes to multithreaded programming, we cannot avoid solving the occasional synchronization need. Furthermore, we're not all rocket scientists,[12] and multithreaded programming is among the toughest domains in computer programming. This means that it's highly recommended to know and use the abstractions for interthread communication included in the new `java.util.concurrent` package in Java 5, rather than to invent our own wheels on top of low-level locks and the wait/notify methods.

We've seen some of the standard synchronization objects in action earlier in this chapter. We'll now cover all of them briefly, so we know roughly what's there and what kinds of problems we can solve with readily available objects.

Let's start with the simplest of them all, the semaphore.

7.3.1 Semaphores

A *semaphore* is essentially a limited set of permissions. Threads acquire a permission from a semaphore in order to do something. When the thread is done with whatever it was doing, it releases the permit back to the semaphore, making it available for another thread to acquire.

Perhaps the most common use for a semaphore is a *counting semaphore*, where the semaphore holds multiple permits, thus limiting the maximum number of threads concurrently doing something protected with the semaphore in question.

[12] I promise to cut back on using this particular metaphor.

As an example of where a counting semaphore might be used, we could build a peer-to-peer application supporting a limited number of simultaneous downloads by having each download thread acquire a permit before proceeding. A completed or cancelled download would result in the permit being released back to the semaphore so that the next download in queue can acquire it, and so forth.

The other type of semaphore is one with a single permit, which essentially boils down to the classic synchronization lock—allowing only one thread access a shared resource to perform some critical work at a time.

When a simple semaphore does not cut it, we can turn to the more sophisticated synchronizers, such as a latch.

7.3.2 Latches

A latch is like a dam. It keeps all threads reaching the latch from going forward until the latch—or the dam, if you will—is released. And when the latch has been released, it stays open forever. In other words, latches are disposable synchronization points.

The `java.util.concurrent` package includes the `CountDownLatch` class, which releases itself after having received the predetermined number of countdown calls. We've already seen a `CountDownLatch` being used in several code listings (such as listing 7.15), mainly for blocking the main thread until the parallel threads have reached a certain point in their execution.

7.3.3 Barriers

Barriers can be considered a special breed of latches. Perhaps the most fundamental difference between a barrier and a latch is that whereas a latch is disposable, the `CyclicBarrier` class allows us to reuse the same barrier instance multiple times. Additionally, although a latch could be released before all threads have passed it, a barrier typically requires all threads to meet at the barrier before releasing them in one big batch.

We could implement a poor man's reality TV show using barriers by creating a `CyclicBarrier` for, say, five threads. Each thread would upon startup call `await` on the barrier object, effectively waiting until all competitors are ready for a common start. When all parties reach the barrier, the barrier breaks, and all five proceed to carry out the next task, eventually reaching the barrier—again waiting for all the other competitors before proceeding to the next leg of the competition.

In addition to the `CyclicBarrier`, the `java.util.concurrent` package provides the `Exchanger`, which is a special kind of barrier for two threads exchanging data at the barrier. The canonical example of how we might use the `Exchanger` is an I/O component with separate threads for reading data from one source and writing the data to another. The two threads would basically swap buffers at the barrier when the reader thread has filled its buffer and the writer thread has written the old one.

Speaking of exchanging data, there's one more standard synchronizer we'll cover before moving on—futures.

7.3.4 Futures

Futures, represented by the `Future` interface and implemented by the `FutureTask` class, are essentially cancelable asynchronous tasks that produce a result. Instead of building a homegrown callback with the appropriate synchronization, we can share a `Future` between the calling thread and the thread that computes the result in the background. The calling thread can invoke `get` on the `Future`, blocking until the result is available (or timing out if using the overloaded method for a configured timeout).

These four synchronizers—semaphore, latch, barrier, and future—are the basic building blocks that we can use for constructing multithreaded behavior relatively easily into our applications. And knowing about them certainly doesn't hurt our ability to test-drive our multithreading programs!

And now, time for a short summary of all the things we've seen and learned in this chapter.

7.4 Summary

This chapter's title refers to test-driving unpredictable code. The two most important categories of unpredictable are time-dependence and multithreaded functionality.

We started off by investigating a simple example of a logging component, which needs to print a timestamp along with the log messages. We devised a couple of solutions for testing the logging component's correct behavior, including fuzzy matching for the timestamp portion of the log output as well as isolating the time-dependent part of the code and overriding it with a known value we can trivially assert against.

Along with these more primitive approaches, we also discussed a way of turning time from being something unpredictable into something predictable by abstracting the system time behind an interface we can control. Introducing a custom class into a code base to represent system time can make many seemingly complex testing targets significantly less difficult to write tests for and to test-drive.

After solving the whole thing with time being somehow outside of our control, we turned our attention to testing multithreaded programs. More specifically, we started by clarifying what it is about multithreaded programs that make it different from sequential code.

We dedicated most of the rest of the chapter to discussing how we can test-drive the various aspects of concurrent behavior we are looking for in our code. We discussed ways of testing for thread-safety and proper synchronization of access to shared resources. We discussed ways of testing for blocking behavior (and how to unblock), and we figured out ways to test for threads being started and stopped as expected. Finally, we learned how to test for asynchronous execution and how interthread synchronization essentially breaks down to simple problems we already know how to solve.

To give more ammunition for our forthcoming challenges with concurrent programs, we finished with a brief tour of the basic synchronizer objects provided by the standard Java API.

All in all, concurrent tests are sometimes more intimate with the code they're testing—and arguably somewhat more complex—than their sequential counterparts; but as we've seen, we can employ test-first programming and build confidence in our multithreaded code. As a matter of fact, it is specifically the relative complexity of concurrent programming that makes having tests that much more important. And there's no better way to ensure testability than by writing the tests first.

8 *Test-driving Swing*

Design is not just what it looks like and feels like. Design is how it works.

—Steve Jobs

I have spent most of my programming career developing backend systems. That is, things without a face—a user interface. Such systems are easy to write automated tests for because there's always some kind of a technical interface to automate. Things aren't as straightforward when there's a graphical user interface (GUI) involved, however. With GUIs, it's not just about the behavior of the widgets laid out on the screen. It's also about the GUI being easy to learn and use by a human being. It's also about the GUI looking good.

In this chapter, we will explore test-driven development in the context of Java Swing development. We'll begin by asking ourselves what to test in a Swing user interface. We're asking because there are aspects of a GUI that don't make sense to try to verify with automated tests—and similarly don't make sense to test-drive into the code base. After we've created an understanding of what kind of things we'd like to test for in a GUI, we'll introduce a couple of design patterns for the presentation layer that help us test-drive our GUI code.

After determining what we'd like to test for and how we'd go about structuring our Swing GUI, we then move on to figure out what kinds of tools we should consider adopting for testing our Swing code, taking a closer look at one open source tool—Abbot. Finally, we'll test-drive a bit of Swing code from scratch by using plain JUnit and the Abbot library.

Ready to improve your swing?

8.1 What to test in a Swing UI

What kind of things should we test for in a graphical user interface? That's not the easiest of questions unless you'll accept "it depends" as the answer. Although there's no simple answer or a universal testing guideline for the Swing developer, we can identify a number of disparate categories or properties of Swing code and come up with some answers by focusing on just one of those categories at a time.

Let's consider the following aspects of a Swing GUI:

- Internal plumbing and utilities
- Rendering and layout
- Interaction

Next, we'll run through each of these three items and discuss whether and how we might want to test our Swing code for or in relation to those aspects. Let's start with the internal plumbing because it's a nice low-hanging fruit.

8.1.1 Internal plumbing and utilities

Although user interfaces mainly deal with presentation and visual aspects in general, that doesn't mean that there wouldn't be plenty of tiny bits of code that are practically identical to the stuff we might write when developing backend systems, batch processing programs, or other less visuals-oriented systems.

Swing user interfaces need to perform validations and type conversions for user input, format strings for presentation, and so forth. This is typically stuff that has nothing at all to do with the Swing API, and it's just as easy to test-drive as the plain old Java code we write for any other domain—and it makes just as much sense to test-drive this kind of code as it does in other domains!

Conversely, where Swing user interface development differs from other domains is where we need to work with the Swing API, which leads us to the next of our three aspects: rendering and layout.

8.1.2 Rendering and layout

The Swing API is all about the rendering and layout of GUI components. If we want a button on the screen, we place a button component into a layout. If we want to display a lot of content in a small physical space, we wrap the component containing the content into another component that knows how to render scrollbars for navigating the content. If we want to display a graph plotting data from a database, we create a custom canvas component that knows how to place and connect the dots appropriately. This is the visual aspect of a Swing GUI. Now the question is, what kinds of things should we test for from the perspective of correct rendering and layout?

> **TIP** Don't test for looks or layout.

As a rule of thumb, I don't test for layout. That is, if I'm developing a panel widget that contains two buttons, I don't write a test for the first button's dimensions beginning 3 pixels from the top and 5 pixels from the left. Testing for such a pixel-precise layout seems to (most of the time) slow me down more than it would help improve the code base's internal quality. In other words, I'd rather leave correct layout to be verified as part of the visual inspection we need to do for the GUI[1] anyway.

---

[1] An exception to the rule might be a library of widgets that you publish to third parties. In that case, it might make sense to have automated tests for the precise locations and dimensions of your widgets when deployed into various kinds of layouts.

What I've sometimes done is test for rough layout. That is, I might write a test that says "button A should be above button B when panel C is rendered" or "button A and button B should have the same width when rendered on screen." These tests are less precise but also more robust because small visual changes in the component under test don't blow up all of my tests (for example, because the component's width decreased from 200 pixels to 196 pixels).

Having said that, there are occasions when it makes sense to test pixel-precise. An example of such an occasion might be the plotting canvas component. We might write a couple of pixel-precise tests to nail down aspects like a small circle being drawn around the center of each plot or the color of a line being green or red depending on whether one of its ends is plotted below the zero level on the Y-axis, and so forth.

When writing pixel-precise tests, we need to remember not to overdo it. For example, for our plotter component we should probably write most of our tests by verifying against an internal model—the plotting data—and have only a couple of tests that draw on a canvas using simple plotting data. If it's not truly necessary to test by examining pixels on the screen, don't do it.

Utility code, rendering, and layout aren't the only aspects of a Swing GUI, however. Utility code is just that—isolated utilities and functions—and the rendering and layout are basically read-only stuff. What we haven't discussed yet is the *write* operations for a GUI—the interactions that happen between different GUI components as a result of external input from the user or triggered by a background thread.

8.1.3 Interaction

Buttons, drop-down selections, and other nifty GUI widgets would be useless on a GUI if the user couldn't use them to interact with the application. The widgets are supposed to receive user input and alter the application's state. Sometimes, the widgets are supposed to interact with other GUI components—for example, to filter out available selections from a drop-down widget based on the state of another widget.

This kind of interaction is not as trivial to test for as the utility code that doesn't have any dependencies on the Swing API. It doesn't require a PhD in astrophysics either, though, because we can test for the desired interactions easily as long as we know the Swing API. For example, we need to know how a Swing component receives user input in order to simulate or expect it in our unit tests.

It's far more effective to describe ways of testing for this kind of interaction through an example, which we'll get to later in this chapter. Before we go there, however, we need to talk about a couple of design patterns for user interface code in order to separate presentation from the behavior of our GUI widgets.

8.2 Patterns for testable UI code

We cannot talk about user interface implementation patterns without mentioning the Model-View-Controller (MVC) architecture that emerged from Smalltalk-80 and that has been a major influence on the way we build GUI applications still today. To cut the story short, figure 8.1 describes the relationships among the three components of MVC.

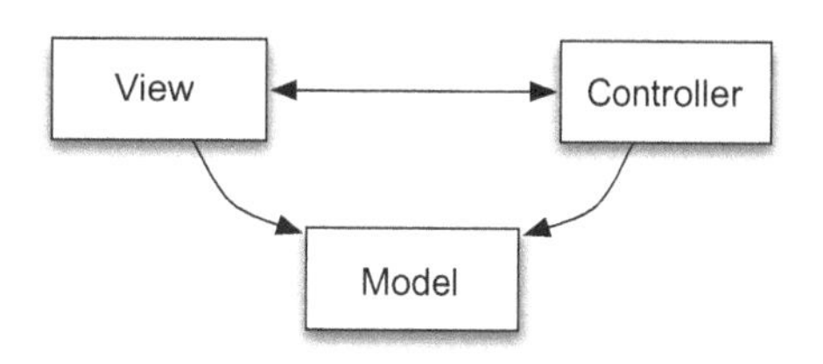

Figure 8.1 The MVC triad and its relationships. The controller acts on the model based on input from the view, the model worries about domain logic unaware of any details of the view or the controller, and the view registers with the model for change notifications and renders the data it obtains from the model.

In MVC, the controller's responsibility is to capture user input from the view's widgets and inflict the appropriate changes to the model, causing the view to update. The model's only job is to encapsulate domain logic and, if using the Observer pattern, notify registered views of the change. What's left to the view is the presentation—displaying the data it gets from the model.

Java Swing was heavily influenced by MVC, although it cannot be described as MVC as such. This is because the separation of the view and the controller in Swing has been collapsed into a single object "because the view and controller parts of a component required a tight coupling."[2]

The collapsing of the view and the controller into a single object is also what can make the traditional quasi-MVC blueprint architecture for Swing UIs slightly troublesome to test. The culprit is that we cannot test the controller logic separately from the view—and, to paraphrase Martin Fowler, visual objects are usually harder to test than non-visual ones. In most cases, it's possible (and strongly recommended) to test the controller and view logic by instantiating the appropriate widgets into a simple container window and then to operate the widget programmatically to simulate user interaction.

This approach doesn't work in all cases, though, or it introduces inconveniences such as slower test execution and difficulties in setting up an automated build on a headless server. Thus, if possible, we'd obviously prefer something that lets us test the controller logic and the presentation separately. Luckily, there are some close cousins of MVC that do just that.

Next, we're going to briefly describe three interrelated patterns that help structure our UI code in a way that supports testability and thus enables easier test-driven development of the UI for our rich client applications. Those patterns are:

---

[2] http://java.sun.com/products/jfc/tsc/articles/architecture/.

- Classic Model-View-Presenter
- Supervising Controller
- Passive View or The Humble Dialog Box

These are all more or less variations of the same theme—moving logic away from the view, making it as dumb as possible and, thus, alleviating the testability problem. In fact, we could consider the latter two to be variations of the classic Model-View-Presenter pattern.

Let's look at the patterns in a bit more detail, starting from a quick overview of the Model-View-Presenter and continuing with a closer look at how the Supervising Controller and the Passive View (a.k.a. The Humble Dialog Box) twist the generic MVP to their slightly different advantages.

8.2.1 Classic Model-View-Presenter

Model-View-Presenter (MVP) is a pattern that emerged from the work of Taligent, Inc., back in 1996.[3] In Taligent's MVP, the widgets that make up the view receive user input only to delegate them to a presenter object, which is ultimately in charge of handling the event. View state in this classic MVP was handled by the view listening to model updates using an Observer pattern.

The view is left devoid of any logic beyond rendering a face for the model, which makes the view straightforward to test with test doubles for the presenter and model. Similarly, the presenter has no dependency whatsoever on the Swing API and can be tested easily by passing in event objects and verifying that the model receives the expected changes.

In practice, this classic MVP pattern is more often implemented in one of the variations documented by Martin Fowler, the author of a number of popular design and architecture-related books. These variations are called *Supervising Controller* and *Passive View*. Let's take a look.

8.2.2 Supervising Controller

The Supervising Controller pattern[4] is a variation of MVP where the presenter (or *controller*) is responsible for handling all user input (the view delegates all user gestures directly to the registered presenters), and the majority of view-model synchronization happens through data binding, typically using something like the

---

[3] Mike Potel, "MVP: Model-View-Presenter, The Taligent Programming Model for C++ and Java," Taligent Inc., 1996, http://www.arsip.or.id/free_doc/m/mvp/mvp.pdf.

[4] http://www.martinfowler.com/eaaDev/SupervisingPresenter.html.

Observer pattern where model objects notify registered listeners—the presenters—of changes, who in turn trigger view widgets to pull the changed data from the model.

In practice, this organization of the presenter and view objects leaves little logic in the view layer. This, in turn, is important because view-layer code is generally somewhat harder to test than plain ol' Java objects. Not much, mind you, but difficult nevertheless.

Let's look at an example to see if it'll make things clearer. Let's say we're developing a GUI for a unit-testing framework. Such things cannot exist without a pretty green bar, so we definitely need one. Figure 8.2 depicts our Supervising Controller-based design for our green-bar UI.

In figure 8.2, as the basis of everything we have a domain object named `GreenBarModel`. The `GreenBarModel` is our model object and represents the most recently executed test run, which our green-bar widget should visualize. The `GreenBarSupervisingController` listens to changes in the `GreenBarModel` object and tells the `GreenBarView` to update its color according to the results of the `GreenBarModel`—the model. `GreenBarSupervisingController` also registers through the view for handling user gestures (in our case, let's say clicks of a Run button).

Listing 8.1 shows how our simple presenter class could look.

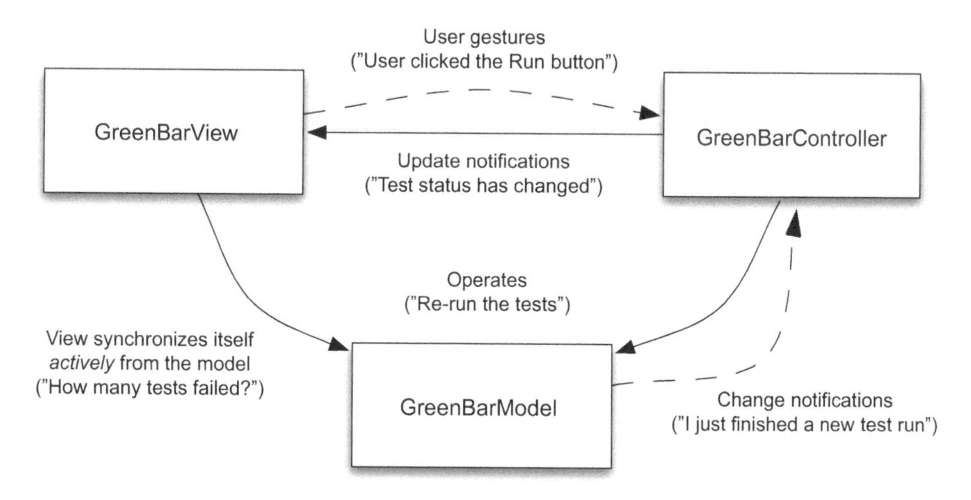

Figure 8.2 Diagram showing the interactions between the Supervising Controller MVP-triplet for a green bar user interface

Listing 8.1 The presenter implemented in a Supervising Controller style

```
public class GreenBarSupervisingController {

    private final GreenBarModel model;
    private final GreenBarView view;

    public GreenBarController(GreenBarView view,
        GreenBarModel model) {
        this.view = view;
        this.model = model;
        view.addRunButtonListener(new RunButtonListener() {
            public void onRunButtonClick() {
                model.runTests();
                updateView();
            }
        });
        updateView();
    }

    private void updateView() {
        view.update(model);
    }
}
```

❶ Register for user gestures

❷ Operate on model objects

❸ Tell view to update itself

As we can see from listing 8.1, the responsibilities of the presenter class are to ❶ register handlers for the various user gestures coming from the view, to ❷ operate on the model objects as appropriate in response to the user gestures, and to ❸ trigger view updates. Considering that the `GreenBarView` is an interface and that the `GreenBarModel` is a plain ol' Java object, the presenter is just as easy to test (and test-drive!) as any regular Java code. Also note that there's not a single `javax.swing.*` interface in sight—that's all left to the view.

Speaking of the view, let's take a quick look at the `view` interface for a Supervising Controller-style MVP triad—the `GreenBarView`, that is:

```
public interface GreenBarView {

    public void addRunButtonListener(RunButtonListener listener);

    void update(GreenBarModel model);
}
```

That's a pretty simple interface. There's one method for registering new user-gesture handlers and one for telling the view to update itself from the given `GreenBarModel`. We can imagine the concrete Swing implementation of the `GreenBarView` interface will be easy to test:

- Instantiate the `view` class, register a listener, simulate a click on the Run button, and verify that the registered listener received the event.
- Instantiate the `view` class, pass it a model to update from, and verify that the appropriate widgets now hold the new data.

We're going to look at how to implement these tests soon. For now, though, let's focus on the presenter and the overall pattern.

Notice how in listing 8.1 the presenter throws the whole model object to the view for synchronizing its widgets? That's just how I decided to do it for this example. In practice, the presenter could trigger view updates on a much finer-grained level. The trade-off is between coupling and performance (and becomes much more relevant when talking about complex UI panels rather than a simple one like our green bar).

Coarse-grained full-screen updates can be a serious performance and usability issue, which we could avoid by triggering more focused updates of only those parts of the screen that need to update. On the other hand, more detailed updates create more coupling between the controller and the view, which we'd obviously like to avoid. In practice, I'd recommend starting with updates as coarse-grained as feels natural; over time, if the performance becomes an issue, split up the update events as necessary.

That was the Supervising Controller variation of the MVP pattern. Let's see how the Passive View twists the MVP triad, making the view even thinner (and thus easier to test) than with the Supervising Controller.

8.2.3 Passive View

The Passive View pattern[5] (also known as the Humble Dialog Box, according to Michael Feathers' seminal article of the same name[6]) is a variation of MVP where the presenter is responsible for both handling user gestures *and* updating the view. The view only needs to capture user gestures and pass them on to the presenter; if something needs to change in the view, the presenter will explicitly tell the view what data it should present. In other words, there's no connection at all between the view and the model objects.

The advantage of Passive View is that the view layer has even less code to test than with the Supervising Controller variation of MVP. The view objects literally can't do anything else but display what they're told. This is also illustrated in figure 8.3.

---

[5] http://www.martinfowler.com/eaaDev/PassiveScreen.html.

[6] http://www.objectmentor.com/resources/articles/TheHumbleDialogBox.pdf.

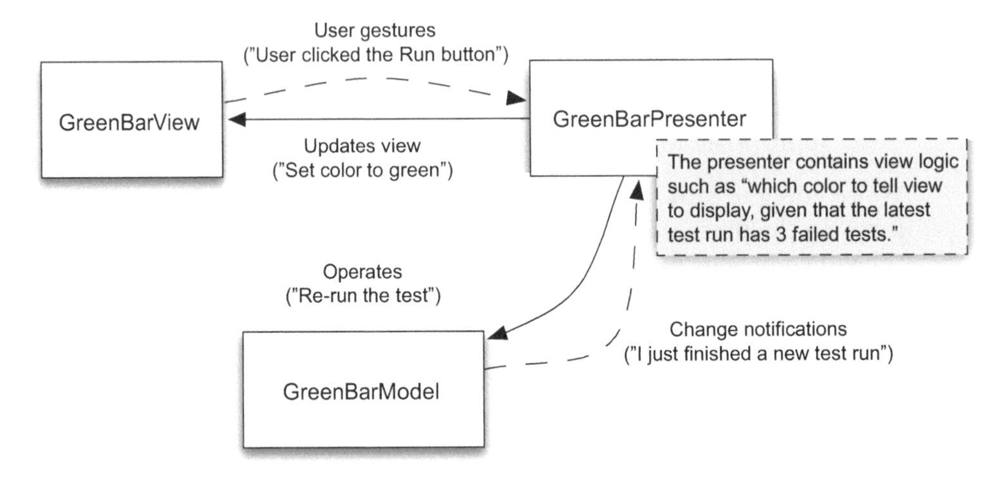

Figure 8.3 Passive View (or The Humble Dialog Box) makes the view as thin as possible, encapsulating as much view logic as possible into the presenter.

In our Passive View–based design in figure 8.3, we once again have a domain object named `GreenBarModel` as the basis of everything. In this second variation of MVP, the `GreenBarPresenter` listens to changes in the `GreenBarModel` object, figures out based on the state of the model which color the bar should display, and then tells the `GreenBarView` to update its bar color. Just like in the Supervising Controller variation, the `GreenBarPresenter` also registers through the view for handling user gestures.

Listing 8.2 clarifies figure 8.3 by showing one possible presenter implementation.

Listing 8.2 The presenter implemented in a Passive View style

```
public class GreenBarPresenter {

    private final GreenBarModel model;
    private final GreenBarView view;

    public GreenBarPresenter(final GreenBarModel model,
                             final GreenBarView view) {
        this.model = model;
        this.view = view;
        view.addRunButtonListener(new RunButtonListener() {
            public void onRunButtonClick() {
                model.runTests();
                updateView();
            }
        });
```

❶ Register for gestures
❷ Operate model
❸ Update view

```
        updateView();
    }

    private void updateView() {
        Color newColor = (model.numberOfFailures() == 0)
                         ? Colors.testsPassed()
                         : Colors.testsFailed();
        view.setBarColor(newColor);
    }
}
```

❹ View logic is in presenter

Looking at listing 8.2 and comparing it to listing 8.1, there's not that much difference. We still ❶ register for handling user gestures from the view, we still ❷ operate on the model based on the gestures, and we still ❸ update the view. What's different is that instead of asking the view to update itself from the model, it's the presenter that's now ❹ doing the work of figuring out what to display.

In the Passive View variation of MVP, the view doesn't even know that there's a model involved—all it knows is that somebody is telling it to paint the bar with a given color. The following code snippet shows our passive `GreenBarView` interface to confirm just that:

```
public interface GreenBarView {

    public void addRunButtonListener(RunButtonListener listener);

    public void setBarColor(Color color);
}
```

As we can deduce from listing 8.2 and the previous `view` interface, the Passive View pattern moves even more view logic from the view into the presenter, reducing the view's responsibilities to delegating user gestures to registered listeners and displaying what it's told to display. This makes the view implementation even simpler to test than with the Supervising Controller:

- Instantiate the view class, register a listener, simulate a click on the Run button, and verify that the registered listener received the event.
- Instantiate the view class, pass it a piece of data to display, and verify that the appropriate widget now holds the new data.

I think we've talked enough about patterns for now. Although the different variations of the MVP pattern (and many others, I'm sure) help us by separating concerns cleanly to allow for easier unit-testing and test-driven development, it should be noted (to the delight of Swing developers working on legacy code bases) that Swing code can generally be unit-tested even without a proper separation of the *M*, *V*, and *C*.

The stepping-stone for being able to do that is the low-level access we can get to the component hierarchy of a Swing application using a variety of open source testing tools, which we'll look at next.

8.3 Tools for testing view components

In the previous section, we talked about making the view layer of our Swing application as thin as possible so that the only two things we need to test are that user gestures are captured and passed on the registered listeners and that the component displays on the screen what it's supposed to display. What we didn't talk about was how to do this. And this is where the need for tools comes into play.

8.3.1 Why do we need tools?

Why do we need tools? In order to answer that question, I'm afraid we need to do a bit of legwork. Let's look back at one of the view interfaces we saw earlier, shown again here:

```
public interface GreenBarView {

    public void addRunButtonListener(RunButtonListener listener);

    public void setBarColor(Color color);
}
```

Now, say we'd like to implement the view in question as a `javax.swing.JPanel`. How would we go about it?

We want the UI to have two widgets: a button for running tests and some kind of a colored box to serve as our green bar. The first steps in programming a unit test for the view implementation are simple and shown in listing 8.3.

Listing 8.3 How to verify that the view works?

```
public class TestGreenBarViewImpl {

    private GreenBarView view;
    private boolean listenerReceivedClick;      <-- (1) Check for received events

    @Before
    public void setUp() {
        view = new GreenBarViewImpl();
        view.addRunButtonListener(new RunButtonListener() {
            public void onRunButtonClick() {
                listenerReceivedClick = true;
            }
        });
```

```
    }

    @Test
    public void viewShouldDisplayTheBarInTheGivenColor()
            throws Exception {
        view.setBarColor(Color.GREEN);                    <-- Simulate the
        // How to verify that the bar really is green?  (2) presenter
    }

    @Test
    public void viewShouldDelegateGesturesToListener()
            throws Exception {
        // How to simulate a click on the "Run" button?
        // How to know whether the button is there at all?
        assertTrue(listenerReceivedClick);     <-- Check for received events (1)
    }
}
```

Listing 8.3 illustrates how we have easily solved half of both of our problems but neither completely. We can easily ❶ register our own handler for the user gestures passed on from the view, but we don't know how to trigger a user gesture on the button. In fact, we don't even know how to test that the button exists in the component. On the other hand, we can easily ❷ simulate the presenter telling the view what to display, but we don't know how to verify that the view does what it's told.

Let's think about some options. Essentially, what we need is access to the Run button for triggering a click event and access to the bar widget for comparing its color to the expected color. We *could* have our tests announce that those particular components are public fields on the `view` class or are accessible through public `accessor` methods. But we don't want to do that. Even without mentioning the word *encapsulation* and the standard Swing idioms of creating anonymous classes all around the place, we'd be exposing individual widgets by and large for the sole purpose of being able to operate them from our unit tests. No thanks.

Fortunately, there's another way made possible by Swing's component hierarchy and Java's powerful Reflection API. Having a reference to a top-level container such as a `JFrame`, we can use the Reflection API to recursively search through the nested container components until we find the one Swing component we want to manipulate.

If that sounds like a lot of work, you're right. It is. And that's why Other People™ have created tools for automating the grudge of the work! Let's talk a bit about what we want from such a tool, compare two of the most popular such tools, and then have a closer look at one of them in particular.

8.3.2 TDD-friendly tools

What do we want from a tool for testing and test-driving Swing components? It's obvious that we want to find components from a hierarchy and operate on them. The different ways we'd like to be able to do that are various, however.

Most of the time, we can probably just refer to a component by its unique name or identifier; but sometimes we want to be less specific and, say, refer to a relative position in the hierarchy. Sometimes we'd like to just get the only button on the pop-up window with a specific title, and sometimes it'd be nice to find the component based on its class. The more of these different ways a tool supports, the better.

What about manipulating the widgets? We need to be able to click buttons and change the content of text fields, but there's more. In some cases, we don't want to just change the content of a text field. Sometimes we want to t-y-p-e into one, keystroke by keystroke, and verify that the field reacts as expected. We want to simulate durations. We might want a component to accelerate whatever it's doing the longer the user keeps a key pressed down. And then there's the mouse, which has many more gestures we might need to simulate.

It's obvious that there's a lot to expect from a Swing test automation library. At the moment there are two libraries in particular that satisfy our needs well. They're called Abbot and Jemmy, they're both open source, and they're both mature projects and have seen plenty of usage around the world. Let's start our tour with the latter. Oh, and before we start the tour, the goal is not to learn both of these APIs throughout but rather to get an idea of what the APIs *look like.*

Jemmy

Jemmy (http://jemmy.netbeans.org/) is a library originally developed by the NetBeans team for their own use[7] and later open sourced to the benefit of the whole Swing-developing Java community. In short, Jemmy provides an API for accessing the internals of a Java Swing UI. It does this by hooking onto the Swing event queue, listening for events, and locating individual components through those events. Having a reference to a component, we can then use Jemmy's API for simulating keystrokes and mouse gestures or interrogate components for their precious data from our unit tests.

[7] There's also an extension to Jemmy called JellyTools (http://jellytools.netbeans.org), also developed by the NetBeans team, which provides additional features for working with NetBeans platform-specific components.

Listing 8.4 shows how we might've implemented the tests from listing 8.3 using the Jemmy API.

Listing 8.4 View tests implemented with Jemmy

```
import org.netbeans.jemmy.operators.JButtonOperator;
import org.netbeans.jemmy.operators.JComponentOperator;
import org.netbeans.jemmy.operators.JFrameOperator;

public class TestGreenBarViewWithJemmy {

    private int buttonClicks;

    private GreenBarViewImpl view;

    private JFrameOperator frameOp;

    @Before
    public void setUp() {
        view = new GreenBarViewImpl();
        buttonClicks = 0;
        view.addRunButtonListener(new RunButtonListener() {
            public void onRunButtonClick() {
                buttonClicks++;
            }
        });
        showFrame(view);
    }

    @After
    public void tearDown() {
        frameOp.dispose();
    }

    private void showFrame(Component component) {
        JFrame frame = new JFrame();
        frame.getContentPane().add(component);
        frame.pack();
        frame.setVisible(true);
        frameOp = new JFrameOperator(frame);
    }

    @Test
    public void viewShouldDisplayTheBarInTheGivenColor()
            throws Exception {
        Color desiredColor = Color.GREEN;
        view.setBarColor(desiredColor);
        JComponentOperator barOp = new JComponentOperator(
                frameOp, new NameBasedChooser("bar"));
        assertEquals(desiredColor, barOp.getBackground());
```

1 Display component in JFrame

2 Dispose of frame afterward

3 Locate components using operators and choosers

```
        assertEquals(desiredColor, barOp.getForeground());
    }

    @Test
    public void viewShouldDelegateGesturesToListener()          ❸ Locate
            throws Exception {                                     components
        JButtonOperator buttonOp = new JButtonOperator(            using operators
                frameOp, new NameBasedChooser("run_button"));      and choosers
        assertEquals(0, this.buttonClicks);
        buttonOp.doClick();                        <-- Simulate user gestures
        assertEquals(1, this.buttonClicks);            with operators
    }
}
```

In listing 8.4, our test class's setup method creates the view component we want to test and ❶ places it into a JFrame for display onscreen. Because we're creating new frames in the setup, we also need to get rid of them by ❷ disposing of the frames in the teardown method. This is the kind of common plumbing code that we should move into a common base class as soon as we create our second Jemmy test case.

Now, how do we solve our problem of getting access to the widgets we want to manipulate? With Jemmy, we do that with the help of two good friends—a *component operator* and a *component chooser*. As we can see in listing 8.4, in both test methods we're ❸ creating some kind of an operator object, passing in a JFrameOperator and a NameBasedChooser as arguments. What's happening here is that we're telling, for example, the constructor of the JButtonOperator class to search through the components inside a given container—the JFrame—and consult the given chooser object regarding which of the child components is the one we're looking for. In the case of the NameBasedChooser, the component is identified by its name property, accessed using Component#getName.

An essential part of the API is the ComponentChooser interface, and in listing 8.4 we're using a concrete implementation named NameBasedChooser. This is not part of the Jemmy API; it's part of our own implementation, shown in listing 8.5.

Listing 8.5 Custom name-based ComponentChooser implementation for Jemmy

```
import org.netbeans.jemmy.ComponentChooser;

public class NameBasedChooser implements ComponentChooser {

    private final String name;

    public NameBasedChooser(String name) {
        this.name = name;
```

```
    }

    public boolean checkComponent(Component c) {
        return name.equals(c.getName());          <-- Identify desired
    }                                                  component by name

    public String getDescription() {
        return "Component named '" + name + "'";
    }
}
```

From listing 8.5, we can see that the ComponentChooser interface is probably not among the biggest we've seen. It defines a checkComponent method, which we've implemented in listing 8.5 by comparing the return value of the candidate component's getName method to the one we're looking for. The other method defined in the ComponentChooser interface is called getDescription and exists purely for informative purposes—Jemmy by default prints out what it's doing to the standard output using the different component choosers' getDescription method to provide a meaningful description. Also, when an operator doesn't find what it's looking for within the configured timeout, Jemmy uses the chooser's description to render a meaningful failure message.

Basic component-finding implementations such as the one in listing 8.5 are arguably something that a tool such as Jemmy should provide. The different ComponentChooser implementations we typically need aren't too difficult to implement, however, so it's not exactly a showstopper.

I've been using Jemmy for as long as I can remember and haven't looked back all that much—it's easy to use, and once the initial plumbing is in place, it just works (which can't be said about all of the tools I've used along the years). Having said that, Jemmy does have a worthy competitor in Abbot, which we'll introduce next.

Abbot

Abbot (http://abbot.sourceforge.net) is not a new player in the Swing-testing scene. Its development has, however, recently picked up (including the support for the Eclipse Standard Widget Toolkit [SWT] graphics library in addition to Swing). Abbot uses a slightly different approach compared to Jemmy. Whereas Jemmy works its magic on the Swing event queue, Abbot makes more use of operating-system-level events. This gives Abbot the benefit of being closer to the real thing, although the difference isn't that significant in my experience.

What's perhaps a more important difference is that Abbot provides explicit support for unit testing. This is illustrated to some degree in listing 8.6, which uses Abbot to re-implement the test we saw earlier in listing 8.4.

Listing 8.6 View tests implemented with Abbot

```
import junit.extensions.abbot.ComponentTestFixture;
import abbot.finder.matchers.NameMatcher;
import abbot.tester.ComponentTester;

public class TestGreenBarViewWithAbbot extends
    ComponentTestFixture {

    private GreenBarViewImpl view;
    private int buttonClicks;

    @Override
    protected void setUp() throws Exception {
        super.setUp();
        view = new GreenBarViewImpl();
        buttonClicks = 0;
        view.addRunButtonListener(new RunButtonListener() {
            public void onRunButtonClick() {
                buttonClicks++;
            }
        });
        showFrame(view);          // (1) Ask Abbot to place component in frame
    }

    public void testViewShouldDisplayTheBarInTheGivenColor()
            throws Exception {
        Color desiredColor = Color.GREEN;
        view.setBarColor(desiredColor);
        Component bar = componentNamed("bar");      // (2) Locate components by names
        assertEquals(desiredColor, bar.getBackground());
        assertEquals(desiredColor, bar.getForeground());
    }

    public void testViewShouldDelegateGesturesToListener()
            throws Exception {
        Component button = componentNamed("run_button");
        assertEquals(0, buttonClicks);
        new ComponentTester().actionClick(button);    // (3) Simulate user gestures with ComponentTester
        assertEquals(1, buttonClicks);
    }

    private Component componentNamed(String name)
        throws Exception {
        return getFinder().find(view, new NameMatcher(name));
    }
}
```

In listing 8.6, we can observe some of Abbot's main features in action. For starters, after creating and configuring our view component in the setup method, we ❶ ask Abbot to put our component into a `JFrame` so that we can test it. In our two test methods, we can see how Abbot lets us locate components using what Abbot calls *matchers*. In both tests, we ❷ use a name-based matcher to find the Run button and the green bar. Finally, in `testViewShouldDelegateGesturesToListener`, we ❸ use Abbot's `ComponentTester` utility to simulate a click on the Run button.

As you may have noticed, although the Jemmy project only provides a library for connecting to Swing components, the Abbot project also provides these nice little utilities, such as a base class to extend our own tests from, moving some plumbing away from our eyes.

One such base class that's especially handy is the `ComponentTestFixture`, from which our test in listing 8.6 extends. In addition to giving us access to the component finder and the `showFrame` method, the `ComponentTestFixture` also, for example, catches exceptions thrown on the event dispatch thread and re-throws them as test failures—which is an ugly business to do yourself.

All in all Abbot has a lot going for it, and it's being developed further. When push comes to shove, either of these two tools we've seen can pull through, so it's more about personal preference regarding which of the two slightly different APIs seems to fit your hands better.

We've now talked about making our views as thin as possible with design patterns such as Passive View and Supervising Controller. We've also seen two open source libraries that facilitate testing view components, giving us access to widgets we can operate. So far we haven't, however, written much view code. It's time to correct that by test-driving a view component from scratch, making use of everything we have in our TDD trick bag—including Abbot and Jemmy, the two Swing testing libraries we just learned about.

8.4 Test-driving a view component

To finish this chapter, we're going to test-drive a view component. Exactly what kind of a view component? That's a good question, and I'm glad you asked. We're going to build a *plot map* component. What do I mean by a plot map component? Let's pull up some virtual pen and paper and look at figure 8.4.

Let's go through the individual UI widgets shown in the design sketch one at a time. First of all, there's a canvas on which the component should draw a series of plot points connected with straight lines. In the bottom-left corner of the UI are two text fields for typing in the X and Y coordinates for a new plot point; this adds a button with the text *ADD* on it for adding the plot point. In addition to the

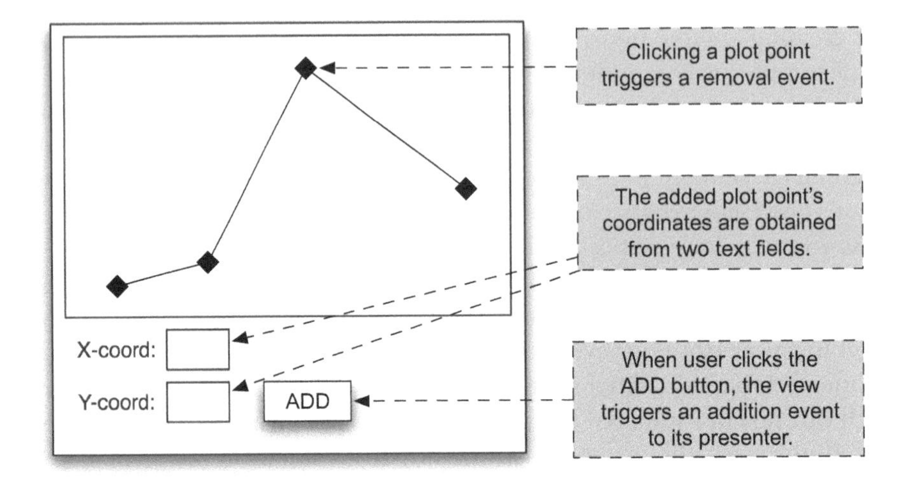

Figure 8.4 UI design sketch for the plot map component explaining the desired responses to user gestures

text fields and the button, the plot points drawn on the canvas should respond to mouse clicks, triggering the removal of the plot point in question.

In the following sections, we will set out to develop this small graphical component with test-driven development. We'll begin by laying out the bits and pieces of our MVP-based design and then proceed to building up the widget. We'll first drive the component widgets, such as text fields and buttons, into the view and wire them up with behavior. Then, we'll add a bit of custom-drawn graphics and eventually make the widget react properly to user gestures on our graph.

Now, let's talk about what should happen under the hood when we're done.

8.4.1 Laying out the design

At this point, we have some kind of a sketch drawing of the widget and an idea of what the widget needs to do. Now, we need to fill the pretty picture with something concrete: code.

Technically speaking, our widget will be connected to a model object that consists of a series of points described in terms of X and Y coordinates. The model class is called `PlotMapModel`; we'll assume that we've already implemented it.

The view component we need to implement should implement the `PlotMapView` interface, shown here:

```
public interface PlotMapView {

    void registerAdditionListener(PlotAdditionListener listener);

    void registerRemovalListener(PlotRemovalListener listener);

    void drawPlotMap(PlotMapModel model);
}
```

From this interface, we can already deduce that there will be two kinds of user gestures the view should delegate to its registered listeners (the presenter): the user *adding* a new plot point and the user *removing* an existing plot point. The `drawPlotMap` method is how the presenter tells the view to update itself.

The two listener interfaces are also straightforward, as can be seen from the following snippets:

```
import java.awt.Point;

public interface PlotAdditionListener {

    void plotWasAdded(Point plot);
}

public interface PlotRemovalListener {

    void plotWasRemoved(Point plot);
}
```

When an addition or removal event reaches the plot map component's presenter, the presenter will modify the underlying `PlotMapModel` accordingly and subsequently invoke the `PlotMapView`'s `drawPlotMap` method to synchronize the view.

For the sake of completeness, listing 8.7 shows the outline of the model class, `PlotMapModel`.

Listing 8.7 The model class in all of its simplicity

```
import java.util.*;
import java.awt.Point;

public class PlotMapModel {

    private List<Point> plots = new ArrayList<Point>();

    public void add(Point plot) {
        plots.add(plot);
    }

    public void remove(Point plot) {
        plots.remove(plot);
```

```
    }

    public List<Point> points() {
        return plots;
    }
}
```

Looking at listing 8.7, the `add` and `remove` methods are invoked by the presenter, and the `points` method will be used by the view for pulling the plot points it needs to draw.

We should now have an idea of what we need to bring into life. It comes down to the following three features:

- *Adding plot points*—Add a pair of text fields and a button that, when clicked, triggers the expected event.
- *Drawing plot points*—Given a series of plot points, the view should draw them on its canvas.
- *Removing plot points*—Given a set of plot points drawn on the canvas, clicking one of them should trigger a removal event for that specific plot point.

How about working on the list top down, starting with adding plot points?

8.4.2 Adding and operating standard widgets

We're about to drop some serious UI development-fu. The first move will be getting those text fields and the Add button in there.

Using Abbot for setting up our test harness, we whip up the plumbing shown in listing 8.8.

Listing 8.8 Plumbing for a test operating the view implementation

```
import junit.extensions.abbot.ComponentTestFixture;
import abbot.finder.matchers.NameMatcher;
import abbot.tester.ComponentTester;
import java.awt.Point;
import java.awt.Component;

public class TestPlotMapViewImpl extends ComponentTestFixture
        implements PlotAdditionListener {          <-- Test class acts as listener

    private Point addedPoint;

    public void plotWasAdded(Point plot) {      |  Keep added point
        addedPoint = plot;                      |  for tests to assert
    }
```

```
    public void setUp() throws Exception {
        super.setUp();
        addedPoint = null;
        PlotMapViewImpl view = new PlotMapViewImpl();
        view.registerAdditionListener(this);
        showFrame(view);
    }
}
```

What we have here is a test class similar to what we saw earlier when discussing Abbot. Perhaps the biggest difference is that this time I've decided to use the Self Shunt pattern,[8] making the test class act as a test double—this time, registering as a `PlotAdditionListener`. What's most important is that when the test methods begin their execution there's a `PlotMapViewImpl` waiting for them on the screen.

Now, let's write a test. With listing 8.9, we add a test for the registered listener. It receives an addition event for the correct plot-point coordinates when we type some coordinates in the text fields and click a button.

Listing 8.9 Test for typing in coordinates and clicking the Add button

```
public class TestPlotMapViewImpl extends ComponentTestFixture
        implements PlotAdditionListener {
    ...
    private ComponentTester tester = new ComponentTester();

    public void testAdditionEventGetsTriggered() throws Exception {
        Point point = new Point(3, 5);
        typeIntoTextField("x_coord_textfield", "" + point.x);
        typeIntoTextField("y_coord_textfield", "" + point.y);
        tester.actionClick(namedComponent("add_button"));
        assertEquals(point, addedPoint);
    }

    private void typeIntoTextField(String name, String value)
            throws Exception {
        tester.actionKeyString(namedComponent(name), value);
    }

    private Component namedComponent(String name) throws Exception {
        return getFinder().find(new NameMatcher(name));
    }
}
```

[8] http://www.objectmentor.com/resources/articles/SelfShunPtrn.pdf.

Adding just enough of the `PlotMapViewImpl` class, we now have a test that fails because Abbot can't find a component named x_coord_textfield on the screen. Adding the missing components one by one, we end up with our implementation looking like listing 8.10.

Listing 8.10 View implementation with the necessary widgets in place

```
import javax.swing.*;

public class PlotMapViewImpl extends JPanel implements
      PlotMapView {

    public PlotMapViewImpl() {
        add(createTextField("x_coord_textfield"));
        add(createTextField("y_coord_textfield"));
        JButton addButton = new JButton();
        addButton.setName("add_button");
        add(addButton);
    }

    private JTextField createTextField(String name) {
        JTextField field = new JTextField();
        field.setName(name);
        return field;
    }

    public void registerAdditionListener(PlotAdditionListener
        listener) {
    }

    public void registerRemovalListener(PlotRemovalListener
        listener) {
    }

    public void drawPlotMap(PlotMapModel model) {
    }
}
```

We've made `PlotMapViewImpl` create the three widgets and add them into its default layout. This is enough for our test to get one step further, now failing because clicking the button doesn't seem to do anything—which is correct because we haven't wired up any functionality behind the widgets. Let's do that right now and get that test passing.

Listing 8.11 shows the view class implementation that passes our test with flying colors.

Listing 8.11 View implementation for passing our first test

```
import javax.swing.*;
import java.awt.event.*;
import java.awt.Point;

public class PlotMapViewImpl extends JPanel implements PlotMapView {

    private PlotAdditionListener additionListener;   <-- View has listener for addition events

    private JTextField xCoordField, yCoordField;

    private JButton addButton;

    public PlotMapViewImpl() {
        createWidgets();
        add(xCoordField);
        add(yCoordField);
        add(addButton);
    }

    private JButton createWidgets() {
        xCoordField = createTextField("x_coord_textfield");
        yCoordField = createTextField("y_coord_textfield");
        addButton = new JButton();
        addButton.setName("add_button");
        addButton.addActionListener(new ActionListener() {
            public void actionPerformed(ActionEvent e) {
                int x = valueAsInt(xCoordField);
                int y = valueAsInt(yCoordField);
                additionListener.plotWasAdded(new Point(x, y));   <-- Button triggers events to registered listener
            }

        });
        return addButton;
    }

    private int valueAsInt(JTextField field) {
        return Integer.parseInt(field.getText());
    }

    private JTextField createTextField(String name) {
        JTextField field = new JTextField();
        field.setName(name);
        return field;
    }
```

```
    public void registerAdditionListener(PlotAdditionListener
        listener) {
        this.additionListener = listener;     <-- Register listener for addition events
    }

    public void registerRemovalListener(PlotRemovalListener
        listener) {
    }

    public void drawPlotMap(PlotMapModel model) {
    }
}
```

In listing 8.11, the view class's constructor does two things: creates the child widgets and adds them on the screen; there's nothing special about that. What's perhaps more interesting is how we wire the Add button to trigger events on the registered `PlotAdditionListener` by pulling data from the text fields inside the button's `ActionListener`. It's worth noting that the current implementation shown in listing 8.11 makes some assumptions. For example, it assumes that there's going to be exactly one registered listener at any time (and that there's always going to be one).

Also, as I was implementing the `ActionListener` for the Add button, I realized that the user might type non-numeric input into the coordinate text fields. That's something we should prevent, so I added that on my task list. I'm thinking we could have the Add button enabled only while there are valid coordinates in the text fields. And after adding a point to the plot map, we should clear out the coordinate text fields. To keep things interesting, let's leave these as exercises for you and move on to doing something slightly different: drawing custom graphics.

8.4.3 Drawing custom graphics

It's one thing to slap together a bunch of off-the-shelf components to build a UI. It's another thing to build one from scratch, literally drawing your custom component on the screen. That's basically what we're up to with our next task: drawing the plot map on a canvas.

Let's first make sure we've got the big picture in check. What we have in place now in our `PlotMapViewImpl` class is a couple of text fields and a button that triggers an addition event on a registered listener. The view class does not, however, do anything when it's asked to draw the given `PlotMapModel`. Eventually, we'd like to be able to see a canvas with plot points, and connecting lines on it. I'm afraid graphics has never been one of my strong points, and doing all of this in one step sounds like too big a bite to take at once. Thus, we'll divide and conquer.

Isolating the problem

What I'm thinking is that we should separate the drawing responsibility to a separate canvas class and just check that the `PlotMapViewImpl` passes through the request to draw plots to the canvas object. In other words, we won't mix the canvas stuff with the top-level panel component but instead have the `PlotMapViewImpl` hold on to a `PlotMapCanvas`, an interface that we can stub away for now. Shrinking the canvas down to as small a piece of code as possible will make it easier to test.

But we're not yet working on the canvas, so let's focus on the view-canvas interaction. Listing 8.12 presents our next test for verifying the desired interaction between the view component and its canvas component.

Listing 8.12 Testing for the view delegating drawing to a `PlotMapCanvas`

```
public class TestPlotMapViewImpl extends ComponentTestFixture
        implements PlotAdditionListener {
    ...
    private PlotMapCanvasStub canvas;

    public void setUp() throws Exception {
        ...
        canvas = new PlotMapCanvasStub();
        view = new PlotMapViewImpl() {
            @Override
            protected PlotMapCanvas createCanvas() {
                return canvas;
            }
        };
    }

    public void
        testViewPassesModelToSeparateCanvasObjectForDrawing()
            throws Exception {
        Point p1 = new Point(1, 3);
        Point p2 = new Point(2, 1);
        Point p3 = new Point(5, 4);
        PlotMapModel model = new PlotMapModel();
        model.add(p1);
        model.add(p2);
        model.add(p3);
        view.drawPlotMap(model);
        assertEquals(Arrays.asList(p1, p2, p3),
            canvas.plottedPoints);
    }
}
```

❶ Use test double for canvas

❷ View creates its canvas with this method

In listing 8.12, we're ❶ using a test double called `PlotMapCanvasStub` for capturing the expected interaction. I decided to swap it in by ❷ overriding a protected factory method to return our test double. The only thing we need from the fake canvas, shown in listing 8.13, is for it to record what it was asked to draw so that we can compare the actual against the expected in our test.

Listing 8.13 Test double for the `PlotMapCanvas`

```
public class PlotMapCanvasStub implements PlotMapCanvas {

    public List<Point> plottedPoints = new ArrayList<Point>();

    public void plot(Point point) {
        plottedPoints.add(point);
    }
}
```

That's all we need for now to get our test to fail for the right reason—the missing behavior for delegating the drawing of the model to the view's canvas component.

Walking the path of least pain, listing 8.14 shows the handful of lines of code we add to make the test turn green.

Listing 8.14 Making view pass model to a separate canvas for drawing

```
public class PlotMapViewImpl extends JPanel implements PlotMapView {
    ...

    protected PlotMapCanvas createCanvas() {        // Needed to make code compile
        return null;
    }

    public void drawPlotMap(PlotMapModel model) {
        for (Point point : model.points()) {        // Tell canvas to draw model's plot points
            createCanvas().plot(point);
        }
    }
}
```

The astute reader may have noticed a couple of interesting shortcuts in listing 8.14. First, we're returning `null` from the `createCanvas` method (which only exists because of the `@Override` annotation in the test)—that's all we need for now. At some point, we'll want the production code to create a canvas, but we're not there yet.

Second, we're invoking the createCanvas method for each plot point we're drawing. This is obviously not the correct implementation—it passes the test because the overridden createCanvas always returns the same object instance—but I wanted to push myself to write a test that explicitly documents our intention of drawing everything on a single canvas.

Listing 8.15 adds a test that brings this shortcoming to light.

Listing 8.15 Explicitly specifying that a view should create exactly one canvas

```
public void testViewCreatesItsCanvasJustOnce() throws Exception {
    final MutableInt canvasesCreated = new MutableInt ();
    view = new PlotMapViewImpl() {
        @Override
        protected PlotMapCanvas createCanvas() {
            canvasesCreated.increment();
            return new PlotMapCanvasStub();
        }
    };
    PlotMapModel model = new PlotMapModel();
    model.add(new Point(1, 1));
    view.drawPlotMap(model);
    view.drawPlotMap(model);
    assertEquals(1, canvasesCreated.intValue());
}
```

1 Increment a counter

2 Should have been exactly one canvas

By **1** incrementing a mutable counter object[9] on every call to createCanvas and calling the drawPlotMap method on the view several times (and with some points to draw), we can **2** verify that the view only creates one canvas for itself.

Now what do we still need to do before we can move on to implementing the canvas? At least there's the null-returning createCanvas method that we should make create an instance of the real thing. There's also one small glitch in our drawPlotMap method—it doesn't clear out the previously drawn plots before drawing new ones! I think we need to add a clear method to our PlotMapCanvas interface and make the PlotMapViewImpl call that before (re)drawing a model.

We're not going to go there, although I'll be happy to wait while you go ahead writing some tests and fixing those shortcomings. Once you're done with them, we need to move on to implementing our custom canvas object!

[9] I used to write my own until the Jakarta Commons Lang project's (http://jakarta.apache.org/commons/lang) 2.2 release gave me proper mutable primitives.

Testing for physical dimensions

As usual, there are many ways to skin a cat. In the case of trying to develop a graphical component that draws itself like our `PlotMapViewImpl` will need to do, perhaps the easiest place to start is with the dimensions; I'm tempted to start from there. To begin, let's make the canvas a fixed size. Listing 8.16 presents a two-liner that gets the ball rolling, nailing the canvas's size to 200x100 pixels.

Listing 8.16 Testing for canvas size

```
public class TestPlotMapCanvasImpl {

    @Test
    public void testDimensionsShouldBeAutomaticallySet()
            throws Exception {
        Component canvas = new PlotMapCanvasImpl();
        assertEquals(new Dimension(200, 100), canvas.getSize());
    }
}
```

Nice. Quick. Simple. Just like the implementation, shown in listing 8.17.

Listing 8.17 The first incarnation of our canvas class

```
public class PlotMapCanvasImpl
        extends Component implements PlotMapCanvas {

    public PlotMapCanvasImpl() {
        setSize(200, 100);
    }

    public void plot(Point point) {
    }
}
```

Not much special in listing 8.17, either. We set the component's size in its constructor and include default implementations of the interface methods. Our test referred to the canvas component as a `java.awt.Component`, so we inherit from that for now.

The test is now passing, but it turns out that it shouldn't. Why? Because setting the size of a `Component` doesn't mean that its physical size when rendered is that size. This is where our Swing knowledge comes into play—without that knowledge, we'd often find out about such quirks only after we've tried to render the component inside a container. In the case of the component's physical size, the problem can be brought to light by (for example) comparing the component's size with its bounds, as shown in listing 8.18, which reveals that our view isn't a fixed size after all.

Listing 8.18 Comparing size and bounds

```
public class TestPlotMapCanvasImpl extends ComponentTestFixture {

    @Test
    public void testDimensionsShouldBeAutomaticallySet()
            throws Exception {
        Component canvas = new PlotMapCanvasImpl();
        showFrame(canvas);
        assertEquals(new Dimension(200, 100), canvas.getSize());
        assertEquals(canvas.getSize(),
            canvas.getBounds().getSize());
    }
}
```

Use Abbot's base class to render component

The simplest solution I could think of for solving this problem was to extend from `java.awt.Canvas` instead of `java.awt.Component`. Having said that, because the change is such a simple one, let's jump right into our next test without reproducing an implementation almost identical to listing 8.17.

What next? Another low-hanging fruit that comes to mind is the canvas's background color. I'm thinking white.

Nailing down the color

We want our widget to have a clean, white background. That should be simple, right? Our next test in listing 8.19 proves that assumption to be correct.

Listing 8.19 Adding another test for the component's background color

```
public class TestPlotMapCanvasImpl extends ComponentTestFixture {

    private Component canvas;

    @Override
    protected void setUp() throws Exception {
        super.setUp();
        canvas = new PlotMapCanvasImpl();
    }

    @Test
    public void testDimensionsShouldBeAutomaticallySet()
            throws Exception {
        showFrame(canvas);
```

```
        assertEquals(new Dimension(200, 100), canvas.getSize());
        assertEquals(canvas.getSize(),
            canvas.getBounds().getSize());
    }

    @Test
    public void testBackgroundColorIsWhite() throws Exception {
        assertEquals(Color.WHITE, canvas.getBackground());
    }
}
```

As you can see, I also decided to refactor a bit and move the canvas component into a field populated in the setup method. Making this test pass is once again a trivial one-liner, shown in listing 8.20.

Listing 8.20 Setting the background in the component's constructor

```
public class PlotMapCanvasImpl
        extends Canvas implements PlotMapCanvas {
    ...

    public PlotMapCanvasImpl() {
        setSize(200, 100);
        setBackground(Color.WHITE);
    }
    ...
}
```

What's perhaps more interesting than these low-hanging fruits is how we're going to verify that the plots are drawn correctly on the canvas. Somehow we need to test for the actual graphical output.

Testing for graphical output

Testing for graphical output can be a tricky challenge. Again, there are many ways to skin the cat, but not all of those ways are equally good. We could pass a test double for a `java.awt.Graphics` to our component and verify that the expected drawing operations happened. That could work out nicely, but it would also couple our test strongly to our implementation. I'm not that worried about coupling when it's unit tests we're talking about, but there's another option that's powerful in situations where we're not dealing with massive volumes of image data but rather a few pixels here and there.

The other option I'm referring to is to render the component on a buffer, extract a bitmap raster from the buffer, and specify our tests in terms of pixels in the raster. That might sound like a lot of work—it can be—but I'm pretty sure that it'll work out for our case. Before we start worrying about pixel-precise tests, we need to figure out how to render our component on a buffer.

There are a couple of ways to do this, but the one I'm accustomed to using is shown in listing 8.21.

Listing 8.21 Utility class for capturing a bitmap of a Swing component

```
import java.awt.Color;
import java.awt.Component;
import java.awt.Graphics2D;
import java.awt.image.BufferedImage;
import java.awt.image.Raster;

public class Bitmap {

    public static Raster of(Component c) throws Exception {
        BufferedImage image = new BufferedImage(c.getWidth(),
                c.getHeight(), BufferedImage.TYPE_INT_RGB);
        Graphics2D graphics = image.createGraphics();
        graphics.setColor(Color.WHITE);
        graphics.fillRect(0, 0, c.getWidth(), c.getHeight());
        c.paint(graphics);                  <-- 1 Tell component to paint itself on buffer
        graphics.dispose();
        return image.getRaster();       <-- 2 Extract raster from buffer
    }
}
```

The key is to create an in-memory buffer, a `java.awt.image.BufferedImage` that we can ❶ ask the component to paint on. Once the component has painted itself on the buffer, we can ❷ extract the bit raster from the image.

Now, with a little effort we can put together a test for the canvas drawing the plot points to the correct coordinates. Listing 8.22 shows just such a test—one that verifies individual pixels' colors around the specific point where we plotted a point.

Listing 8.22 Test for the canvas drawing the right stuff

```
public class TestPlotMapCanvasImpl extends ComponentTestFixture {
    ...

    @Test
    public void testPlotIsDrawnOnScreen() throws Exception {
        canvas.plot(new Point(2, 2));
        Raster raster = Bitmap.of(canvas);      <-- 1 Capture raster
```

```
        Pixel.in(raster).at(2, 2).shouldBe(Color.BLACK);
        Pixel.in(raster).around(2, 2).shouldBe(Color.WHITE);
    }
}
```

❷ Assert color of individual pixels from raster

In listing 8.22, we're using a couple of utilities for making the test more compact. First, we ❶ capture the bitmap of the component into a raster object using the `Bitmap` class we saw in listing 8.21. Then, we're using another utility class that I've omitted for brevity (check out the book's source code online) to ❷ assert the color of specific pixels in the raster. After plotting a point at the coordinates [2,2], we expect the pixel at [2,2] to be black and everything around it to be white.

This test finally gives us permission to implement the `PlotMapCanvasImpl`'s `paint` method, as shown in listing 8.23.

Listing 8.23 Rudimentary implementation of drawing custom graphics

```
public class PlotMapCanvasImpl
        extends Canvas implements PlotMapCanvas {

    private List<Point> plots = new ArrayList<Point>();
    ...

    @Override
    public void paint(Graphics g) {
        g.setColor(Color.BLACK);
        for (Point p : plots) {
            g.drawLine(p.x, p.y, p.x, p.y);
        }
    }
}
```

❶ Use black color for drawing

❷ Paint pixel at each point

Our test is now passing, and we're drawing plot points onscreen. We do that by ❷ drawing a line in black from the location of each plot point to itself. We're drawing a line because the `Graphics` class doesn't seem to offer a way to color a single pixel. Also, if you're not familiar with the Swing API, we first need to ❶ set the active color to black to let the `Graphics` object know with which color the `drawLine` operation should draw.

And speaking of drawing lines, that's what we still need to do—connect our plot points with lines in the rendered custom canvas. Let's see how that goes.

Testing for patterns

Where are we? We've drawn plot points on the screen, and we need to connect them. The first question is, of course, how can we test for the canvas correctly drawing the connecting lines?

We could, of course, use the exact same approach for verifying the color of 142 pixels as we did for 2 pixels in listing 8.22, asserting each pixel between two coordinates explicitly. The downside is that our test method would rise straight into the hall of fame for historically long methods. Clearly we don't want test methods with line count in the hundreds. We need something simpler, and I can think of at least two ways to write a simpler test than explicitly checking for all 142 pixels along the line:

- Make the line shorter.
- Use an algorithm to find the connecting line.

By using as simple as possible a scenario—an extremely short line—we effectively make it feasible to hard-code assertions for specific pixels into our test. By using an algorithm to find the connecting line, we spend some time and money on implementing an algorithm that takes the starting point and the ending point and figures out whether there's a path of colored points between the start and end points. Because the algorithm can get verbose and we can come up with a reasonably simple scenario for our test, let's go with the first option. Listing 8.24 shows a test for the canvas drawing a connecting line between two points we've plotted.

Listing 8.24 Test for plot points getting connected

```
public class TestPlotMapCanvasImpl extends ComponentTestFixture {
    ...

    @Test
    public void testPlotsShouldBeConnected() throws Exception {
        canvas.plot(new Point(2, 9));
        canvas.plot(new Point(5, 6));
        Raster raster = Bitmap.of(canvas);
        Pixel.in(raster).at(2, 9).shouldBe(Color.BLACK);
        Pixel.in(raster).at(3, 8).shouldBe(Color.BLACK);
        Pixel.in(raster).at(4, 7).shouldBe(Color.BLACK);
        Pixel.in(raster).at(5, 6).shouldBe(Color.BLACK);
    }
}
```

Check manually calculated coordinates

In listing 8.24, we're using the same `Pixel` utility as before to check the color of individual pixels. In this case, we've hard-coded the coordinates between [2,9] and [5,6] to be [3,8] and [4,7]. And that's all. The test case fails correctly and complains about the intermediary pixels not being black, giving us permission to draw the connecting lines, as shown in listing 8.25.

Listing 8.25 Drawing lines between plots

```
public class PlotMapCanvasImpl
        extends Canvas implements PlotMapCanvas {
    ...

    @Override
    public void paint(Graphics g) {
        g.setColor(Color.BLACK);
        Point previous = null;
        for (Point current : plots) {
            if (previous == null) {
                previous = current;
            }
            g.drawLine(previous.x, previous.y,
                    current.x, current.y);
            previous = current;
        }
    }
}
```

❶ First point doesn't have previous

❷ Draw line from previous to current

❸ Prepare for next loop iteration

The implementation in listing 8.25 draws the connecting lines with the exact same `drawLine` method of the `Graphics` object we used before for drawing the single plot points. The difference is that we're now ❷ drawing the line from the `previous` point's coordinates to the `current` point's coordinates inside the loop. We also tackle the problem of the first current point not having a predecessor by proactively ❶ using the same point as the previous and the current point. The remaining points, however, have their `previous` set because we always ❸ update it after drawing a line.

Let's call it a day as far as drawing custom graphics goes and tackle the third and last item on our list: removing plot points from the canvas through user gestures (mouse clicks, in our case).

8.4.4 Associating gestures with coordinates

We want the canvas to capture mouse clicks on it and to notify its container—the `PlotMapViewImpl`—about the event. To be more specific, we'd like the canvas to notify about only those mouse clicks that hit one of the plotted points. So how do we go about this?

First of all, we need some kind of a callback mechanism with which the view can register a handler for the mouse clicks. For this purpose, we create the `PointEventListener` interface:

```
public interface PointEventListener {

    void onPointEvent(Point point);
}
```

We also need a way for the view to register a `PointEventListener` with the `PlotMapCanvas`. That we can provide by adding an `addRemoveListener` method to the `PlotMapCanvas` interface, as follows:

```
public interface PlotMapCanvas {

    void plot(Point point);

    void addRemoveListener(PointEventListener listener);
}
```

We have just quickly designed the necessary interfaces, so let's see how we might write our next failing test by making use of these interfaces.

Simulating and responding to mouse clicks

We want our widget to respond to the user clicking our canvas with the mouse. In order to verify that this behavior is in place, we need a way to simulate mouse clicks. Luckily, the `java.awt.Component` class, which our canvas inherits from, offers a handy method called `dispatchEvent`. The `dispatchEvent` method can be used for simulating pretty much any kind of mouse event, including the simple left-click that we want.

Listing 8.26 shows our next test, simulating a mouse click and registering a test double to listen for the expected remove events.

Listing 8.26 Test handling of user gestures

```
public class TestPlotMapCanvasImpl extends ComponentTestFixture {

    private PlotMapCanvasImpl canvas;

    ...

    @Test
    public void
        testPlotsShouldReactToClicksByTriggeringRemoveEvents()
            throws Exception {
```

```
        final List<Point> removedPoints = new ArrayList<Point>();
        canvas.addRemoveListener(new PointEventListener() {
            public void onPointEvent(Point point) {
                removedPoints.add(point);
            }
        });
        Point point = new Point(5, 20);
        canvas.plot(point);
        canvas.dispatchEvent(new MouseEvent(canvas,
                MouseEvent.MOUSE_CLICKED,
                System.currentTimeMillis(),
                MouseEvent.BUTTON1_DOWN_MASK,
                point.x, point.y, 1, false));
        assertTrue(removedPoints.contains(point));
    }
}
```

❶ Register remove listener

❷ Simulate mouse click

Our test in listing 8.26 is supposed to simulate a mouse click on a plotted point and verify that the proper event is delegated to the registered listener. It accomplishes this by ❶ creating an anonymous implementation of our new `PointEventListener` interface that adds the received `Points` into a `List`. After registering the fake listener, our test ❷ simulates a mouse click using the `dispatchEvent` method.

As expected, our test fails until we get around to implementing the canvas's `addRemoveListener`. Listing 8.27 shows our `PlotMapCanvasImpl` implementation.

Listing 8.27 Canvas delegating mouse clicks to registered listener

```
public class PlotMapCanvasImpl
        extends Canvas implements PlotMapCanvas {
    ...

    public void addRemoveListener(final PointEventListener
            listener) {
        addMouseListener(new MouseAdapter() {
            public void mouseClicked(MouseEvent e) {
                listener.onPointEvent(e.getPoint());
            }
        });
    }
}
```

In listing 8.27, our canvas registers an anonymous `MouseAdapter` implementation with itself to delegate the mouse clicks to calls to the `PointEventListener`.

Because our current canvas implementation draws each plot point as a single pixel—something we might need to change at some point—we can pass the origin point of the MouseEvent as the point to be removed.

There's another issue we realize as we're writing the implementation for the MouseAdapter. We're triggering a remove event for any and all mouse clicks. Instead, we should generate an event only when the user clicks on a plot point.

Making our assertions more precise

Listing 8.28 comes to the rescue with a test that forces out the right behavior along with slightly cleaner, refactored test code.

Listing 8.28 Testing for only certain mouse clicks triggering remove events

```
public class TestPlotMapCanvasImpl extends ComponentTestFixture {
    ...
    private List<Point> removedPoints;

    @Override
    protected void setUp() throws Exception {
        super.setUp();
        removedPoints = new ArrayList<Point>();
        canvas = new PlotMapCanvasImpl();
        canvas.setRemoveListener(new PointEventListener() {
            public void onPointEvent(Point point) {
                removedPoints.add(point);
            }
        });
    }

    ...

    @Test
    public void testClickOnPlottedPointShouldTriggerRemoveEvent()
            throws Exception {
        Point point = new Point(5, 20);
        canvas.plot(point);
        simulateMouseClickAt(point.x, point.y);
        assertTrue(removedPoints.contains(point));
    }

    @Test
    public void testClickOnNonPlottedPointShouldBeIgnored()
            throws Exception {
        canvas.plot(new Point(100, 50));
        simulateMouseClickAt(20, 30);
        assertTrue(removedPoints.isEmpty());
    }
```

❶ Register fake listener for remove events

❷ Clicks on plotted points trigger event

❸ Ignore clicks on non-plotted points

```
    private void simulateMouseClickAt(int x, int y) {
        canvas.dispatchEvent(new MouseEvent(canvas,
                MouseEvent.MOUSE_CLICKED,
                    System.currentTimeMillis(),
                MouseEvent.BUTTON1_DOWN_MASK, x, y, 1, false));
    }
}
```

Just like in listing 8.26, we're ❶ registering a fake `PointEventListener` with the `PlotMapCanvasImpl` that we're testing. This time, however, we're not just testing that ❷ mouse clicks on top of a plotted point trigger a remove event. We're also testing that ❸ a click that's *not* targeted at one of the plotted points will *not* trigger a remove event.

And, sure enough, the test fails because we're not comparing the origins of the mouse events against our list of plotted points inside `PlotMapCanvasImpl`. Listing 8.29 introduces our implementation, which fortunately is still compact and elegant.

Listing 8.29 Comparing the source of the mouse click before triggering events

```
public class PlotMapCanvasImpl
        extends Canvas implements PlotMapCanvas {
    private List<Point> plots;
    ...

    public void setRemoveListener(final PointEventListener
        listener) {
        addMouseListener(new MouseAdapter() {
            public void mouseClicked(MouseEvent e) {
                Point point = e.getPoint();
                if (plots.contains(point)) {       <-- Interested only in plotted points
                    listener.onPointEvent(point);
                }
            }
        });
    }
}
```

Listing 8.29 doesn't introduce much extra code to prevent non-plotted points from triggering remove events for the registered `PointEventListeners`. We check that the `Point` object associated with the `MouseEvent` matches one of the plotted points.

Our canvas object now has the basic functionality in place for drawing plotted points with connecting lines between them, and delegating remove events back to the view component. We're not going to continue further with the example, although there would be a lot of interesting stuff to do (such as making the plotted points draw a more elaborate sprite on the screen than a single pixel). The reason for not continuing is that we could go on for hours; and I'm sure that by now, you've gotten plenty of ideas for structuring and test-driving your custom Swing components—even those that draw themselves!

Let's do a quick summary of what we've learned in this chapter and prepare to shift gears to part 3, which takes us to a whole new level of test-driven development—the acceptance testing level.

8.5 Summary

In this chapter, we have learned about testing and test-driving Swing code. We began by talking about how we should test internal plumbing, utilities, and the interaction or UI logic of our components. Rendering and layout are things we have to verify visually anyway and, considering the higher effort associated with testing such things in a meaningful way, we usually don't test for these aspects.

In order to help us make the things we do want to test as testable as possible, we learned about a handful of design patterns for testable UI code. Based on the classic Model-View-Presenter (MVP) pattern, Supervising Controller and the Passive View make the view as thin as possible, moving almost all logic outside of the view where it's easier to test.

Having figured out how we can test the majority of the logic in our user interfaces easily by employing these design patterns, we still need to test the little logic that remains in the view. To help us succeed in this task, we explored the techniques and tools available for testing visual Swing components. We looked at two tools in particular—Jemmy and Abbot—and acknowledged that they're equally suitable for the job at hand and that making the decision between the two is largely a matter of personal preference.

Finally, we set out to test-drive the visual portion of a simple view component that incorporates both standard widgets, such as text fields and buttons, but also custom graphics. We saw first-hand how to push the desired interactions into the implementation, whether initiated by changes in the model or by user gestures. We also saw how custom-drawn components can indeed be tested in a relatively simple manner. The key is to divide the problem into small pieces that we can conquer easily.

This chapter completes part 2 of the book. In part 3, we'll change our focus from the low-level, code-oriented test-driven development to the product-oriented and team level process of acceptance test-driven development.

Part 3

Building products with Acceptance TDD

Now that we've mastered the art of test-driving any and all kinds of Java code, part 3 turns our attention to the next level of test-driven-ness: acceptance TDD.

In chapter 9, we'll learn about not just acceptance TDD but also user stories, acceptance tests, and what those tests should be testing. We'll also provide a brief overview of the kind of tool support that's available. In chapter 10, we'll discuss how to use the open source Fit framework to implement executable acceptance tests in a handy tabular format. In chapter 11, we'll learn different strategies for connecting our executable acceptance tests into the system under test.

By the time you've flipped the last page of chapter 11, you'll be ready and set for test-driving applications the right way and the smart way. However, it's probably not going to be a walk in the park to adopt these techniques—let alone have your whole team adopt them. For that reason, chapter 12 examines a number of gotchas and techniques for helping you and your colleagues. After all, you're not reading this book just for laughs, are you? That's what I figured. Let's get started!

9 Acceptance TDD explained

In the spacecraft business no design can survive the review process, without first answering the question—how are we going to test this thing?

—Glen B. Alleman, Director Strategic Consulting for Lewis & Fowler

In the previous chapters, we have explored the developer-oriented practice of test-driven development, covering the fundamental process itself as well as a host of techniques for employing TDD on a variety of Java technologies. In this chapter, we'll take the core idea of TDD and apply it to the overall product development process.

TDD helps software developers produce working, high-quality code that's maintainable and, most of all, reliable. Our customers are rarely, however, interested in buying *code*. Our customers want software that helps them to be more productive, make more money, maintain or improve operational capability, take over a market, and so forth. This is what we need to deliver with our software—functionality to support business function or market needs. Acceptance test-driven development (acceptance TDD) is what helps developers build high-quality software that fulfills the business's needs as reliably as TDD helps ensure the software's technical quality.

Acceptance TDD helps coordinate software projects in a way that helps us deliver exactly what the customer wants when they want it, and that doesn't let us implement the required functionality only half way. In this chapter, we will learn what acceptance test-driven development is, why we should consider doing it, what these mysterious acceptance tests are, and how acceptance TDD integrates with TDD.

Acceptance test-driven development as a name sounds similar to test-driven development, doesn't it? So, what's the difference between the two? Surely it has something to do with the word *acceptance* prefixed onto TDD, but is there something else beneath the surface that differentiates the two techniques? What exactly are these acceptance tests? And what are we accepting with our tests in the first place? These are the questions we're going to find answers to as we start our journey into the world of acceptance tests and acceptance test-driven development.

We'll begin by describing a lightweight and extremely flexible requirements format called *user stories*. After all, we need to know how our system should behave, and that's exactly what user stories tell us. From there, we'll continue by exploring what acceptance tests are and what kinds of properties they should exhibit. By then, we will know what our requirements—the user stories—might look like, and we will know how our acceptance tests should look, which means we'll be ready to figure out how we work with these artifacts or what the process of acceptance TDD looks like.

An essential property of acceptance TDD is that it's a team activity and a team process, which is why we'll also discuss team-related topics such as the roles involved and who might occupy these roles. We'll also ask ourselves why we should do this and respond by identifying a number of benefits of acceptance TDD. Finally, we'll talk about what exactly we are testing with our acceptance tests and what kind of tools we have at our disposal.

But now, let us introduce ourselves with a handy requirements format we call *user stories*.

9.1 *Introduction to user stories*

User stories are an extremely simple way to express requirements. In its classic form, a user story is a short sentence stating *who* does *what* and *why*. In practice, most stories just tell us who and what, with the underlying motivation considered apparent from the context. The reason a story is typically only one sentence long (or, in some cases, just one or two words that convey meaning to the customer and developers) is that the story is not intended to document the requirement. The story is intended to *represent* the requirement, acting as *a promise of a future conversation* between the customer and the developer.

9.1.1 *Format of a story*

A number of people have suggested writing user stories that follow an agreed format such as "As a (role) I want (functionality) so that (benefit)." However, I and a number of other proponents of user stories for requirements management recommend not fixing the format as such but focusing on the user story staying on a level of detail that makes sense, using terms that make sense to the customer. This is not to say that such a template would be a bad idea—which it isn't; it's just that one size doesn't fit all, and the people in your organization might feel differently about the format than I do.[1]

On the physical format of user stories

In part because user stories are concise, many co-located teams keep their user stories written on small index cards or sticky notes, managing them on a whiteboard or other task board. This method is beneficial because communication is clear and progress is immediately obvious. Therefore, more and more multisite projects are also adopting such physical *story cards* for managing their work locally. After all, the benefits often far outweigh the hassle of relaying the status from the task board to electronic format for distribution. The use of index cards on an early XP project gave birth to the mnemonic of 3 Cs: card, conversation, confirmation.

9.1.2 *Power of storytelling*

Hannah Arendt, a German political scientist, has said, "storytelling reveals meaning without committing the error of defining it."[2] This particular quote eloquently communicates how user stories focus on meaning without stumbling on nitty-gritty details.

---

[1] Ron Jeffries, "Essential XP: Card, Conversation, Confirmation," *XP Magazine*, August 30, 2001.

[2] Hannah Arendt, *Men in Dark Times* (Harvest Books, 1970).

Inside every story is another one trying to come out

Just like there are multiple solutions to most computing problems, there is always another way to write a given user story. Indeed, it might make sense to take a closer look at a user story before rubberstamping it as a technical story. There is usually a way to express the story in a way that conveys the underlying value—the rationale—of the story. If you can't figure out that value, try again.

User stories are in many ways a form of storytelling, which is an effective medium for transferring knowledge. For one, people like listening to stories. Storytellers are good at keeping our attention—a lot more so than, say, structured documents of equal volume—and it's not just audible stories that have this advantage; prose with a storyline and context is far more interesting reading than a seemingly unconnected sequence of statements.

Let's see how much this property shows through in practice by looking at a couple of examples of user stories.

9.1.3 Examples of user stories

To get a better idea of what user stories look like, here are some examples of the kinds of user stories I personally tend to write:

- "Support technician sees customer's history onscreen at the start of a call"
- "The system prevents user from running multiple instances of the application simultaneously"
- "Application authenticates with the HTTP proxy server"

These user stories express just enough for the customer to be able to prioritize the feature in relation to other features and for the developer to be able to come up with a rough effort estimate for the story. Yet these stories don't burden the developer by prescribing the implementation, and they don't drown the team with excessive detail.

The first story about a technical-support application doesn't tell us what the screen will look like; and the second story doesn't talk about desktop shortcuts, scanning process listings, and so on. They convey *what* provides value to the customer—not *how* the system should provide that value. The third story is a bit different. It's clearly a technical user story, not having much to do with business functionality. It does, however, have enabling value, and it expresses that need in a clear manner. Furthermore, although harder to quantify, some technical stories might create value for the customer through lower total cost of ownership.

That's about all we're going to say about user stories for now. For a more in-depth description of user stories as a requirements management and planning tool, a great pick would be Mike Cohn's book *User Stories Applied* (Addison-Wesley, 2004).

As we already mentioned, the format of a user story doesn't matter all that much as long as it communicates the necessary information—who, what, why—to all involved parties, either explicitly or implicitly. In fact, just like the format of a story isn't one-size-fits-all, using stories as a requirements-management or planning tool isn't in any way a requirement for doing acceptance test-driven development—it's a natural fit.

Now that we know what the mysterious stories are (or what they can be), let's figure out what we mean by *acceptance tests*.

9.2 Acceptance tests

Acceptance tests are specifications for the desired behavior and functionality of a system. They tell us, for a given user story, how the system handles certain conditions and inputs and with what kinds of outcomes. There are a number of properties that an acceptance test should exhibit; but before taking a closer look, let's see an example.

9.2.1 Example tests for a story

Let's consider the following example of a user story and see what our acceptance tests for that particular story might look like. I present you figure with 9.1.

The functionality that we're interested in is for the system to obtain and display the customer's history of records when a call comes through the customer

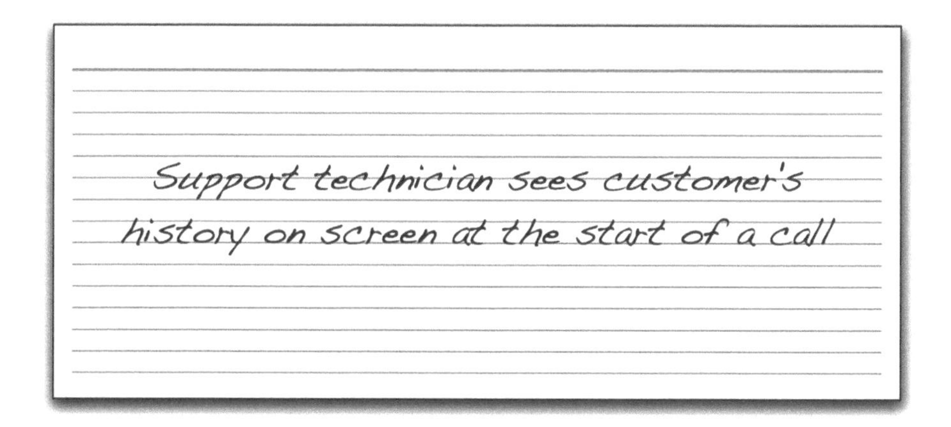

Figure 9.1 Example of a user story, written on a story card

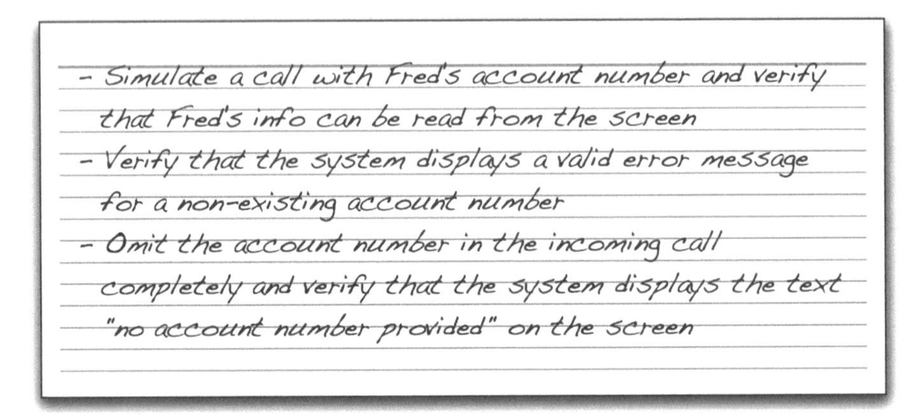

- Simulate a call with Fred's account number and verify
that Fred's info can be read from the screen
- Verify that the system displays a valid error message
for a non-existing account number
- Omit the account number in the incoming call
completely and verify that the system displays the text
"no account number provided" on the screen

Figure 9.2 Example tests for the story, written on the back of the story card from figure 9.1

support system. I might, for example, think of the tests for this story that are scribbled down as figure 9.2.

These three tests would essentially tell us whether the system behaves correctly from the perspective of a user—conditions of satisfaction. They tell us nothing about how the system implements that behavior.

Now, with these example tests in mind, let's look at some essential properties of acceptance tests, starting with who owns them and who writes them.

9.2.2 *Properties of acceptance tests*

So far, you've probably deduced that acceptance tests are typically short and somewhat informal. There's more to the nature of acceptance tests, however, and next we're going to look at some general properties.

To make a long story short, acceptance tests are

- Owned by the customer
- Written together with the customer, developer, and tester
- About the *what* and not the *how*
- Expressed in the language of the problem domain
- Concise, precise, and unambiguous

Let's expand these sound bites one by one and see what they mean.

Owned by the customer

Acceptance tests should be owned by the customer because their main purpose is to specify acceptance criteria for the user story, and it's the customer—the business expert—who is best positioned to spell out those criteria. This also leads to the customer being the one who should ideally be writing the acceptance tests.

Having the customer write the acceptance tests helps us avoid a common problem with acceptance tests written by developers: Developers often fall into the pit of specifying technical aspects of the implementation rather than specifying the feature itself. And, after all, acceptance tests are largely a specification of functionality rather than tests for technical details (although sometimes they're that, too).

Written together

Even though the customer should be the one who owns the acceptance tests, they don't need to be the only one to write them. Especially when we're new to user stories and acceptance tests, it is important to provide help and support so that nobody ends up isolating themselves from the process due to lack of understanding and, thus, being uncomfortable with the tools and techniques. By writing tests together, we can encourage the communication that inevitably happens when the customer and developer work together to specify the acceptance criteria for a story.

With the customer in their role as domain expert, the developer in the role of a technical expert, and the tester in a role that combines a bit of both, we've got everything covered. Of course, there are times when the customer will write stories and acceptance tests by themselves—perhaps because they were having a meeting offsite or because they didn't have time for a discussion about the stories and their accompanying tests.

The same goes for a developer or tester who *occasionally* has to write acceptance tests without access to the customer. On these occasions, we'll have to make sure that the necessary conversation happens at some point. It's not the end of the world if a story goes into the backlog with a test that's not ideal. We'll notice the problem and deal with it eventually. That's the beauty of a simple requirement format like user stories!

Another essential property for good acceptance tests ties in closely with the customer being the one who's writing the tests: the focus and perspective from which the tests are written.

Focus on the what, not the how

One of the key characteristics that make user stories so fitting for delivering value early and often is that they focus on describing the *source* of value to the customer instead of the mechanics of *how* that value is delivered. User stories strive to convey the needs and wants—the *what* and *why*—and give the implementation—the

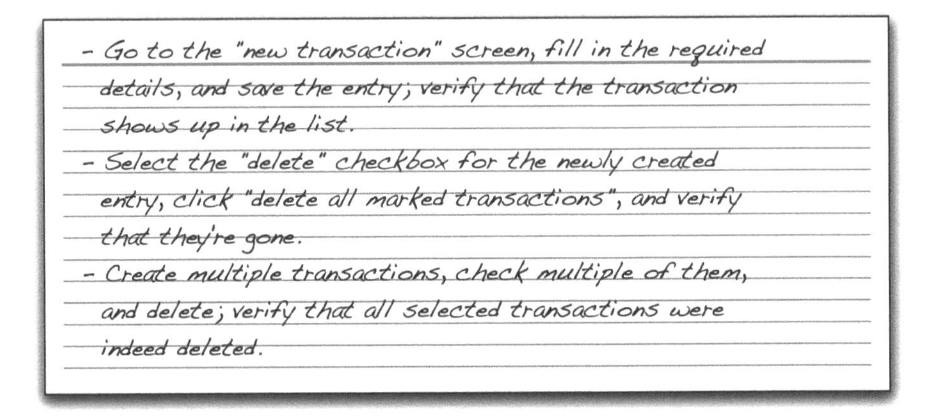

- Go to the "new transaction" screen, fill in the required details, and save the entry; verify that the transaction shows up in the list.
- Select the "delete" checkbox for the newly created entry, click "delete all marked transactions", and verify that they're gone.
- Create multiple transactions, check multiple of them, and delete; verify that all selected transactions were indeed deleted.

Figure 9.3 Acceptance tests focusing too much on the implementation

how—little attention. In the vast majority of cases, the customer doesn't care how the business value is derived.[3]

Let's look at an example to better illustrate this difference between what and why and how. Figure 9.3 shows an example of acceptance tests that go into too much detail about the solution rather than focusing on the problem—the customer's need and requirement. All three tests shown on the card address the user interface—effectively suggesting an implementation, which isn't what we want. While doing that, they're also hiding the real information—"what are we actually testing here?"—behind the technology.

Instead, we should try to formulate our tests in terms of the problem and leave the solution up to the developers and the customer to decide and discuss at a later time when we're implementing the tests and the story itself. Figure 9.4 illustrates a possible rewrite of the tests in figure 9.3 in a way that preserves the valuable information and omits the unnecessary details, which only clutter our intent.

Notice how, by reading these three lines, a developer is just as capable of figuring out what to test as they would be by reading the more solution-oriented tests from figure 9.3. Given these two alternatives, which would you consider easier to understand and parse? The volume and focus of the words we choose to write our tests with have a big effect on the effectiveness of our tests as a tool. We shouldn't neglect that fact.

[3] Well, they shouldn't. Part of the reason many customers like to dictate the *how* is our lousy track record as an industry. It's time to change that flawed perception by showing that we can deliver what the customer wants as long as we get constant feedback on how we're doing.

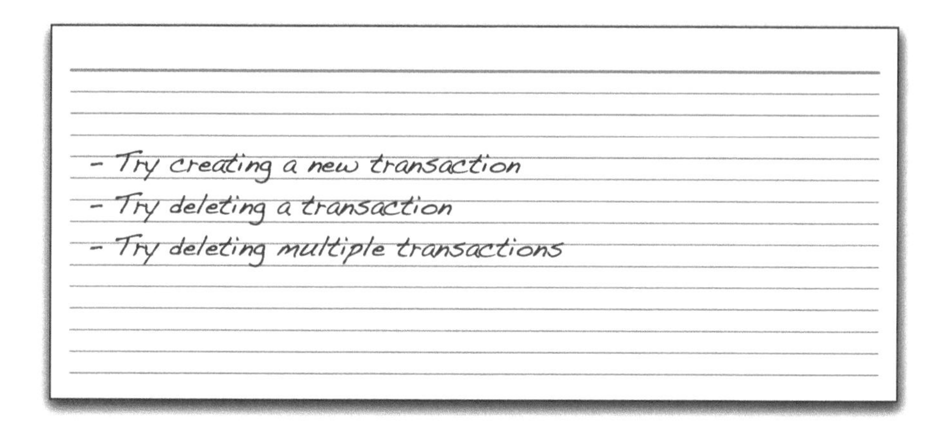

Figure 9.4 Trimmed-down version of the tests from figure 9.3

There's more to words, though, than just volume and focus. We also have to watch for our language.

Use the language of the domain

An important property of acceptance tests is that they use the language of the domain and the customer instead of geek-speak only the programmer understands. This is the fundamental requirement for having the customer involved in the creation of acceptance tests and helps enormously with the job of validating that the tests are correct and sufficient. Scattering too much technical lingo into our tests makes us more vulnerable to having a requirement bug sneak into a production release—because the customer's eyes glaze over when reading geek-speak and the developers are drawn to the technology rather than the real issue of specifying the right thing.

By using a domain language in specifying our tests, we are also not unnecessarily tied to the implementation, which is useful since we need to be able to refactor our system effectively. By using domain language, the changes we need to make to our existing tests when refactoring are typically non-existent or at most trivial.

Concise, precise, and unambiguous

Largely for the same reasons we write our acceptance tests using the domain's own language, we want to keep our tests simple and concise. We write each of our acceptance tests to verify a single aspect or scenario relevant to the user story at hand. We keep our tests uncluttered, easy to understand, and easy to translate to executable tests. The less ambiguity involved, the better we are at avoiding mistakes and the working with our tests.

We might write our stories as simple reminders in the form of a bulleted list, or we might opt to spell them out as complete sentences describing the expected behavior. In either case, the goal is to provide just enough information for us to remember the important things we need to discuss and test for, rather than documenting those details beforehand. Card, conversation, confirmation—these are the three Cs that make up a user story. Those same three Cs could be applied to acceptance tests as well.

Remember the acceptance tests we saw earlier, for the story about a customer support system? Take another look at them, back in figure 9.2.

Would you say these tests are simple and concise? Perhaps you would. Perhaps you wouldn't. Personally, I'd say there are some things in these tests that could be safely omitted while still preserving enough information to carry the original intent, and some things that shouldn't be there. Figure 9.5 shows a revamp of the same tests shown in figure 9.2.

Notice the difference in conciseness? Notice how the developer would still know to test for the right things, provided they can ask the customer for the details, such as what kind of a message should be displayed for a non-existent account number or when the number is omitted altogether? The tests in figure 9.5 can be considered *more accurate* than the tests in figure 9.2 because they omit details that could change by the time we get around to implementing the story.

Obviously, some prefer to have more details written down for the acceptance tests than do others. Whether you're into more text or less, or whether you prefer sketching little diagrams and UI designs as part of your user stories and the accompanying acceptance tests, it's up to you and your team to decide. It's all

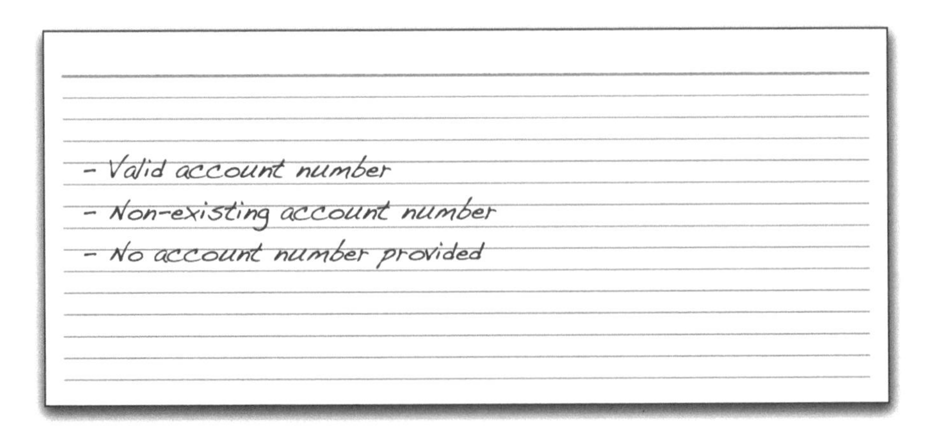

- Valid account number
- Non-existing account number
- No account number provided

Figure 9.5 Revamped acceptance tests from figure 9.2

good as long as you remember to keep your acceptance tests simple and concise, and as long as you avoid writing down ambiguous things that can be interpreted wrongly at a later stage. Specifically, avoid writing down details that are easy to find out later and that don't add crucial information for estimating the size of the story.

The last property of acceptance tests that we'll list here has more to do with automating the tests than the way or form in which they're written.

9.2.3 Implementing acceptance tests

Yet another common property of acceptance tests is that they might not be implemented (translation: automated) using the same programming language as the system they are testing. Whether this is the case depends on the technologies involved and on the overall architecture of the system under test. For example, some programming languages are easier to interoperate with than others. Similarly, it is easy to write acceptance tests for a web application through the HTTP protocol with practically any language we want, but it's often impossible to run acceptance tests for embedded software written in any language other than that of the system itself.

The main reason for choosing a different programming language for implementing acceptance tests than the one we're using for our production code (and, often, unit tests) is that the needs of acceptance tests are often radically different from the properties of the programming language we use for implementing our system. To give you an example, a particular real-time system might be feasible to implement only with native C code, whereas it would be rather verbose, slow, and error-prone to express tests for the same real-time system in C compared to, for example, a scripting language.

The ideal syntax for expressing our acceptance tests could be a declarative, tabular structure such as a spreadsheet, or it could be something closer to a sequence of higher-level actions written in plain English. If we want to have our customer collaborate with developers on our acceptance tests, a full-blown programming language such as Java, C/C++, or C# is likely not an option. "Best tool for the job" means more than technically best, because the programmer's job description also includes collaborating with the customer.

Now that we know something about acceptance tests and we have an idea of who's writing the tests in the first place, let's see how we use them to drive our development. What does acceptance test-driven development look like on paper?

9.3 Understanding the process

Test-driven development gives a programmer the tools for evolving their software in small steps, always certain of the software working as expected. This certainty comes from the programmer expressing their expectations in the form of automated unit tests. In acceptance test-driven development, this certainty is gained not on the level of technical correctness but rather on the feature level of, "does the software do what I want it to do?"

In other words, although in TDD we're first defining the specific behavior we want our code base to exhibit and only then implementing the said behavior, in acceptance TDD we first define the specific user- or customer-valued functionality we want our system as a whole to exhibit and only then implement the said behavior, most likely using TDD as our vehicle of choice.

Because we know what acceptance tests look like, how about if we take a quick tour through the overall process of acceptance test-driven development and then broaden our view and look at what happens on the scale of a whole iteration? After that, we can go back and zoom in on the details of the more interesting bits.

> **About the customer**
>
> You may have noticed that user stories as a requirements-management technique tend to stress having close and frequent interaction with the customer. If you're worried about not having an on-site customer, or having a customer who's not keen on having much to do with developing the software, you can stop worrying. There are ways around this obvious limitation, and we'll talk about those later on. For now, just consider *the customer* as referring to a role rather than a specific person—a role that can be played by, say, one of the test engineers or developers who knows enough about the product's domain to be able to make the kinds of decisions a real customer would make.

But now, I present you with the process of acceptance test-driven development, distilled into four small steps.

9.3.1 The acceptance TDD cycle

In its simplest form, the process of acceptance test-driven development can be expressed as the simple cycle illustrated by figure 9.6.

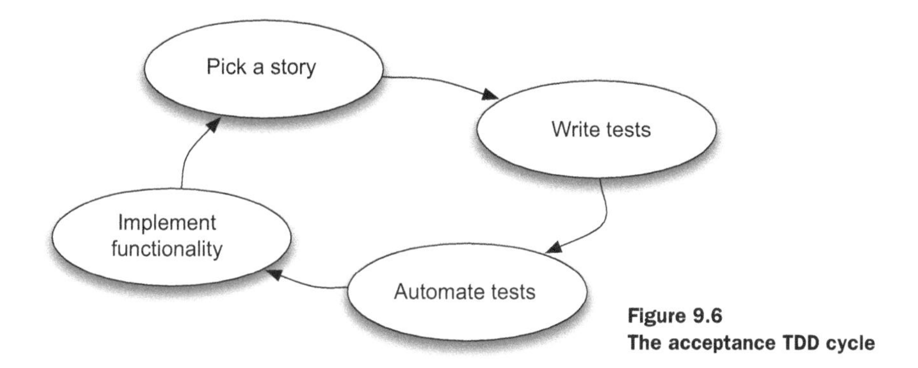

Figure 9.6
The acceptance TDD cycle

This cycle continues throughout the iteration as long as we have more stories to implement, starting over again from picking a user story; then writing tests for the chosen story, then turning those tests into automated, executable tests; and finally implementing the functionality to make our acceptance tests pass.

In practice, of course, things aren't always that simple. We might not yet have user stories, the stories might be ambiguous or even contradictory, the stories might not have been prioritized, the stories might have dependencies that affect their scheduling, and so on. We'll get to these complications later. For now, let's keep our rose-tinted glasses on and continue thinking about the simple steps outlined previously. Speaking of steps, let's take a closer look at what those steps consist of.

Step 1: Pick a user story

The first step is to decide which story to work on next. Not always an easy job; but, fortunately, most of the time we'll already have some relative priorities in place for all the stories in our iteration's work backlog. Assuming that we have such priorities, the simplest way to go is to always pick the story that's on top of the stack—that is, the story that's considered the most important of those remaining. Again, sometimes, it's not that simple.

Generally speaking, the stories are coming from the various planning meetings held throughout the project where the customer informally describes new features, providing examples to illustrate how the system should work in each situation. In those meetings, the developers and testers typically ask questions about the features, making them a medium for intense learning and discussion. Some of that information gets documented on a story card (whether virtual or physical), and some of it remains as tacit knowledge. In those same planning meetings, the customer prioritizes the stack of user stories by their business value (including business risk) and technical risk (as estimated by the team).

What kinds of issues might we have when picking stories from this stack of user stories? There are times when the highest-priority story requires skills that we don't possess, or we consider not having enough of. In those situations, we might want to skip to the next task to see whether it makes more sense for us to work on it. Teams that have adopted pair programming don't suffer from this problem as often. When working in pairs, even the most cross-functional team can usually accommodate by adjusting their current pairs in a way that frees the necessary skills for picking the highest priority task from the pile.

The least qualified person

The traditional way of dividing work on a team is for everyone to do what they do best. It's intuitive. It's safe. But it might not be the best way of completing the task. Arlo Belshee presented an experience report at the Agile 2005 conference, where he described how his company had started consciously tweaking the way they work and measuring what works and what doesn't. Among their findings about stuff that worked was a practice of giving tasks to the *least qualified person*. For a full closure on their experience and an explanation of why this approach works, listen to Arlo's interview at the Agile Toolkit Podcast website (http://agiletoolkit.libsyn.com/).

There can be more issues to deal with regarding picking user stories, but most of the time the solution comes easily through judicious application of common sense. For now, let's move on to the second step in our process: writing tests for the story we've just picked.

Step 2: Write tests for a story

With a story card in hand (or onscreen if you've opted for managing your stories online), our next step is to write tests for the story. If you paid attention earlier in this chapter, we just learned that it's the customer who should be writing the tests. So how does this play out?

The first thing to do is, of course, get together with the customer. In practice, this means having a team member sit down with the customer (they're the one who should own the tests, remember?) and start sketching out a list of tests for the story in question.

As usual, there are personal preferences for how to go about doing this, but my current preference (yes, it changes from time to time) is to quickly scram out a list of rough scenarios or aspects of the story we want to test in order to say that the feature has been implemented correctly. There's time to elaborate on those rough scenarios later on when we're implementing the story or implementing the acceptance tests. At this time, however, we're only talking about coming up with a bulleted list of things we need to test—things that have to work in order for us to claim the story is done.

We already saw a couple of examples of the kind of tests we're referring to when we discussed the properties of acceptance tests. For example, you might want to peek back at figure 9.4, showing three tests on the back of a story card. That is the kind of rough list we're after in this step.

On timing

Especially in projects that have been going on for a while already, the customer and the development team probably have some kind of an idea of what's going to get scheduled into the next iteration in the upcoming planning meeting. In such projects, the customer and the team have probably spent some time during the previous iteration sketching acceptance tests for the features most likely to get picked in the next iteration's planning session. This means that we might be writing acceptance tests for stories that we're not going to implement until maybe a couple of weeks from now. We also might think of missing tests during implementation, for example, so this test-writing might happen pretty much at any point in time between writing the user story and the moment when the customer accepts the story as completed.

Once we have such a rough list, we start elaborating the tests, adding more detail and discussing about how this and that should work, whether there are any specifics about the user interface the customer would like to dictate, and so forth. Depending on the type of feature, the tests might be a set of interaction sequences or flows, or they might be a set of inputs and expected outputs. Often, especially with flow-style tests, the tests specify some kind of a starting state, a context the test assumes is part of the system.

Other than the level of detail and the sequence in which we work to add that detail, there's a question of when—or whether—to start writing the tests into an executable format. Witness step 3 in our process: automating the tests.

Step 3: Automate the tests

The next step once we've got acceptance tests written down on the back of a story card, on a whiteboard, in some electronic format, or on pink napkins, is to turn those tests into something we can execute automatically and get back a simple pass-or-fail result. Whereas we've called the previous step *writing tests,* we might call this step *implementing* or *automating* those tests.

In an attempt to avoid potential confusion about how the executable acceptance tests differ from the acceptance tests we wrote in the previous step, let's pull up an example. Remember the acceptance tests in figure 9.5? We might turn those tests into an executable format by using a variety of approaches and tools. The most popular category of tools (which we'll survey later) these days seems to be what we call *table-based tools*. Their premise is that the tabular format of tables, rows, and columns makes it easy for us to specify our tests in a way that's both human and machine readable. Figure 9.7 presents an example of how we might draft an executable test for the first test in figure 9.5, "Valid account number".

In figure 9.7, we've outlined the steps we're going to execute as part of our executable test in order to verify that the case of an incoming support call with a valid account number is handled as expected, displaying the customer's information onscreen. Our test is already expressed in a format that's easy to turn into a tabular table format using our tool of choice—for example, something that eats HTML tables and translates their content into a sequence of method invocations to Java code according to some documented rules.

Java code? Where did that come from? Weren't we just talking about tabular formats? The inevitable fact is that most of the time, there is not such a tool available that would understand our domain language tests in our table format and be able to wire those tests into calls to the system under test. In practice, we'll have to do that wiring ourselves anyway—most likely the developers or testers will do so using a programming language. To summarize this duality of turning acceptance tests into executable tests, we're dealing with expressing the tests in a format

Action	Parameters
place call	555-1234, account 123456
accept call	555-1234
verify text	123456
verify text	Cory Customer

Figure 9.7 Example of an executable test, sketched on a piece of paper

On style

The example in figure 9.7 is a *flow-style test*, based on a sequence of actions and parameters for those actions. This is not the only style at our disposal, however. A declarative approach to expressing the desired functionality or business rule can often yield more compact and more expressive tests than what's possible with flow-style tests. The volume of detail in our tests in the wild is obviously bigger than in this puny example. Yet our goal should—once again—be to keep our tests as simple and to the point as possible, ideally speaking in terms of *what* we're doing instead of *how* we're doing it.

that's both human and machine readable and with writing the plumbing code to connect those tests to the system under test.

With regard to writing things down (and this is probably not coming as a surprise), there are variations on how different teams do this. Some start writing the tests right away into electronic format using a word processor; some even go so far as to write them directly in an executable syntax. Some teams run their tests as early as during the initial authoring session. Some people, myself included, prefer to work on the tests alongside the customer using a physical medium, leaving the running of the executable tests for a later time. For example, I like to sketch the executable tests on a whiteboard or a piece of paper first, and pick up the computerized tools only when I've got something I'm relatively sure won't need to be changed right away.

The benefit is that we're less likely to fall prey to the technology—I've noticed that tools often steal too much focus from the topic, which we don't want. Using software also has this strange effect of the artifacts being worked on somehow seeming more formal, more final, and thus needing more polishing up. All that costs time and money, keeping us from the important work.

In projects where the customer's availability is the bottleneck, especially in the beginning of an iteration (and this is the case more often than not), it makes a lot of sense to have a team member do the possibly laborious or uninteresting translation step on their own rather than keep the customer from working on elaborating tests for other stories. The downside to having the team member formulate the executable syntax alone is that the customer might feel less ownership in the acceptance tests in general—after all, it's not the *exact* same piece they were working on. Furthermore, depending on the chosen test-automation tool and its syntax, the customer might even have difficulty reading the acceptance tests once they've been shoved into the executable format dictated by the tool.

Just for laughs, let's consider a case where our test-automation tool is a framework for which we express our tests in a simple but powerful scripting language such as Ruby. Figure 9.8 highlights the issue with the customer likely not being as capable of feeling ownership of the implemented acceptance test compared to the sketch, which they have participated in writing. Although the executable snippet of Ruby code certainly reads nicely to a programmer, it's not so trivial for a non-technical person to relate to.

Another aspect to take into consideration is whether we should make all tests executable to start with or whether we should automate one test at a time as we progress with the implementation. Some teams—and this is largely dependent on the level of certainty regarding the requirements—do fine by automating all known tests for a given story up front before moving on to implementing the story.

Some teams prefer moving in baby steps like they do in regular test-driven development, implementing one test, implementing the respective slice of the story, implementing another test, and so forth. The downside to automating all tests up front is, of course, that we're risking more unfinished work—inventory, if you will—than we would be if we'd implemented one slice at a time. My personal preference is strongly on the side of implementing acceptance tests one at a time rather than try getting them all done in one big burst.[4]

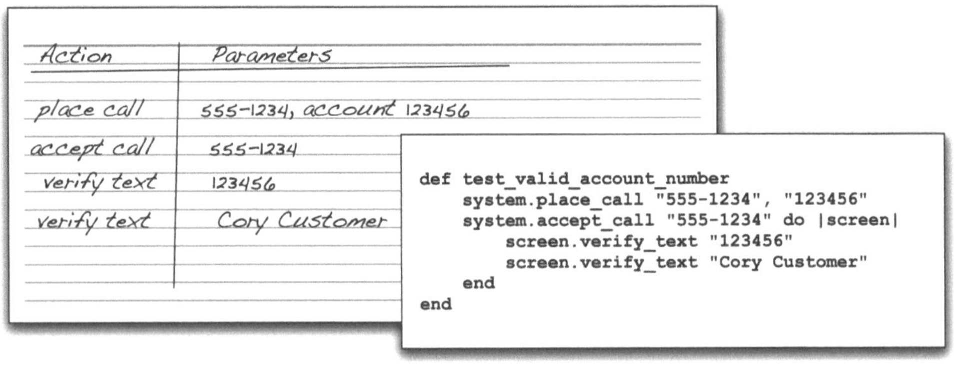

Action	Parameters
place call	555-1234, account 123456
accept call	555-1234
verify text	123456
verify text	Cory Customer

```
def test_valid_account_number
    system.place_call "555-1234", "123456"
    system.accept_call "555-1234" do |screen|
        screen.verify_text "123456"
        screen.verify_text "Cory Customer"
    end
end
```

Figure 9.8 Contrast between a sketch and an actual, implemented executable acceptance test

[4] It should be mentioned, though, that elaborating acceptance tests toward their executable form during planning sessions could help a team understand the complexity of the story better and, thus, aid in making better estimates.

Many of the decisions regarding physical versus electronic medium, translating to executable syntax together or not, and so forth also depend to a large degree on the people. Some customers have no trouble working on the tests directly in the executable format (especially if the tool supports developing a domain-specific language). Some customers don't have trouble identifying with tests that have been translated from their writing. As in so many aspects of software development, it depends.

Regardless of our choice of how many tests to automate at a time, after finishing this step of the cycle we have at least one acceptance test turned into an executable format; and before we proceed to implementing the functionality in question, we will have also written the necessary plumbing code for letting the test-automation tool know what those funny words mean in terms of technology. That is, we will have identified what the system should do when we say "select a transaction" or "place a call"—in terms of the programming API or other interface exposed by the system under test.

To put it another way, once we've gotten this far, we have an acceptance test that we can execute and that tells us that the specified functionality is missing. The next step is naturally to make that test pass—that is, implement the functionality to satisfy the failing test.

Step 4: Implement the functionality

Next on our plate is to come up with the functionality that makes our newly minted acceptance test(s) pass. Acceptance test-driven development doesn't say how we should implement the functionality; but, needless to say, it is generally considered best practice among practitioners of acceptance TDD to do the implementation using test-driven development—the same techniques we've been discussing in the previous parts of this book.

In general, a given story represents a piece of customer-valued functionality that is split—by the developers—into a set of *tasks* required for creating that functionality. It is these tasks that the developer then proceeds to tackle using whatever tools necessary, including TDD. When a given task is completed, the developer moves on to the next task, and so forth, until the story is completed—which is indicated by the acceptance tests executing successfully.

In practice, this process means plenty of small iterations within iterations. Figure 9.9 visualizes this transition to and from test-driven development inside the acceptance TDD process.

As we can see, the fourth step of the acceptance test-driven development cycle, implementing the necessary functionality to fix a failing acceptance test, can be expanded into a sequence of smaller TDD cycles of test-code-refactor, building up the missing functionality in a piecemeal fashion until the acceptance test passes.

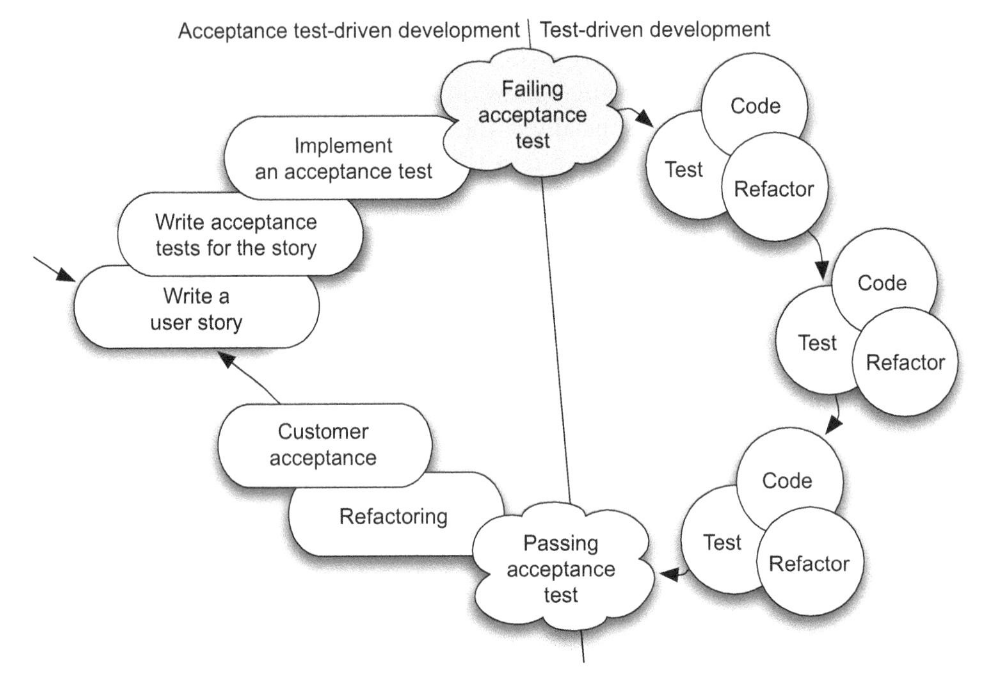

Figure 9.9 The relationship between test-driven development and acceptance test-driven development

The proportions in the figure should not be considered to reflect reality, however. Whereas the TDD cycle might range from one minute to a dozen, we might be chopping out code for a couple of hours or even the whole day before the acceptance test is passing.

While the developer is working on a story, frequently consulting with the customer on how this and that ought to work, there will undoubtedly be occasions when the developer comes up with a scenario—a test—that the system should probably handle in addition to the customer/developer writing those things down. Being rational creatures, we add those acceptance tests to our list, perhaps after asking the customer what they think of the test. After all, they might not assign as much value to the given aspect or functionality of the story as we the developers might.

At some point, we've iterated through all the tasks and all the tests we've identified for the story, and the acceptance tests are happily passing. At this point, depending on whether we opted for automating all tests up front (which I personally *don't* recommend) or automating them just in time, we either go back to Step 3 to automate another test or to Step 1 to pick a brand-new story to work on.

It would probably not hurt to walk around a bit and maybe have a cup of coffee, possibly check out your email. Getting acceptance tests passing is intensive work. As soon as you're back from the coffee machine, we'll continue with a broader view of how this simple four-step cycle with its small steps fits into the bigger picture of a complete iteration within a project.

9.3.2 Acceptance TDD inside an iteration

A healthy iteration consists mostly of hard work. Spend too much time in meetings or planning ahead, and you're soon behind the iteration schedule and need to de-scope (which might translate to another planning meeting...ugh!). Given a clear goal for the iteration, good user stories, and access to someone to answer our questions, most of the iteration should be spent in small cycles of a few hours to a couple of days writing acceptance tests, collaborating with the customer where necessary, making the tests executable, and implementing the missing functionality with our trusted workhorse, test-driven development.

As such, the four-step acceptance test-driven development cycle of picking a story, writing tests for the story, implementing the tests, and implementing the story is only a fraction of the larger continuum of a whole iteration made of multiple—even up to dozens—of user stories, depending on the size of your team and the size of your stories. In order to gain understanding of how the small four-step cycle for a single user story fits into the iteration, we're going to touch the zoom dial and see what an iteration might look like on a time line with the acceptance TDD–related activities scattered over the duration of a single iteration.

Figure 9.10 is an attempt to describe what such a time line might look like for a single iteration with nine user stories to implement. Each of the bars represents a single user story moving through the steps of writing acceptance tests, implementing acceptance tests, and implementing the story itself. In practice, there could (and probably would) be more iterations within each story, because we generally don't write and implement *all* acceptance tests in one go but rather proceed through tests one by one.

Notice how the stories get completed almost from the beginning of the iteration? That's the secret ingredient that acceptance TDD packs to provide indication of real progress. Our two imaginary developers (or pairs of developers and/or testers, if we're pair programming) start working on the next-highest priority story as soon as they're done with their current story. The developers don't begin working on a new story before the current story is done. Thus, there are always two user stories getting worked on, and functionality gets completed throughout the iteration.

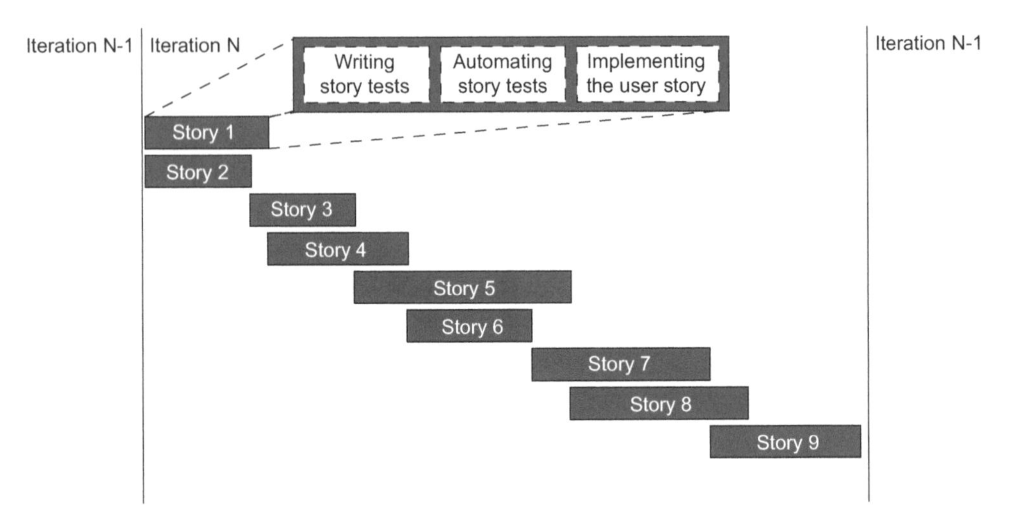

Figure 9.10 Putting acceptance test-driven development on a time line

So, if the iteration doesn't include writing the user stories, where are they coming from? As you may know if you're familiar with agile methods, there is usually some kind of a planning meeting in the beginning of the iteration where the customer decides which stories get implemented in that iteration and which stories are left in the stack for the future. Because we're scheduling the stories in that meeting, clearly we'll have to have those stories written before the meeting, no?

That's where continuous planning comes into the picture.

Continuous planning

Although an iteration should ideally be an autonomous, closed system that includes everything necessary to meet the iteration's goal, it is often necessary—and useful—to prepare for the next iteration during the previous one by allocating some amount of time for pre-iteration planning activities.[5] Otherwise, we'd have long-lasting planning meetings, and you're probably not any more a friend of long-lasting meetings than I am.

In practice, these pre-iteration planning activities might involve going through the backlog of user stories, identifying stories that are most likely to get scheduled for the next iteration, identifying stories that have been rendered obsolete, and so

[5] Suggestions regarding the time we should allocate for this continuous planning range from 10–15% of the team's total time available during the iteration. As usual, it's good to start with something that has worked for others and, once we've got some experience doing things that way, begin zeroing in on a number that seems to work best in our particular context.

forth. This ongoing pre-iteration planning is also the context in which we carry out the writing of user stories and, to some extent, the writing of the first acceptance tests. The rationale here is to be prepared for the next iteration's beginning when the backlog of stories is put on the table. At that point, the better we know our backlog, the more smoothly the planning session goes, and the faster we get back to work, crunching out valuable functionality for our customer.

By writing, estimating, splitting if necessary, and prioritizing user stories before the planning meeting, we ensure quick and productive planning meetings and are able to get back to delivering valuable features sooner.

When do we write acceptance tests?

It would be nice if we had all acceptance tests implemented (and failing) before we start implementing the production code. That is often not a realistic scenario, however, because tests require effort as well—they don't just appear from thin air—and investing our time in implementing the complete set of acceptance tests up front doesn't make any more sense than big up-front design does in the larger scale. It is much more efficient to implement acceptance tests as we go, user story by user story.

Teams that have dedicated testing personnel can have the testing engineers work together with the customer to make acceptance tests executable while developers start implementing the functionality for the stories. I'd hazard a guess that most teams, however, are much more homogeneous in this regard and participate in writing and implementing acceptance tests together, with nobody designated as "the acceptance test guy."

The process is largely dependent on the availability of the customer and the test and software engineers. If your customer is only onsite for a few days in the beginning of each iteration, you probably need to do some trade-offs in order to make the most out of those few days and defer work that can be deferred until after the customer is no longer available. Similarly, somebody has to write code, and it's likely not the customer who'll do that; software and test engineers need to be involved at some point.

Sometimes, we might do a couple of test sketches during iteration planning in order to have a basis for better estimates. As a rule of thumb, however, we begin translating our acceptance tests from behind the story cards (or from whatever medium we've settled on for authoring your requirements) into automated acceptance tests as soon as we have finished iteration planning.

When do we write acceptance tests? *(continued)*

We start from those stories we'll be working on first, of course, and implement the user story in parallel with automating the acceptance tests that we'll use to verify our work. And, if at all possible, we avoid having the same person implement the tests and the production code in order to minimize our risk of human nature playing its tricks on us.

Again, we want to keep an eye on putting too much up-front effort in automating our acceptance tests—we might end up with a huge bunch of tests but no working software. It's much better to proceed in small steps, delivering one story at a time. No matter how valuable our acceptance tests are to us, their value to the customer is negligible without the associated functionality.

The mid-iteration sanity check

I like to have an informal sanity check in the middle of an iteration. At that point, we should have approximately half of the stories scheduled for the iteration running and passing. This might not be the case for the first iteration, due to having to build up more infrastructure than in later iterations; but, especially as we get better at estimating our stories, it should always be in the remote vicinity of having 50% of the stories passing their tests.

Of course, we'll be tracking story completion throughout the iteration. Sometimes we realize early on that our estimated burn rate was clearly off, and we must adjust the backlog immediately and accordingly. By the middle of an iteration, however, we should generally be pretty close to having half the stories for the iteration completed. If not, the chances are that there's more work to do than the team's capacity can sustain, or the stories are too big compared to the iteration length.

Learning from our mistakes, we've come to realize that a story's burn-down rate is constantly more accurate a source of prediction than an inherently optimistic software developer. If it looks like we're not going to live up to our planned iteration content, we decrease our load.

Decreasing the load

When it looks like we're running out of time, we decrease the load. We don't work harder (or smarter). We're way past that illusion. We don't want to sacrifice quality, because producing good quality guarantees the sustainability of our productivity, whereas bad quality only creates more rework and grinds our progress to a halt. We also don't want to have our developers burn out from working overtime, especially when we know that working overtime doesn't make any difference in the long run.[6] Instead, we adjust the one thing we can: the iteration's scope—to reality. In general, there are three ways to do that: swap, drop, and split.

Swapping stories is simple. We trade one story for another, smaller one, thereby decreasing our workload. Again, we must consult the customer in order to assure that we still have the best possible content for the current iteration, given our best knowledge of how much work we can complete.

Dropping user stories is almost as straightforward as swapping them. "This low-priority story right here, we won't do in this iteration. We'll put it back into the product backlog." But dropping the lowest-priority story might not always be the best option, considering the overall value delivered by the iteration—that particular story might be of low priority in itself, but it might also be part of a bigger whole that our customer cares about. We don't want to optimize locally. Instead, we want to make sure that what we deliver in the end of the iteration is a cohesive whole that makes sense and can stand on its own.

The third way to decrease our load, splitting, is a bit trickier compared to dropping and swapping—so tricky that we'd better give the topic its own little section.

Splitting stories

How do we split a story we already tried hard to keep as small as possible during the initial planning game? In general, we can split stories by function or by detail (or both). Consider a story such as *"As a regular user of the online banking application, I want to optionally select the recipient information for a bank transfer from a list of most frequently and recently used accounts based on my history so that I don't have to type in the details for the recipients every time."*

Splitting this story by function could mean dividing the story into "...from a list of recently used accounts" and "...from a list of most frequently used accounts." Plus, depending on what the customer means by "most frequently and recently used," we might end up adding another story along the lines of "...from a weighted list of most frequently and recently used accounts" where the weighted list uses an algorithm specified by the customer. Having these multiple smaller stories, we could then start by implementing a subset of the original, large story's functionality and then add to it by implementing the other slices, building on what we have implemented for the earlier stories.

Splitting it by detail could result in separate stories for remembering only the account numbers, then also the recipient names, then the VAT numbers, and so

[6] Tom DeMarco and Timothy Lister have done a great favor to our industry with their best-selling books *Slack* (DeMarco; Broadway, 2001) and *Peopleware* (DeMarco, Lister; Dorset House, 1999), which explain how overtime reduces productivity.

forth. The usefulness of this approach is greatly dependent on the distribution of the overall effort between the details—if most of the work is in building the common infrastructure rather than in adding support for one more detail, then splitting by function might be a better option. On the other hand, if a significant part of the effort is in, for example, manually adding stuff to various places in the code base to support one new persistent field, splitting by detail might make sense.

Regardless of the chosen strategy, the most important thing to keep in mind is that, after the splitting, the resulting user stories should still represent something that makes sense—something valuable—to the customer.

Now that we have an idea of acceptance TDD as a process and about what's in it for us, let's talk about what powers that process: the team.

9.4 Acceptance TDD as a team activity

Because we're talking about a process for software development, which is inherently a people business, we cannot bypass the topic of team structure. Regardless of your professional background, I'm sure you have questions about the kind of team a project employing acceptance test-driven development might have, what kinds of roles there would be, and who would be doing what. Let's start from the single most important role a software project has: the role of the customer.

9.4.1 Defining the customer role

Having seen a variety of businesses, from big to small, from high-tech to brick-and-mortar, I've seen many variations on who the customer is for a software project. In some places, the customer is the one who pays, in some it's the one who will be using the system, and in others it's the one who will be selling the system. The customer may be the one who knows most about the application domain; or if management can't come up with anything else for someone to do, they may make that person the customer.

With perhaps the exception of that last example, all of these are potentially valid, smart ways to decide who will act as the customer. Generally speaking, the customer should derive direct or indirect benefit from the end product, although, especially in commercial settings (and even more so when talking about shrink-wrap software products) the level of indirection is rather deep.

Note that we're talking about *customer* as a role, not as an individual. Although the majority of projects might have a single person who acts as the customer, it doesn't have to be so. Indeed, many systems span multiple domains that might be far too complex for one person to understand thoroughly. In such contexts a team of customers typically occupies the customer role. When dealing with such a setup, it is crucial that the customer team has the necessary mechanisms to make and negotiate decisions quickly.

To better describe the ideal customer for a software project, let's look at some properties we would like to see in our customer(s).

Shared interest in success

The ideal customer shares the team's interest in the overall success of the project. Sharing that interest is essential in making sure that the team and the customer are working toward the same goal. Without that shared interest, it is difficult to sustain the high-bandwidth communication and heavy involvement of the customer in the daily work of the project team—doubly so if the customer has other commitments in addition to your project. When we have the right customer, they're an integral part of the team rather than an outsider expressing requests about what the team should be doing.

Authority to make decisions

Although getting empathy is better than facing cold ignorance, a customer without the authority to make decisions is not much more than a messenger between the team and the real customer. In an agile project relying on the ability to react to changes as they happen, having the authority to make decisions within the team (after all, the customer *is* part of the team) is essential. Decisions regarding prioritization and what a given user story entails must be made in a timely manner if we're to keep up with our capacity of delivering working software—after all, we need to know what to build in order to build it.

Ability to understand implications

Making decisions is not enough. Those decisions must be—within certain limits—smart decisions based on the best knowledge at that time and considering the implications of such decisions. For a customer on a software project, this might require consulting the development team with regard to technical implications of present alternatives, including the estimated cost and effort associated with a given decision.

Ability to explain the domain

An important characteristic—and unfortunately an aspect often lacking the attention it warrants—of a customer is the ability to explain the application domain to the team. The team is expected to speak the customer's language using the business domain's own terms, but they should not be expected to learn the domain on their own. After all, it could take years to learn a domain well enough without continuous interaction with the customer. Having a customer that's able to communicate effectively with the team is an essential building block for success.

We now have an idea of what is expected from the customer role. Earlier, we mentioned that the customer works with members of the development team in writing acceptance tests. This rather vague wording begs the question, who is this member of the development team that the customer collaborates with so closely in writing acceptance tests?

9.4.2 Who writes tests with the customer?

In some teams, it might be the customer and a tester who together create acceptance tests. In others, it might be the customer and a developer. In still others, it might be the customer and a group consisting of any combination of testers and developers. My personal experience has been with teams where developers take significant responsibility in testing their software beyond unit testing and TDD, so I've mostly seen teams where it's the customer and a developer who write acceptance tests. There are certain advantages, however, in having testers work on the acceptance tests with the customer and developers.

Perhaps the main differentiator in having a tester versus having a developer write acceptance tests with the customer comes from the slightly different perspective these team members generally possess for the system being developed. The developers are intimately familiar with how the system is structured, what kinds of changes will be required to support a given story, and so forth. That helps enormously in formulating possible solutions to fulfill the customer's need. The testers, on the other hand, are more familiar with the system as a whole and—typically—with the application domain in general. This makes testers ideal candidates for writing acceptance tests, because they already have the right perspective for defining how the system should work.

In practice, however, there is no hard and fast rule here either. In most cases, it seems, the ideal would be to have the whole team participate in writing acceptance tests. The benefits from doing so include not just spreading the knowledge but also the building of relationships between individual team members and the customer. The more people work together, the more fluent their collaboration becomes, and again that's essential in determining how well the team is able to build the features the customer wants.

9.4.3 How many testers do we need?

Some organizations—Microsoft being probably the best known—have established a practice of pairing a dedicated tester for each developer. Whether this is a good idea for your organization or not, I don't know. According to my experience, most teams do well with one tester per two developers or so, and most teams fare OK with even fewer testers as long as the developers are good at wearing the tester hat. (This isn't that easy, really: Professional testers often have a different mindset than most professional programmers.) In short, I'd suggest starting out with one tester per two to three developers and scaling up or down from there as you gain experience in your particular environment.

By now we know acceptance TDD is a team-level process that affects the way a whole team produces software together. We haven't talked about the benefits of acceptance TDD, however, beyond a passing mention of "better software faster." I think it's about time to discuss those benefits in more detail now that we have an idea of the process in general.

9.5 Benefits of acceptance TDD

Why were we doing this acceptance test-driven thing again? The reason is simple—it helps us write better software, the right software, and it helps us do that without spending our precious time and money on things of secondary importance. It sounds good all right. How about a closer look at how this support realizes itself?

To a large degree, the benefits of acceptance TDD could be seen as a direct extension of many of the benefits of user stories—being able to focus on the right things, getting the important stuff done while minimizing the waste in the process, and maximizing the value our customer gets out of the whole process. With that in mind, let's see how acceptance TDD expands on that already huge potential.

9.5.1 Definition of "done"

In a class about project management, one of the first things we learn is that projects have a beginning and an end. Otherwise, they're not projects. Quite likely, in the same class we're told about Parkinson's Law, which says, "Work expands to fill the time available for its completion." What do these two teachings have to do with acceptance TDD, you may ask? The key issue here is, *knowing where we are* and *knowing when to stop.* We need a definition of *done,* and acceptance TDD gives us a simple binary criterion that does just that: "Do all tests for the story pass?"

NOTE If you're familiar with the Scrum process, for example, you're probably already familiar with this concept. The definition of *done* is one of the first things a Scrum coach will ask the team to come up with if there is none. A mutual, shared working agreement about what counts as *done* is a must-have for reliable measures of progress.

With our acceptance criteria expressed as automated (or automatable) acceptance tests, we have a lot of the means necessary to set ourselves up for productive software development as far as knowing when we're done is concerned. Not all acceptance criteria are written down as automated acceptance tests, however. Some of them remain as the result of objective manual testing and evaluation by the customer. A good example is user interfaces.

User interfaces are not done until a human being says so

The user interface created for exposing functionality developed as part of a given story might be as crucial to get right—in some cases even more crucial—than implementing the functionality itself 100% correctly. If the user cannot access the functionality, or if the user interface is so horrid that they give up halfway through, the value of having the functionality is far less than if it was accessible.

The acceptable level of usability of a user interface is difficult to translate into an automated test. Instead of a set of automated tests, we might end up expressing the acceptance criteria as a combination of simple *constraints* such as "a maximum of three mouse-clicks required to access feature X" or "implementation must validate against modern web standards" and a sequence of *subjective evaluations* by the customer as we make progress with implementing the story (or, if that doesn't scale too well in a particular environment, once the developers feel sufficiently confident they've satisfied the story's usability requirements). In a sense, such subjective evaluations could be considered acceptance tests that define *done* as "when Simon says so" (which goes for all stories, by the way—it's never done until Simon says so, although the passing acceptance tests are a pretty darn good indicator).

Whatever the means of determining when we're done, the important thing is for everyone to know and agree to the way of determining when a given task is considered completed—whether it's a matter of all acceptance tests passing or a more complicated scenario involving subjective evaluations. In any case, acceptance TDD puts the act of thinking about and specifying those tests and evaluations in the beginning of the development cycle of implementing a user story. It makes it a heck of a lot easier to work effectively when we know how to tell when we're done.

And this feeds back to our two key issues: *knowing where we are* and *knowing when to stop.*

Knowing where we are

Acceptance tests don't drive development quite as the unit tests in TDD do. Instead, they drive development by giving us a concrete goal to aim at and the means to know when we've accomplished that goal. Similarly to unit tests in TDD, our acceptance tests keep us honest about what's needed and thus help us avoid scope creep and gold plating. Acceptance tests tell us exactly what we need to do, and they tell us when we're done leaving no room for ambiguity. But that's not all there is to knowing where we are—it's also about *the customer* knowing where we are.

With acceptance TDD, the customer can always tell where the development is going. As acceptance tests are added to the continuous build results and, as acceptance tests start passing, the customer gets valuable and trustworthy information about the progress the team is making. All they need to do is look at which acceptance tests are passing and which are not.

Knowing when to stop

Having our acceptance criteria clearly spelled out in the form of acceptance tests not only helps us know when we're done, but it also helps us avoid the classic gold-plating disease to which we developers often are subjected. It's a lot more difficult to "quickly add this little cool UI feature" when we have a set of tests passing, effectively shouting "you're done—have the customer look at it so we can move on!"

Then again, sometimes we're not done even though the tests say so. In these situations, when it's clear that the tests are lacking some essential aspect of the story, we see that the missing aspect gets implemented. Sometimes, that means consulting the customer about the details of how that missing part of the story should work. Sometimes, that leads to adding new acceptance tests as well, before we eventually implement the missing aspect.

Again, the mere existence of a set of acceptance tests aids us a great deal in stopping when we should. Not a moment too soon. Not a moment too late.

9.5.2 Cooperative work

One less obvious benefit of acceptance TDD is that it creates a more cooperative environment because everyone is working with the same goal at the same time. If testing is carried out after the development (and by a tester), then it often happens that the developer is already doing other stuff when the tester finds a bug. The goals of the developer and tester then conflict in a way.

Contrast this with a scenario where developers and test engineers are working together for a common goal of producing high-quality software that solves the right problem. This is a much more effective way to work, especially considering how each individual brings their unique knowledge and skill set into solving the problem.

9.5.3 Trust and commitment

In acceptance TDD, we write acceptance tests to specify what it means when that given user story has been implemented correctly. Having the customer write those acceptance tests together with the development team significantly solidifies the meaning of user stories. This is because there's a direct connection between what the customer specifies and what they get.

Part of this solidified meaning of user stories is also coming from the association of the customer seeing the development team implementing exactly what they ask for without holding them hostage to things they've said before or things they wrote down as requirements earlier. Part of it is coming from the developers seeing the customer write the acceptance tests, which clearly communicates the value coming out of completed code.

In short, the customer sees that their needs are indeed being met, and the developers see that the work they're doing is valued by the customer. Demonstrating the implemented user stories to the customer together with running (and passing!) acceptance tests is by far the best way I know to accomplish just that.

The ways in which tests are written in acceptance TDD do have significance. So much significance, in fact, that the next benefit of acceptance TDD on our list is *specification by example.*

9.5.4 Specification by example

An important aspect of acceptance tests is that they represent *specification by example,* a way to express requirements by the way of comprehensible examples rather than complex formulas and ambiguous prose. This brings us a number of advantages.

Generic descriptions that are full of ambiguity and subject to interpretation are an order of magnitude harder to translate into executable tests. Furthermore, for the customer it is much more difficult to validate whether a test is correct when they need to interpret the original intent among the ambiguities.

In short, tests expressed with concrete examples are easier to read, easier to understand, and easier to validate—not to mention easier to write in the first place! That last advantage becomes critical when our goal is to have the customer involved in specifying and writing tests for our system.

9.5.5 Filling the gap

Regardless of how well our unit tests cover our production code, they are not testing our system. They are testing our code and components in isolation. To put it another way, unit tests give us a good indication of whether our code works; but without some additional testing, we don't know whether our software as a whole works as it should work. In fact, in most cases our unit tests don't even tell us whether the individual components we're testing work together, although judicious use of contracts and interaction-based tests help close this gap. Although unit testing—especially in the form of test-first programming—is an enormously helpful practice in producing quality software, we often need something more to put our whole system under an automated test harness.

Some have even questioned the need for unit tests in the presence of a thorough acceptance test suite. Some successful programmers rely solely on automated acceptance tests to give them feedback and guard for regression during development. Personally, I feel that even though automated acceptance tests can indeed provide good enough protection for regression in some situations, the other benefits of writing unit tests to support TDD are more than enough to justify writing them. Generally speaking, one size does not fit all.

I'd go as far as warning you about the looming danger of using acceptance tests like unit tests in TDD—it might happen that we lose sight of the big picture of what's needed for the story, or we might stop writing good unit tests, effectively chewing away at our ability to refactor efficiently as we no longer have as thick a safety net as we used to with TDD. Acceptance test-driven development accompanies test-driven development—it doesn't replace it.

Now that we have an idea of the overall process of acceptance TDD and who's doing what, I think it's a good time to dig deeper into what exactly—technically speaking—we are testing with our acceptance tests.

9.6 What are we testing, exactly?

Just saying acceptance tests test user stories is often not enough to convey the idea of what exactly acceptance tests should test. Yes, acceptance tests are meant to verify that a user story is implemented correctly as specified. However, there are many ways to do that. We'll explore these ways further in chapter 11, but let's understand the fundamentals right now in order to create a crisp picture of what we should be testing with our acceptance tests.

9.6.1 Should we test against the UI?

Perhaps the most common question regarding acceptance tests is whether they should exercise the system under test through the real user interface (or the external interface of a machine-to-machine system) or some kind of an API beneath the user interface. The answer is, of course, "it depends." In general, however, our goal is to gain as much confidence as possible with as little effort as possible. Whether this is best achieved by writing end-to-end tests or by a divide-and-conquer strategy of writing smaller, more isolated tests is very much context-dependent.

When trying to decide whether to write acceptance tests against the system's real interface, against an abstract user interface (for example, when using the Presenter pattern described in chapter 8), or against some sort of a service layer exposing the business logic to the user interface, we might ask ourselves questions such as the following:

- How easy is it to write tests against the selected interface?
- How fragile will the tests be if written against the selected interface?
- Is the performance of the selected interface an issue?

For some systems, and especially for machine-to-machine–style backend systems, testing against the external interface is the best option. This is because those interfaces are typically well defined and do not exhibit as much turbulence as user interfaces. In general, machine-to-machine interfaces are easy to test.

Graphical user interfaces (GUIs) are a much more difficult class of interfaces from a testing perspective. One of the reasons for this is that GUIs often change more frequently than machine-to-machine interfaces as new functionality is added. This problem can be mitigated to some degree with careful design of the GUI implementation as well as that of the implementation of the tests themselves. Most often, however, it's not a question of technology that leans our decision in either direction.

Not a question of technology

With the tools available for the modern developer, moving a button on the screen or otherwise changing the basic layout is rarely a big issue for the maintainability of acceptance tests written against the GUI. Some extra care must be given, however, to avoid ending up with tests that are far more complex and verbose than the associated business logic would imply. In practice, it often makes sense to map a concise testing language on top of the technical interface to keep the complexity of tests in check. This way, we can keep the effort of writing acceptance tests against the GUI close to the effort of writing the same tests against an internal API.

Performance might matter

Sometimes, the motivation for having our acceptance tests bypass the real interface and go directly against the internal API is performance. The external interface could be a serial port with limited bandwidth, and we might have tens of megabytes of data to push through the thin pipe while executing our acceptance tests. In this type of scenario, it often makes sense to execute the tests without going through the bottleneck, effectively trading coverage for speed of feedback.

Even if we end up running our tests against an internal API, we still want to run at least some of our tests (although maybe not as often as the rest) against the real thing. Things are rarely either-or when talking about software development. In practice, we typically have acceptance tests operate on all available layers from the GUI, through internal APIs, and all the way down to isolated business logic.

A somewhat similar situation warranting testing against an internal API is the complete lack of access to the real thing. For example, we might not have the device with which our system is accessed. We might not have the exact hardware on which our system is supposed to be deployed. This leads us to the next question regarding what we're testing, exactly.

9.6.2 Should we stub parts of our system?

For many of the same reasons as for writing our tests against an internal interface instead of the external one, there are certain situations where we feel like replacing some part of our system—not necessarily just the external interface—with a fake implementation.

For example, our tests might require that a database be set up with large datasets before each test, and the particular database could prove to be too slow to do this while still retaining a fast enough feedback cycle. In this situation, we might be tempted to have our application use an in-memory database instead of the real one in order to avoid the cost of hitting the wire every time our tests or the application itself touches the database. Or we might be tempted to use a local database running on the same machine as the application in order to at least minimize the cost of network I/O.

The question remains: Should we do that? Should we replace some parts of the system with fake or alternative implementations in the name of convenience or speed?

Sufficiently close to the real thing

Whether we should stub or not is a question for which the answer is mostly dependent on the degree of certainty we have in the specific replacement being close enough to the real thing from the tests' perspective. In our example of replacing the real database with one that's physically located on the same machine as the application instead of on a separate one, the difference between the real thing and the replacement is insignificant. Replacing the real database product with a different one—or sometimes even using the same database in in-memory mode instead of running it as a server—is already more complex decision to make.

Differences in the SQL syntax supported by different databases, differences in how each database product handles certain data types, and so forth can be big enough risks to bite the bullet and use the real thing—even if the acceptance tests run slower with it. Whether to stub or not is ultimately a subjective decision, and there's no blanket answer that would be globally correct. We need to evaluate the trade-offs involved and make a decision case by case.

Sometimes a stub is our only option

Some situations remain where the stub is our only viable option, however. For example, some teams developing embedded or highly hardware-dependent software can be constrained because the sheer cost of a particular hardware chip or device is prohibitive. Another perhaps more common scenario is one where the constrained hardware is available infrequently and only for short periods of time. In situations like that, it's often better to run your acceptance tests on top of a simulator instead of only being available to run your tests for three hours every two weeks.

The question of stubbing parts of our system when running acceptance tests is more complex than defining what's close enough to the real thing, however. Acceptance tests are not all alike, and not all aspects of what our customer is interested in involve system-level properties. A good example of this is domain-specific business logic, which is a topic of its own.

9.6.3 Should we test business logic directly?

Just as traditional testing is not only about testing against functional requirements but also non-functional requirements, acceptance tests are written to cover a range of aspects of the system being developed. Perhaps the majority of acceptance tests are functionality-oriented, specifying correct behavior for a variety of different interaction sequences. Usually, a smaller portion of acceptance tests are those that specify systemic and non-functional requirements, such as the system's ability to handle simultaneous connections or to survive a crashing database or network downtime. Yet another class of acceptance tests specifies the core business logic—the stuff that happens behind the curtains when we interact with the system.

Thinking from the customer's perspective, testing domain-specific business logic directly makes a lot of sense. In many domains, the business logic involved is more than enough to warrant isolation and focus. It is much easier to wrap our heads around the logic when it's no longer muddled with irrelevant information related to populating forms, for example. From the developer's perspective, it's the exact same outcome—by focusing on the business logic directly, we are much more able to understand what the system needs to do.

To summarize, if your particular domain involves non-trivial business logic, by all means, specify and test it directly rather than hide it behind a sequence of actions through an external interface.

Speaking of summaries, before we wrap up this chapter, let's take a little tour through the various tools we have at our disposal for supporting the implementation of acceptance tests as part of acceptance TDD.

9.7 Brief overview of available tools

As in so many other aspects of software development, using the right tools can make the difference between night and day. What we are typically looking for in a tool for acceptance testing is support for:

- Writing our tests
- Implementing our tests
- Running our tests
- Reporting test results

Writing our tests refers to our need for a customer-friendly format that facilitates effective collaboration between developers, testers, and customers. The tool also needs to help us convert that customer-friendly format into something executable (if it isn't already) and to execute them—after all, that's what *automated* means. There is more to running our tests than that, though.

Because we will likely want to incorporate our acceptance tests into a continuous integration server to be run as a background job at configured intervals, the tools should support running the tests in batch mode—that is, without any manual intervention by whomever wants to run the tests. Finally, there's little use in running tests if we don't know whether they passed or not. Therefore, our toolset should also provide a way to report test results.

There are a variety of tools available for acceptance testing that all meet the previous requirements in one way or another. I'll introduce some of the more common ones briefly before diving into one of them in more detail.

9.7.1 Table-based frameworks

The latest fad in acceptance-testing tools is to express the tests in the form of tables. The common use case is that the customer (usually together with the developer) creates a table consisting of rows and columns, which is then interpreted by the testing framework based on the semantics and data embedded into the table cells. The customer could, for example, author the test table with the same office productivity tools with which they're already familiar and then save the document into a format that can be read and parsed by the testing framework—often either HTML (if using Microsoft Word) or XLS (if using Microsoft Excel).

Examples of tools in this category include Fit, FitNesse, and Selenium.

Fit: smart parsing for simple tables

Fit (Framework for Integrated Tests) was developed by Ward Cunningham to bridge the gap between the customer and the developer in the context of authoring acceptance tests. Fit essentially provides syntax for constructing test fixtures from HTML tables and a way to hook those fixtures into their implementations in various programming languages, such as Java, C#, Python, and so forth.

Given an HTML document, Fit parses the document looking for tables and, when it finds one, invokes the underlying code associated with the specific table. Finally, Fit renders the input document with all the table cells colored according to test results—a cell containing an assertion that failed would be colored red, and a cell containing an assertion that passed would be colored green. Anything that's not a table is considered narrative and is not processed by Fit. Fit is currently rather popular among teams adopting agile methods and, especially, Extreme Programming.

FitNesse: Fit in a Wiki

The guys at ObjectMentor built FitNesse to make writing Fit tests easier. FitNesse is essentially a combination of a web server, Fit, and a wiki web application that lets users edit web pages online using a more compact wiki syntax instead of raw HTML (which is a pain to edit by hand without graphical tools). The lightweight and simple markup language used to structure tables, headings, bulleted lists, and so forth can be a remarkable boost in productivity when working on the acceptance tests because the tests are more malleable and readily editable.

Selenium: controlling a browser

Selenium is a tool focused on testing web applications through the real user interface. What makes Selenium relatively unique is the way it accomplishes this, however.

Selenium tests are written as HTML tables just like in Fit and FitNesse, but they are implemented under the hood in JavaScript and executed by the JavaScript engine of the real web browser, such as Internet Explorer or Mozilla Firefox. This provides certain advantages over tools and libraries that exercise a web application by simulating a browser—specifically because of the varying level of support for JavaScript by the libraries and because of the differences in JavaScript support by the various browsers.

It is worth noting that Selenium also includes a remote-control mode, which allows for writing the tests in a programming language like Java or a scripting language like Ruby, while still executing the tests through a live web browser.

9.7.2 Text-based frameworks

Although table-based frameworks might be the mainstream right now, they are not the only class of frameworks suitable for acceptance testing. Not everyone likes authoring tests as tables. The text written into the cells of test tables is often close to written English, but the table structure brings with it a degree of syntax. Fortunately, some tools exist that let us author our tests in plain text instead of structured documents such as HTML.

Exactor: simple keyword-driven testing

Brian Swan of Exoftware developed a framework named Exactor to aid the developers in writing automated acceptance tests in a concise manner while still not restricting the test implementation too much. Instead of structuring tests into cells in an HTML table, Exactor tests are expressed in plain text files following a couple of simple rules: Every line that's empty or starts with the hash character is considered narrative, and all other lines represent a combination of an action and its parameters, separated by the tab character. The framework maps the names of actions into names of Java classes, and the parameters are passed to the `execute` method of an instance of the resolved class.

TextTest: testing with logs

Another testing framework based on raw text in contrast to structured documents is TextTest, written by Geoffrey Bache. TextTest's approach is unique in that its tests are written as log files. The fundamental idea is that the customer can express tests in a plain text file using whatever language he wishes, and the developer then implements the tests by adding logging statements to appropriate places in the production code. TextTest then verifies the correct functionality by comparing the expected and log files after running a test.

9.7.3 Scripting language-based frameworks

There is another category of acceptance-testing tools that can offer a great deal of power through the flexibility and friendliness of a scripting language. These tools are typically frameworks that attempt to deliver the promise of a domain-specific language through a generic scripting language such as Python or Ruby.

The obvious downside of these tools is that they're limited by the selected scripting language's suitability in defining a custom vocabulary within the limits of the language syntax. On the other hand, if the more complex syntax is not an issue (for example, if the customer possesses enough programming skills to be able to deal with the syntax), these tools enable an enormous scale of possibilities in terms of implementing tests—a full-blown scripting language is available, after all.

A good example of this category of tools is Systir,[7] which makes use of the Ruby scripting language's malleable syntax for building reasonably good, custom-domain–specific languages.

9.7.4 Homegrown tools

One important class of testing tools is those that are created in-house according to a specific development team's specific needs. Homegrown tools are in the core of the buy versus build dilemma. Writing our own testing framework does have its associated cost (both in building as well as maintaining it), and it might take some time to get started writing tests if we also need to implement a framework as you go.

The advantage of writing our own is, of course, that it will be tailor fit and will likely serve our needs better than a tool built by someone else on the other side of the globe. Also, the cost of writing our own testing framework is often less than we'd expect. I once wrote in one day a basic table-based testing framework for testing a web application according to a test script expressed as an Excel sheet. With that in mind, my suggestion would be to first evaluate whether it would be that costly to write your own instead of using a readily available framework that's slightly awkward to use in your particular context.

There's a thin line between homegrown and off-the-shelf testing tools or frameworks. In fact, most projects tend to grow some sort of a testing framework—sometimes from scratch and sometimes on top of an existing tool such as Fit. It's a question of how much third-party software you leverage beneath your custom test automation assets, be it tests or tooling.

OK, enough talk about tools. Let's wrap up the chapter with a quick summary.

9.8 Summary

By now, we know that user stories are a useful, lightweight technique for managing requirements. In this chapter, we discussed their connection with what we call acceptance tests—automated tests that can be used to drive development on the feature level a bit like we do on the code level with unit tests and test-driven development.

We started by clarifying to ourselves what acceptance tests are and what they should look like. From there, we continued to examine the process of acceptance

---

[7] http://atomicobject.com/pages/System+Testing+in+Ruby.

test-driven development, getting familiar with the four steps involved: picking a story, writing acceptance tests for it, automating those tests, and implementing the functionality to make the tests pass. We also looked at how this four-step cycle fits into the bigger picture of a whole iteration of an agile process and the kinds of activities related to stories and acceptance tests that we perform throughout the iteration.

After discussing the benefits of acceptance TDD, we turned our attention to the team and some common questions related to acceptance TDD: specifically, the customer's role in the process. Finally, we briefly talked about what we are testing with our acceptance tests and took a quick tour of available open source tools for implementing acceptance tests.

Now that we're aware of this fascinating technique called acceptance test-driven development and how it works, it's time to take a closer look at one specific tool for automating acceptance tests. In the next chapter, we'll introduce Fit, one of the open source tools we mentioned earlier and possibly the most used acceptance testing framework today. Once we know how Fit works and how we can use it for authoring and automating acceptance tests, we'll dedicate chapter 11 to discussing various strategies for implementing acceptance tests—that is, how to connect the test logic into the system under test.

10 Creating acceptance tests with Fit

We are searching for some kind of harmony between two intangibles: a form which we have not yet designed and a context which we cannot properly describe.

—Christopher Alexander,
father of the Pattern Language movement

It is safe to say that, at the time of writing this book, the Fit framework is by far the most popular acceptance-testing framework in use. It also happens to be good at what it does. For that reason, we'll be using Fit in this book to demonstrate how we can go about automating acceptance tests with a tool that supports customer collaboration as well as lending a hand to the programmer or tester for automating the tests' execution. Before getting down to the business of acceptance test-driven development with Fit, we need to know something about how Fit works and how to express acceptance tests with Fit. That is the goal of this chapter.

We'll begin by drawing the big picture of what Fit is, what it does, and how it can be used in acceptance TDD. We'll continue by familiarizing ourselves with the core concepts of Fit—*test documents* and *fixture tables*. From there, we'll continue with studying how Fit turns *fixture tables* into executable tests by binding the tables it encounters to *fixture classes*. We'll gain understanding of the way Fit does this by looking at three built-in fixture types called the `ColumnFixture`, `RowFixture`, and `ActionFixture`.

Having learned about the three built-in fixture types, we will shortly discuss how fixtures can (and should) be extended and customized for our specific needs. We'll also look at a couple of additional fixtures provided by an extension to Fit called *FitLibrary*. Finally, we'll look at how we can execute our Fit tests from the command line and as part of an automated build using Apache Ant.[1]

For a more thorough exploration into the Fit framework, I highly recommend picking up a copy of *Fit for Developing Software* (Addison-Wesley, 2005) by Ward Cunningham and Rick Mugridge, the original authors of Fit and FitLibrary, respectively. That book is the definitive tome that documents Fit's features in far more depth and breadth than what is possible within the constraints of a single chapter. Having said that, once reaching this chapter's summary, we will already have good enough a grasp of Fit's concepts and underpinnings to be able to start automating acceptance tests on our project.

And now, let's get Fit.

10.1 What's Fit?

Fit, originally an acronym that stood for Framework for Integrated Tests, was developed by Ward Cunningham a couple of years ago to help getting customers involved in writing acceptance tests. Fit is available for a number of mainstream

[1] http://ant.apache.org.

(and not quite so mainstream) programming languages and is essentially a thin framework that parses table-based documents and interprets and translates them into a sequence of method calls into the underlying *fixture classes* implemented with a programming language such as Java, C#, Python, or Ruby. Fit also supports reporting test results by producing a user-friendly, color-coded output of the test document, highlighting the fail/pass status of each table row with a green or red background color for each respective table cell.

Before we get any more tangled with who interprets what and what translates to what, let's talk a bit about how Fit fits into the process of acceptance TDD.

10.1.1 Fit for acceptance TDD

To quote the Fit homepage,[2] "Fit creates a feedback loop between customers and programmers. Fit allows customers and testers to use tools like Microsoft Office to give examples of how a program should behave—without being programmers themselves. Fit automatically checks those examples against the actual program, thus building a simple and powerful bridge between the business and software engineering worlds."

This feedback and collaboration build around the ability of the customers to stay within their familiar productivity tools using the familiar table structure within a document to describe the wanted program behavior and verify for themselves whether a given behavior is in place or not. However, there's still a way to go from a document containing text in tables to the computer executing code that checks the specification against the system under test. Figure 10.1 gives an overall picture of what happens when a team follows acceptance TDD in this way.

Looking at figure 10.1, the process for creating an executable acceptance test using Fit starts from the top-left corner. Let's go through what's happening in each of these steps.

Customer creates a sketch

The first step is for the customer (possibly in collaboration with a member of the development team) to write an initial sketch of the test document. *Sketch* in this context means that the document probably isn't yet in its final, executable format but it already describes the desired behavior for a user story, providing examples of that behavior in the form of tables.

---

[2] http://fit.c2.com/.

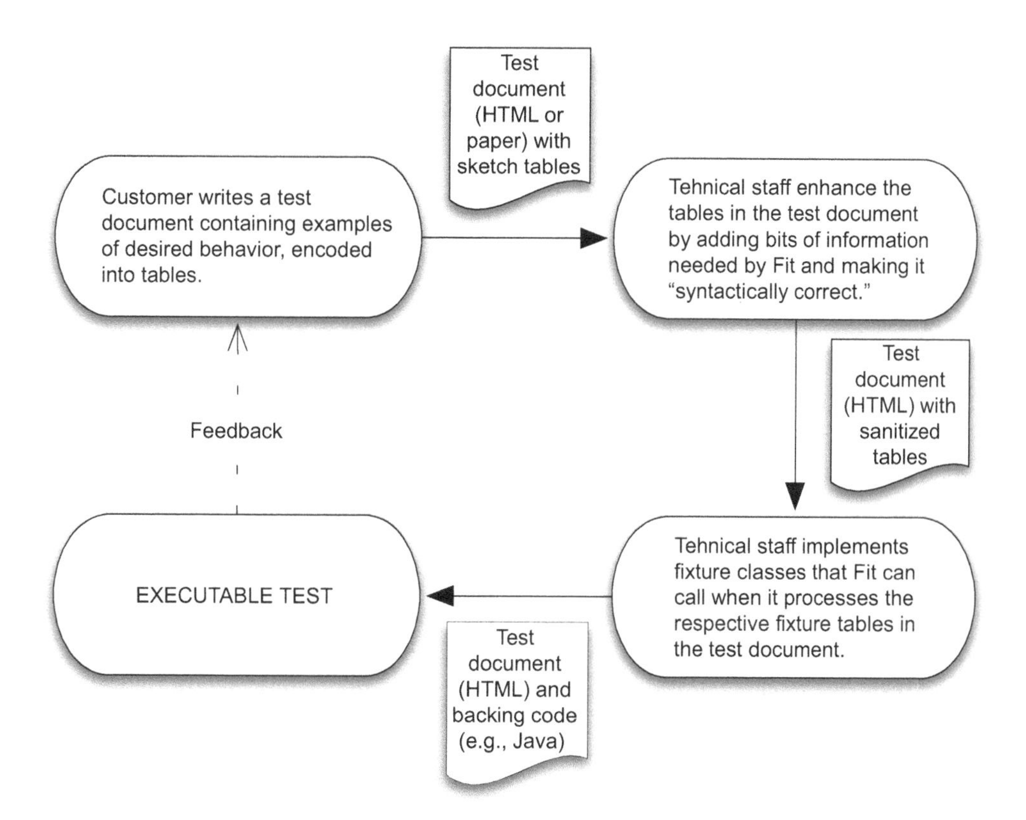

Figure 10.1 The transitions from a test document informally described by the customer to an executable test. After the customer has created the initial test document, the development team first sanitizes the tables so that Fit can interpret it correctly. With a syntactically valid test document, the development team next implements the backing code—the fixture classes—so that Fit has something to invoke when processing the test document. When all three of these steps are done, we have an executable test in the form of the combination of a document containing fixture tables and code that implements the tables.

In this sketch stage, the test document should first and foremost act as a tool for the customer to express their vision. Thus, even if the document is written together with a technical staff member, the focus should not be on creating the examples' tables in a format understood by Fit. Some teams like creating these sketches on paper, leaving the conversion to electronic format to be carried out in the next step—cleaning up the sketch tables.

Team cleans up the sketch tables

In the second step, the development team (developer, testing engineer, business analyst—anyone familiar with Fit and the already existing fixture classes) takes the sketch and enhances it so that it's ready for Fit to process.

In practice, this often means adding a header row to the tables created by the customer with some metadata for Fit (later we'll see why), altering the exact wording used by the customer to match suitable pre-existing fixture classes, splitting a table created by the customer into two tables for technical reasons, and so forth.

Although the test document can experience a lot of refactoring as tables get touched up, split up, and moved around, the team should take care to retain the customer's original intent. In other words, although the sketch needs to be sanitized enough for Fit to be able to process it, the document must also remain understandable by the customer. This might mean that, for example, a certain amount of duplication between multiple tables should be allowed in the name of readability rather than mercilessly removing the duplication with the side effect of making the examples more difficult to follow.

After the development team is finished cleaning up the test document, Fit is able to parse and process the document. However, at this stage the vast majority of tests are typically failing because Fit doesn't know what "accumulated interest" or "number of bonds in portfolio" means in terms of the technical implementation of the system under test. This is why we need the third step in figure 10.1, which we'll discuss next.

Team implements backing code

Once the customer has described examples of the desired behavior as tables and the development team has cleaned up the tables for Fit, it is the programmer's job to implement the underlying fixture classes to glue the tables in the test document into the system under test. Figure 10.2 illustrates the translation that takes place, carried out by the Fit framework.

When Fit parses a test document and encounters a table, it needs to process the table somehow. The problem is, of course, that the table describes the desired behavior in the customer's language (for example, English); however, the system under test only understands ones and zeros, so some kind of translation is needed.

The Fit framework acts as a dumb translator that understands the format and structure of the fixture tables and, following certain rules, knows how to feed the bits and pieces in a fixture table to someone else—that someone else being a fixture class. The fixture class then does whatever it needs to do—Fit doesn't care—

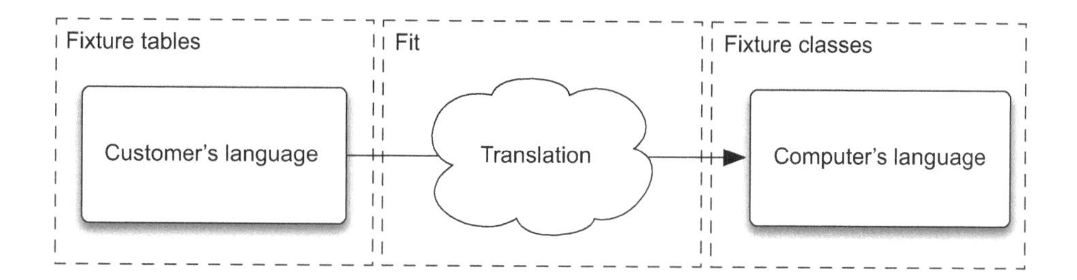

Figure 10.2 The Fit framework translates the customer's language encoded in fixture tables into the computer's language encoded in fixture classes. The fixture classes can be implemented with a variety of programming languages, typically—but not necessarily—in the same language as the system under test is implemented. Scripting languages, for example, are often a good candidate for implementing the backing code for fixture tables due to their flexibility and ability to integrate with other technologies.

and communicates back following certain rules.[3] We'll look at these rules later in this chapter when we talk about a number of concrete fixture classes.

In order to connect fixture tables to the system under test, Fit needs to have a matching fixture class for each fixture table. Luckily, most fixture classes can and will be used in more than one test document. Or, the other way around, sometimes the team doesn't need to implement new fixture classes for a test document because the document uses fixture tables that are backed by existing fixture classes.

We've already mentioned in passing the concepts of a *test document, fixture table,* and *fixture class*. Let's see what those peculiar things look like, starting from the documents and tables.

10.1.2 Test documents contain fixture tables

In Fit, the concept of a test is loosely defined through a test document containing an arbitrary mixture of narrative text and executable fixture tables. When we're running such a test document with Fit, the narrative text sections are ignored, and the fixture tables are interpreted, one by one, in the order Fit encounters them in the document.

Although it is possible to author these test documents in other formats, HTML is by far the most common among projects using Fit. Some teams, for example, choose to author their test documents using Microsoft Word, saving the documents as HTML. Figure 10.3 shows an example of an HTML test document opened in Microsoft Word for editing.

[3] For example, a fixture class throwing an exception generally means that the test has failed....

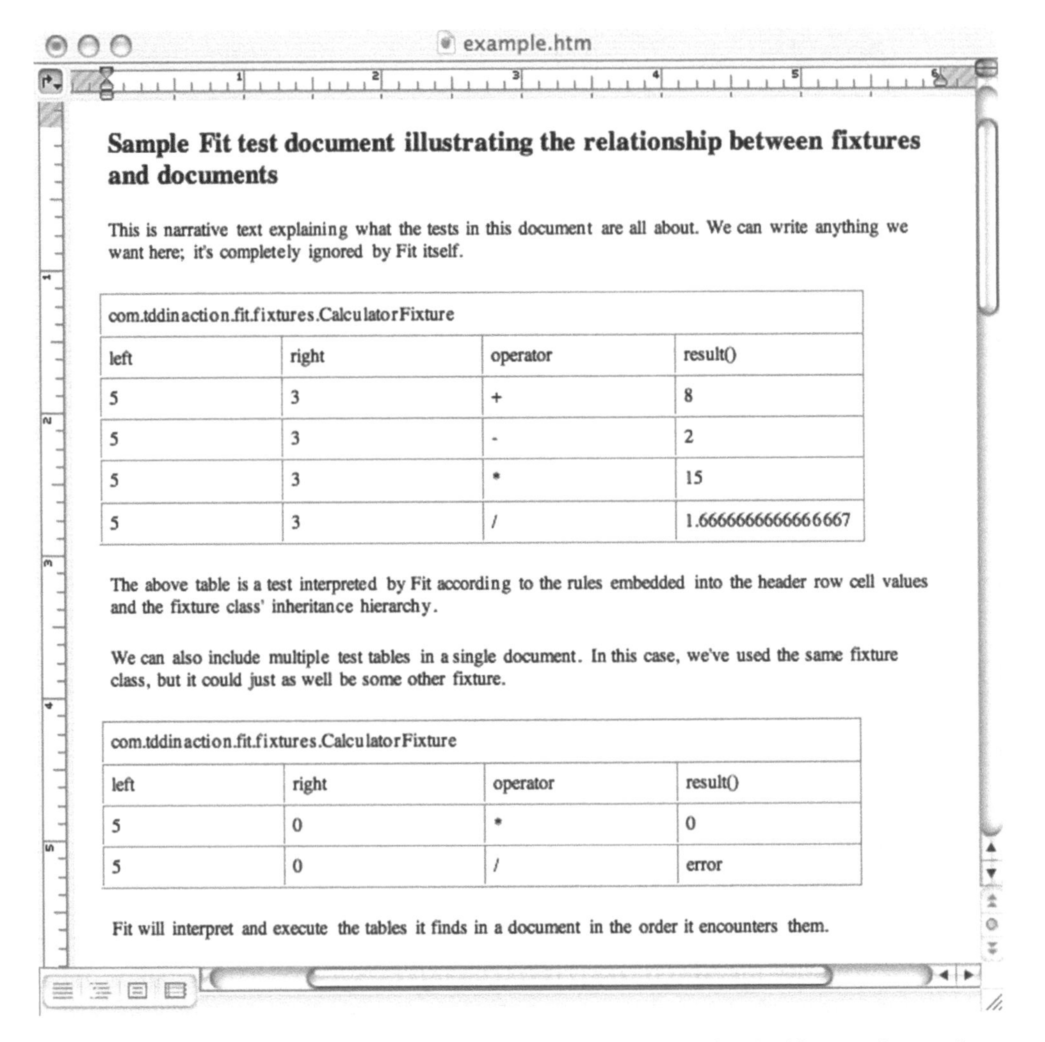

example.htm

Sample Fit test document illustrating the relationship between fixtures and documents

This is narrative text explaining what the tests in this document are all about. We can write anything we want here; it's completely ignored by Fit itself.

com.tddinaction.fit.fixtures.CalculatorFixture			
left	right	operator	result()
5	3	+	8
5	3	-	2
5	3	*	15
5	3	/	1.6666666666666667

The above table is a test interpreted by Fit according to the rules embedded into the header row cell values and the fixture class' inheritance hierarchy.

We can also include multiple test tables in a single document. In this case, we've used the same fixture class, but it could just as well be some other fixture.

com.tddinaction.fit.fixtures.CalculatorFixture			
left	right	operator	result()
5	0	*	0
5	0	/	error

Fit will interpret and execute the tables it finds in a document in the order it encounters them.

Figure 10.3 Fit test documents are regular HTML files that can be edited with a regular word processor. The example document shown here illustrates how the format allows for mixing executable test or fixture tables with narrative text around them.

As you can see, the document contains two tables mixed with narrative text. The document contains headings—which are considered by Fit to be part of the narrative—and there could be any other HTML markup, such as images (screenshots of the UI prototype, for example), links to external documentation, and so forth. In

> **Creating a common template for test documents**
>
> Although there's no technical requirement for test documents to look the same, most projects end up creating some kind of a template for their Fit tests. For example, one project always included a special table in the top of the document, recording information such as the associated use case and the number of the iteration in which the test was created. In practice, this table was just another fixture table from Fit's perspective, so the people working on the project needed to have a backing fixture class for it. As far as I can remember, though, the fixture class didn't do anything because the table's purpose was to document the test itself, not to test the system.

short, Fit doesn't care. What Fit does care about is the two tables present in the document, which represent something Fit needs to execute somehow.

The two tables in figure 10.3 represent the executable portions of the test document and are the infamous fixture tables to which we've already alluded to. *Fixture* is arguably a loaded word in the world of test automation. As we learned in part 1, a fixture in the context of unit-testing is the state or a set of objects used by a test class for carrying out an automated test. In the context of Fit, however, the word *fixture* has a different meaning. Let's talk about that next.

10.1.3 Fixtures: combinations of tables and classes

What we've learned about Fit's nomenclature so far is that the tables in a test document are called *fixture tables*. From a programmer's perspective—or whomever carries out the final step of implementing the backing code for a fixture table—the two tables in figure 10.3 represent instances of a class named `CalculatorFixture`, which the programmer creates for mapping the table data into method calls to our system under test. We could say that fixtures are the programming language *implementations* of the abstract fixture tables in a test document. Let's look at figure 10.4 for a close-up of one of the tables in figure 10.3 and see what it tells us.

The first cell on the first row is the name of a *fixture class*, in this case, `com.tddinaction.fit.fixtures.CalculatorFixture`. When it encounters a table, Fit loads a class with the name indicated in the first cell and instantiates an object of that class using the default (no-argument) constructor. The fixture class is what makes a fixture table "alive," giving Fit something to invoke when encountering a fixture table that references the class. What happens when Fit encounters

com.tddinaction.fit.fixtures.CalculatorFixture			
left	right	operator	result()
5	3	+	8
5	3	-	2
5	3	*	15
5	3	/	1.6666666666666667

Figure 10.4 One of the fixture tables from the test document captured in figure 10.3. The first row on the table tells Fit which *fixture class* to use to execute this table. The interpretation of the remaining rows depends on the fixture class.

a fixture table is dependent on the specific fixture class; but whatever that is, the Fit table parser drives it by feeding the table rows to the fixture object one by one.

We have fixture tables and fixture classes. What about just plain *fixture*? If you visit a team that's using Fit, they're probably talking about *fixtures* whether their finger is pointing at an HTML document or a Java class. Some people use the term *fixture* as shorthand for *fixture table* or *fixture class*, trusting that the meaning can be deduced from the context. There's another way to look at it, though.

If we consider the whole journey from the customer's first sketch to an actual, running, automated acceptance test, we're all the time working on a unit that is represented by a table (customer's view) or a class (programmer's view) or both. In that sense, and considering that the fixture table and fixture class are tightly coupled, we can generally refer to the combination of a fixture table and the backing fixture class as *a fixture.*

That's pretty much all there is to say about fixtures in general. It's time to introduce some concrete fixture classes in order to extend our understanding of what fixtures are and what they can do. How about starting with the three built-in fixtures?

10.2 Three built-in fixtures

Fit comes with three built-in fixture classes: `ColumnFixture`, `RowFixture`, and `ActionFixture`. The idea is that projects will create their own, application-specific fixture libraries to support their particular application domain, preferences, and so forth. Before we begin creating custom fixtures, however, we should first learn about the three most basic ones by taking a little tour through the available built-in fixture classes and the kinds of fixture tables they support.

That's what we'll do next. We'll begin with perhaps the most intuitive one of the triplet—the ColumnFixture. Once we've grokked how the ColumnFixture can be used for specifying expected outcome with a given input for the logic under test, we'll move on to discover RowFixtures, a more data-oriented colleague of the ColumnFixture. Finally, we'll shake hands with the last of the three built-in fixtures, the ActionFixture, which facilitates expressing interaction-oriented tests.

First up: the ColumnFixture.

10.2.1 ColumnFixture

The ColumnFixture is perhaps the simplest[4] of the three built-in fixtures. Its simplicity stems from the straightforward mapping Fit performs between columns in a fixture table to public fields and methods on the underlying fixture class in order to let the fixture class carry out simple calculations based on the table's contents. Before you start wondering how that mapping works, let's look at the structure of a ColumnFixture table.

The second row of a ColumnFixture table—the one right after the fixture class name—is called the *header row*. The column values in the header row indicate to Fit what it should do with the rest of the rows on the table. If a cell on the header row has the value left, Fit knows that, for that column in the following rows, it should set the cell's content as the value of a public field named left on the underlying fixture object. Figure 10.5 highlights the essential pieces of the ColumnFixture table we saw in figure 10.4.

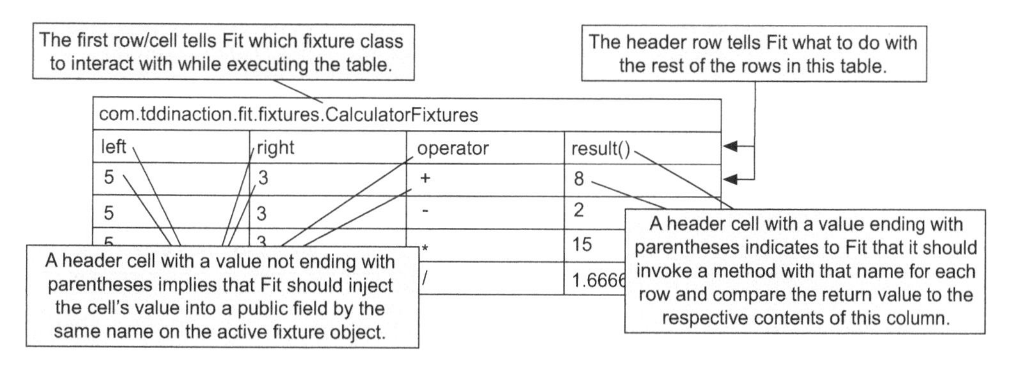

Figure 10.5 The column fixture table from figure 10.4 with explanations of the meaning of key elements of the table structure

---

[4] Simplest does not mean the least powerful, though. Some might argue that **ColumnFixture** is the most adept of the built-in fixtures to support testing business logic.

If a cell on the header row has the value `result()` (note the parentheses), Fit knows it's an *expected result* column. This means for that column and for each row, Fit will call a method named `result` and compare its return value to the expected value indicated in the current row's cell value. Due to this way of mapping columns to field and method access, the `ColumnFixture` is mostly used for relatively simple calculation-style tests, which are focused on verifying the correct results of executing specific business rules for a variety of different kinds of input.

Our fixture class from the sample Fit document, `CalculatorFixture`, is a subclass of `fit.ColumnFixture`. Let's look under the hood and figure out exactly how Fit performs the previous mapping of table data to the fixture class and where we write the glue code that interacts with the system under test. Considering the `CalculatorFixture` table in figure 10.5, the fixture class implementation could look like listing 10.1.

Listing 10.1 CalculatorFixture.java

```
public class CalculatorFixture extends fit.ColumnFixture {

    public double left;
    public double right;
    public char operator;

    public double result() {
        Calculator calculator = Calculator.getInstance();
        switch (operator) {
            case '+': return calculator.add(left, right);
            case '-': return calculator.subtract(left, right);
            case '*': return calculator.multiply(left, right);
            case '/': return calculator.divide(left, right);
        default:
            throw new IllegalArgumentException(
                      "Unknown operator: " + operator);
        }
    }
}
```

❶ Fields for input

❷ Methods produce output

❸ result() method has access to row's data

In listing 10.1, we can see the ❶ three public instance variables to which Fit binds our fixture table's input columns. Note how the "left" and "right" columns' contents are converted to primitive `double` values and how the "operator" column's symbol is converted into a `char`. Most of the basic types like Java's primitives and basic data types from the `java.lang` package are converted automatically. For the rest, we need to perform the conversion ourselves. (But that's a topic for another book.)

Looking at the ❷ `result` method, we can see how columns that have a trailing "()" are mapped to public methods that don't take any arguments and return something. Again, Fit doesn't care about the method's return type—after first populating a row's values from input columns to instance variables, Fit invokes the methods matching each expected result column, comparing the actual return value to the expected one that is defined in the fixture table. In other words, ❸ the methods have full access to the values of the current row's input fields.

With the `CalculatorFixture` class (and the production code[5]) implemented, we can now tell Fit to run our test document against the fixture implementation to test our production code. We'll talk about how we can run Fit tests later in this chapter. For now, let's skip directly to the outcome. Figure 10.6 shows an example of what kind of a result document Fit could produce from our test run.

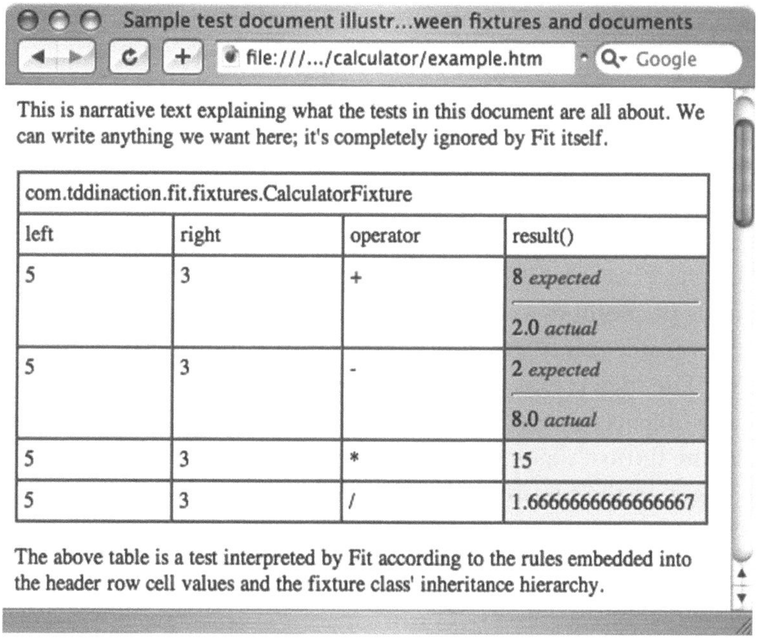

Sample test document illustr...ween fixtures and documents

file:///.../calculator/example.htm

Google

This is narrative text explaining what the tests in this document are all about. We can write anything we want here; it's completely ignored by Fit itself.

com.tddinaction.fit.fixtures.CalculatorFixture			
left	right	operator	result()
5	3	+	8 *expected* 2.0 *actual*
5	3	-	2 *expected* 8.0 *actual*
5	3	*	15
5	3	/	1.6666666666666667

The above table is a test interpreted by Fit according to the rules embedded into the header row cell values and the fixture class' inheritance hierarchy.

Figure 10.6 As Fit executes our tests, the relevant table cells are colored to indicate success and failure. For any mismatch, both the expected and actual values are displayed next to each other.

[5] We could, of course, run the test without the production code in place. It's just that it wouldn't make much sense because our fixture class wouldn't be testing anything or wouldn't compile.

Figure 10.6 demonstrates how Fit renders variations between the expected and actual output of the expected result cells with a pink background and both the expected and actual values separated with a horizontal line. (The colors don't appear in this book's black-and-white images, but you can discern them from their gray shading.) Apparently we "mistakenly" wired addition and subtraction the wrong way around. How clumsy of us... (In practice, we expect most errors in our Fit tables to be about missing functionality, not trivial programming errors like this.)

Passing checks, on the other hand, are indicated by light green background. Note that all the other cells are left alone because they're not performing any assertions—they're just set up for the assertion (result) cells of that specific row.

I think we've seen enough of `ColumnFixture` for now. Let's look at the next built-in fixture, the `RowFixture`.

10.2.2 RowFixture

The `RowFixture` can be used to compare the results of more complex queries, typically to verify the system's *state* after having prior fixtures simulate interaction with or invoke functionality in the system. As an example, we will use the `RowFixture` to verify that our calculator remembers the last five computations.

Like `ColumnFixture`, the `RowFixture` is to be subclassed by our own, custom fixture class. `RowFixture` differs from `ColumnFixture` in that it doesn't map columns to fields or methods on the fixture class. Instead, a `RowFixture` is used to compare the results of *a single query method* on the fixture class to the rows of the fixture table. The idea is that each row represents a single domain object, and the list of domain objects formed by the rows in our fixture table should match the list returned by the fixture's `query` method.[6] Fit then compares the returned domain objects and rows in the fixture table using reflection.

As an example, let's write a test for checking our calculator's short-term memory. That is, when queried for the operation history, the `Calculator` object returns a list of objects that matches what we have written into the fixture table. Figure 10.7 presents a fixture table we might write for such functionality.

---

[6] For more details about the actual algorithm with which Fit determines whether the lists match, refer to http://fit.c2.com/wiki.cgi?RowFixture and the source code for **`fit.RowFixture`**.

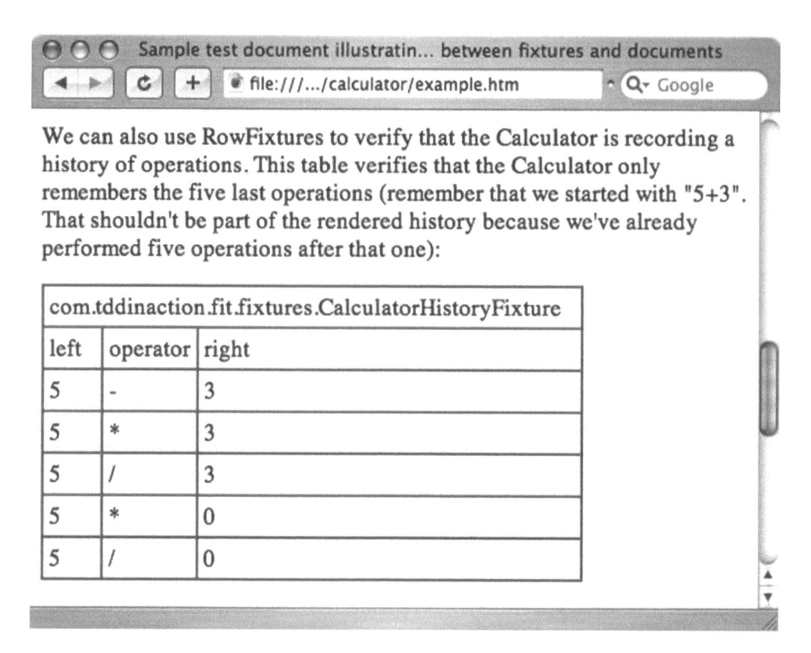
Sample test document illustratin... between fixtures and documents

file:///.../calculator/example.htm

We can also use RowFixtures to verify that the Calculator is recording a history of operations. This table verifies that the Calculator only remembers the five last operations (remember that we started with "5+3". That shouldn't be part of the rendered history because we've already performed five operations after that one):

com.tddinaction.fit.fixtures.CalculatorHistoryFixture		
left	operator	right
5	-	3
5	*	3
5	/	3
5	*	0
5	/	0

Figure 10.7 The `RowFixture` can be used to compare larger datasets easily. The `RowFixture` compares the set of objects described by the table rows to the set of objects returned by a query method on the fixture class.

Note that our test is verifying that the calculator only remembers the last five operations performed. The fixture class, shown in listing 10.2, is straightforward to implement.

Listing 10.2 Example `RowFixture` verifying that calculator records history correctly

```
public class CalculatorHistoryFixture extends fit.RowFixture {

    public Class getTargetClass() {
        return Operation.class;
    }

    public Object[] query() throws Exception {
        java.util.List history =
            Calculator.getInstance().getOperations();
        return history.toArray(new Operation[history.size()]);
    }
}
```

Return Operation objects (annotates `return Operation.class;`)

Query method that Fit calls (annotates `public Object[] query() throws Exception {`)

From listing 10.2, we see that our `RowFixture` advertises that its target class is `Operation`. Internally, Fit uses this information to determine which fields or methods it should compare between the objects in the table and the objects returned by the fixture's `query` method.

Listing 10.3 presents the `Operation` class, using public fields to represent column values.

Listing 10.3 The domain object class returned by the `query` method

```
public class Operation {
    public int index;          <-- Location in history

    public double left;
    public double right;
    public char operator;
}
```

Domain object class representing performed operation

Because we haven't yet implemented the limitation of history size, the matching algorithm of `RowFixture` notices that the returned list and the table contents don't match, reporting them appropriately with the pink background in figure 10.8.

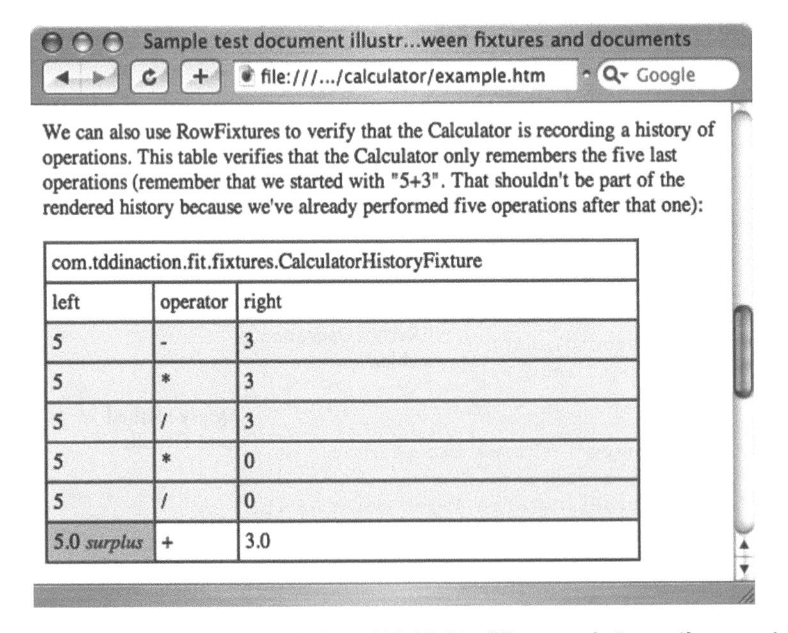

com.tddinaction.fit.fixtures.CalculatorHistoryFixture		
left	operator	right
5	-	3
5	*	3
5	/	3
5	*	0
5	/	0
5.0 *surplus*	+	3.0

Figure 10.8 `RowFixture` **finds and highlights differences between the expected and actual data by invoking a `query` method that returns an array of objects, comparing it to the array of objects constructed from the fixture table's rows. Any surplus or missing records will be highlighted with a pink background while the matching records get the familiar green shade.**

The output in figure 10.8 indicates that the `RowFixture` found a surplus object from the array returned by our fixture's query method, compared to what we expected. If we had returned a list missing some of the operations, we would've gotten a similar output with the message *missing* to indicate that the returned array was missing some rows that we expected it to contain.

As I believe you've already deduced from this example, the `RowFixture` is particularly well-suited for comparing datasets and, as such, is a nice (although not too commonly used) companion for the more computation-oriented `ColumnFixture`. However, when using the `RowFixture` for comparing datasets, we should know that the fixture table's rows and the objects returned by the `query` method are sorted before matching the expected with the actual. In practice, this means that the order of the returned objects is ignored—an important feature of the `RowFixture`, which isn't too clearly spelled out in Fit's documentation! In other words, the `RowFixture` isn't the right tool for the job if you want to test the order, too.

Next up is the oddball of Fit fixtures—the `ActionFixture`.

10.2.3 ActionFixture

The `ActionFixture` is a more action-oriented alternative compared to the other built-in fixtures. Originally created for writing fixtures to test graphical user interfaces, the `ActionFixture` has become an all-round workhorse that people extend and use for a variety of purposes; but still, at its heart, it models interaction with at least an abstract user interface.

Let's make sure we understand the standard functionality provided by the `ActionFixture`, before getting ahead of ourselves by extending it.

Unlike `ColumnFixture` and `RowFixture`, `ActionFixture` does not depend on a header row. The only concern the `ActionFixture` has is that the first column on each row contains a *keyword*—the name of an action. These actions are mapped by Fit to method calls on an object called "actor" in Fit nomenclature. The actor object is typically the `ActionFixture` itself or some other object capable of delegating our actions to the system under test—sometimes the actor object can be a part of the system under test, if the method names in our production code base are on a suitable level of abstraction (that is, if they make sense from the perspective of the user, for example).

The `ActionFixture` class comes with a set of four built-in actions: "start", "enter", "press", and "check". Here's a brief description of each:

- *start*—The equivalent of navigating to a screen for the first time. When the `ActionFixture` encounters the "start" action, it replaces the current actor object with a new instance of the class of which the name is in the second column following the "start" keyword. From that point on, all actions are invoked on this new actor object.
- *enter*—Like typing information into a text box. When the `ActionFixture` encounters the "enter" action, it tries to call a method on the current actor object with the method's name indicated in the second column after the `enter` keyword. The arguments passed into the method are collected starting from the third column.
- *press*—Like clicking a button on a user interface. When the `ActionFixture` encounters the "press" action, it tries to call a simple, no-argument method on the current actor object with the method's name indicated in the second column after the `press` keyword.
- *check*—Like saying, "compare these two values—they should be equal." When `ActionFixture` encounters the "check" action, it calls a no-argument method on the current actor object with the method's name indicated in the second column after the `check` keyword and compares the return value to the value of the third column.

To see these actions in action (pun intended), look at the fixture table in figure 10.9, which exercises our `Calculator` class in an imperative manner, simulating a user pushing the buttons on the calculator and asserting that the calculator's display is showing the correct output after certain sequences of input.

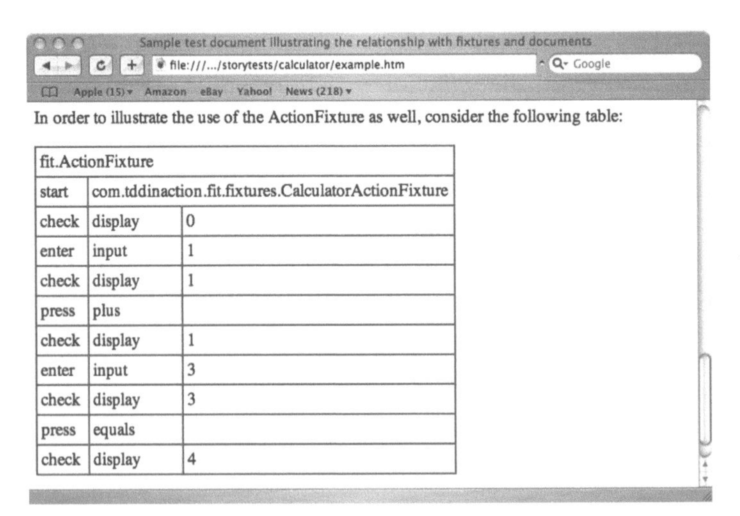

fit.ActionFixture		
start	com.tddinaction.fit.fixtures.CalculatorActionFixture	
check	display	0
enter	input	1
check	display	1
press	plus	
check	display	1
enter	input	3
check	display	3
press	equals	
check	display	4

Figure 10.9 **`ActionFixtures`** **are, as their name implies, action-oriented and are suited for modeling interaction with the system under test. The four available actions to use in the fixture table are "start", "check", "enter", and "press".**

This table would translate to roughly the following execution sequence on behalf of the Fit framework:

1. Create an instance of `CalculatorActionFixture`, and set it as the current actor.
2. Call `display` on the `CalculatorActionFixture` instance, expecting 0.
3. Call `input` on the `CalculatorActionFixture` instance, which takes 1 as the parameter.
4. Call `display` again—it should now return 1.
5. Call `plus` on the `CalculatorActionFixture` instance.
6. Call `display` again, and verify that it's still returning 1.
7. Call `input` on the `CalculatorActionFixture` instance, which takes 3 as the parameter.
8. Call `display` again, and verify that it's now returning 3.
9. Call `equals` on the `CalculatorActionFixture` instance.
10. Call `display` one last time, this time verifying that it returns 4, which is our final result.

Under the hood, our custom `ActionFixture` class translates these application-oriented actions such as display, input, plus, and equals, into method calls to the system under test. For example, if we're launching the system under test inside the same process our Fit tests are running in, we could create a new instance of the calculator user interface in our fixture class's constructor. Following such an approach, the `CalculatorActionFixture` class could look like listing 10.4.

Listing 10.4 CalculatorActionFixture.java

```
public class CalculatorActionFixture extends fit.ActionFixture {

    private CalculatorPresenter presenter;

    public CalculatorActionFixture() {
        actor = this;                                  <- Associate ourselves as current actor
        presenter = new CalculatorPresenter(new Calculator());   <- Obtain reference to system under test
    }

    public double display() {
        return presenter.display();                    | Actions map directly to methods on code
    }

    public void equals() {
```

```
        presenter.evaluate();
    }

    public void input(double input) {
        presenter.inputValue(input);
    }

    public void plus() {
        presenter.plusClicked();
    }
}
```

Actions map directly to methods on code

The four built-in actions of the ActionFixture are enough to construct tests for even surprisingly complex functionality. However, the intent is to build fixture classes to support our specific application and domain as well as possible. In practice, that's likely something other than "start", "enter", "press", and "check", although we still use the same fundamental logic of the ActionFixture and its action keywords in the first column. For example, we might extend the built-in ActionFixture by overriding certain parts, effectively giving us an option of saying "verify display is showing | X" instead of "check | display | X" or just "plus" instead of "press | plus".

Although the three built-in fixtures, ColumnFixture, RowFixture, and ActionFixture, are somewhat sufficient for building any kind of tests from a purely technical point of view, the reality is that we don't want to limit our tests to using just these three fixture classes. Instead, we extend them and create our own, tailored fixtures for our specific needs—a bit like we've done with the three different Calculator fixtures we've already seen but also tweaking the fixture tables' execution. Let's spend a minute looking at an example illustrating what we mean by that.

10.2.4 Extending the built-in fixtures

The three built-in fixtures each provide their own way of extending themselves to solve a specific type of test-authoring problem. Sometimes, however, the extension facilities provided by these fixtures aren't the perfect match we're looking for. This means we'll need to go one step further and dig into the built-in fixtures' source code to find alternative extension points.

Example: setting up data for our tests

For instance, we might want to create a fixture that lets us define data to be populated into a database. We could abuse the standard ColumnFixture to do so by using a combination of input fields receiving the data to populate and having an "add()" column that maps to a method call that inserts the record into the system. The "add()" column's only function would be to offer us a hook into the appropriate point in time when we have all the data from a row. In essence, this would be an unwanted extra column in our test document—noise we'd rather not have there.

A better solution would be to create a custom fixture that extends from `ColumnFixture` and overrides the `reset` and `execute` methods to accomplish the same end result—a record being added for each row in the table. Listing 10.5 shows a rough sketch of what this approach would look like in Java code.

Listing 10.5 Extending `ColumnFixture` to create a data-population fixture

```
public class HandmadeSetUpFixture extends fit.ColumnFixture {

    public String name;          Fields collect
    public String email;         data to populate

    @Override
    public void reset() throws Exception {
        name = null;             Reset data
        email = null;            before each row
    }

    @Override
    public void execute() throws Exception {
        // ...         <-- Populate data
    }                      in execute()
}
```

As we can see in listing 10.5, we're not providing an `add` method to trigger the data population, but instead we're overriding two methods (`reset` and `execute`) in order to accomplish the same thing without littering our test document with unnecessary columns. These two methods happen to get invoked in the appropriate phases of the fixture's lifecycle: `reset` gets called before processing each row, and `execute` gets called when all input columns of each row have been processed and Fit is about to start going through the output columns (which we don't have). The `execute` method is the perfect match for taking the data we've received so far for the current row and stuffing it into a database of some kind.

Better test specs with extra code

In the previous example, we're doing the same thing in `execute` that we'd do in some other void, no-argument method if we'd add an extra output column just to perform the data population. In addition, we need to implement the `reset` method to null out the previous row's data—this is something we wouldn't need to do with our uglier approach. The added effort, however, is negligible compared to the improvement in our fixture table's usability, removing the need for an extra column with just a couple of lines of code.

Speaking of needs, there are some common needs that haven't been attended to by the built-in fixtures (or that are more cumbersome than we'd like). Fit is open source, and extending the built-in fixtures is probably not among the hardest programming tasks you've encountered. However, it's work we'd rather not need to do. Fortunately, Professor Rick Mugridge from Auckland University has already put in the effort of creating a library of handy add-ons for Fit—add-ons that are much appreciated and widely used by the Fit community.

10.3 Beyond the built-ins with FitLibrary

An ongoing effort by Rick Mugridge and Ward Cunningham, the FitLibrary project[7] includes plenty of extensions and utilities that provide a solid stepping stone and make Fit more accessible to the beginning acceptance tester. Although the FitLibrary consists of more than these, we'll focus on two fixtures from the FitLibrary with specific characteristics—`DoFixture` and `SetUpFixture`.

10.3.1 DoFixture

Those who have set out to extend the built-in `ActionFixture` class to provide a test-definition language closer to the business's own lingo may have noticed that `ActionFixture` is not the easiest class to extend. There are subtle limitations coming from `ActionFixture`'s handling of the table structure, which shows in us being able to build keywords that are close to but not quite what we'd like them to be like. `DoFixture` brings a great relief in this regard, in being a superior base from which to start building our own flow-style fixtures.

Writing tests in natural language

What makes `DoFixture` different from `ActionFixture`? First, `DoFixture` allows us to mix keyword cells with argument cells in our table, effectively allowing us to write tests that spell out almost as natural language. For example, compare the following row in a regular `ActionFixture` table

transfer	100,00	AC0001	AC0002

[7] http://sourceforge.net/projects/fitlibrary.

to one with the keywords intertwined with variable data in a `DoFixture` table row:

transfer	100,00	dollars from	AC0001	to	AC0002

The difference in syntax reaches beyond the table and to the Java code backing our fixture tables. First, the classic version:

```
public void transfer(float amount, String from, String to) {
    ...
}
```

And then the `DoFixture` version:

```
public boolean transferDollarsFromTo(float amount, String from,
    String to) {
    ...
}
```

The logic used by `DoFixture` to construct the method name from the columns is surprisingly straightforward: It expects the columns to alternate between being a keyword and an argument, applying the usual camel-casing logic to the resulting list of words. Doesn't get much simpler than that!

Although we could use a more meaningful name for the action in our custom `ActionFixture` class, effectively making the backing code equivalent to the `DoFixture` version, there's a huge advantage in terms of the readability of our test documents with `DoFixture`'s intertwined syntax, which makes it a clear winner in my eyes compared to `ActionFixture`.

This added flexibility and power come with a cost, however. The implementation of `DoFixture` requires that it be the first fixture on the test document. This is rarely an issue, though, and certainly a price I'm willing to pay for the improved ability to construct flow-style tests with something that reminds us of natural language.

Delegating to child fixtures

Another advantage gained by using the `DoFixture` is the ability to easily split parts of the fixture into separate tables in the test document. This is largely due to the fact that, by default, all tables in a test document are handled by the initial `DoFixture` without an explicit fixture class declaration row for each table. Actions on the `DoFixture` can choose to return a fixture object. When this happens, Fit uses the returned fixture object to handle the remainder of a table. One of the most common uses for this feature of `DoFixture` is to run another useful addition from FitLibrary—`SetUpFixture`—which we will look into in a minute.

Figure 10.10 shows an example of a test making use of `DoFixture`. The document consists of several fixture tables of different kinds, showcasing some of the main features of `DoFixture` including two different types of `SetUpFixtures`, rows representing actions, assertions about the system's state, and usage of the alternating cells' syntax for the kind of natural language actions we just discussed.

com.tddinaction.fit.fixtures.ReviewsDoFixture

setup book data			
title	edition	ISBN	authors
JUnit Recipes	1	1932394230	J.B. Rainsberger, Scott Stirling
Spring in Action	1	1932394354	Craig Walls, Ryan Breidenbach
Ajax in Action	1	1932394613	Dave Crane, Eric Pascarello, Darren James

setup review data			
title	edition	review date	review text

go to front page		
ensure	text present	Found reviews for 0 books

setup review data			
title	edition	review date	review text
JUnit Recipes	1	2005-01-05	First review of JUnit Recipes
JUnit Recipes	1	2005-08-10	Second review of JUnit Recipes
Spring in Action	1	2005-05-28	Review of Spring in Action
Ajax in Action	1	2006-02-08	Most recent review

Note that there are four reviews in all, but two of them are for the same book!

go to front page		
ensure	text present	Found reviews for 3 books
ensure	text present	JUnit Recipes
ensure	text present	Spring in Action
ensure	text present	Ajax in Action

Check that the books with most recent reviews are listed before the ones with older reviews.

verify that	Ajax in Action	is before	JUnit Recipes
verify that	JUnit Recipes	is before	Spring in Action

Figure 10.10 Example of a test making use of a custom `DoFixture` and `ReviewsDoFixture`, showcasing some of `DoFixture`'s additional features compared to the built-in `ActionFixture`. Although the document contains multiple fixture tables, they're all handled by the `ReviewsDoFixture`, activated with the first table on the page. The remaining tables and rows map to methods on the `ReviewsDoFixture` instance, except when such a method returns a `Fixture`. When the method returns a `Fixture` object, that particular `Fixture` object handles the remainder of that table.

The first table on the page in figure 10.10 declares to Fit that this document will be handled by an instance of `ReviewsDoFixture`, our custom `DoFixture` class. After this bit, Fit knows that (unless the `DoFixture` tells it otherwise) all the remaining tables on the page shall be handed to the `ReviewsDoFixture` for processing.

The next table begins with an action named "setup book data" with no arguments. Fit maps this action to a method called `setupBookData` on the `ReviewsDoFixture` class. In this case, the `setupBookData` method returns a `SetUpFixture` for setting up test data for the system under test, as illustrated in listing 10.6.

Listing 10.6 `DoFixture` returning `SetUpFixture` to handle remainder of table

```
public class ReviewsDoFixture extends fit.DoFixture {

    public Fixture setupBookData() throws Exception {
        return new BookSetupFixture();
    }
}
```

This effectively means that the remaining four rows of the table are handled by the `BookSetupFixture` (a subclass of `SetUpFixture` that we'll talk about in the next section) that we passed back to Fit. Similarly, the first action on the next table, "setup review data", maps to another method on the `ReviewsDoFixture` class because the scope of the `BookSetupFixture` doesn't span across table borders. Adding that to our `ReviewsDoFixture` class, we're looking at the piece of code in listing 10.7.

Listing 10.7 `DoFixture` from listing 10.6, returning two different `SetUpFixtures`

```
public class ReviewsDoFixture extends fit.DoFixture {

    public Fixture setupBookData() throws Exception {
        return new BookSetupFixture();
    }

    public Fixture setupReviewData() throws Exception {
        return new ReviewSetupFixture();
    }
}
```

The next table after our two initial `SetUpFixture` tables is closer to a regular `ActionFixture` again, with two actions mapping to methods `goToFrontPage` and `textPresent(String)`. Here's the corresponding Java code for reference:

```
public class ReviewsDoFixture extends fit.DoFixture {
    ...

    public boolean goToFrontPage() {
        ...
    }

    public boolean textPresent(String expected) {
        ...
    }
}
```

But wait. We can't see that *ensure* word from our table anywhere in the Java code. That's because "ensure" is one of a few special actions supported by `DoFixture`. It's basically saying to Fit that this particular action's outcome should be checked for success (return a value of `true`). Other such keywords include, for instance,[8] `check`, which compares the return value of the action to the value in the last column on the row, and `reject`, which checks that the action fails, as expected.

The rest of the table is mostly a combination of using a `SetUpFixture` again to add reviews to the system and the same two regular actions: "go to front page" and "text present". The last table, however, is an excellent example of how we can mix keywords with their arguments to produce readable tests. Not to mention our ability to add descriptive blocks of text in between the tables, of course.

Enough about `DoFixture`. Let's take a closer look at those `SetUpFixtures` we've already seen used in the previous example.

10.3.2 SetUpFixture

`SetUpFixture`, another addition to our toolbox from `FitLibrary`, has a self-descriptive name. Its main purpose is to make creating setup tables as intuitive as possible—a lot like our homegrown data population fixture in listing 10.5. Let's dissect the "setup review data" table from our previous example, shown in figure 10.11.

setup review data			
title	edition	review date	review text
JUnit Recipes	1	2005-01-05	First review of JUnit Recipes
JUnit Recipes	1	2005-08-10	Second review of JUnit Recipes
Spring in Action	1	2005-05-28	Review of Spring in Action
Ajax in Action	1	2006-02-08	Most recent review

Figure 10.11 This fixture table from figure 10.8 shows an example of a `DoFixture` on the first row creating and returning a `SetUpFixture` object to handle the remaining five rows.

[8] For a full list of supported special actions, refer to FitLibrary documentation in the download.

Here, the "setup review data" action is part of the DoFixture, creating and returning an instance of our setup fixture class, ReviewSetupFixture. In other words, the first table row from figure 10.11 processed by our ReviewSetupFixture object is the header row listing names for the columns in the rest of the table. SetUpFixture uses the values on this header row to figure out the method name to call upon parsing each row, meaning that, in our example, the ReviewSetupFixture would get a call to a method named titleEditionReviewDateReviewText with four arguments, for each data row in the table.

Listing 10.8 shows the Java code matching the fixture table.

Listing 10.8 Example of a SetUpFixture

```
public class ReviewSetupFixture extends fit.SetUpFixture {

    public ReviewSetupFixture() throws Exception {
        super.registerParseDelegate(
                Date.class, new SimpleDateFormat("yyyy-MM-dd"));
        deleteReviewData();
    }

    private void deleteReviewData() throws Exception {
        // implementation omitted for brevity
    }

    public void titleEditionReviewDateReviewText(String title,
            int edition, Date date, String text) throws Exception {
        // create a Review object from the arguments and
        // persist it to the system under test
    }
}
```

Configure date format

Delete existing data before processing table

Handle rows in setup table one by one

The method titleEditionReviewDateReviewText takes not just String arguments but also integers and java.util.Date values. Fit knows how to parse strings into integers and other numeric values, but it doesn't know which date format we want to use in our test documents; we have to tell it explicitly by invoking the registerParseDelegate method, inherited from SetUpFixture.

Listing 10.8 also illustrates a common pattern in SetUpFixtures—the fixture removes all existing data from the system in the constructor (executed when encountering a setup table) and adds new data one by one in the add method (in our example, titleEditionReviewDateReviewText).

It's worth noting that the same kind of setup could be performed with the built-in ColumnFixture by adding an "add()" column to the table (or overriding the `execute()` method from the superclass), effectively mapping to our `titleEditionReviewDateReviewText` method in listing 10.8. The benefit of using a `ColumnFixture` like that would be that the Java code remains relatively clean, especially for large setup tables with a long list of arguments for the `add` method. The downside, on the other hand, is the extra column just to know when to create and store an object from whatever field values have been populated at that time.

10.3.3 There's more

The previous two fixtures, `DoFixture` and `SetUpFixture`, are not the only useful additions to our toolbox from the FitLibrary. There are additional fixtures for dealing with ordered and unordered lists, and fixtures for supporting tests that verify business logic through calculations, checking constraints, and combinations. There's also support for file system-based comparisons, images, and whatnot.

In addition, one of the FitLibrary's most useful contributions has not been mentioned yet, but we'll get to that in a moment. You see, it's related to running Fit tests, and that's what we're going to discuss next.

10.4 Executing Fit tests

We've now seen the three built-in fixtures of the Fit framework with examples of the fixture tables and their associated fixture class implementations as well as of the output generated by Fit when running the tests. Next, we'll look at how we run those tests! But first, some basics.

What artifacts do we need in order to run our Fit test documents? We need the test documents themselves, of course, and we need the fixture classes that are referenced from our test documents' fixture tables. We also need the production code and any library dependencies for our fixture classes to be able to connect to the system under test. How all of these artifacts are created depends on the programming language with which we've decided to implement our fixture classes. In the case of Java, we need to compile our fixture classes before we can run our test documents, and we need to provide all of the mentioned artifacts—except the test documents—in the class path when running Fit.

If the test documents aren't put into the class path, then where are they located? That's a good question, and we should say something about storing test documents before we start talking about the different ways of executing them.

If our customer is to be able to write and update test documents on their own, they had better be in a place where they can access them—a shared network drive, for example. Another way could be to employ a web-based solution, such as Fitnesse. The simplest solution, in my opinion, is to keep the Fit test documents in the same place as the source code—in the configuration-management tool. As long as the customer is onsite and has access to the repository, that's more than enough.

Although we might end up using a more elaborate solution, we'll likely start with a plain vanilla "Fit and HTML files on the local disk" approach. Let's look at how to run our tests in such a setup—first for running a single Fit test document, then for running a whole folder structure of tests, and, finally, for running Fit tests as part of an Apache Ant-based build script.

10.4.1 Using a single test document

The Fit distribution includes a basic test-runner class for Fit tests called `fit.FileRunner`. The basic usage is to pass the `FileRunner` a path to a test document and the path to where we want the result document to be generated. Here's an example of how we might invoke the `FileRunner` from the command line:

```
$ java -classpath fit.jar:classes:. fit.FileRunner \
    src/story/tests/example.htm testresults/example.htm
```

Running this command produces a result summary output into *stderr* that looks like the following:

```
$ java -classpath fit.jar;classes;. fit.FileRunner ...
23 right, 4 wrong, 0 ignored, 0 exceptions
```

This is all the output that the `FileRunner` produces on the console—a summary of how many tests passed, how many had failing assertions, how many tests were ignored, and how many unexpected exceptions were thrown during the test run. The result document contains the details, of course, so this simplicity is nice.

The `FileRunner` also adjusts its exit code according to the number of failed ("wrong" and "exceptions") tests. If no test failed, the exit code is 0; if five tests failed the exit code is 5; and so forth. This is nice to know if we plan on integrating our Fit tests into our build cycle using shell scripts, for example!

10.4.2 Placing all tests in a folder structure

Obviously, running a single Fit test document is not always enough for everyone. Although we typically work with a single story, perhaps running a single Fit test document at a time (at which point using the `FileRunner` from within the IDE or on the command line can be sufficient), in some cases we would like to run all of our acceptance tests—or a subset of them—in an automated manner with as little manual effort as possible. For that purpose, Rick Mugridge developed the FolderRunner class that is part of the FitLibrary.[9]

The usage of FolderRunner is remarkably similar to that of FileRunner. The only difference is that instead of passing in the path to a test file and the result file, we pass in a path to a folder containing test files and the path to a folder where we want the result files written, respectively:

```
$ java -classpath fit.jar:fitlibrary.jar:classes:.
    fit.FolderRunner src/story/tests/ testresults/
```

If the source folder contains a hierarchy of subfolders with test documents, the FolderRunner will create the exact same directory structure under the result folder with a test result HTML document for each source HTML document. The FolderRunner also produces a handy report of the whole test run, showing summaries for all levels of the hierarchy of executed test documents.

The FolderRunner also supports a relatively sophisticated setup/teardown. We can place test documents named setup.htm and setup.html (or setup.xls—the FolderRunner supports Excel sheets as well) into our test folders, and the FolderRunner will execute each setup document higher or on the same level in the source tree as the current test document. And the same goes for teardown documents named teardown.htm, teardown.html, and teardown.xls. This allows us to avoid duplicating special setup fixtures in each of our test documents and concentrate on the essential.

10.4.3 Testing as part of an automated build

We could certainly do away with invoking Fit's test-runner classes from the command prompt, and we could encapsulate those commands into shell scripts, but that is far from being an ideal solution in certain aspects. For one thing, maintaining the scripts for multiple platforms such as Windows and Linux is a hassle we'd like to avoid; and we wouldn't want to edit the script every time we add a new package or a new library to our project, meaning that we'd have to resort to some advanced shell-scripting to traverse through the file system in order to construct the appropriate class path, for example.

In practice, the Java projects of today more often than not choose to use a modern build tool such as Apache Ant or Apache Maven (http://maven.apache.org), in part because of a need to easily execute their Fit tests as part of an automated

---

[9] An ongoing effort by Rick Mugridge and Ward Cunningham, the FitLibrary project provides plenty of other utilities in addition to the **FolderRunner**, as we've seen in the previous sections of this chapter.

build. Although the Fit distribution doesn't currently come with a custom Ant task (or a Maven goal, for that matter) for running Fit tests, it's straightforward to wrap command-line tools we've already seen into an Ant target, as shown in listing 10.9.

Listing 10.9 Running Fit with an Ant build script

```
<project name="SampleProject" default="...">
    ...
    <path id="myclasspath">
        <path location="classes" />
        <fileset dir="lib" includes="*.jar" />
    </path>

    <target name="acceptance-test" depends="compile, unit-test">
        <java classname="fit.runner.FolderRunner"
              classpathref="myclasspath">
            <arg line="src/fit-tests" />
            <arg line="reports/fit" />
        </java>
    </target>
</project>
```

Depend on Fit, FitLibrary, and our fixtures

Execute FolderRunner

Specify source and result directories

The nice thing about Ant is that we have all of Ant's power in our hands with regard to constructing the necessary class path for running Fit, and we have all the file system-manipulation tasks at hand for, say, creating missing output directories, deleting the results of a previous test run, and so forth.

Running our Fit tests as part of the automated build is often not enough, however. Whereas we could get a binary result of "some tests failed" versus "all tests passed" by letting the `<java/>` task fail our build if the `FolderRunner` exits with a non-zero return code (to signify the number of assertion failures and unexpected exceptions during the test run), the more important information is often the test documents, annotated with colors and exception messages, as appropriate. A common way of making these reports accessible for an automated build is to copy them to a web server. The following listing shows one way to do that, using Ant's optional FTP task:

```
<ftp server="ftp.ourserver.com" port="21"
     remotedir="/www/reports/acceptance"
     userid="coder" password="java1">
    <fileset dir="reports/fit">
        <include name="**/*.html"/>
    </fileset>
</ftp>
```

Another common approach to publishing the generated reports would be to let a continuous integration server such as CruiseControl take care of publishing the files on the web server, but that's a topic for another whole book.

That's enough Fit for now. We'll learn more about the intricacies of Fit in the following chapter, and what we've seen so far should be more than enough to get started.

10.5 Summary

Phew. That was a compact run-through of Fit, the acceptance-testing framework *de choix* for what possibly represents a majority of software projects out there using agile methods.

We began by discussing how Fit fits (sorry) into the acceptance test-driven development process, describing the three steps involved in translating a user story or a use case into an automated acceptance test: sketch a test document with examples described in tables, clean up the fixture tables in the test document, and implement the backing fixture tables. After having gained an understanding of how Fit can be used to test-drive features, we switched our focus to studying the Fit framework itself.

Fit test documents consist of a mixture of narrative text and different types of executable fixture tables. Fit comes with three built-in fixture types for binding the test tables into the system under test—`ColumnFixture`, `RowFixture`, and `ActionFixture`—which we can extend for our project's needs.

One of the most essential additions to our Fit toolbox is the FitLibrary extension, which provides a whole bunch of additional fixtures we can use and extend. Finally, we can easily execute our tests from the command prompt or as part of an automated build using Ant, in large part due to the handy `FolderRunner` that's part of the FitLibrary. The `FolderRunner` lets us organize our Fit tests into a directory structure with multilevel setup fixtures and informative summary reports.

This was just a glimpse at the features and intricacies of Fit and the FitLibrary. You might want to pick up the official Fit bible, *Fit for Developing Software* (Addison-Wesley, 2005) by Ward Cunningham and Rick Mugridge, for a more thorough tutorial and reference. And don't forget to check out the FitLibrary and Fit websites at http://sourceforge.net/projects/fitlibrary and http://fit.c2.com, respectively.

Now that we know the essential concepts of Fit and have an idea of what's involved in writing and automating Fit tests, we're ready to take Fit into use in our, real-life software projects for improving the communication both within our team as well as with our stakeholders. There's more to acceptance testing, however, than just selecting a tool and running with it. There's also the question of how to connect our tests with the system under test—not always a straightforward decision to make. Largely for that reason, the next chapter is dedicated to discussing the ins and outs of different approaches to making that crucial connection.

11

Strategies for implementing acceptance tests

Drawings help people to work out intricate relationships between parts.

—Christopher Alexander, father of the Pattern Language movement

We've now been introduced to acceptance tests, and we've gained an understanding of how to work with acceptance tests in the context of a team using an agile or iterative process. We've also taken a brief look into the Fit framework, which is probably the most popular acceptance-test tool around. Along the way, we saw what the technical representation of our acceptance tests might look like and roughly what is involved in automating those tests. In this chapter, we'll change our focus toward the technical gotchas of making our acceptance tests—fixture classes, in the case of Fit—interact with the system under test.

The traditional craft of quality assurance (QA) with manual testing and scripted test cases[1] has long taught us to think of testing as being about testing the system as a whole, end to end, in order to verify functionality. And it makes sense. After all, we want to know that the system as a whole works correctly rather than that all the pieces work correctly in isolation. The world has more shades of gray than that, however. There is clearly value in testing on levels beneath the whole system. More than anything, it's a question of cost versus value.

In order to explore the alternatives at our disposal, we'll first discuss the variables that influence our decisions, three general approaches to connecting acceptance tests with the system under test, and a couple of lower-level techniques that support the more general approaches. Once we've clarified the playing field a bit in terms of these general approaches, we'll move on to examining some specific technologies and how they can affect the way we connect our tests with the system. Finally, we'll answer some frequently asked questions regarding the practicalities of how to set up automated tests.

Let's get started.

11.1 What should acceptance tests test?

One of the first questions that comes to mind is what to test. Yes, we want to know that our system works correctly and that there are no defects and that the system is usable. But are these aspects the kind of stuff we want to verify with our automated acceptance tests?

There's a saying about using the best tool for the job at hand, and that rings true in the case of testing. We cannot omit manual, visual testing, because computers aren't good at evaluating the usability and attractiveness of our applications. Or, perhaps more accurately, we humans aren't good at telling the computer how to determine what pleases our eye and intuition. Similarly, humans

[1] "Scripted" in the sense of "documented steps to carry out," not in the sense of automating tests into executable scripts.

aren't good at performing mundane, repeating tasks indefinitely, which makes a good case for automating the majority of our regression tests. The best tool for the job... Or, the other way around, acceptance tests don't need to test *everything*!

Professional tester wanted

No matter how much we preach about the importance of test automation for sustainable software development, no automated test can have the intuition and smarts of a good tester. A good tester can use their skills to identify scenarios and interaction sequences where a system might behave unexpectedly. To free their intuition, however, they must be freed from the burden of routine test repetition. That's exactly what our automated regression tests are for. They nail down the risks we have already identified while the human brain is given a chance to focus on identifying new risks we haven't yet found.

The answer to "what should acceptance tests test?" is simple: They should test the correct fulfillment of requirements as specified by our user stories (or whatever medium is in use). Sometimes, that might mean testing algorithms. For some, it might mean testing user action sequences. Ask yourself what kind of test would be just enough to tell you that this specific user story has been implemented properly. In other words, focus on the essential. It's good to have functionality end-to-end under automated tests, but not at any cost.

To make smart decisions about what to test and how, we need to consider three things: the story, turbulence, and technology. In this section, we'll figure out how to do just that. Let's start with the story.

11.1.1 Focus on what's essential

If the requirement for which we're implementing tests is about calculating something correctly, it's likely that we should focus on the logic related to the calculation rather than go through the UI and see the correct numbers on the screen for each and every interesting case. Whether the numbers are displayed is one thing; whether the numbers are correct is another. No need to mix the two—it'd make things more difficult to change in the long run if we hardwired domain logic together with presentation.

Let's say we've got a user story about checking out a shopping cart in our online store using a Visa or MasterCard. We need to check that the application rejects invalid card numbers, verification numbers, and more. We've written our acceptance tests so that they log on through the web interface and navigate to the correct page, filling in the invalid data, submitting the form, and checking for the expected rejection message. We're not interested in all that other stuff, so why should we write our acceptance tests in terms of it? It doesn't make sense.

Some stories, on the other hand, should be tested through the actual UI. For instance, a story about the user getting redirected to our online store's login page when their session has timed out is a good candidate for a test that would operate through the web interface, simulating an end-to-end scenario. Although we'd likely make the user's session expire right after logging in rather than waiting for 20 minutes, it would make sense to test this kind of functionality in terms of the user operating a web browser.

The story itself can tell us something about what its tests should be testing. There's more guidance available, however, if we take into consideration the aspect of turbulence—something, that makes it even more important for us to be testing the right things!

11.1.2 Avoid turbulent interfaces

The biggest danger with automated tests is that they can become a maintenance nightmare. A huge influencer in that respect is the kind of turbulence we can expect around the parts where our acceptance tests connect with the system under test. We don't want to increase the effects of any such turbulence we might have to go through. This brings us back to the point about not mixing domain logic with presentation.

Let's think about the credit-card validation story again. What if our customer wants us to add support for American Express in addition to the two existing card types? Do we want to write all that web-page navigation stuff again? I wouldn't. Even if the navigation would be nicely encapsulated[2] into a single piece of code that our tests invoke as a one-liner as part of our setup, it would still be noise around the signal—noise we'd rather do without.

Suppose we added support for American Express, and we now support three difference credit cards. Next, our customer wants to redo the whole checkout process. We realize that we'll have to update all of our credit-card validation tests because they're exercising the functionality through the checkout form—which is now getting scrapped. If we'd tested the validation directly, without going through the UI, we'd only need to update that one test we had that verified that the credit-card validation is invoked as part of the checkout instead of updating all of them. And we certainly don't want to have to edit a whole bunch of acceptance tests when something completely unrelated changes.

---

[2] Although our tests might operate through the user interface, they should still be expressed in terms of the story and the domain, hiding the implementation and the user interface.

Things change fast in software development, so there will always be turbulence. If we're not testing on the proper level for a given story, the turbulence just gets worse. That's why we need to consider how turbulent our chosen interface for acceptance tests is. And how much rework will be needed when the system changes. The cost of change aspect is not all there is, however. We also need to consider how easy or difficult it is to create those tests in the first place. And that's where technology has a big role to play.

11.1.3 Cross the fence where it is lowest

Technology is just a means to achieving greater goals. Yet the limitations and biases of the available technology also constrain our options in reaching for those goals. Technology is also something we must take into consideration when making decisions about our approach to acceptance testing. Sometimes it makes sense to cross the technological fence where it is lowest, and sometimes it makes sense to climb higher because of a truly greener pasture on the other side.

We can start our considerations by determining the hard limits set by technology. If the software we're building runs on a proprietary embedded operating system, we're limited to what the operating system provides. If the software we're building is written in C, we're limited to the tools that the C language, compiler, and the underlying platform provide us. In the other extreme, the more entry points the technology platform offers, the more alternative interfaces the system under test exposes and the less constrained we are with regard to the approaches available.

When we know the hard limitations of what is possible to do with the technology, we can then evaluate whether our chosen technology stack supports some specific approach or approaches to automated testing better than the others. Virtual machine-based technologies such as Java with dynamic reflection capabilities tend to facilitate intrusive white box–style techniques better than non-intrusive access to UI components on the operating system level, for example. On the other hand, technologies making use of native UI components tend to make interrogating and operating upon the UI widgets easy, while simultaneously making it relatively far more laborious to provide API-level access to the application's functionality.

Although technology can have a significant effect on our options and their relative advantages and disadvantages, we can affect the influence our technology imposes on us in many ways. By designing our systems to be testable on the unit and module level and by evolving the software architecture appropriately, we can effectively give ourselves more options to choose from as we make entirely new ways of accessing the system possible. For example, by structuring our application with a clean service layer fronting our business logic and infrastructure services, and by exposing that service layer to our tests, we create for ourselves the opportunity to implement our tests against the domain-level functionality rather than the UI.

Technology is a central variable in the equation, and connecting acceptance tests with the system under test is largely about technology. We will continue discussing this subject in more detail in the context of specific types of systems later in this chapter. Before we do that, however, it is useful to identify the main high-level approaches to connecting with the system under test.

11.2 Implementation approaches

There are probably as many ways to test a system as there are technologies and teams to do so. However, as in many other domains, patterns emerge from the swirling chaos. We have identified a handful of classes of approaches or styles of acceptance testing that we believe cover the majority of teams doing acceptance test-driven development.

Paying our respects to the fine tradition of coining fancy terms for simple things, we'll call the first three of these styles *going end-to-end*, *crawling under the skin*, and *exercising the internals*. These three approaches represent higher-level strategies. There are also fourth and fifth supplemental strategies that we'll discuss after the higher-level strategies. They should be considered complimentary approaches and work well with any of the three higher-level strategies.

Let's begin with the first of our triplet, *going end-to-end*.

11.2.1 Going end-to-end

Ideally, when we test a system, we're testing the system as a whole. In other words, the system is exercised as is, just like it will be used when deployed to the production environment. We're testing the functionality through the real interface, be it a GUI or a machine-to-machine type of technical interface. We're testing end-to-end, including any and all components that make up the system. Even though we might be drilling directly into the database backend, for example, to check correct behavior, we're testing the application itself end-to-end in black box style, as illustrated in figure 11.1.

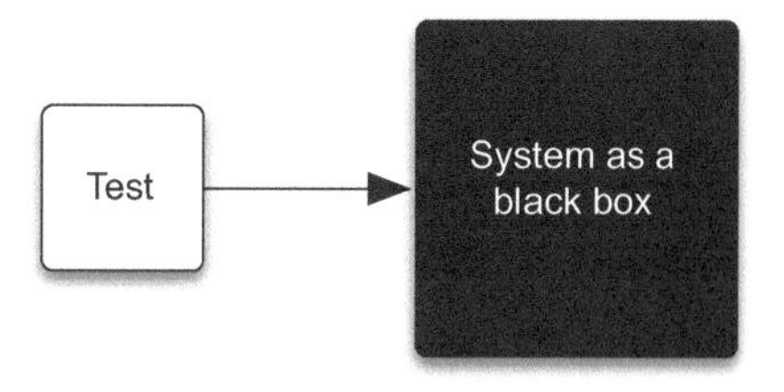

Figure 11.1 End-to-end test scenario with the test accessing the system through its external interface, knowing nothing about the system's internals

A typical example of an end-to-end scenario is to write acceptance tests for a web application using a library, such as jWebUnit. The jWebUnit source repository includes a Fit fixture class for using jWebUnit with Fit.[3] In practice, we would extend from jWebUnit's `WebFixture` and create our own vocabulary on top of jWebUnit's API, as illustrated in listing 11.1.

Listing 11.1 Example of an end-to-end oriented fixture class for testing web applications

```
public class WebFixture extends
        net.sourceforge.jwebunit.fit.WebFixture {

    public boolean goToFrontPage() {
        beginAt("/home");
        return true;
    }

    public boolean logInAs(String username) {
        page("/login");
        enter("j_username", username);
        enter("j_password", TestConfig.getPasswordFor(username));
        submit();
        tester.assertTextPresent("Welcome");
        return true;
    }

    ...
}
```

Depending on the available tools and libraries for connecting to the system under test, fixture classes like the one in listing 11.1 can be straightforward to implement, with the fixture classes' main purpose being translating the customer's language to lower-level steps in navigating the web application being tested.

Why test the whole system?

In the beginning of this section, we said, "Ideally, when we test a system, we're testing the system as a whole." Why *ideally*? The main reason is that end-to-end testing is the type of testing that's most representative of the system's real-world setting. In other words, end-to-end testing tends to cover the system as broadly as possible. It's also the most intuitive strategy for nontechnical stakeholders to understand because the tests operate on the system as a black box—which is how the said

[3] The jWebUnit project is currently undergoing significant change, and the jWebFit subproject seems to have been left without much attention lately. You might need to patch the code available from the project's repository in order to get it working.

stakeholders perceive the system. Being able to map the tests directly to the user-accessible functionality and operations of the system reduces the risk of having the stakeholders become estranged from the system.

These are benefits that we'd like to take advantage of. However, this strategy has a downside as well. Perhaps the biggest handicap of the end-to-end approach is that the tests tend to be more brittle than they could be, because they're dependent on the UI, which typically changes more frequently than the business logic underneath—and in ways that should not affect the correctness of the logic underneath. Furthermore, writing the tests in the first place can be a laborious task because of the need to satisfy the UI's requirements, effectively clicking our way through to the functionality we want to test.

Another factor to consider is the speed of test execution.

Trading speed for certainty

Such tests are also often up to a magnitude slower compared to tests that bypass the UI and otherwise loosen up the concept of treating the system under test as a black box. The speed of test execution is not something we can dismiss. While implementing a user story, we want to be able to run the associated acceptance tests quickly and easily, again and again until they pass. Preferably, we'll also run the full suite of acceptance tests before moving on to other tasks. Every second counts, because larger projects can easily have hundreds or thousands of acceptance tests.

Not being able to run the full test suite means we're forced to make a trade-off between the certainty of the overall system correctness and the pace of development, as illustrated in figure 11.2.

We're effectively delaying the full feedback to our continuous-integration system, which dutifully churns through the full test suite in the background while we're already starting on the next story. As the time between a question and its answer increases, so does the cost of asking the question. That is, we're trading a bit of time from each integration cycle, accepting the risk of the occasional hit of a test failing after we've already moved on—making it more costly to respond to the failing test.

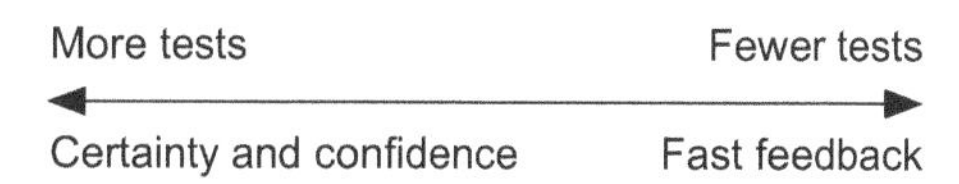

Figure 11.2 We often face a trade-off between running the full suite of tests that provide a high level of certainty and running fewer tests that provide less feedback (certainty) but do it faster.

The end-to-end strategy for acceptance tests is an admirable goal that yields great benefit as long as we can work around the risk of brittle and burdensome tests that are slow to run. We can reduce these risks through careful design and merciless refactoring of our acceptance tests and their implementation. However, a slightly different strategy can sometimes yield more bang for the buck. Testing through the UI is the biggest culprit of the end-to-end strategy with regard to brittleness and slowness; we call such a strategy *crawling under the skin.*

11.2.2 Crawling under the skin

Crawling under the skin means just that: having our tests crawl under the system's skin (the UI). We could think of it as introducing a new, alternative UI—an abstract UI—to connect with the core of the system under test. The main driver for this strategy could be considered the main downsides of the end-to-end strategy as described previously, largely related to testing through the UI.

Avoiding needless change

By interfacing our acceptance tests against the application and domain logic instead of the concepts of the UI, or against an abstract UI instead of a concrete and technology-specific one, we can reduce the risk of ending up with a pile of high-maintenance test code that cries for our attention every time we touch the skin of our system. Again, that risk can be minimized even if we do test against the real UI—it's just much easier if we bypass the UI or at least couple our tests with UI *concepts* instead of concrete *widgets.*

Figure 11.3 illustrates a test not just accessing the UI but also going beneath the skin to operate an abstract UI or internal APIs.

In figure 11.3, the tests are exercising the system under test through three different channels: the external UI, an abstract UI, and an internal service layer API. Whether all of these make sense for a given system depends largely on the architecture of the system. Listing 11.2 shows some examples of how these different approaches to crawling under the skin might look from the fixture class's point of view when testing a weblog application.

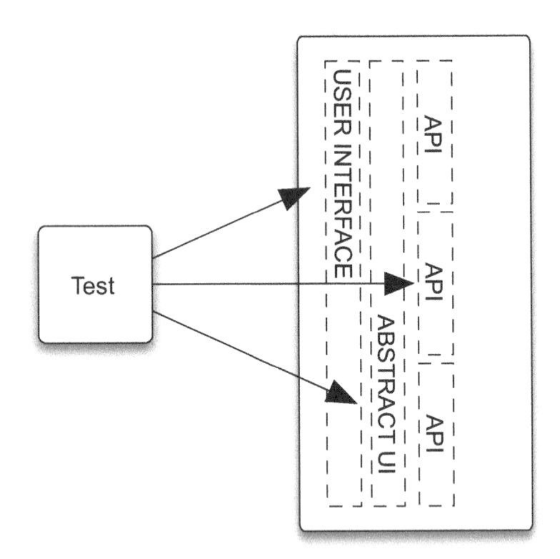

Figure 11.3 Test operating against an internal API or an abstract UI in addition to or instead of the real UI

Listing 11.2 Examples of different styles of crawling under the system's skin

```
public class WeblogApplicationFixture extends fit.DoFixture {
    ...

    public boolean subscribeForAnnouncements(String email) {
        InitialContext ctx = new InitialContext(serverConfig);
        Subscriptions bean = (Subscriptions)
                ctx.lookup("ejb/Subscriptions");
        bean.subscribe(email);
    }

    ...

    public boolean postNewBlogEntry(String title, String content) {
        BlogEntry entry = new BlogEntry();
        entry.setTitle(title);
        entry.setContent(content);
        BloggingAPI api = applicationContext.getBloggingAPI();
        api.saveEntry(entry);
    }

    ...

    public boolean undo() {
        Command command = new UndoLastEdit();
        applicationEventQueue.append(command);
        command.waitForCompletion();
    }
}
```

❶ Bypass UI and connect to service API directly

❷ Access API in same JVM

❸ Operate abstract UI through internal event queue API

Let's see what kinds of approaches we use in listing 11.2 to skin the weblog. The first action method, `subscribeForAnnouncements`, ❶ performs a Java Naming and Directory Interface (JNDI) lookup to a remote application server where the system under test is running. This approach exploits the system's architecture that happens to make the internal API easily accessible also from tests running in a remote Java Virtual Machine (JVM).

The second method, `postNewBlogEntry`, on the other hand, ❷ accesses an internal service layer directly using a normal Java API call, which is possible when the tests are running within the same JVM as the system under test.

The third method, `undo`, is an example of accessing not an internal service layer API but rather an internal, abstract UI API. In our example, there is an event queue to which the real interface would delegate application-specific command objects, which in turn should trigger some kind of behavior in the application. In this approach, we ❸ create the abstract command objects ourselves and append them to the event queue rather than using the real UI.

None of these three alternatives to implementing acceptance tests for our weblog should be affected by a change in the UI such as renaming a submit button or replacing a radio group with a drop-down selection—because they're expressed in terms of abstract UI concepts or the underlying business logic rather than widgets and other concrete UI details.

Acceptance tests implemented against a programming interface just beneath the UI help us sustain our pace all the way until and through the long maintenance phase. Are there other advantages to count for this strategy than cheaper maintenance? Yes.

Easier implementation

In addition to such tests being less costly to maintain, they also tend to be easier to implement. This is where things get a bit unintuitive at first. We're accustomed to thinking about the system through what *we* can do with it. Why, then, is it easier to write our acceptance tests against something other than the level of abstraction we're naturally wired to think in?

The main reason lies in the impedance mismatch between a human looking at a visual interface and a computer looking at a sequence of zeros and ones. In order to be able to write robust tests against a UI, we need to accommodate for the acceptance tests to be able to hook onto and operate the relevant bits of the interface. This could be almost a deal-breaker for productivity or it could be no big deal, largely depending on the actual UI technology and the availability of testing tools that are able to interface with our chosen technology stack.

For a web application, for example, we might need to devise naming conventions for specific elements on a set of dynamically generated web pages. Otherwise, how else are we going to automate a test, which involves clicking the correct link on a database-driven list of products? We could of course determine that we should go for the fourth link in a given panel, but that would render our test helpless in the face of someone adding some new test data into the database.

Now, consider the same test involving selecting a specific product, this time not operating through the web interface but through a programming API. We no longer need to tweak regular expressions and come up with all sorts of heuristics for identifying the link we want to click. Instead, we pull a list of product objects through an API, identify the product we're interested in with all the expressiveness of the programming language of our choice, tell a service interface to set the given product as selected, and so forth. Depending on our design, we can achieve remarkably robust tests with this approach.

Acceptance tests that go against a programming interface are also generally faster to execute, compared to end-to-end tests going through the UI. Surely there must be some downsides to crawling under the skin, right? Yes. Let's take a quick tour.

Downsides to skinning the app

Although we might consider testing only the essential functionality to be a good thing, it's not always that black and white. The downside is that we're compromising the admirable goal of having the system tested in its natural habitat. We're skipping an essential part of the puzzle—the UI—and we have to balance that fact with manual testing. Granted, computers are lousy at evaluating the quality of graphical UIs, and techniques like context-driven and exploratory testing are helpful in spending our manual testing efforts where they're most likely to yield new information. Nevertheless, we must acknowledge the consequences—the risks—of our chosen strategy.

One of those risks is that by skipping the UI, we're slightly more vulnerable to alienating our nontechnical stakeholders. One side of the solution is to not compromise the language with which we *express* our tests even though the *implementation* of the tests would be purely technical. The other side of the same solution is to focus on creating a mutual, domain-specific language, which lets nontechnical stakeholders discuss and understand the acceptance tests even though there is no mention of buttons, links, sliders, and other UI widgets.

This strategy also poses a challenge for technical team members. Just as the users, the customer, and other nonprogrammers are treading foreign landscape when we drop the UI from the picture, the programmers face a similar change of thinking around the test implementation. This shows best in the need to expose functionality through such a test interface just for testing, because we haven't traditionally needed to expose our internals to more than one client.

The challenge is in this practice conflicting with our long culture of promoting strict encapsulation and design based on the *need to know*. The added exposure also boasts some positive side effects, however. The need to expose our domain logic to a test interface as well as the real UI can help us develop a good, testable, modular design for that critical section of our software.

Knowing that we're living in a world full of different shades of gray, we must ask, does this path lead further? Is there still some slice of bad influence that we could shave off of our acceptance tests? Perhaps not surprisingly, yes, there are situations where an even slimmer profile for an acceptance test can be well-suited for our purpose. We call this third strategy to implementing acceptance tests *exercising the internals*.

11.2.3 Exercising the internals

Exercising the internals is all about testing a specific internal portion of the system's business or application logic, without going through any UI or API designed for the purpose. It's kind of like crawling under the skin taken to the extreme.

Good examples of this strategy would be acceptance tests that verify a bunch of business rules related to a user story.

For example, we might have separate acceptance tests for checking the user-visible functionality through tests like "try with valid input," "try with missing info," and "try with invalid info." We also might have separate, internals-targeted acceptance tests that would test (and document!) the exact validation rules directly against the validation logic, rather than indirectly in the context of a user operation.

Figure 11.4 visualizes how a test might probe the system's business logic directly, bypassing the UI (whether concrete or abstract) and other external APIs. Again, let's see how this approach might look in a Fit fixture class. Listing 11.3 presents an example fixture class for testing credit-card validation logic.

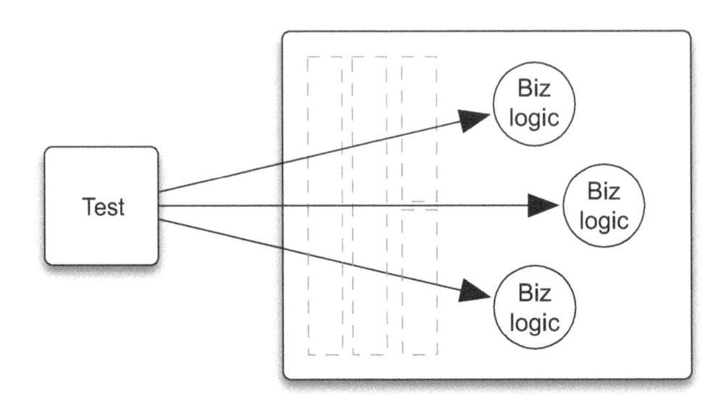

Figure 11.4 Acceptance tests can also access a system's business logic directly, bypassing any external interface or API.

Listing 11.3 Example of a Fit fixture class that digs right into the core business logic

```
public class CreditCardValidationFixture extends fit.ColumnFixture {

    public String cardNumber;

    public boolean isValid() {
        return "".equals(validationMessage());
    }

    public String validationMessage() {
        try {
            CreditCard card = new CreditCard(cardNumber);
            return "";
        } catch (ValidationException e) {
            return e.getMessage();
        }
    }
}
```

The `ColumnFixture` presented in listing 11.3 is certainly not a manifestation of a heavyweight acceptance test pulling in the whole system under test and half of the network. It's so simple and isolated that it looks like a unit test!

The main advantage of this strategy is the precision of testing exactly what we want to test and nothing more. The number and complexity of the business rules present in today's enterprise systems can be mind-boggling, and isolating the business rules into these high-precision tests can be of significant help in keeping track of them. Without any unnecessary clutter around the business rules, we are able to express them more clearly, making it easier for the development team and the customer to pick up discrepancies and missing variations in the specification (that is, in the tests).

What is the difference, then, between these internals-exercising acceptance tests and unit tests? First, although unit tests are written in the language of the implementation, all acceptance tests—even the likes of these—should be written in the language of the business domain. Even though we might effectively be testing a single class or a small set of closely related classes with our acceptance tests, just as we do in our unit tests, there is a difference. It's mostly semantic, but still. The point is that the unit tests were written for the developer, and the acceptance tests were written for (and sometimes by) the customer—and the vocabulary they use should reflect the audience's interested in the tests' results.

Just as unit tests alone aren't usually sufficient for verifying that a system works as it should, the kind of acceptance tests that only exercise the internals in a selective manner are also not sufficient. In practice, we are likely following one of the first two strategies—going end-to-end or crawling under the skin—for most of our acceptance tests, and we only employ the internals-oriented strategy to a select few places dominated by business rules or other logic of interest to the customer. Speaking of supplementary strategies, there's another one we'd like to discuss: stubbing out irrelevant components that are making life difficult for our tests.

11.2.4 Stubbing out the irrelevant

One important card to have in our sleeve is what we call *stubbing out the irrelevant*. This means testing the system not in its full, production-like setup but rather with some non-essential components replaced with stubs, simulators, or alternative implementations in favor of testability. Replacing the production database with an in-memory database is a common example of such a replacement.

Most of the time, the parts we stub out for our acceptance tests with an alternative implementation are external resources such as relational databases, third-party web services, directory services, and so forth. Figure 11.5 shows a scenario where we have stubbed out a web service proxy.

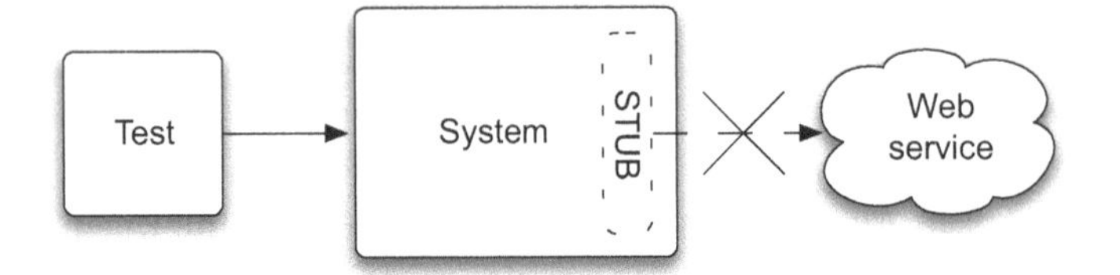

Figure 11.5 Testing a system with a less relevant component replaced with a testing-friendly, fast-executing stub

Sometimes, however, we also stub out integral parts of the system under test. Reasons might include speed of execution, ease of manipulating the system's state in our tests, or the specific component not being available (which might be because it just doesn't exist or because the component costs $1 million a pop and the millions aren't growing on trees).

Like exercising the internals, stubbing the irrelevant is also a supplementary strategy for acceptance tests. We cannot risk going to production with a system that has never been deployed with the correct database, which has never connected to the third-party payment gateway, and which has never endured a load test with the CPU or I/O heavy component in place. It's obvious that we need to test these integrations at least to some degree.

Most of the time, we opt for running the majority of our acceptance tests against the stubbed system and run only a small, focused set of tests with the difficult components in place. Having an architecture and design that modularize these stubbed-out components nicely is crucial from a risk-management point of view. We want to be confident that the system works when put together and into production. A design that's simple and built for the purpose is a great aid in achieving that confidence because we are able to analyze the overall coverage of our tests: "A and B have been tested working together, and B and C as well, which means that when we plug together all three, they will indeed work."

Many motivations for stubbing a component for our acceptance tests have something to do with the limitations and constraints of technology. If our system is reading and writing to disk a lot, it can make sense to abstract away the file system and supply a blazing-fast in-memory implementation for testing only. Slow I/O is but one example of a technology constraint. Technology influences not just how and when we stub out parts of the system for acceptance testing; it influences our application of the other strategies as well.

Technology can also create opportunities and enable us to exploit yet another strategy in implementing our acceptance tests. J.B. Rainsberger likes to call them *testing backdoors.*

11.2.5 Testing backdoors

Every now and then, it makes sense to use a backdoor. In the context of computer systems and acceptance testing, a *backdoor*—a *testing backdoor*—is a sort of alternative interface through which an outsider, such as an acceptance test, can peek inside the system to verify something or possibly to reorder some digital furniture for a test that isn't satisfied by the interiors designed for the previous test.

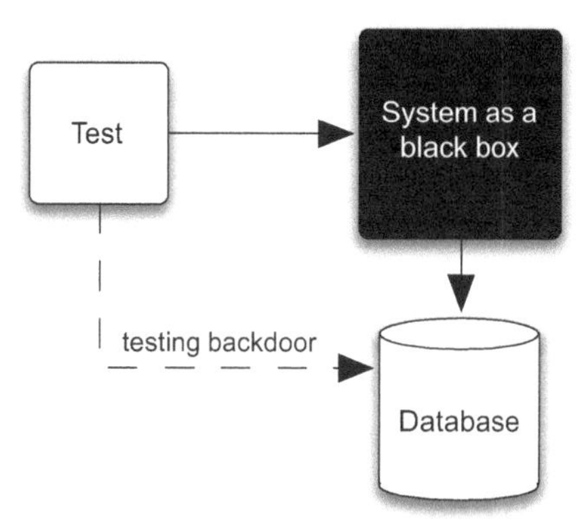

Figure 11.6 Making use of a testing backdoor in our acceptance tests

A typical case of a testing backdoor in modern enterprise systems is the database, also illustrated in figure 11.6. The database is part of the system as a whole, but it also happens to have an external interface that's equally visible to our acceptance tests as it is to the rest of the system under test. This means that we can, for example, set up test data by pushing it directly into the database rather than using the system's API. Sometimes there isn't such an API, and connecting directly to the database is our only option. On the other hand, a testing backdoor such as the database might be the only feasible way of verifying desired side effects of an acceptance test.

It is also not unheard-of for something that started life as a testing backdoor to evolve into a part of the system's public API, allowing the application to develop into new directions. For instance, a backdoor that was born due to a need for tests to be able to register to receive notifications of failed transactions might over time grow into groundbreaking monitoring and fault-management functionality that tips the market and flushes out the competition.

In short, testing backdoors are solutions created for overcoming a technical limitation, but the technology can take on a life of its own as something more than a small just-for-testing hack.

Speaking of technology, let's change our focus and do some tech-talk in order to find out how exactly certain mainstream technologies affect our acceptance testing strategies.

11.3 Technology-specific considerations

As we've already established, technology cannot be ignored when deciding on our strategy of connecting acceptance tests with the system under test. There are hard limits, and there are less-hard limits. There is a little extra effort, and there are major overhauls. There are all sorts of annoyances big and small, most of them having to do with technology. In this section, we're going to talk about how the strategies discussed earlier in this chapter mingle with the main categories of software we're building today, ranging from simple programming libraries to user applications to distributed systems.

We'll start from the simpler end of the spectrum: programming libraries intended for use by developers in building applications that depend on the library. From there, we'll move on to user-oriented applications, covering applications with both console-based and graphical user interfaces. Finally, we'll check up on networked, distributed systems and what strategies might work well in that domain.

11.3.1 Programming libraries

Programming libraries are the building blocks with which we create larger software without having to implement everything from scratch ourselves. Programming libraries are written by a developer, for a developer, and that's something that makes our life much easier in some respects, regarding the practice of acceptance tests.

Let's say we're developing an XPath[4] engine for pulling out information from XML documents with simple XPath expressions rather than traversing through a DOM tree or resorting to incomprehensible regular expressions. Our user stories are worded in technical terms and for a good reason—our customer is a programmer. For example, one of the stories could be about pulling the value of a named attribute from an identified XML element. For such a story, one of the first acceptance tests could involve an XML document like the following, with the test verifying that our library is able to return `value` when we ask for the `root` element's attribute named `attr`:

```
<root attr="value" />
```

How do we implement such a test? Should we go through the UI or go under the skin? Should we operate directly on the internals? The relative simplicity of choosing a strategy for testing programming libraries is that there isn't much choice. In essence, for programming libraries, we're always going under the skin because there is no skin, but we're also going end-to-end because the public programming interface is our UI. The only real decision to make is whether some pieces of logic within the library should be tested directly even though it would not be exposed directly through the public API.

---

[4] http://www.w3.org/TR/xpath.

For this test, our implementation might well be a snippet of Java code like the one shown here:

```
public class XPathTest {
    @Test
    public void retrievingValueOfAttributeFromEmptyRootElement()
            throws Exception {
        Document doc = parse("<root attr=\"value\" />");
        assertEquals("value",
            XPathEngine.valueOf("root/@attr", doc));
    }
}
```

The question remains whether the example test is on the level of abstraction we'd like to have for our acceptance tests. What do you think? Could you refactor the test to be more expressive? I'm pretty sure you can think of at least something. But would we go so far as to replace JUnit as a testing framework and try something less technical? Would it make sense to use, say, a table-based tool such as Fit for the acceptance tests of such a programming library? Perhaps it would, perhaps it wouldn't. I consider it likely that most teams would stick to JUnit and effectively merge their unit tests and acceptance tests. I would not, however, be too surprised to meet a team that would consider it valuable to be able to express its tests in a more accessible format than Java code with all those escaped quote characters and line feeds.

What about stubbing, then? Should we sometimes consider it an option to stub parts of the library for our acceptance tests? Sure. Why not, if it makes sense? For example, it might make our lives a lot easier if we'd decide to stub out the system clock for the duration of our acceptance tests or if we'd plug in a logging component that would keep all output in memory instead of writing it to disk.

That's about all we can say about acceptance testing programming libraries, so let's move on to bigger things with some kind of distributed elements—applications with a networking interface.

11.3.2 Faceless, distributed systems

In today's world of corporate IT, practically all software does some kind of communications over a network connection. We have all sorts of specialized web applications serving client applications with static or, more commonly, dynamic data transmitted over the HTTP protocol. We have web services exposing our system's capabilities to the neighboring department's systems over standards like SOAP.[5]

---

[5] SOAP, a specification maintained by the World Wide Web Consortium (http://www.w3.org), used to stand for Simple Object Access Protocol. In the latest version of the specification, however, the name no longer stands for anything—it's just SOAP.

There might be a continuous stream of updates coming from our ERP system over a proprietary communications protocol and API. These are effectively new interfaces to our system—the system we want to be able to test for correctness. It's clearly a lot more involved than testing a programming library. The question is, how does that added complexity in terms of external interfaces show in our decisions about our acceptance-test implementation strategy?

First, even though the software in distributed systems can be arguably a lot more complex than in typical programming libraries, and a large portion of that extra complexity lies in the areas directly adjacent to the network, we're still mostly interested in the actual functionality rather than in how that functionality is accessed. This would imply that perhaps we should write most of our tests under the skin, accessing internal APIs instead of talking to a network socket, and only implement some end-to-end tests as a sanity check for the overall architecture and for the networking libraries in the opposing ends of the wire being able to understand each other. Figure 11.7 illustrates this hybrid approach with boxes and arrows.

Then again, most machine-to-machine interfaces are relatively easy to automate, partly because they are designed to be used by a machine and, thus, do not require advanced pattern recognition and artificial intelligence in order to fake a human user. Part of it is because machine-to-machine interfaces are often specialized and focused on a single service. Thanks to this relative simplicity and easy automation, the added cost or effort of going for an end-to-end acceptance-testing strategy might not be too big.

An exception to this could be a proprietary, closed interface, which we'd either have to reverse-engineer first before implementing our own testing library for it or have to operate using the vendor's client-side API—assuming such a thing is

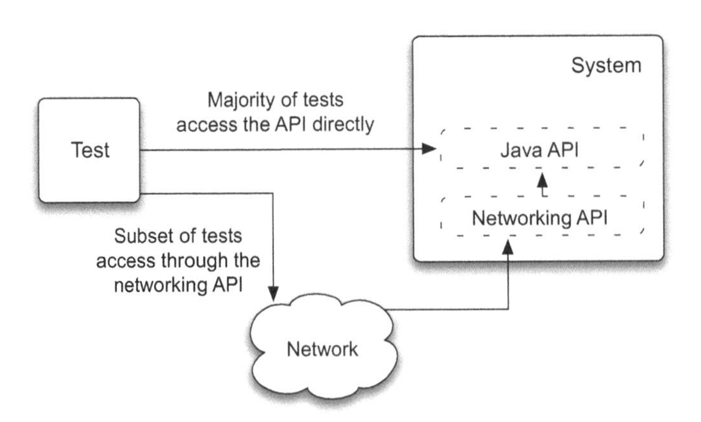

Figure 11.7
Networking is slow compared to direct access to a Java API, which suggests that we should consider implementing most of our acceptance for a "faceless" system against internal APIs and let a smaller subset of tests verify that the networking API processes incoming data correctly and renders the system's response properly back to the wire.

available; or, perhaps we'd be forced to test through the client-side application's UI! Luckily, most of the time, we can fare well with having our acceptance tests bombard the network interface. In those rare cases where this is not feasible, crawling under the skin isn't a bad option either.

Now, if it's the nature of machine-to-machine interfaces that makes faceless distributed systems easy to automate and thus easy targets for the end-to-end strategy of acceptance testing, what about applications with UIs? Let's start our excavation from the original archetype of applications with UIs—console applications.

11.3.3 Console applications

The simplest of UIs these days are found in the so-called *console applications*, also known as command-line interface(CLI) applications. Let's pick an example many of us are familiar with. Consider a command-line FTP client—the universal file-transfer tool, which nowadays ships along with practically all operating systems.

Most command-line FTP clients have an interactive text-based UI, which essentially works by the way of the application prompting the user for a command and then proceeding to execute the given command, eventually returning with a prompt for the next command. Listing 11.4 illustrates this with a sample sequence of interactions between a user and an FTP client.

Listing 11.4 Sample interaction with a CLI application

```
$ ftp ftp.myserver.com
Connected to ftp.myserver.com
220 ProFTPD 1.3.0rc2 Server [123.123.123.123]
User (ftp.myserver.com:(none)): lasse
331 Password required for lasse.
Password: *****
230 User lasse logged in.
ftp> help
Commands may be abbreviated.  Commands are:

!               delete          literal         prompt      send
?               debug           ls              put         status
append          dir             mdelete         pwd         trace
ascii           disconnect      mdir            quit        type
bell            get             mget            quote       user
binary          glob            mkdir           recv        verbose
bye             hash            mls             remotehelp
cd              help            mput            rename
close           lcd             open            rmdir
ftp> quit
Bye.
$
```

The interaction in listing 11.4 shows how we start the application from the operating system's shell or console, give our credentials when prompted for them, execute the `help` command, and then exit the program with the `quit` command.

Most of the functionality of such an application could be mapped to the available commands and variations of their arguments. For example, assuming we were building the world's greatest command-line-based FTP client, we might have a story and the accompanying acceptance tests for uploading a file from the local file system, which would effectively map to using the `put` command with the path of the local file given as an argument. Similarly, we might have acceptance tests for handling error situations like displaying a descriptive error message if the given path doesn't point to any existing file on the local file system. Which strategies might we use for implementing such acceptance tests?

An end-to-end strategy would be relatively easy to implement, considering how trivial the UI is—an interactive prompt of ASCII characters to which we could easily feed automated input and from which we could parse the application's response. The semantic overhead introduced by the UI on top of the actual application domain (network file transfer, in our case) is often minimal with console-based applications—uploading a file to the server from the local file system has a one-to-one mapping to a single put command.

We could, of course, bypass the UI even if it's this thin, and implement our "upload file from local disk" acceptance test directly against the programming API beneath the console prompt. This would likely be also a relatively trivial task, assuming the presentation has been properly separated from the application logic. If we did that, we'd need to test the UI separately, which might or might not present more work compared to an end-to-end approach, considering both the effort in implementing the tests as well as the expected frequency and impact of changes to the system under test over time.

Again, we might have some aspects of the application's functionality that would make more sense to test directly, going for the internals rather than verifying it indirectly through externally visible operations. Similarly, we might want to stub out some pieces of the application in order to help us more easily verify expected behavior in error situations like when the network connection is pulled out in the middle of an upload, for example. In most cases, however, I'd vote for implementing acceptance tests for a console application against the UI, following the end-to-end strategy.

If this is more or less the situation with console-based applications, how about the ones with a fancy GUI?

11.3.4 GUI applications

When we talk about GUI applications, we are talking about the rich-client type of desktop applications such as Microsoft Outlook, Adobe Photoshop, and Mozilla Firefox. Fortunately, most GUI applications developed in the corporate world aren't as big as Outlook or Photoshop. Having said that, they're not far behind in complexity. Speaking of complexity, desktop GUI applications probably have the most complex semantics in their UI, and this is what makes GUI applications one of the most difficult types of systems to write automated tests for.

Semantic complexity

By semantic complexity, we are referring not just to the endless variety of different custom widgets found in such applications, but also to their nature as event-driven applications with a significant portion of all functionality happening in the background multithreaded. In practice, this means that testing correct behavior following an end-to-end approach might not be possible by typing text into an input field, clicking a button, and verifying that a file was written to disk or that a warning message was removed from a status bar. The catch is that we don't know when those things will happen. In other words, we have to wait for an arbitrary time before checking for the expected behavior to have happened, and that is bound to make our tests not just slower but also more brittle than we'd like.

The multithreaded nature of GUI applications and the short waits we likely need to inject into our test code are not the main obstacles for following the end-to-end strategy, however. Most often, the biggest challenge for GUI teams in automating their acceptance tests through the UI is being able to locate and manipulate the UI components. For example, a Java Swing application only exposes to the underlying operating system and other applications the top frame of the GUI and its title and not much else.

Let's see what approaches and twists we could use in tackling this semantic complexity with our acceptance-test implementation, going from the purest end-to-end approach to the less pure and the more "under the skin"–style approach.

Triggering operating system–level events

With desktop GUI applications, the technical UI is most often the keyboard and the mouse. How would we simulate the user in this scenario, assuming we'd like to follow the end-to-end strategy for acceptance testing? We could fake the same UI events that a real user would create by sending raw operating system-level events through a native, operating system-specific API. Such events would need to be targeted to specific coordinates within our application window, however, which effectively means we're testing blind, trusting that our hard-coded coordinates are correct.

In practice, coordinate-based test automation is a swamp I don't recommend entering. The tests are brittle, and their maintenance is a nightmare. Also, for Java Swing applications, for example, asserting the state of the application has to be done through interrogating the internals using tools such as Jemmy or Abbot (similarly to what we did in chapter 8). This is because Swing components are not visible to the underlying windowing system—unless we introduce some kind of logging code into the application only for testing purposes and verify expected behavior by examining a log file. It sounds unattractive, and it most often is. In short, implementing our acceptance tests with this approach can be considered our last straw.

What if we would be able to see all the UI components of the application under test from outside the process? What would our options look like then?

Using a native API

Certain GUI technologies, which use native widgets for rendering the text fields, the buttons, and so forth, offer a possibility to test the application end to end through a native API. In other words, we can write code that looks up a component by its name and type from a given application window, send some events to it (for instance, "click the left button"), and also interrogate the components' state ("What's this text field's current value?" "Is that button enabled?").

This approach gives us a chance to test the application as a black box, without meddling with the internals. The downside is, of course, exactly that—we can't meddle with the internals. At least, this complicates our test implementation when we need to communicate both with the native API for operating on the widgets and with the internals through a custom hook we've exposed in order to facilitate the necessary interprocess communication.

Personally, I find this kind of a black-box approach less than optimal for testing GUI applications. In the vast majority of cases, we have to (or at the least we'd like to) be able to operate on the internals anyway. Second, having to express our tests through what's available in the UI is somewhat limiting, considering that we'd like to be able to test our application throughout the project, not just in the end.

Having brought this up, let's explore the idea of exposing hooks from the application a bit farther.

Exposing hooks from the application

The fundamental idea behind exposing different types of *hooks* from the application is to give our tests—running separately from the application under test—

access to locating, operating, and interrogating specific parts of our UI as well as the application logic and state beneath. Testing through hooks exposed by the application can effectively facilitate testing things that it isn't possible to test through the existing UI. This can basically be a form of crawling under the skin or a testing backdoor, in terms of the strategies we discussed earlier.

But what kind of hooks are we talking about, technically speaking? Well, in one project, we ended up exposing the full component hierarchy of a Java Swing application to the outside world by having the application start a Remote Method Invocation (RMI) server and register an implementation of our testing interface as an RMI object. With this remoting scheme in place, we could connect to the running application over an RMI connection and traverse the component tree however we wanted.

Exposing hooks does not, however, need to mean such an elaborate low-level access. Just giving a remotely accessible interface for initiating a predefined set of operations, assertions, and so on can be enough. Such hooks would aid us in keeping our tests written on the proper level of abstraction—the level of user-valued functionality—rather than falling prey to the temptations of implementation details, such as a specific UI component's name.

The main downside to exposing hooks from our application is the potential effort required to do so. Implementing a facility for remote access to your application's widgets and internal state can be a significant investment, especially for smaller projects. Furthermore, splitting our test implementation into two places—the test code and the hooks it uses—can slow things down. This notion brings us to question whether we could avoid splitting the work somehow. We know at least one way to do that: by bringing the test code and the application inside the same process.

Merging tests and the application

We could consider embedding our tests into the application itself as a natural progression on the path from pure black-box testing toward the lighter shades of gray, eventually reaching a pure white-box approach. We already moved from the end-to-end class of strategies into the domain of crawling under the skin when we started exposing hooks instead of going through the real UI—even if our hooks would operate on the GUI components using whatever API they're built with. With this in mind, could there be a more honest and simple way to crawl under the application's skin than to deploy our test code inside the application?

There are two ways of putting our test code together with the application code. We can either embed our tests into the application or embed our application into our tests.

The latter approach of letting the tests launch the application programmatically, as illustrated in figure 11.8, is perhaps better suited for automated testing because we are already well-equipped to execute our tests as part of automated builds, for example, and because our development tools also integrate the dominant testing frameworks. In short, it's trivial for us to launch our tests and have the tests launch the application they're testing, whereas we'd have to do more work in order to be able to launch the application and then somehow initiate the tests' execution and collect the test results.

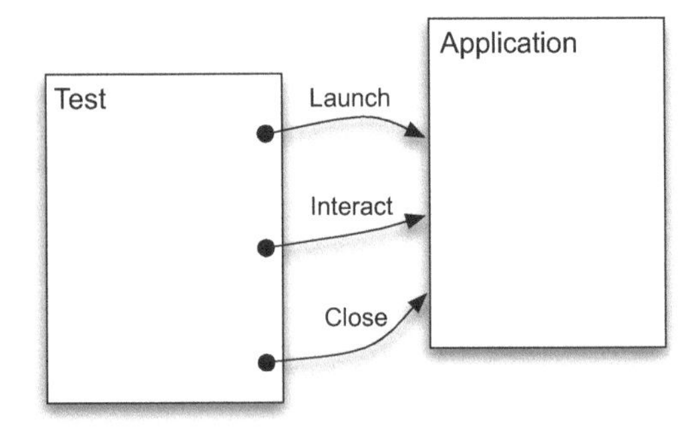

Figure 11.8 Application is started from the test

Sometimes, however, it makes more sense to go with the former approach, embedding our tests into the application, and to put in that extra bit of work to be able to launch the tests within the application, as illustrated in figure 11.9.

A recent example of a situation where we opted for this approach was a Java WebStart application. Java WebStart applications are essentially Swing applications, except that they're started with a special WebStart client that knows how to download the application's resources and even the correct runtime based on a configuration file placed on a web server. Thus, we should be able to use the same testing libraries that we'd use for a regular Swing application.

However, because the WebStart application's deployment configuration (mainly dependencies and security settings) was considered a source of risk—having created late-found problems with previous releases—we wanted to launch the application through the actual WebStart client instead. The solution we ended up with was to embed a specific test module into the application, which could be invoked from an outside process, running all of our automated tests and reporting them back to the external process. This is more laborious than we'd hoped, but certainly doable and something we considered worth the effort.

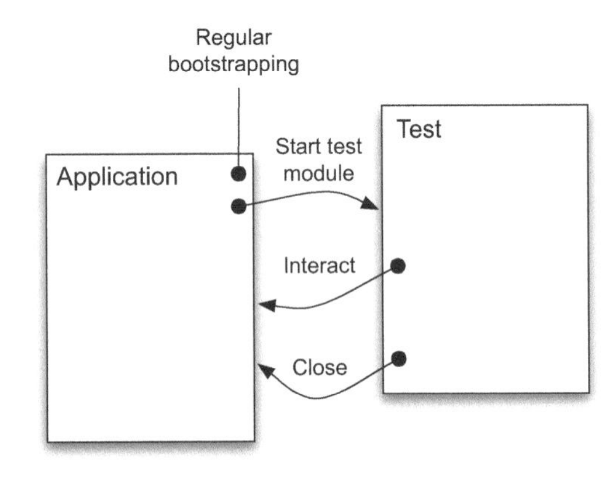

Figure 11.9 Tests are embedded into the application through a plug-in mechanism.

Again, as usual, some features are best suited to be tested directly against the internals, and we might want to stub or replace some components for our tests. This is something the embedded approach supports well because we're typically using a unit-testing framework, and the same programming language as the application itself has been written for implementing our tests.

Unfortunately, this approach also means that our tests are effectively hidden from nontechnical stakeholders, such as end users and the customer. The risks of ineffective or otherwise lacking collaboration are much higher than if we would be able to collaborate on the tests directly and use that same medium—the acceptance tests—as both a communication tool as well as an executable specification.

Enough talk about desktop applications. There's a specific brand of applications with graphical UIs we haven't yet discussed—web applications. Let's take a look at how or whether web technology changes the way we should think about our acceptance test implementation strategy.

11.3.5 Web applications

Web applications are perhaps the most essential category of enterprise applications developers around the world are trying to tackle in today's world of e-this and online-that. Web application development today is characterized not just by the distributed nature of the web or the request-response–based protocol that is HTTP, but also by the vast number of standards and the even broader range of different implementations of said standards. The fact that web browsers handle especially the more recently introduced features of web standards differently affects our acceptance-testing strategy by simultaneously putting more weight on end-to-end testing with the real browser and making it more difficult to accomplish just that. In short, it complicates things.

We can apply the same strategies of testing some details directly by exercising the internals that we use for testing any other types of applications. We can stub out components or resources that would be difficult to control. What piques our interest about implementing acceptance tests for a web application is the age-old decision between testing through the UI or beneath it and, if we opt for the end-to-end approach, whether we should implement our acceptance tests by *simulating* a web browser or *controlling* the real browser.

Through the UI or under the skin?

The main reason web applications tend to put more weight on being able to test through the UI is the relatively essential role of the presentation layer, HTTP sessions, JavaScript, and other web infrastructure in achieving the application's desired behavior. Having automated acceptance tests go through the actual HTTP interface would likely help us catch at least some of the errors we may introduce in our web plumbing code or in the presentation layer—including browser compatibility issues.

Regardless of these incentives for going end-to-end with our acceptance tests, testing through the UI requires extra effort and tends toward larger tests, which consequently translates to more brittle tests. Furthermore, testing a web application built on top of an application server platform such as Java EE or .NET through the UI also introduces a performance hit in terms of test execution speed—starting the application server and deploying an application can take many more precious seconds than we'd like.

Choosing to crawl under the web application's skin might give us the upper hand on both test brittleness and the slowness associated with bouncing the application server and deploying the application. Although the more intuitive approach to crawling under the application's skin might be to use some kind of remoting technology, perhaps the more valuable proposition is to embed the tests into the same process as the application itself and to run the application raw without the real application server. For example, we could choose to hook our acceptance tests into a service layer behind the web plumbing, dropping the application server startup and application deployment from the picture.

Knowing the advantages and disadvantages of following the end-to-end strategy for implementing acceptance tests for a web application, and assuming that we've decided to go end-to-end, the other interesting question is whether we should simulate a web browser or control a real web browser.

Simulating or controlling a browser

The main point to consider when pondering simulating a web browser versus running a web browser under the control of our acceptance tests is whether existing simulation libraries (such as jWebUnit for Java or Twill for Python, for example) can handle our use of JavaScript or other technologies that are often not supported at all or only partially supported by the available libraries.

These simulation libraries fake the HTTP traffic toward the web application and parse and interpret the returned HTML pages, offering an object hierarchy of the page elements that we can then operate on. Such libraries have to duplicate all the functionality of actual web browsers except the rendering (because they don't need to display the pages). That's why using a simulation library is not fully representative of a real web browser.

Listing 11.5 shows an example of an acceptance test written using JUnit and the jWebUnit library; it connects to a remote web server and interacts with it using the HTTP protocol, but there's no web browser whatsoever involved.

Listing 11.5 Example of using the JWebUnit library to test the Manning website

```
import net.sourceforge.jwebunit.junit.WebTestCase;
import org.junit.Before;
import org.junit.Test;

public class TestWebApplicationWithJWebUnit extends WebTestCase {

    @Before
    protected void setUp() throws Exception {
        getTestContext().setBaseUrl("http://www.manning.com/");
        setScriptingEnabled(false);
    }

    @Test
    public void testManningWebsiteWithJWebUnit() throws Exception {
        beginAt("/");
        assertLinkPresentWithText("Ordering Info");
        clickLinkWithText("Ordering Info");
        String[] paymentOptions = { "Visa", "MasterCard",
                                    "American Express",
                                    "Discover Card",
                                    "eCheck", "PayPal" };
        for (String option : paymentOptions) {
            assertTextPresent(option);
        }
    }
}
```

The advantage of using simulation libraries like the ones mentioned is that they're built for the purpose of testing and, thus, they incorporate plenty of built-in assertions and operations. In other words, the API they give us is sufficient for most of our needs, and they yield enough power to us so that we can add what's missing ourselves.

Simulation tools give us an easy-to-use framework to build our tests with, but they're not sufficient for all applications, especially those that make heavy use of the more advanced features of web technologies like JavaScript. For example, Ajax[6] techniques are likely to cause headaches for tools like jWebUnit. Could we

[6] Ajax (or AJAX) stands for Asynchronous JavaScript and XML and represents the latest trend in Web 2.0 development. The best resource on all things Ajax I'm aware of is *Ajax in Action* (Manning Publications, 2005), written by my friend Eric Pascarello and David Crane. Dave also co-authored another fresh Manning title, *Ajax in Practice* (Manning Publications, 2007), which takes a cookbook approach to conquering the world of JavaScript.

avoid these pitfalls by programmatically controlling the real web browser instead? Yes, to some degree, although that approach isn't without drawbacks.

The prerequisite for us to be able to control a web browser like Internet Explorer, Mozilla Firefox, or Safari is that the browser—a native application—exposes an API that is rich enough for us to use for testing purposes.

Fortunately, Internet Explorer on Windows does a decent job at this through the COM component model. In essence, Internet Explorer is registered with the Windows operating system as a COM component, and we can launch a new instance of Internet Explorer by obtaining a new instance of the COM component. From there, we can invoke any operations exposed by the COM interface. This is the premise on which tools like Watir (for Ruby), jWatir (for Java), Pamie (for Python), and Samie (for Perl) base their implementation.

The problem is that, at the time of writing this, no cross-platform solution is available that works on all major development platforms (Windows, Linux, and Mac OS X). For instance, on Mac OS X, our only option for controlling a browser seems to be SafariWatir, a Watir extension for controlling Safari, the default browser on Mac OS X. Figure 11.10 shows the SafariWatir extension in action.

The Mozilla project does have its XPCOM, modeled after Microsoft's COM, which should be cross-platform; but it's far from being ready for mainstream adoption. There's also a plug-in for Mozilla-based browsers that lets an external process control the browser over a Telnet connection; however, the only available version of the plug-in is for the Windows operating system.

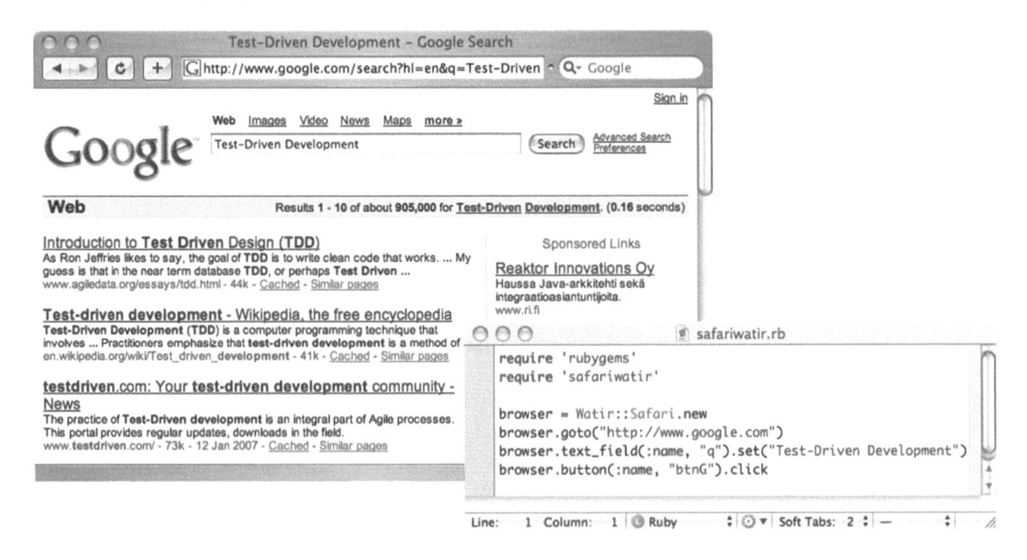

Figure 11.10 A Ruby script controlling a Safari web browser on Mac OS X using the SafariWatir library

The Selenium project is well on its way toward this admirable goal, although its reporting and build-integration capabilities are still lacking at the time of writing this book. We're also missing glue for making Selenium tests support active customer collaboration better, but I'm sure the situation will improve over time.

Another problem with this approach of controlling an actual web browser is speed—we're adding yet another variable into the picture, and the communication between the testing library and the browser can be sluggish. Furthermore, we'd often like to start a fresh session for every test, which might require launching a fresh instance of the browser, again adding to the duration of our tests. If these aren't an issue for you, though, controlling a real browser can be a good alternative implementation for an end-to-end acceptance testing strategy.

In conclusion, there are no easy choices with regard to an acceptance-test implementation strategy for web applications. Not that the choice would be any easier with other types of applications with UIs. Although technology does have its say in our decisions, an important factor should be our team's preferences and skills. After all, software development is a people business, and the way we support collaboration through our acceptance tests does carry some weight.

Before we wrap up the chapter, it would probably make sense to cover some frequently asked questions that are bound to come up when setting out to implement test automation, whether you're doing it test-first or not.

11.4 Tips for common problems

Implementing acceptance tests for complex systems is not the easiest of tasks. Many enterprise systems deal with enormous volumes of data, semantically complex calculations with a slew of variables, and exceptions to the rule. I have seen projects quickly build up a test suite that's almost as complex as the system they're testing, because it's so easy to forget that we should design and refactor our acceptance tests just like we design and refactor our production code and unit tests.

The potential complexity of acceptance tests is not the only problem I see a lot. Performance—the duration of test execution—is a real issue for many teams. One client has an eight-hour build, most of which goes into running hundreds and hundreds of end-to-end acceptance tests.[7] Such long test duration means that it might take a full working day before a team finds out that their changes have broken something elsewhere in the system.

Clearly, there are a lot of issues that we'd like to avoid. The following sections are intended to help you see the roadblock early on while you still have

[7] Eight hours isn't *that* bad, though, considering that it used to be somewhere around 48 hours!

time to maneuver. Let's start by looking at how we could perhaps speed up our test suite.

11.4.1 Accelerating test execution

A slow acceptance test suite is the most common problem I've seen lately with projects that are adopting automated acceptance tests. It's usually not just that the tests take a long time to execute. It's also that setting up the system before running the tests takes time and that restoring the system back into a known state in between tests takes time.

A colleague once shared a word of wisdom with me after I had poured my frustration on him regarding having too much work to do within regular office hours. His advice was to "do less." Doing less is indeed the key to speeding up test execution as well. Let's take a look at a handful of ways to do less.

Organizing tests

If you have a long-running setup routine for your test suite, one of the first things you should do is to look at your tests and determine whether all of the tests need that much setup. It's often the case that you can find a number of subsets of tests, some of which could do with less (faster) setup.

One specific categorization that might help cut the overall test duration significantly is to split your test suite into tests that have side effects and tests that don't have side effects. For example, tests that verify business or validation rules are probably not writing to the database—thus, those tests can be safely executed in the "no side effects" suite before tests that do require repopulating the database, as illustrated in figure 11.11.

Other useful categorizations can be found by examining the target system's internal boundaries. For example, tests for an e-commerce system that only touch on the customer-related tables may not need to run the full setup for customer *and* product tables and vice versa.

There's another way of speeding up the test suite that's directly related to databases and persistence. I call it *cheating on persistence.*

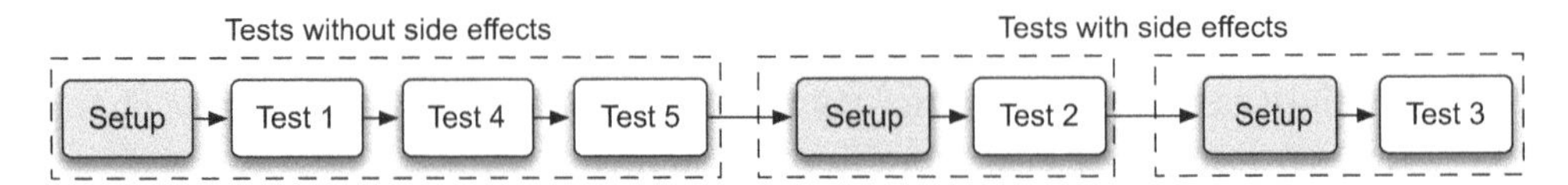

Figure 11.11 Tests without side effects can be executed one after another without running the full setup in between each test. Tests with side effects can then be executed as usual, with the setup before each individual test.

Cheating on persistence

Disk I/O is often the single biggest source of slow performance. And it's usually the relational database or some other persistence solution that does most of the disk I/O. Thus, if we could make our persistence solution do less disk I/O, we should be able to accelerate our test suite quite a bit.

We could, for example, run our acceptance tests against a system that's configured to use the database in in-memory mode (cheating on persistence in that we're not writing to disk and therefore not *persisting* anything) or tweak its configuration so that our tests initiate fewer disk writes from the database.

A less suspicious-sounding trick to doing less work is to share the workload among multiple workers. Let's talk a bit about distributing work.

Distributing work

Delegation can also be a form of doing less (yourself). For accelerating our acceptance test suite, we might implement this idea by distributing test execution to a grid of several machines running tests in parallel. This would mean that each individual machine has less to do, each finishing its slice of the test suite in a fraction of the time it takes for a single machine to run the full suite.

When distributing the work, it should be noted that the advantage comes from having more disk I/O and more CPU cycles available for the computation required to execute the test suite. Generally speaking, it's not the tests that drain on these resources—it's the system under test that spins the disk and crunches the numbers. With this in mind, the distributed test farm wouldn't make much sense unless we scale the number of instances of the system under test. In practice, we're talking about one of the following options:

- One-to-many
- Many-to-many
- Many-to-many-more

Let's quickly discuss the relative pros and cons of the three patterns, starting from the one-to-many scenario illustrated in figure 11.12.

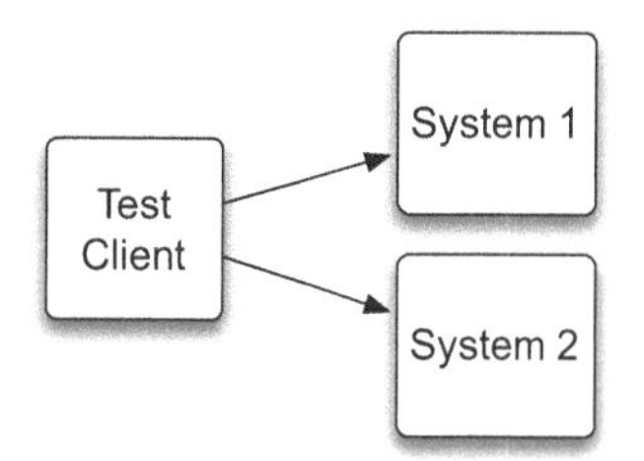

Figure 11.12 Single test client load-balancing test cases between multiple target systems

In the one-to-many scenario, the test client is load-balancing individual test cases between multiple target systems. This setup has the benefit of the test client being able to run another test case while the other is blocked, waiting for the system under test to respond. In practice, this is a simple setup that only requires a simple multithreaded test runner and that scales well as long as the source of slowness is mostly within the system under test (such as test setups populating the underlying database) and not, for example, in the communication overhead or in the test parsing the system's responses.

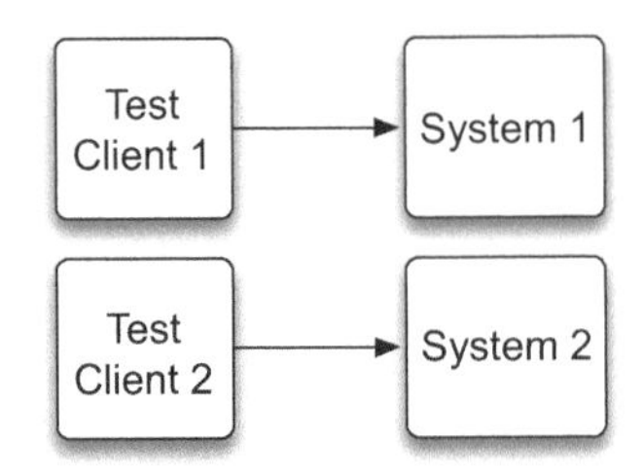

Figure 11.13 Multiple test clients executing their subset of tests against their dedicated target system

Another relatively simple way to distribute work is to have multiple test clients running their slice of tests against their own dedicated target system, as illustrated in figure 11.13. This is just a matter of coordinating multiple machines to execute tests in parallel and organizing your acceptance tests into roughly equal-sized test suites or, alternatively, making the coordinating test runner smart enough to feed test cases to the test clients as they complete their previous test case. This approach of having multiple test clients also means that the coordinating test runner needs to be able to collect the test-execution results for a combined report.

If neither one-to-many nor many-to-many yield enough time savings to bring the overall duration to an acceptable level, you might consider combining them into our third scenario: having many test clients load-balance to their dedicated sets of target systems. This scenario is depicted in figure 11.14.

By having multiple test clients and even more target systems, we can scale our test farm in all directions. We can add target systems until the test clients become the bottleneck. At that point, we add a new test client, making the ratio of test clients to target systems such that the bottleneck is no longer the test client, and so forth. The downside to this approach is, of course, that the complexity of our test farm is far bigger than either of the previous two scenarios alone.

Speaking of complexity, our next way to do less is also a trade-off of getting faster test execution in exchange for increased complexity.

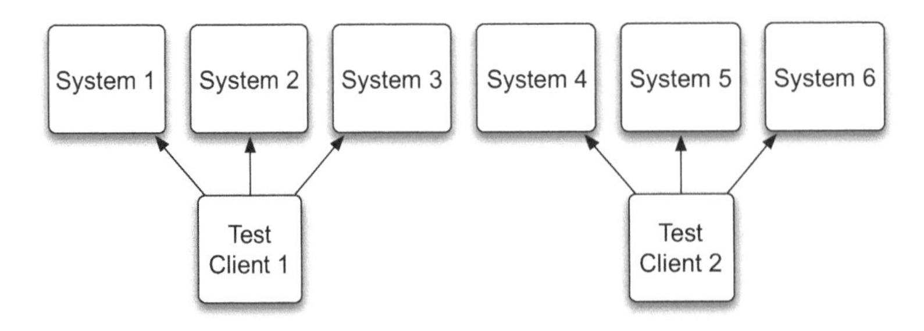

Figure 11.14 Multiple test clients load-balancing test cases between multiple target systems

Minimizing setup with dependent tests

For many enterprise systems, the amount of setup performed before each test causes a significant drag on test execution times. This setup typically involves populating a database with a known data set or stopping and starting a server. We can do less by performing this kind of setup just once. For example, we could populate the underlying database in the beginning of our test suite. This approach is illustrated in figure 11.15.

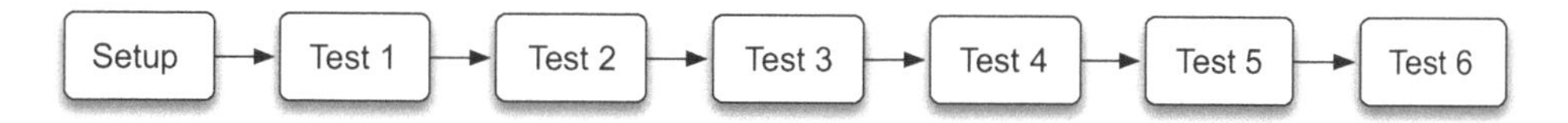

Figure 11.15 With ordered, dependent tests, we can perform a common setup just once in the beginning of the test suite. However, each test case may have assumptions about the side effects of earlier tests.

In practice, this typically creates a number of dependencies between individual tests because the tests affect the system's internal state. For instance, test T1 might verify that our online shop's shopping cart handles successful purchases correctly, effectively creating a bunch of orders into the underlying database. If test T2 is supposed to check that the sales statistics are correct, we have a dependency between tests T1 and T2 because changing T1 means that we need to change T2 as well.

Although we can easily speed up the overall test execution, there are significant downsides to creating dependencies between tests. Perhaps the most significant of these downsides is that our maintenance load grows exponentially as we add more tests and more dependencies. Nobody likes editing several dozen tests just to be able to add a new test.

Another issue with dependent tests is reporting. With dependencies between tests, a single real test failure often triggers failures in most tests that depend on the failing test—even though there's nothing wrong with the functionality those dependent tests are trying to verify—as illustrated in figure 11.16. In practice, this means that our test reports give us far less information than they could if only legitimate test failures were reported.

Figure 11.16 Test suite with dependencies between tests has test failures. Without analyzing test logs and wielding psychic powers, it's impossible to say which of the four failing tests are failing for a legitimate reason and which are failing because a dependent test failed.

With dependent tests, the best we can do is to make the test runner ignore tests for which a dependency failed to complete successfully. We'd basically know that there are failing tests, but we'd have no idea how many!

Although dependent tests are certainly not among my favorite techniques for speeding up test execution, they are an option nevertheless. Just be aware of what you're trading off if you choose to create those dependencies.

Now, let's look at a less risky way of speeding up our acceptance tests—specifically, those that modify the contents of a database.

Rolling back transactions

Acceptance tests often need to populate a database again and again with a known data set because the previous tests may have changed the data. A trick we learned in chapter 6 may come in handy with acceptance tests as well: rolling back a transaction after a test to restore the database to its original state.

The point behind rolling back a transaction instead of dropping the full database and repopulating it from scratch is that a rollback is typically several magnitudes faster. We gain a lot of speed from this technique, but it's not one of the easiest approaches to implement. First, it requires an architecture that gives the acceptance tests access to the transaction. Second, this approach works only if each test works within a single transaction—which is hardly the case with a lot of the systems I've seen.

To summarize, this approach has a lot of potential but is feasible only in a rare few cases. Nevertheless, it's a technique worth being aware of! Now, let's move on to our last way of doing less to speed up—the soft boot.

Soft booting

It's not that rare to encounter a software development project where acceptance tests frequently restart the target system to reset its internal state. Although this is usually a trivial thing to do with a couple of lines of Perl or Bash, it's not a snap to restart a full-blown Java EE application server, for example. Instead of doing a full restart, try to find a way to do a *soft boot*.

A soft boot is one that doesn't involve stopping processes, reallocating hundreds of megabytes of memory, re-reading a gigabyte of data from the database into an application-level cache, or performing other intensive and slow operations. A soft boot is a smart operation that does less—one that does the absolute minimum set of tasks required in order to bring the system back into a known state.

A typical example of where the soft-boot technique fits in is a gateway system that processes and forwards network traffic, sitting between two networks. Instead of restarting the whole system, we might, for example, flush the gateway's internal caches and queues.

The soft boot might not always be feasible. It might require careful architectural design and refactoring to ensure that the full state is indeed reset. Again, it isn't an approach that does the trick for all cases but is certainly another handy tool in our toolbox for speeding up our test suite.

We've now covered a handful of ways to accelerate our test suites' execution, and it's time to move on to our next common problem—that of complex test cases.

11.4.2 Reducing complexity of test cases

Verbose, complex acceptance tests are a problem with many a team. There's duplication all over the place; it's difficult to see the forest for the trees when the test setup is 40 lines of code and talks about low-level implementation details instead of concepts from the associated user story. How can we reduce this complexity?

Beyond the usual rules of refactoring away duplication, renaming things to communicate better (and in the appropriate language), and structuring our acceptance tests into cohesive units with common fixtures as we do for unit tests, there's not much advice to give—those same techniques will get you far if done properly.

Having said that, acceptance tests for web applications, for example, can often be simplified by turning common setups into *context objects* that know how to take the target system and the test case into that state. Now, instead of creating a hierarchy of test cases with inherited setups, a test case can point to a context and say, "take me there." Different contexts can build on top of each other, possibly creating an inheritance hierarchy, but the inheritance hierarchy is now hidden from the test cases.

Taking the context-object pattern further, it's possible to speed up test execution by implementing what I call a *caching context object*, illustrated in figure 11.17.

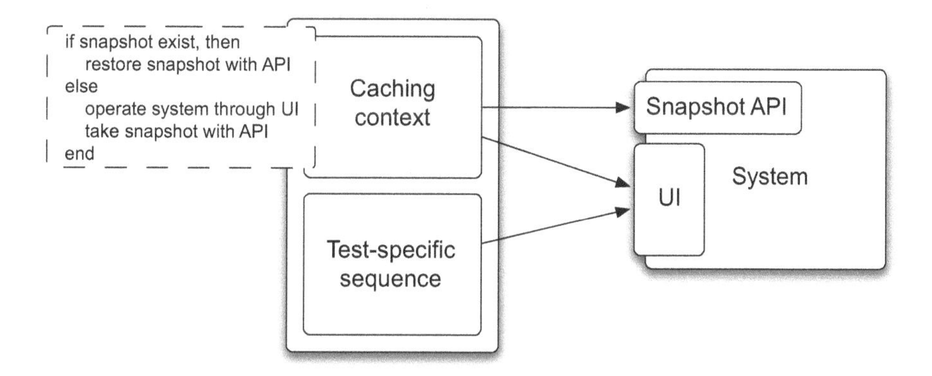

Figure 11.17 A caching context object not only knows how to operate the system into the correct state but also takes a snapshot of the system state after reaching the desired context. The snapshot can be used in later tests using the same caching context to restore the state quickly without redoing the full sequence of steps.

A caching context object differs from a regular one by its ability to take a snapshot of the session state after first execution and to restore the snapshot on subsequent runs, effectively skipping a number of potentially long-lasting HTTP requests. In practice, the implementation of such caching context objects needs to rely on the target system to expose an API for taking and restoring named snapshots of session data on the server-side.

The caching context object is relatively simple to implement as long as the state to be restored doesn't include external systems such as relational databases. Speaking of databases, the last common problem we'll discuss is how to manage test data.

11.4.3 Managing test data

It's one thing to maintain a beautiful code base of automated, executable acceptance tests. It's a different matter to maintain test *data*—the data our test setups push into the database and the data our acceptance tests assume exist in the database. There's no escape from the fact that managing test data will be more laborious than we'd like. However, we do have some simple guidelines to consider for keeping our test data as manageable as possible:

- Use a single data set.
- Generate the data set.
- Version-control our data.

Let's see what we mean by these one-liners.

Using a single data set

The first of our guidelines for managing test data is to have only a single data set for acceptance tests. The point about having a single data set is that our test data is probably massive enough already—and starting to duplicate data for individual test cases will make things worse. Furthermore, keeping several data sets in sync with each other is not what I'd call an easy task. I've found it much easier to extend a single data set when new requirements pop up—for example, when a new acceptance test needs a specific case that isn't found in our current data set.

But doesn't common knowledge about maintainable code and design suggest that we should not have monolithic entities, whether it's a class or a data set? Yes, we should try to partition our test data into smaller assets that, when combined, build up the full data set. At some point, our data set may grow beyond our ability to handle it as a single asset. Having said that, we should not do that partitioning without considering the price tag. If we're going to partition, it has to happen around boundaries that don't add too much to our cognitive load for managing the overall data set.

One possible way to partition the data set is to switch from a static definition of test data (such as SQL scripts, human-editable dump files, and so on) into a dynamic definition. For example, we could generate the test data.

Generating the data set

The main benefit of generating test data versus defining the data statically is volume. A script that generates data can be several magnitudes smaller in size, therefore making it more manageable and easier to keep track of.

One specific pattern that I've personally found useful is to generate test data using the target system's own persistence implementation. For example, if the system uses Hibernate or an equivalent ORM solution for persisting domain objects, we could easily use the same domain classes and the same ORM solution for generating the base data set for our acceptance tests. The obvious benefit of this approach is that our data set is described in terms of the domain, not in terms of schemas, tables, columns, and SQL statements.

For our third guideline for managing test data, whether you're using a static or dynamic approach, you should version-control your data set definition—and in a usable manner.

Version-controlling your data

One of the trickiest challenges we can face in relation to test data is figuring out after the fact what was changed in the data set between two test runs. With this in mind, we should strive to, first of all, version-control our data-set definition. But it doesn't stop there—we need to version-control the definition in a format that we can effectively work with. Specifically, we need to be able to *diff* two versions of the definition: that is, figure out which lines differ between the two versions.

This effectively suggests that our data-set definition must use a text-based format rather than a binary dump file, for example. It might be blatantly obvious, but I've seen plenty of projects maintaining their test data definitions in binary files or, even worse, having the data as a schema on a running database server. Forcing developers and testing engineers to use a database client and SQL statements to explore and modify test data must be among the most effective ways of hampering a team's productivity.

I think we've covered test data well enough for now. There's clearly no magic spell or silver bullet that will solve all of your test data-related problems but I hope that these guidelines will give you ideas for keeping your troubles to a minimum. Let's wrap up the chapter and move on.

11.5 Summary

We set out in the beginning of this chapter to explore our options for connecting acceptance tests with the system under test. We started by identifying the three main factors to take into account when making a decision: the nature of the feature and acceptance tests we want to implement, the expected turbulence or frequency and volume of change, and the technology involved. We discussed how these factors might influence our preferences through simple examples.

After mapping out the surrounding area of what kind of forces are in play, we discussed some strategies for implementing our acceptance tests. We started from the most intuitive alternative of testing the application end to end, going through the actual UI just like (or a bit like) a real user would. We continued by moving a notch closer to the metal, getting to know the approach we called crawling under the application's skin, or testing right beneath the UI. Finally, we quickly discussed the other end of the spectrum between pure black-box and pure white-box testing, in the form of exercising the internals directly and, where appropriate, stubbing out the irrelevant stuff that makes our application difficult to test or slows our tests down too much. We also touched on the use of testing backdoors for verifying expected behavior and desired side effects.

Next, we dove a bit deeper into the realm of the third major influence in our strategy—technology. We enumerated through some major types of software including programming libraries, distributed systems, console applications, desktop applications with GUIs, and web applications. By looking closer at our possibilities in implementing acceptance tests for these kinds of systems, we've now built up a foundation based on which we are able to make smart, informed decisions about our acceptance testing strategies.

To finish the chapter, we waded through a number of tips and tricks for tackling common problems teams face when their acceptance test suites grow into a mess that's as fast as a snail and too complex to grasp.

Writing good acceptance tests is difficult, and implementing them into executable tests well is not far behind. You should now feel better equipped to face this challenge and not be afraid to explore the topic further.

In the next chapter, we'll change focus once again, ending our journey through the world of test-driven development and acceptance test-driven development by concentrating on how to successfully adopt—and sustain—personal and team-level practices like TDD and ATDD.

12 Adopting TDD

They say that time changes things, but you actually have to change them yourself.

—Andy Warhol

You're reading this book, so it's likely that you're already interested in TDD and quite possibly already in the process of adopting the technique in your work. It's also likely, however, that not all of your co-workers share your interest in test-driven development. Having the rest of the team adopt test-driven development would obviously support your own adoption, not to mention the benefits to the organization as a whole—which is why you'd probably want your colleagues to get infected with the test-first bug as well. This chapter's purpose is to help you both in your personal adoption of TDD and in getting others aboard the adoption train.

We won't focus too much on TDD itself, because the dynamics of personal adoption are universal regardless of the actual change being suggested. What we're going to cover are factors that influence our ability to lead change on a personal level, whether for ourselves or for our colleagues—colleagues who are possibly on our client's payroll, if we're in the role of an external consultant.

Let's begin by discussing what it takes to adopt a technique like TDD.

12.1 What it takes to adopt TDD

Adopting a new development technique is not an easy task, especially when the technique is as radically different from our old ways as TDD is. Further, it's not enough to adopt the technique and master it once. We need constant rehearsal and practice in order to keep learning and improving. It all takes a lot of discipline. And it's worth every bit of the effort.

Let's begin by taking a look at some of the factors that influence our ability to sustain lasting change in our personal adoption of TDD (or pretty much any other technique, for that matter).

12.1.1 Getting it

Many of the best software engineers I know suffer from some weird programmer-specific form of attention deficit disorder, which lures them to constantly try out new things, only to abandon the new tool, framework, or technique a couple of weeks later.

A key factor in sustainable change is for the individual to really understand the dynamics underlying the change. Understanding *why* a technique is beneficial and should be considered is key. Lacking this understanding may lead to the technique being dropped when the individual faces external pressure. As such, it is extremely important to discuss our ideas and thoughts with others to make sure we're really getting it.

First-hand experience is also important for understanding the *why*. Repeating a mantra such as "TDD is good for you" doesn't go far in creating a lasting change.

The change becomes real when we see with our own eyes how we just prevented an angry customer from busting in through the phone line because we wrote our tests first. We created the solution one small step at a time and realized something we wouldn't have thought of if we had designed the whole solution up front.

Having said that, it can be extremely difficult to truly appreciate the rationale and benefits of a change if there's no immediate need for improvement, no sense of urgency.

12.1.2 Sense of urgency

W. Edwards Deming, father of the Japanese post-war industrial revival and author of *Out of the Crisis* (MIT Press, 1982), once said, "It is not necessary to change—survival is not mandatory." This quote mirrors the way we often see changes such as adopting a new development technique. We might be aware of the benefits that the change would bring, but the benefits are easy to forget if there's no immediate need for improvement. For most people, change represents a degree of risk. As long as there's no immediate problem that needs solving or something that needs changing, we are happy with the status quo because we don't want to risk making things worse.

Unfortunately, we typically don't have the sense of urgency we seek. That's not to say that there wouldn't often be a sense of urgency in the form of pressure from management, though. It just tends to be focused on short-term goals, such as completing a project on time, rather than sustained improvements in the organization's delivery capability. We can, however, *create* a sense of urgency for ourselves.

The sense of urgency we can create for ourselves has to build on our desire to improve our skills as craftsmen, to improve our ability to deliver what we promise when we promise it, and to fulfill our clients' needs. Having said that, the sense of urgency must be something practical and concrete enough that we feel we can do something about it every day.

Here's an example of creating a sense of urgency: A pair of developers decided to tackle their growing list of defects once and for all. In just a couple of weeks, the defects were all either fixed, closed, or assigned up-to-date priorities, and the rate of incoming defects had almost ground to a halt. Another example of a self-initiated sense of urgency involved a developer who finally got fed up with having to go back and fix bugs from code they had written and so decided to stop making bugs. They ramped up their testing practices and eventually adopted TDD, and the centralized testing function no longer revealed programming errors by that developer.

This kind of change requires discipline and determination for which a sense of urgency is a great source of energy. Such a change, such discipline and determination does not last forever, however, unless we get frequent positive feedback to reassure us that we are indeed making progress. In other words, we need a sense of achievement.

12.1.3 Sense of achievement

We don't particularly like doing things that we're bad at. At least I don't. And we love doing things we're constantly improving at. It is the frequent small wins and the accumulating sense of achievement that keep our motivation high.

The power of a sense of achievement is at the heart of a sustainable change. We must choose goals that are small enough and concrete enough that we can achieve them quickly and often. And when we do achieve a goal, no matter how small, we should celebrate it and give ourselves credit for the accomplishment. When you finally get that legacy class instantiated in your test harness, get up and grab a cup of coffee (or tea, or Jolt—whatever tickles your fancy). When you've managed to test-drive code all day without lapses to the dark side, treat yourself by eating out.

The exact prize or reward isn't all that important. What's important is that we acknowledge that our achievement and concrete rewards, however small, are excellent motivators. Plus, your peers will also take note of your wide smile, the giant ice cream, the spontaneous "Yippee!" and other small tokens of your progress.

With all of the celebration and patting ourselves on the back, we must not, however, turn a blind eye toward the occasional setbacks and ignore our failures. More specifically, we must exhibit integrity with our actions.

12.1.4 Exhibiting integrity

When adopting a new technique or practice in a team environment, it might not be enough to internalize the fundamental reasons why we're using the technique. Peer pressure is one of the biggest influences; and because we humans are bad at accepting things we don't understand, it is crucial to exhibit true integrity with our actions and behavior. An integral part of exhibiting integrity is being consistent with our actions and words and being open about what we do and what kind of results we're seeing.

Being congruent

Picture yourself as a tourist somewhere far from home, asking for directions to your hotel from a local passing by. At first, the local points to their left. Wanting to be sure you got it correct, you point at your little street map with your finger, and the local starts waving to their right. Unsure about whether it's left or right, you ask again, and the local now waves to their left. How confident do you feel at this point about the local having any idea of where your hotel is?

If we are to convince others of the advantages of our adopting a new practice, we must be consistent with our communication as well as our actions. Behaving arbitrarily seriously harms our credibility as well as that of our arguments for the change we're leading. Issuing blanket statements, for example, makes little sense because we'll eventually have to correct ourselves, effectively decreasing any weight our message may have had in the eyes of others. If we're promoting TDD to our colleagues, we'd better practice it ourselves, too. If we're having trouble keeping up the practice when working on some area of the legacy code base, we should be open about it and explain what we are doing to try to make it easier in the long run. For example, we may decide to refactor and investigate potential tools that could help alleviate the pain.

With this in mind, even more critical than avoiding constant reformulation of the message we're communicating with our words and actions, the message must not be one-sided and focused only on the positive. We need to be truly open in order to gain trust for what we're doing.

Being open

It's easy to publicize success, but openness has to include our failures and setbacks as well. People recognize and won't give a positive response to propaganda. Furthermore, our goal should not be convincing others of how insanely great the change we're leading is. Our goal should be convincing others that we are rational about the change—and to communicate our experience truthfully and objectively.

In addition to how we talk the talk and walk the walk, *when* we walk the walk can have a big impact on the chances of a lasting change. Let's talk about selecting the right time for the change before moving our attention toward getting others involved in our change.

12.1.5 Time for change

Change happens all the time. Among the things that change are the properties of an environment where we aspire our envisioned change to take place. Thus, we shouldn't blindly forge ahead with a change but instead spend a moment looking ahead and identifying the right time for the change.

Pressure and challenging schedules

Considering the previous factors, it is important to choose a suitable time for starting the change. Adopting a new technique a week before a major deadline on a high-pressure project might not be the best idea.

Although we might personally understand how the change would improve our productivity, the improvement will probably follow a learning curve as we (and our coworkers) are adapting to and becoming familiar with our new way of doing things. Furthermore, the added pressure of a looming deadline is certainly not helping our peers and management understand the reasons for the change and will probably not yield their support. The utmost question in their mind would likely be, "Why now, when we're already neck-deep with the upcoming release?"

It is often best to introduce big changes at natural change boundaries, where change is seen as something to be expected rather than as something that presents a risk.

Natural boundaries and piggybacking

In general, change is easiest to initiate at natural change boundaries rather than in the middle of an activity such as a software project, especially if the group's ability to absorb risk is already lowered due to an external pressure of some kind.

Some of the more obvious natural boundaries for change include the beginning of a new project, a new release, or pretty much any restructuring of the team. Other less ideal but nonetheless attractive natural boundaries can be iteration boundaries, holiday seasons, or even off-site team events.

These natural boundaries essentially represent other changes that we've already accepted. Piggybacking a new change on top of another change (a change we've already accepted and are not questioning) works well because there's already the notion of something new starting. Therefore, our mental wiring is already in a state that's susceptible to an additional change—be it a new IDE or a development technique like TDD or writing acceptance tests before implementation.

All of these factors we've discussed so far—really getting it, having a sense of urgency and achievement, exhibiting integrity with what we do, and recognizing the right time for the change—have an influence on how easy or difficult it is for us to lead sustainable change. These factors are equally important in getting others aboard the change, perhaps even more so because it's likely that not everyone is as excited about the change as we are.

12.2 Getting others aboard

Getting others aboard the change we're leading (adopting TDD, for example) involves extending our own understanding of the change into the collective understanding of a group of people—the "us," if you will. Part of this task entails the individuals in the group going through their own personal adoptions. The same forces are in play—it's just that the balance is a bit different and there's someone else championing the change and (we hope) looking after the health of each individual's adoption process.

The champion is an important role, because they serve as the ultimate source for motivation and energy. Luckily, the role of the champion can (and should, at least eventually) be distributed among several individuals who are able and willing to take on this task. Speaking of roles, the change champion is a virtual role that is added to the individual's formal roles and responsibilities, and these other roles affect our chances of getting others aboard. Let's take a closer look at how the formal role of a champion can influence that person's ability to lead change within the group.

12.2.1 Roles and ability to lead change

Change can be initiated and lead from a variety of roles, although the underlying dynamics in these situations differ to some degree. The common goal is to help build an environment that facilitates sustainable change, including a sense of urgency as well as a frequently felt sense of achievement. Although change champions are typically senior colleagues acting in roles such as technical architect, tech lead, or senior engineer, the champion role can be taken by an individual or individuals in nontechnical as well as junior technical roles.

Instead of focusing on a group of arbitrarily selected job titles, let's approach these different formal roles from the perspective of influence, which often correlates with seniority or authority in general within the group. We can identify three main domains of influence: influence toward junior colleagues, influence toward peers, and influence toward higher-ups. Let's go through these one by one.

Mentoring junior colleagues

Perhaps the most common relationship of influence during a change is a senior staff member mentoring a junior staff member (note that "junior" does not necessarily mean younger). The formal role of the senior individual might be a tech lead, a project manager—even a business manager. Motivating junior colleagues and supporting their personal adoption processes is naturally made easier because of the leadership brought by seniority, be it through years of experience or merely through organizational hierarchy.

For a senior mentoring a junior, it is important to steer away from yielding too much control over the individual being mentored. The junior colleague must have enough time and space to take ownership over their personal adoption. The job of the mentor is to provide information, validation, feedback, and support in general. A mentor might give a junior colleague a link to a website that discusses unit-testing patterns, teach their colleague pair-programming, perform peer reviews, or simply make themself available for questions—all the while assuring the junior colleague that there's no such thing as a stupid question.

Although it might be necessary to push somewhat more in the beginning, if the mentor isn't able to let go soon, there's something wrong with one of the fundamental forces driving the mentored individual's personal adoption. They might not recognize the benefits of the change, or there might be a mismatch between the adoption program and the employee's incentives program. For example, an employee might get a bonus based on how many billable hours they put in for their current client, whereas TDD might decrease the billable hours (by improving productivity). Whatever the cause, it is the mentor's job to keep an eye out for these kinds of issues and act upon them.

A mentoring relationship between a senior and junior staff member is commonplace and natural, but it isn't quite as easy to build up between two peers—that is, two individuals with no perceived seniority.

Leading peers through change

I hope we've all had the chance to work with peers we really synched with. These are the kinds of working relationships where there is a constant spring-boarding of ideas and open sharing of great accomplishments and miserable failures. These are also the kinds of relationships where the necessary authority and mutual respect are already in place for one peer to be able to lead change and mentor the other—and vice versa. Not all relationships between peers are like this, however, and this is where it gets tricky for the change agent.

Lacking an existing supporting relationship, we need to create one before we can be effective. There's no magic recipe for creating the necessary trust in a relationship overnight, but the eventual success invariably requires openness and integrity. Between technical craftsmen, the best way of creating trust and respect is to do as you say and demonstrate that you are knowledgeable about your craft and proficient in what you do.

They say, "It takes one to know one." When it comes to developers and change, it often takes one to *lead* one. In short, we need to show that what we're promoting works for us; and we must be sensitive enough to know how much we can push without invading our colleagues' safe zone, letting them come through at their own pace.

When it comes to influencing our peers, we can't come off as pushy know-it-alls. We must learn to listen to our colleagues, understand and respect their views of the change, and adapt our communication accordingly. Listening is also important for the last of the three domains of influence—the higher-ups.

Managing upward

Everyone has a boss. At least, most of us do. And our boss is likely interested in the change we're leading. We must manage upward, or we'll risk failure resulting from lack of understanding from above. The amount of managing upward required will undoubtedly vary a lot from one organization and culture to the next, but one thing is sure—our manager will have a different perspective on the change than we do.

Let's say I'm a software developer and I report to a project manager. The project manager is responsible for shepherding the project through to completion on time, on budget, and without sacrificing quality. There's no doubt that the project manager wants to know how the change—say, the adoption of TDD will affect the project's progress. If I'm the project manager and driving the change from that position, I probably have a business manager (account manager, sales director, product manager, whatever) who's going to want to know whether the change will affect their work.

Furthermore, these higher-ups are not likely to understand the same language as our peers and junior colleagues. We must take note of finding out what exactly worries them and then formulate our message to answer those specific concerns. Without helping our superiors understand our change, we won't get their commitment and support—often the opposite, because we generally resist things we don't understand.

This brings us to one of the obvious but also amazingly easy-to-forget pieces of advice for a change agent: Expect resistance and be prepared for a long battle, because change takes time.

12.2.2 Change takes time

Very few changes in our behavior happen overnight. As change agents, promoting the adoption of a technique such as TDD means changing the way a professional software engineer works. That change might involve unlearning several decades' worth of experience doing things the old way. For that software engineer, the change is almost certainly not going to be an easy one. People change slowly, and we must be patient to be able to support our colleagues through their journey until they're ready for the change.

In addition to change taking calendar time, change also takes the time of the change agent. With this in mind, we should avoid trying to support too many individuals simultaneously. It's often easier to lead one person at a time or one team at a time through a change than to spread the change immediately to four teams and not be able to support any of the four teams properly. Furthermore, the more resistance we face from the individuals we are supporting, the fewer individuals we can support. After all, it takes a lot more effort, attention, and energy to support a resisting individual than it takes to guide an enthusiastic colleague to make the change.

Speaking of resistance, Woodrow Wilson once said, "If you want to make enemies, try to change something." In other words, not everyone will like us suggesting that they should start developing software in a radically different way from what they're used to doing. There will almost certainly be resistance against the change; and, as change agents, we must face the resistance and try to overcome it.

In the next section, we'll discuss ways of both recognizing resistance and responding to it. And if you're even remotely as anxious as I am to learn to deal with resistance, I think I'd better stop babbling and let us move on.

12.3 How to fight resistance

"Resistance is futile." I'm afraid that's not how most change agents in corporate environments see it. I certainly didn't consider the overwhelming resistance I saw everywhere a futile activity when I first tried to create a lasting change in myself. In fact, knowing how to fight resistance effectively is possibly the single most important skill for a change agent.

In this section, we'll learn about a number of techniques for fighting resistance. Before we can respond to resistance, however, we need to recognize the resistance and its root causes. For this reason, let's first discuss how we can recognize resistance.

12.3.1 Recognizing resistance

Although you would think that I would recognize that there will be resistance for most change, I am constantly getting blind-sided by the kind of resistance I see when entering a new environment or even helping initiate change in a familiar one. Slowly, I'm getting better at spotting resistance earlier and adapting my behavior accordingly. It isn't easy, though, because resistance comes in at least as many forms as there are people involved.

It's easy to spot obvious forms of resistance, such as outright refusal to do things differently. Here are a few categories of resistance that might not be so obvious at first.

Coinciding change

I once joined a software project that had been going on for several months already. There was clear ownership of parts of the code base, and people were basically working in their own pods eight hours straight, only pausing for lunch and the occasional status meeting. To get to the point, my trying to promote pair-programming in this project didn't go down too well. A few weeks after basically giving up, I started to see things I hadn't noticed before.

One of the developers had started coming to work earlier than usual, thereby also leaving for home earlier. At first, I hadn't given it a second thought—people often do that in Finland during the summer when the sun starts to rise earlier. This developer also started having lunch earlier than others. Again, that didn't strike me as odd. I started wondering if this was a coincidence or whether it had something to do with me pushing for more pair-programming on the project. Not too long after, over an after-work beer, I learned that this particular developer indeed didn't feel comfortable pair-programming and that part of the motivation for him changing his daily rhythm was to gain a couple of hours of time when he would be guaranteed to get to work alone.

This wasn't the only instance of resistance against change on that project, but it is a prime example of resistance appearing cloaked, in a form I most certainly didn't expect and didn't notice at first. The key lesson for me was that we should try to improve our awareness for coinciding change and see if there's a relevant connection with the change we're trying to facilitate. We might learn something we might otherwise never find out.

Look for actions beyond words

In addition to looking out for coinciding change, we should look for change in what people do, rather than simply in what they say. A seemingly common form of resistance to change is false agreement. I visited a team for two days to do a quick health check and advise on possible improvements in their working practices, and everything seemed to go smoothly with the team nodding in concert with pretty much anything I said.[1]

A couple of weeks later, when checking in with the client, it turned out that nothing had changed as a result of my visit. The team had held a meeting where they'd basically talked themselves out of every single one of my suggestions. This particular gig taught me more than a couple of things about the craft of consulting, but perhaps the most relevant one in this context was that words (or other gestures) don't mean a thing if there's no concrete action to match those words. Look for those missing actions. But also listen for missing words.

Listen for the missing words

No matter what they say about silence being a sign of approval, it can actually mean either yes or no. Especially in the context of introducing a change that affects the way people work, silence should be considered a warning sign—a potential indicator of the individual in question having reservations they're not

[1] This should've been the give-away for me—nobody ever agrees with *everything* I say!

bringing forth. Sure, it could be just that this particular individual doesn't like to speak as much as their peers do. The worst alternative is to ignore the silence and assume it means approval. It is much better to bring it up with the individual in question, ideally in private and in a neutral surrounding as to not put them into an uncomfortable position.

Another case of missing words might be where someone is not giving full closure—that is, they're hiding information and thereby letting others create a flawed understanding of how things really are. Just as it is natural for us to resist change we don't feel ownership over, it is natural for us to avoid confrontation that puts us into an uncomfortable situation. Being, say, the only member of a team that does not want to adopt TDD can involve a lot of hidden peer pressure—pressure that nobody is knowingly creating but that exists nevertheless.

Again, we should see that the necessary confrontation takes place (and in a supportive setting) so that we can overcome the roadblock and proceed with the team's adoption process. Note that overcoming the roadblock might not mean that the individual in question goes with the flow. Sometimes, the best solution is to appreciate differences in views and live and let live. Bob and Chris, for example, can adopt TDD, even if Dave doesn't think much of it. Simply making everyone aware of the situation is already a much healthier situation and facilitates progress.

Yet another form of resistance related to words is one where we hear the right words but in a passive context.

The conditional "yes"

The conditional "yes" is one that comes with an "if." Let's say you're explaining to your boss an idea about running the upcoming project using acceptance test-driven development, and they reply with, "I'll back it 100% if you'll put together a risk analysis and figure out a way to sell this to the customer and my boss." Although your boss might be truly with you and the proposed change, it might be that they're skeptical; and instead of confronting you with their doubts, they're trying to postpone the confrontation to the indefinite future by asking you to do stuff.

A common pitfall for an enthusiastic change agent hearing these words is to dive right in, only to find out later that all the extra work they've been asked to do on top of their normal responsibilities is not addressing the boss's real doubts. The key once again is to listen carefully and patiently before rushing to conclusions. A wise man once said that the gap between "yes" and "maybe" is much bigger than the gap between "no" and "maybe." Understanding the perspective from which our peers and superiors are looking at the change is essential to identifying and confronting the right issues.

In large organizations with lots of bureaucracy, it might be nothing out of the ordinary to spend time writing piles of documents in order to make change happen. One contributor to the apparent difficulty in implementing change is also that the parties who need to agree about the change are somewhat detached from each other—an issue that often gets highlighted with our next example of a not-so-obvious form of resistance.

Things that "can't"

When discussing a suggested change with others, we sometimes hear the words, "we can't." Quite a number of times after hearing those words, I have immediately responded with something along the lines of, "Oh, you're right. We can't do that." Some of those times, I probably should've replied with, "Why?" By getting down to the root cause of "can't," we can get rid of self-imposed constraints and flawed assumptions that are feeding the resistance.

"We can't" can mean a whole lot of things. Sometimes it really means we can't, but sometimes it means we won't—or *I* won't. In these situations, we should try to find out the underlying fear, expectation, or assumption that is at the source of this resistance. We could dig around with questions such as, "What's going to happen if we do?" and see if we could tackle or eliminate the bad things that would result from that. It is likely that when TDD on a particular piece of code is referred to as "impossible," it is really just "difficult" or something with which we are unfamiliar—and therefore uncomfortable.

Generalizations in general are fertile ground for uncovering potential by reframing the solution space. Ask "Why?" a few times, and see where you end up. You just might find yourself looking over a brand new scenario.

Stream of higher priorities

One of the trickier forms of resistance I've seen over my years in consulting has been the higher-priority syndrome. The symptoms of the higher-priority syndrome include the change at hand frequently getting overtaken by things that "are of higher priority."

For instance, the database administration group of one client (an extremely traditional, large organization) seemed to be overwhelmed with all sorts of emergencies whenever they were supposed to collaborate with our development team on putting together a development environment with private database schemas for everyone. It turned out that the apparent busyness of the database administrators was largely a result of them feeling uncomfortable with the new setup, not having had such an environment before. Again, the higher priorities might indeed be valid issues that need taking care of, but they may represent resistance nevertheless.

Setting up barricades

One of our natural reactions to change that we feel threatening our safety or comfort is to respond defensively or with an attack. This defensive behavior might display itself in the form of words, actions, body gestures, or—perhaps more commonly—all of them. What this behavior is essentially doing is building a barricade to protect the individual from the perceived threat of the suggested change.

When facing a barricade, we must resist becoming defensive ourselves. Instead, we need to address the resistance by disarming ourselves and responding with openness. Acknowledge the resisting individual's fear, and talk about that instead of the suggested change. By making explicit the connections between the change and the fear fueling the resistance, we are creating a safe environment for discussion where both parties are sitting on the same side of the table. Sooner or later, the barricade serves no purpose and will get torn down.

With all of these different kinds of resistance we might face as change agents, are there any more tricks to put in our sleeves for tackling them? Obviously I wouldn't be asking if there weren't.

12.3.2 Three standard responses to resistance

Although it's good—no, it's downright essential—to be able to recognize and identify the real source of resistance, we also need to tackle it. The big question is, of course, how? Unfortunately, there's no magic formula for overcoming resistance beyond having an eye for social skills and psychology in general.

The following, however, is a list of things that are commonly applied by change agents and are known to have worked at least once for everyone—whether in our professional careers, with domestic issues involving the purchase of the latest overpriced electronics, or in the kindergarten courtyard.

Logic

The first line of defense against resistance is every geek's best friend: logic. It can do miracles to simply go through what the proposed change means in practical terms and to unravel the logic behind the change leading to the expected benefits. It is especially important to focus on things that directly affect the individual's own work, again, in practical terms. After all, people will accept change for their own reasons and their reasons alone. This is why we need to be able to show and tell how TDD, for example, contributes to improved productivity and work life.

Trial

When good ol' logic doesn't cut it, we can always try to persuade the resisting individual to just "give it a shot." It is far easier to say yes to something that's perceived as a temporary solution, a prototype, or a pilot rather than say yes to a decision that we'll have to live with for the rest of our lives. It's much easier to give in to trying TDD for one month than to "start using it," because for the individual the sentence might implicitly continue with "from now to eternity." Once the individual has agreed to give it a shot, we must not leave it at that, though. We also need to make sure that we support the individual throughout the one shot and see that it has a chance of being successful.

Appeal

Even if you don't happen to have a puppy-eyes look that makes grown men shed tears, there's a good chance that you can appeal to the resisting individual. Useful alternatives include appealing to the common good (that of the team, the company, and so forth) or to the individual's professionalism. "Do it for me, Jake" has also worked before. Again, getting the individual to agree to give it a try is just the first step and motivating the appealed party during the adoption can be hard work.

Beyond these obvious strategies for overcoming resistance, we also have more indirect and, perhaps, less obvious techniques to consider.

12.3.3 Techniques for overcoming resistance

Although the techniques of logic, trial, and appeal are sometimes enough for the change agent to get by, sometimes these basic techniques fail to get us over the resistance we're facing. What follows is a collection of techniques and thought-provokers that might yield extra leverage. Let's start with changing the goal to support the suggested change.

Supporting change with goal setting

When facing resistance to change, it is sometimes good to expand the solution space by changing the situation. We can potentially eliminate the issue by changing the surroundings to be more favorable for the suggested new way of doing things. By asking for something that's easier to achieve using test-driven development than via the preexisting test-last practice, we are making it easier for the individual to accept the change and make it their own.

What we're asking for should not be obviously made up just for getting that someone back into the ranks. People don't like having their arm twisted, and doubly so if the twister does so behind our backs. We need to express our requirements in terms of the results we want, not in terms of the way to achieve those results.

Listen—really listen—and empathize

It is often said that the most important part of being able to converse effectively is listening. When we address another individual about their resistance, it is extremely important for us to show that we care by really listening to what the other has to say and showing that we're trying to understand their perspective.

A useful listening technique is to reformulate what we think we heard the other say in our own words, thereby getting confirmation for whether we got it right—a mutually significant piece of information—and perhaps to ask whether we left something out. Furthermore, we can try to empathize with the individual by prompting for confirmation for our interpretation of and the sources of their feelings.

Having a relationship helps enormously in our ability to empathize with each other, not least because assuming the best of others becomes easier the better we know each other. It is amazing how problems magically shrink after we walk down the corridor to sit with that someone we've so far known only as an email handle, really listening to and empathizing with what they have to say.

Don't think of it as resistance

When facing resistance, explicitly labeling it as such might help resolve the problem. Or it could hold us back from resolving the problem. The problem with thinking of resistance as resistance is that of a *frame of reference.*

The frame of reference in which we present a problem affects the way we think of the problem. Using a different frame of reference can yield new tools and put new solutions at our disposal or even dissolve the problem altogether. In general, it is much better to think of resistance as useful information. In fact, sometimes we might learn that we ourselves are the ones whose resistance needs to be overcome—it just might be that the change agent themself holds the key to resolving the problem at hand.

It might be that we're promoting quality-oriented techniques to an organization that thrives not by delivering good software fast but rather by delivering bloated software in long time frames with massive teams of consultants, effectively generating the company a nice little cash cow in the form of maintenance contracts. Techniques like TDD or ATDD might be one of the last things in that specific organization's interest. In such a situation, we should choose to back off politely and focus on creating lasting change somewhere else.

Speaking of choice, sometimes having a choice is all that's needed to overcome resistance.

Give choice

They say that a great consultant always lets the client come up with the solution to the problem. The same could be said about change agents.

People rarely resist an idea they've invented themselves or a proposed change they have been developing. This bias toward easier acceptance of things that we feel ownership over also affects the sustainability of a change. Thus, sometimes it makes sense to create options, alternative solutions if you will, and step back, letting the resisting individual make a choice. Once they have made that choice, they're likely much more committed to it than if they'd been talked into the change by someone else.

So choice creates ownership. Having choice is not, however, guaranteed to make it any easier for the resisting individual to overcome their underlying fears. With this in mind, we should also consider providing a degree of familiarity with the proposed change before presenting the alternatives.

Provide familiarity

Related to our earlier notion of frames of reference, sometimes we can overcome resistance that is caused by unfamiliarity with the suggested change by framing the change in familiar terms or by associating it with a previous change, possibly championed by the resisting individual in question.

For example, if the resisting individual happens to be a proponent of test automation in the domain of system testing, it might be worth it to try to explain the rationale for TDD through the same benefits gained from system-level test automation instead of going on and on about incremental, emerging design.

Another path to the desired sense of familiarity might be through small, safe experiments where the resisting party can toy with the suggested change without being constrained by the source of their resistance. Some of my clients have adopted the practice of organizing a weekly *coding dojo*,[2] a form of structured group-programming session to support the adoption of TDD. Such sessions are typically considered a special environment where it's generally acceptable to goof off a bit and where it's possible to fail in a safe environment. As such, these sessions are a good vehicle for providing familiarity to TDD through a shared experience.

Another useful frame of reference to consider as a thinking tool for dealing with resistance is to look at your situation through the Satir Change Model.

Satir Change Model

The Satir Change Model describes change as a transformation through four states: the old status quo, chaos, practice and integration, and the new status quo. Change starts from the current state of practice, moves to the chaos state as the foreign element—the change—is introduced into the system, eventually stabilizes into practice, and, at some point, becomes the new status quo. One of our problems as

[2] For more information, see the Agile Finland wiki (http://wiki.agilefinland.com). We'll also talk about coding dojos later in this chapter when discussing ways of facilitating change.

change agents is that we're likely in a different phase of this transformation than are our colleagues.

Let's say we're coaching a team with their TDD adoption. We might have several years of active test-driving experience under our belts, whereas the team member sitting next to us might've heard of TDD for the first time the day before. Our personal experience of going through the chaos of turning the design-code-test sequence around took place so long ago that we are less able to empathize with the feeling. Yet we need to appreciate that the people around us might be experiencing that chaos very vividly right now and spending a significant amount of energy and brainpower in changing the way they think about programming.

In the words of Dale Emery, a fellow consultant, "You see the beauty and splendor of your vision. They see confusion, pain, and risk immediately ahead." We need to accept this difference and adjust our thinking in that frame of reference. Fears that seem unfounded to us can be very real to others. One technique that can do wonders for bridging this gap between different perspectives is to concretize the transition with a story.

Tell stories

Storytelling is central to how we humans learn. It is far easier to associate with a story than with raw facts laid out in tables or bullet points. As such, storytelling should also have a place in our toolbox for dealing with resistance. By telling a story, we can help our audience relate to the protagonist in the story and use the plot as a medium for illustrating the feasibility and benefits of the suggested change. Listening to a little story can help us think about our situation in ways that weren't available to us before.

I have found that storytelling can be extremely effective even if the story doesn't directly relate to the particular individual's source of resistance. I once told a developer a story of how another team I had trained and coached was having problems with one of the testing engineers vocally resisting the idea of acceptance TDD and how the team eventually got to the root cause of the resistance. The developer I told the story to wasn't resisting acceptance test-driven development but TDD. Yet, me telling the story about another team got the developer thinking analytically and reflecting about what was happening on that other team—and, as luck would have it, he was able to continue applying the same analytic thinking to his own situation, digging out the root cause for his own resistance. Telling a story might help even if it's not about a situation *identical* to the present.

Whether in telling a story or in a discussion with an individual resisting the suggested change, it is important to adjust the weight of our words to the context in which they're said. Most often, we should lighten up in order to improve our ability to influence.

Lighten up

Those of us who have led a management role in a command- and control-oriented environment are perhaps most vulnerable to using unnecessarily strong wording to help deliver "the message." In some cases, stressing a point with strong, absolute words can be the last straw that tips the scale our way. In other cases, however, the added pressure of our words only grounds both parties deeper into their respective positions. Using lighter words leaves us with more space for constructive discussion. After all, our chances of resolving resistance suffer if we're not willing to change ourselves.

This handful of techniques for overcoming resistance has helped many a change agent make way for a lasting change. For more useful tips and techniques, you may want to find a copy of *Fearless Change* by Mary Lynn Manns and Linda Rising (Addison-Wesley, 2004). Right now, however, we need to talk about something we may need to do when the resistance proves to be more than we can handle.

12.3.4 Picking our battles

It's not easy to come up with the right strategy for overcoming resistance—largely because there's never a single best strategy. Sometimes the right thing to do is to be persistent and persuasive rather than pushing harder, and sometimes we really should just step back and slow down. And sometimes we simply need to pick our battles.

Tale from the real world

I was once called in to train and coach a development team in TDD. I was faced with the usual mix of skills and enthusiasm, but one team member in particular got my attention because of his rather vocal indications of resistance to TDD. Throughout my tenure with the team, he kept expressing his skepticism without providing real arguments. I kept trying to argue the benefits and feasibility of TDD with the team member but, unfortunately, without success.

This experience taught me something important: some battles are not worth fighting. The troublesome team member represented what I consider a battle that couldn't be won—or, to be more accurate, a battle that couldn't be won in time. After all, I had a limited amount of time available for helping the team as best I could; and, in hindsight, I ended up spending way too much time fighting a lost battle.

Compromise can make sense

Not all people will adopt TDD, for example, no matter how hard we try to pick their brain and find solutions for the source of their resistance. Although certainly not the first option to fall back on when seeing the slightest resistance, it should be considered a valid outcome to make up a compromise that allows for the willing to continue with successful adoption and the not-so-willing to continue with their old ways.

This is not to say that such compromises would be easy. It's usually not a problem to choose a specific portion of the project where the motivated team members can employ TDD to its fullest. What typically causes problems, however, is the interface between the TDD and non-TDD domains. For example, test-driving code around a code base that suffers from bad testability is not the most trivial of problems for a beginning test-driven developer. Similarly, the difference in the rhythm of integrating changes between those who develop test-first and those who don't is often a source of schism because the latter group typically has to perform large merges while the former sees no problems whatsoever.

Picking our battles is something we'd like to avoid but sometimes cannot, especially in large organizations with significant variations in people's backgrounds and attitudes towards their craft.

12.4 How to facilitate adoption

Although no single intervention technique or strategy is a silver bullet, there are a number of potential interventions that we carry in our proverbial change agent tool belts. We already discussed some such interventions earlier in this chapter, and the following should be considered additional tools from which to choose the most suitable. Furthermore, some of these tools are effectively extensions or abstractions of those we have discussed earlier.

Let's start from what often happens to be among the first interventions leading to the change—evangelizing for the change.

12.4.1 Evangelize

One of my largest clients is in the middle of a significant change involving the transformation of software-intensive product development toward agile methods. The change was started with a series of free-of-charge, open seminars being announced within the product-development organization. The intent of these seminars was to increase awareness of agile methods and to solicit interested parties to stand up and get in contact with the change agents representing an internal quality organization. These seminars were run by a well-known consultant and were well-attended, acting as an essential stepping-stone in triggering change throughout the organization.

These seminars were pure evangelistic events designed to push a message—to tell a positive story about how the future could be transformed by adopting the change—and to create pull for the change from the audience.

DICEE

Guy Kawasaki, the original Apple evangelist turned venture capitalist, coined the acronym DICEE[3] to describe the characteristics of a great product:

- *Deep*—A great product is deep.
- *Indulgent*—A great product is a luxury.
- *Complete*—A great product is more than a physical thing.
- *Elegant*—A great product has an elegant user interface.
- *Emotive*—A great product incites you to action.

Although we as change agents in software development organizations are more likely to evangelize engineering practices and methodologies than products in the traditional sense, we can extract important points from these characteristics to help us as we evangelize for change.

Let's see how these aspects of evangelism might positively affect the target audience. In fact, let's make things a bit more concrete by using TDD as our context—as the thing we're evangelizing.

Show depth

First of all, we should seek to present TDD as a deep solution that doesn't run out of gas after the first five miles. As evangelists, we should show how TDD improves quality and productivity, and how it works not just in a few special cases but as a holistic way of economically developing high-quality software. This means anticipating and preparing for the inevitable objections starting with "But that won't work in our environment, because...." We should also pack an array of real-life examples, testimonials from early adopters within the same organization, pointers to external resources, and so forth—because our audience will want to see evidence.

Make it special

Second, we want to present TDD as a luxury. We like to feel special; and by portraying the proposed practice as something special, as "something the best developers do,"

[3] Guy Kawasaki, *Rules for Revolutionaries: The Capitalist Manifesto for Creating and Marketing New Products and Services* (Collins, 2000).

we're bringing our audience that much closer to taking the first step toward adopting the practice. To paraphrase Guy, the audience should feel like they're rewarding themselves by buying our product, which in this case means adopting TDD. This means that we should be talking not just about improving the technical quality of the code we produce or about the pragmatic conciseness of avoiding gold plating, but also about how TDD makes our work more exciting and meaningful.

Make it complete

Great evangelists don't focus too much on the details but instead show their audience how the proposed change fits nicely into the big picture. By offering a complete solution with no glaring gaps, we can tackle a lot of natural resistance to "unsafe" new things. Completeness shows that we have thought it through and we're not just talking to keep ourselves warm, leaving the really tough problems for others to solve. This completeness includes not just the message but also our support continuing forward. The audience wants to know that we're there when they need help and support—whether that means off-the-shelf training, coaching and consulting, management sponsorship, or simply fighting the bigger power battles for them.

Show the elegance

Although the "Elegant" in DICEE refers to an elegant user interface, we have an equivalent need for elegance in evangelizing practices and methodologies. To quote Guy again, "Things work the way you'd think they would. A great product doesn't fight you—it enhances you." What this means in our context of evangelizing TDD is that we must not fail to show how TDD works for us and how it aligns with our thinking. When weu're giving a live demonstration to a room full of developers, we don't stop at describing what we're doing. We describe what we're thinking—describe *why* we are doing what we are doing. Getting inside the thought processes of someone using TDD is a great way of showing the intuitive elegance of the technique.

Make it emotive

Great products sell themselves once we've gotten the first box on the market. As evangelists, one of our primary goals is to turn our audience into evangelists for our "product." This means we need to make the practice we're evangelizing emotive—something that creates excitement and the urge to tell others. For someone evangelizing TDD, making the product emotive is largely about conveying our own excitement and the benefits of TDD as clearly as possible. Focus on how great it is and get people to try it for themselves, ensuring that they'll also experience the thrill of developing test-first. A key in ensuring this thrill is to have some low-hanging fruits for the audience to start from.

Speaking of low-hanging fruits and getting started with the change, let's move on from evangelization to our next intervention technique, which we call *lowering the bar.*

12.4.2 Lower the bar

A frequent sense of achievement is important for keeping a change alive and well. We could argue that the single most important of these frequent achievements is the first one. Making the proposed change seem like something that's hard to achieve is opposite to our goals. Instead, we need to make it as easy as possible to take the first step, removing or lowering any and all barriers to entry.

Quick path to first success

As a concrete example of what this could be in practice, we might want to provide prepackaged, supported turnkey solutions for setting up a development environment to support the new development practice. We might want to provide templates and sample code. We might provide a five-minute screencast to go with the thorough but less accessible online documentation.

The quick first victory is only the beginning, of course. We must lower the proverbial bar not just for the first hurdle but for the whole first run. We do this by creating *slack.*

Slack

Chances are you've at least heard of the term *slack* in the context of Tom Demarco's best-selling title *Slack: Getting Past Burnout, Busywork, and the Myth of Total Efficiency* (Broadway, 2001). Slack, as Demarco defines it, is "the degree of freedom in a company that allows it to change."

This slack is the ingredient that makes it possible for an individual to take time to reflect on the change at hand and to avoid feeling unnecessary pressure to perform. Without enough slack, an individual generally has to take a leap of faith in order to adopt a new way of working—because it's their neck on the line if the improvements promised by the new tool or technique aren't realized fast enough to balance out the initial drop in productivity.

Slack could be realized in many ways. For a team in the process of adopting TDD, management could create slack simply by protecting the team from external interruptions such as fixing defects in previously released versions of the software. Another simple way might be to explicitly add a safety buffer by allocating less work for the team until they've had time to get up to speed with TDD.

Having slack is important for an organization for many reasons, but it is perhaps most essential for change to succeed. Which takes us to the third component of lowering the bar—making failure an acceptable outcome.

License to fail

Slack goes a long way in creating a runway for change to take off. No matter how long or wide the runway is, however, the perceived risk will never be completely eliminated. Therefore, we need to make sure that the individuals facing change have a license to fail—and that they themselves know about having that license!

I was once talking to an ex–project manager who had later become the Scrum Master (a process coach) for a team that was adopting Scrum, an agile method. Soon, he started seeing the need for improving the quality of code they were delivering and started promoting TDD. All of the promotion didn't seem to go anywhere, however: Only one developer started programming test-first, and the rest wrote unit tests after the fact.

Interestingly, the ex–project manager was very suspicious of my suggestion to be explicit with the team about failure being an option. For him, mentioning failure as an option was the equivalent of giving the devil a finger—"they'll start slacking off if I say that!" Obviously I didn't agree with that notion, and neither should you. In fact, not giving the team a signal that it's OK to fail will likely have a negative effect on the team's productivity because the team members may feel the need to cover their own butts in case the change doesn't deliver the expected improvements.

We've talked about three ways to lower the bar in this section—the barrier to entry, if you will. The early success, slack, and a license to fail are tools that work for many barriers, but they don't instantaneously make everything alright. They also don't work unless we are able to recognize the barrier. The best way to recognize barriers to entry—the obstacles that are keeping our audience from taking their first step toward adoption—is to engage in conversations with our audience. These conversations might take place right after an evangelistic event, or they could take place at the water cooler a week later. These conversations could (and should) also take place after the audience has taken their first step—a step that often involves training and education.

12.4.3 Train and educate

The next step after evangelizing change is often to organize training. From a motivation point of view, having management that encourages projects and people to sign up for training is an important act of commitment. Just make sure that you're not promising what you can't deliver—if training resources are limited to only a handful of teams during the next months, say so.

Having a great evangelist running through an organization and going on about the next big thing without being followed by proper training can be more devastating to a company's productivity than a natural disaster. After getting people excited about a change, we must not leave them alone as they look for the path to righteousness. We need to be there to provide guidance and direction.

Over time, as the adoption is proceeding within a group, the role of training tends to change as well. I've seen a number of successful transitions that started with larger-scale, general training sessions for introducing the organization to the fundamentals of the change being adopted. As the teams gained experience with the new practices and processes, the training leaned more and more toward specific point solutions as responses to specific needs (for example, how to test-drive when we have a lot of legacy code or how to test-drive Swing code).

Although training is an economic way of moving information and knowledge, typically only a tiny portion of all the information being passed during a training course sticks with any given individual. The good news is that the group as a whole tends to catch a much larger portion of the information load. Related to this fact, our next intervention is all about spreading that information within the group.

12.4.4 Share and infect

As Jerry Weinberg, the consultants' consultant, has taught us, the wider you spread your raspberry jelly, the thinner it gets.[4] Although evangelists speaking to large audiences and experienced practitioners giving training classes are resources not to be ignored, the most intensive learning happens on a completely different level through personal, hands-on experiences. Considering that we all learn and see things differently, being able to share our learning with others is something to which we need to pay attention.

We can identify three distinct levels of sharing: personal, team-level, and organizational. We'll next introduce a handful of tools for facilitating sharing through all of these levels, starting from the power of proximity and then moving from the center of our circle of influence toward the outside.

Sit together

One of the easiest ways to increase sharing is to encourage the flow of information throughout the team[5] by sitting together. *Together* doesn't mean adjacent cubicles. *Together* means close by with a clear line of sight to our co-workers. What we're looking for is an environment with not the slightest barrier to asking a question or sharing that handy little keyboard shortcut you just figured out. If we can always

---

[4] Gerald M. Weinberg, *Secrets of Consulting: A Guide to Giving and Getting Advice Successfully* (Dorset House Publishing Company, 1986).

[5] Alistair Cockburn, the creator of the Crystal family of agile methods, refers to this phenomenon as *osmotic communication* in *Agile Software Development* (Addison-Wesley, 2001).

see whether our colleagues are busy (on the phone, for example) and make a decision about whether we can interrupt them with a question or useful information, we're more likely to interact with them. If, on the other hand, we have to walk down the hall to speak to someone, we may be disinclined to do so.

The obvious progression from sitting close enough to engage in spontaneous discussions is to work together in pairs.

Pair up

In the context of sharing our personal knowledge, working in pairs is about as personal as it can get. Specifically, when dealing with development techniques such as TDD, pair programming helps enormously in spreading good practices. In addition to all the cool keyboard shortcuts and programming tricks and idioms, pair-programming with our peers provides immediate feedback, moral support, and a fresh pair of eyes that contribute to supporting our personal adoption and understanding of good practices.

Having said that, it is also essential for people to have time and space for absorbing the flux of change, letting them take personal ownership of the change. Speaking of time and space, on a team level, we can and should consider putting aside some time for the whole team to sit down and share.

Organize sharing sessions

Modern software development is very much a people-oriented activity—teamwork. One of the components of effective teamwork is acting as a unit with shared goals, shared understanding, and—to some degree—shared opinions. In the middle of a change, reinforcing the team's consensus about its development practices is as important as ever. Some examples of the kind of sharing sessions that we might want to consider include *brown bags* and *coding dojos*.

Brown-bag sessions derive their name from people carrying their lunch into a meeting room in little brown bags, the idea being that people could listen to a colleague talking about some interesting topic while they're eating their lunch. In most companies, however, the brown bags have turned to more or less regular sessions that take place after lunch or after office hours rather than during regular lunch (probably because people like having their lunch served on real plates).

Coding dojos, on the other hand, are more interactive sessions where software is developed on a single, shared machine, projecting the screen for everyone to see. The original[6] coding dojos were more like presentations, with someone walking

[6] The nice folks in the Paris XP community started running weekly gatherings in 2005 and named them the Coding Dojo.

through a rehearsed development scenario, explaining every step along the way and thus sharing their thinking and technique with others. Since then, other coding dojos have been organized using a more interactive format, where the session is given a problem to solve and the participants develop the solution as a group, rotating a pair of developers on the keyboard while others observe.

Brown-bag sessions and coding dojos are good for spreading knowledge and creating a supportive, open environment where people feel safe to experiment and learn from their peers. There's no reason to restrict such sessions to only individual teams or projects, however. These same session formats can be used equally well for spreading knowledge on the organizational level.

Spread out

As change progresses to multiple little islands within the organization, sharing knowledge between these islands increases in importance. By organizing open sharing sessions that can be attended by anyone across organizational boundaries, we can start to build up communities of practice that help keep the change alive and give direction. As the change grows beyond the capacity of the original change agents, having a network of communities of practice facilitates continuing support for those taking their first steps and provides a sounding board for those farther along in their adoption.

So far, we have discussed interventions ranging from the more abstract means of evangelizing to the more personal level of sharing knowledge. Along with these techniques, it is almost always a good idea to provide fresh perspective and a nurturing touch to teams' adoption process through coaching and facilitation.

12.4.5 Coach and facilitate

Along with off-the-shelf–style training and formal forums for sharing information, it often makes sense to engage teams with a coach or facilitator. Whereas training tends to focus on providing information and on honing skills, coaching and facilitation is more about taking a step back and looking at what we're doing from an outsider's perspective. Coaching helps us learn things about ourselves and our behavior—and about coping with these findings—rather than about the change we're adopting.

Get a coach

Effective coaching requires a degree of detachedness from the context in which the coaching is happening. Even the most experienced coaches are vulnerable to bias and blind spots when they are part of the context. Thus, one of the first steps in our quest for providing effective coaching for our team is to get a coach from outside the team. The coach doesn't have to be an external consultant, though, as long as they have the skills, experience, and authority necessary to work effectively in a coaching role using inquiry, introspection, and discussion.

An experienced coach can work with the team and individuals, helping them find solutions for the problems at hand and pointing out problems the team isn't able to see from where they're standing. The coach is not a consultant in the traditional sense, because they don't bring solutions. Rather, they help clients find solutions. The coach should not be just thrown at the team, however, because a key ingredient to a successful coaching relationship is a mutual agreement over the scope and goal of the coaching. In other words, make the coach available, but don't force them down the team's collective throat.

The coach's job is to listen and observe and then to advise, educate, and act as a mirror for the team to reflect on their feelings and behavior. One specific area where the skills of a professional coach can be especially helpful is in facilitating meetings.

Facilitate meetings

There's more to facilitating meetings than keeping track of the agenda and other practical arrangements. In the context of helping a team through change, a much more important aspect of facilitating meetings is in helping participants understand all alternatives and the underlying forces when making decisions. The facilitator plays an important role in increasing the participants' awareness of their own behaviors and biases in conflict situations, smoothing the team's way toward a consensus.

The facilitator needs to stay aware of the undercurrents below the ongoing interactions, making sure that everyone participates and that the team is aware of all the issues—all the while ensuring that the environment remains safe and supportive rather than hostile and disruptive. In order to reach the meeting's objectives, the facilitator needs to balance the meeting's structure, pace, and style of interaction. In some cases, the focus should be on keeping the meeting enjoyable; in others, our focus should be on results and getting the job done. Sometimes this might mean focusing on external threats in a cooperative mode, and other times the best approach might be more competitive.

Helping participants unleash their untapped resources is part of the coach's job, and techniques such as introspection and reflection are essential tools in achieving that. Let's talk a bit more about the essence of stopping to talk.

Stop to talk

A specific type of meeting we can use in coaching a team—or an individual—is the reflection or retrospective meeting. A regular reflection meeting establishes a space where participants can freely speak their minds about past successes and failures and about conflicting opinions, and generally feel safe in bringing forth issues about the team's way of working. By looking at how we're doing with our adoption, we keep the change alive and show ourselves that change is indeed happening. This can be surprisingly important. I have more than once walked out of a reflection meeting wondering, "Who are all these strange people?" after seeing the team's energy level jump from near-zero to way up there simply because they finally had a chance to speak up and talk things through.

Coaching and facilitation are very much involved with increasing participation. As our next concrete intervention, let's look at increasing participation and commitment by giving the resisting individual a role that makes them part of the change.

12.4.6 Involve others by giving them roles

As we've learned by now, people resist change more when they aren't involved in that change. As such, it is obvious that we can reduce resistance by making people part of the change. One of the ways of doing that includes giving people roles.

Involve stakeholder groups

Think of an organization that is trying to adopt acceptance TDD and is facing strong resistance from the centralized QA department, whose team members are feeling their jobs are at stake and cannot accept that "automated acceptance tests can replace professional test engineers." We know that this is not what the change is about—test engineers remain an important group of people with specialist skills—but the test engineers might not know that.

In this scenario, we should invest in educating the QA department about what exactly acceptance TDD is and how the change will and will not affect them. In addition to enlightening the QA department, we can engage in a collaborative system of transforming the processes involved in moving toward acceptance TDD. Part of that process involves giving the test engineers new roles.

Turning threats into opportunities

For example, test engineers with programming skills could become responsible for automating test scenarios and consulting developers on the system's testability. Test engineers who are lacking programming skills, on the other hand, could focus on exploratory, context-driven testing as a complementary testing practice for automated tests, or have their new roles focus more on the customer-facing part of the equation. Their responsibilities might revolve around developing specifications with the customer representatives, analyzing test scenario coverage, coordinating non-functional testing, and so forth.

With a little thought, we can turn threats that are acting as a source of resistance into exciting opportunities for personal development. When giving people new roles, it is also important to pay attention to *who* we are giving what kinds of roles. *Social leaders* are an especially powerful group in this situation.

Identify social leaders

Every group has informal, social leaders. Although the social leaders are often people who others look up to and rely on for advice, they are not necessarily the most experienced or the most skilled individuals in the group. People who have a natural tendency to motivate others and generally keep the pack together are often great social leaders. By giving a suitable role to such a social leader, we essentially create a "deputy change agent" and give them a megaphone to run with.

Getting a social leader excited about the change is like throwing fuel on a fire—it can blow up obstacles faster than an external change agent ever could. Giving roles can also be used for bringing about change because doing so destabilizes the status quo by, for example, assigning roles outside of the individuals' skill sets.

12.4.7 Destabilize

Status quo is about stability and safety. In order to disrupt the status quo and to encourage change, we can intentionally make the current safe place less safe, thereby causing people to seek for a new stable state—a safe place—through change. The logic behind this strategy is in our fundamental need for safety, control, and certainty. As long as these needs are met, a change will cause resistance. When some or all of these are already lacking, further change will likely cause much less of a reaction—especially if the announced change purports to restore these needs.

We can disrupt the status quo in many ways, but all of them involve raising awareness of what's really happening. For example, by moving the focus from perceived threats within the organization to the real threat coming from the competition, we can often turn resistance into powerful collaboration towards a common goal—survival. One approach that has woken up resisters before is to present hard numbers about the company's less-than-favorable financial performance, showing how the competition is kicking ass. Yet another effective disruption has been to bring developers in contact with an angry customer. Just be wary of destabilizing too much—the shock might make people freeze or rebel rather than push for change that we're after.

As our final intervention technique before summing up, let's discuss delayed rewards.

12.4.8 Delayed rewards

By now, we should realize the importance of people like the internal change agents, external coaches, and social leaders. All of these roles have a lot to contribute to a successful adoption of change. Similarly, losing some of these key people might prove to be disastrous for the adoption process. (We've likely all witnessed at least one initiative that has quietly faded away after such a key person left the company or moved on to other tasks.) One way to minimize the risk of this happening is to use delayed rewards.

The core idea behind delayed rewards is that there will be incentives for the key people to see the whole thing through. The delayed reward might be pure fame and glory, a promotion, or cold hard cash, possibly tied to improvements in the company's financial performance. The important things to remember are that these rewards must be balanced and that the delayed rewards are not meant as a substitute for regular compensation but an extra on top. In other words, it doesn't mean not rewarding your key people—and everyone else involved in the change—early and often!

12.5 Summary

In this chapter, we learned that the chances of successful personal adoption are greater when we know our stuff, understand why we should be interested in adopting the suggested change in the first place, have a sense of achievement throughout the adoption process, and exhibit integrity and openness all the way in order to shield ourselves from unnecessary external pressure. We also learned that, although timing is perhaps not everything, it certainly matters.

Talking about getting others aboard, we recognized three directions we need to manage as change agents in different roles—upward, downward, and horizontally—and we discussed some of the distinct pitfalls we should avoid in each of these roles.

We also enumerated a number of indicators for not-so-obvious resistance, including spoken and unspoken communication and actions that masquerade resistance as something else. We also discussed a number of techniques for dealing with resistance, starting from a handful of standard responses—good ol' logic, a temporary agreement, and the power of appeal—and moving on to more indirect ways of overcoming resistance, such as thinking tools and more effectively adapting our behavior to the situation.

To finish our journey through being agents for organizational change, we went through a number of possible interventions for facilitating adoption. We studied the secrets of evangelizing effectively, and we shared some tips for getting change started by lowering the bar and by providing support in the form of training and education. We further discussed ways to share our knowledge and infect peers and peer groups with this change. Finally, we talked about what we can achieve with coaching and facilitation, as well as by giving and communicating roles to those involved. To top it off, we also threw in the possibility of encouraging change by destabilizing the status quo, and we reminded ourselves about the need to keep key people involved, possibly using delayed rewards.

Leading change is one of the toughest jobs in any organization or culture. Yet it is one of the key capabilities for the continued survival of a company. As a final piece of advice for an aspiring change agent, be persistent. It's going to be a rough ride, whatever you do. Just keep your eyes and ears open, know your toolbox, and use your brain—and you'll do just fine.

Plus, even if you feel like you're stumbling and constantly falling in the mud puddle, check your pockets—you might have caught a lot of fish without knowing it.

appendix A: Brief JUnit 4 tutorial

```
import static org.junit.Assert.*;        ❶
import org.junit.*;
import java.io.*;

public class TestConsoleLogger {        ❷

    private static final String EOL =
        System.getProperty("line.separator");
    private ConsoleLogger logger;
    private PrintStream originalSysOut, originalSysErr;        ❸
    private ByteArrayOutputStream sysOut, sysErr;

    @Before public void createFixture() {        ❹
        logger = new ConsoleLogger();
        originalSysOut = System.out;
        originalSysErr = System.err;
        sysOut = new ByteArrayOutputStream();
        sysErr = new ByteArrayOutputStream();
        System.setOut(new PrintStream(sysOut));
        System.setErr(new PrintStream(sysErr));
    }

    @After public void resetStandardStreams() {        ❺
        System.setOut(originalSysOut);
        System.setErr(originalSysErr);
    }

    @Test public void infoLevelGoesToSysOut()        ❻ ❼
        throws Exception {
        logger.info("msg");
        streamShouldContain("[INFO] msg" + EOL, sysOut.toString());
    }

    @Test(timeout = 100)        ❽
    public void errorLevelGoesToSysErr() throws Exception  {
        logger.error("Houston...");
        streamShouldContain("[ERROR] Houston..."
            + EOL, sysErr.toString());
    }

    private void streamShouldContain(String expected,        ❾
        String actual) {
        assertEquals("Wrong stream content.",        ❶
            expected, actual);
    }
}
```

❶ We get assertion methods from JUnit's `Assert` class through a static import.

❷ The name of the class should indicate that it's a test—for example, have the class name start with `Test`.

❸ The instance variables set up in the `@Before` method represent the common fixture for the test methods.

❹ We can prepare a known state for the test by tagging a public method with the `@Before` annotation.

❺ We can clean up after our test by tagging a public method with the `@After` annotation.

❻ All public void methods tagged with `@Test` are considered test cases by the JUnit 4 TestRunner.

❼ Test methods can declare any exceptions—JUnit catches them.

❽ The `@Test` annotation also allows for timing tests, testing for expected exceptions, and so on.

❾ We can declare any number of helper methods as long as they don't look like test methods.

appendix B: Brief JUnit 3.8 tutorial

```
import java.io.*;

public class TestConsoleLogger extends                    ❶❷
    junit.framework.TestCase {

    private static final String EOL =
        System.getProperty("line.separator");
    private ConsoleLogger logger;
    private PrintStream originalSysOut, originalSysErr;
    private ByteArrayOutputStream sysOut, sysErr;

    @Override protected void setUp() {         ❹❺             ❸
        logger = new ConsoleLogger();
        originalSysOut = System.out;
        originalSysErr = System.err;
        sysOut = new ByteArrayOutputStream();
        sysErr = new ByteArrayOutputStream();
        System.setOut(new PrintStream(sysOut));
        System.setErr(new PrintStream(sysErr));
    }

    @Override protected void tearDown() {      ❺❻
        System.setOut(originalSysOut);
        System.setErr(originalSysErr);
    }

    public void testInfoLevelGoesToSysOut() throws Exception {
        logger.info("msg");                                       ❼
        streamShouldContain("[INFO] msg" + EOL, sysOut);
    }                                                             ❽

    public void testErrorLevelGoesToSysErr() throws Exception {
        logger.error("Houston...");
        streamShouldContain("[ERROR] Houston..." + EOL, sysErr);
    }

    private void streamShouldContain(String expected,     ❾
            ByteArrayOutputStream stream) {
        assertEquals("Stream content doesn't match expected. ",   ❿
                expected, stream.toString());
    }
}
```

❶ The name of the class should indicate that it's a test—for example, have the class name start with `Test`.

❷ We extend from JUnit's `TestCase` class.

❸ The instance variables set up in the `setUp()` method represent the common fixture for the test methods.

❹ We can prepare a known state for the test by overriding the protected `setUp()` method.

❺ If using Java 5, it's good to add the `@Override` annotation to `setUp()` and `tearDown()` to avoid typos.

❻ We can clean up after our test by overriding the protected `tearDown()` method.

❼ All public void methods starting with `test` are considered test cases by the JUnit 3.8 TestRunner.

❽ Test methods can declare any exceptions—JUnit catches them.

❾ We can declare any number of helper methods as long as they don't look like test methods.

❿ Extending `TestCase` gives us, among other things, a bunch of assertion methods such as `assertEquals()`.

appendix C: Brief EasyMock tutorial

```
import static org.easymock.EasyMock.*;          ❶
import org.easymock.EasyMock;
import org.junit.Test;

public class TestInternetRelayChat {

    @Test
    public void messagesAreOnlyDeliveredToOtherClients()
            throws Exception {
        String msg = "Maisk Maisk!";

        Client koskela = EasyMock.createMock(Client.class);
        Client freeman = EasyMock.createMock(Client.class);   ❷
        Client himberg = EasyMock.createMock(Client.class);

        expect(himberg.onMessage("lasse",                ❸
            msg)).andReturn(true);

        freeman.onMessage("lasse", msg);                 ❹
        expectLastCall().andReturn(true);

        replay(freeman, koskela, himberg);               ❺

        InternetRelayChat irc = new InternetRelayChat();
        irc.join("inhuman", freeman);
        irc.join("vilbert", himberg);                    ❻
        Prompt prompt = irc.join("lasse", koskela);
        prompt.say(msg);

        verify(freeman, koskela, himberg);               ❼
    }
}
```

❶ Import static utility methods from EasyMock and the class itself.

❷ Ask EasyMock to create mock objects for the given interface.

❸ Record expected interactions.

❹ This is an alternative, functionally equivalent syntax for the previous syntax.

❺ When we're done recording expectations, we move the mocks to replay mode.

❻ With everything set up, we exercise the code under test.

❼ We ask the mock objects to verify that the expected interactions took place.

appendix D: Running tests with Ant

Apache Ant is the de facto build tool used by Java developers all around the world. Not surprisingly, Ant has had JUnit integration as long as I can remember. Here's a quick tutorial for creating an Ant script that runs our unit tests and cranks out a pretty HTML report of the results. If you're not familiar with Ant, please refer to the online documentation[1] or grab one of the excellent books on the topic.[2]

Let's start our little tutorial and see what kind of a project we're dealing with.

> **Apache Ant and JUnit 4 compatibility**
> JUnit 4 support was introduced in the 1.7 release of Apache Ant, which means that you'll need to downgrade your tests to use JUnit 3.8 if you don't have or cannot upgrade your Ant version to the 1.7 branch. The versions of Ant and JUnit you're using do not, however, affect your build script.

D.1 Project directory structure

From the perspective of build scripts, we're not interested in what our Java classes can do. We only care about the code compiling, us being able to run all automated tests as part of our build, and getting a nice report out of the test run, which we can browse for details on test failures and so forth. The project's directory structure dictates a lot of what our build script needs to do. Consider the relatively simple directory structure depicted in listing D.1.

Listing D.1 Sample directory structure

```
/SampleProject
  /src
    /main
      /com/tddinaction/.../ProductionCode.java    ❶ Production code under src/main
    /test
      /com/tddinaction/.../TestCode.java          ❷ Test code under src/test
  /bin
    /classes-main
      /com/tddinaction/...                        ❸ Compiled code follows similar separation
    /classes-test
      /com/tddinaction/...
```

---

[1] Especially the User's Manual (http://ant.apache.org/manual) and the Ant Wiki (http://wiki.apache.org/ant).

[2] I would personally recommend *Ant in Action* by Steve Loughran and Erik Hatcher (Manning Publications, 2007). It's basically a 2nd edition of their earlier book, *Java Development with Ant* (Manning Publications, 2002).

```
/lib
  /main
    commons-logging.jar
  /test
    junit.jar
build.xml
```

❹ **Dependencies separated for production and test code**

❺ **Build script in root of project directory**

Our source code is split into two directories: ❶ src/main and ❷ src/test. Having separate source trees provides for an easier distinction between test code and production code and also because makes writing build scripts a lot easier—everything under X is about X, everything under Y is about Y.

We also have a similar split for compiled class files. ❸ Compiled production code goes to bin/classes-main, and compiled test code goes to bin/classes-test. Not surprisingly, ❹ the libraries we depend on are separated under lib/main and lib/test. Once again, the separation makes it easier to manage the different sets of dependencies for runtime and development and simplifies the act of creating a deployment archive, which should only contain compiled production code and only runtime dependencies.

The Ant build script, ❺ build.xml, is located in the root of the project directory. And speaking of the build script, we're ready to look inside it. Let's start with the first step of getting all code compiled.

D.2 The basics: compiling all source code

For this project, the build.xml used for compiling all source code to their respective output directories might look something like listing D.2.

Listing D.2 build.xml for compiling all code for the `SampleProject`

```
<project name="SampleProject" default="compile">

    <path id="classpath.main">
        <fileset dir="lib/main" includes="**/*.jar" />
    </path>

    <path id="classpath.test">
        <path refid="classpath.main" />
        <pathelement location="bin/classes-main" />
        <fileset dir="lib/test" includes="**/*.jar" />
    </path>

    <target name="clean">
        <delete failonerror="false" includeemptydirs="yes">
            <fileset dir="bin" includes="classes-*/**" />
```

Different compilation class paths for production and test code

❶ **Target for cleaning up compilation artifacts**

```
        </delete>
    </target>
                                              ❷ Target for compiling
                                                 all source code
    <target name="compile">
        <mkdir dir="bin/classes-main" />
        <javac srcdir="src/main" destdir="bin/classes-main"
               debug="on" classpathref="classpath.main" />     Different
                                                               compilation
        <mkdir dir="bin/classes-test" />                       class paths for
        <javac srcdir="src/test" destdir="bin/classes-test"    production
               debug="on" classpathref="classpath.test" />     and test code
    </target>

</project>
```

This is familiar to those who have seen Ant build scripts. The script in listing D.2 provides the developer with two *targets* to execute: ❶ `clean` and ❷ `compile`. With Ant installed, typing `ant clean` on the command prompt deletes all compiled class files. Typing `ant compile` compiles all .java source files into the bin directory. Typing `ant clean compile` first deletes existing class files and then compiles everything from scratch. And, because the project's default target is configured as compile, just typing `ant` is the same as typing `ant compile`.

But what about running those tests we're now compiling?

D.3 Adding a target for running tests

JUnit is integrated into Ant through the `<junit/>` *task*. In order to make running our unit tests part of our build, we need to add a new target to build.xml, which uses the `<junit/>` task. Listing D.3 shows an example of what this new target might look like.

Listing D.3 build.xml with a `test` target using Ant's standard `<junit/>` task

```
<project name="SampleProject" default="test">          Use test target as
                                                        default from now on
    <property name="junit.data" value="reports/junit/data" />
    ...
                                                   Use property for ❶
                                                     output path to
    <target name="test" depends="compile">        reduce duplication
        <mkdir dir="${junit.data}" />
        <junit printsummary="yes" fork="true" haltonfailure="no">
            <classpath>                                          Need everything
                <path refid="classpath.test" />                  in class path
                <pathelement location="bin/classes-test" />      including compiled
            </classpath>                                         test code
```

```
            <formatter type="xml" />
            <batchtest haltonfailure="no"
                todir="${junit.data}">
                <fileset dir="src/test"
                    includes="**/Test*.java" />
            </batchtest>
        </junit>
    </target>

</project>
```

❶ Use property for output path to reduce duplication

❷ Collect all classes that match pattern for execution

Without going to too much detail, the new target in listing D.3 uses the `<junit/>` task to ❷ collect all unit tests from src/test for execution and generates a bunch of XML files under ❶ the configured reports/junit/data directory. These XML files describe the test execution environment, which tests were run, and with what kind of results. Those XML files aren't user-friendly, though. We need a pretty report to look at.

D.4 Generating a human-readable report

We can generate a nice, compact HTML report from the output of the `<junit/>` task by using another built-in task, `<junitreport/>`. All it needs to know is where to find the test results, where we want the report to be generated, and in what format—there are a couple of options.

Listing D.4 presents the necessary modifications to our existing build script for both running the tests as well as for generating the HTML report.

Listing D.4 build.xml with a target for running tests and generating the report

```
<project name="SampleProject" default="test">

    <property name="junit.data" value="reports/junit/data" />
    <property name="junit.html" value="reports/junit/html" />
    ...

    <target name="test" depends="-test-run, -test-report" />

    <target name="-test-run" depends="compile">
        <mkdir dir="${junit.data}" />
        <junit printsummary="yes" fork="true" haltonfailure="no">
            <classpath>
                <path refid="classpath.test" />
                <pathelement location="bin/classes-test" />
            </classpath>
            <formatter type="xml" />
```

"test" target coordinates test and reporting

```
            <batchtest haltonfailure="no" todir="${junit.data}">
                <fileset dir="src/test" includes="**/Test*.java" />
            </batchtest>
        </junit>
    </target>

    <target name="-test-report" depends="-test-run">
        <mkdir dir="${junit.html}" />
        <junitreport todir="${junit.data}">
            <fileset dir="${junit.data}"
                includes="TEST-*.xml" />
            <report format="frames" todir="${junit.html}" />
        </junitreport>
    </target>

</project>
```

"test" target coordinates test execution and report generation

<junitreport/> generates aggregated XML in data directory...

...and produces HTML report in frames format under reports/junit/html

That's it. We now have an Ant build script for compiling our code, running our unit tests, and producing a pretty report of the results!

resources

Works cited

Alur, Deepak, Dan Malks, and John Crupi. *Core J2EE Patterns: Best Practices and Design Strategies.* Prentice-Hall, 2003.

Ambler, Scott W. and Pramodkumar J. Sadalage. *Refactoring Databases: Evolutionary Database Design.* Addison-Wesley, 2006.

Cohn, Mike. *User Stories Applied: For Agile Software Development.* Addison-Wesley, 2004.

Cooper, Alan. *The Inmates Are Running the Asylum: Why High Tech Products Drive Us Crazy and How to Restore the Sanity.* Sams, 1999.

Crane, Dave, Bear Bibeault, Jord Sonneveld, Ted Goddard, Chris Gray, Ram Venkataraman, and Joe Walker. *Ajax in Practice.* Manning Publications, 2007.

Crane, Dave, Eric Pascarello, and Darren James. *Ajax in Action.* Manning Publications, 2005.

Cunningham, Ward and Rick Mugridge. *Fit for Developing Software: Framework for Integrated Tests.* Addison-Wesley, 2005.

DeMarco, Tom. *Slack: Getting Past Burnout, Busywork, and the Myth of Total Efficiency.* Broadway, 2001.

DeMarco, Tom and Timothy Lister. *Peopleware: Productive Projects and Teams.* Dorset House Publishing Company, 1999.

Feathers, Michael. *Working Effectively with Legacy Code.* Addison-Wesley, 2004.

Fowler, Martin, Kent Beck, John Brant, and William Opdyke. *Refactoring: Improving the Design of Existing Code.* Addison-Wesley, 1999.

Gamma, Erich, Richard Helm, Ralph Johnson, and John Vlissides. *Design Patterns: Elements of Reusable Object-Oriented Software.* Addison-Wesley, 1995.

Hillenius, Eelco and Martijn Dashorst. *Wicket in Action.* Manning Publications, 2007.

Kawasaki, Guy. *Rules for Revolutionaries: The Capitalist Manifesto for Creating and Marketing New Products and Services.* Collins, 2000.

Kerievsky, Joshua. *Refactoring to Patterns.* Addison-Wesley, 2004.

Kuchana, Partha. *Software Architecture Design Patterns in Java.* Auerbach, 2004.

Larman, Craig. *Agile & Iterative Development: A Manager's Guide.* Addison-Wesley, 2003.

Loughran, Steve and Erik Hatcher. *Ant in Action: Java Development with Ant, Second Edition.* Manning Publications, 2007.

Mann, Kito. *JavaServer Faces in Action.* Manning Publications, 2005.

Manns, Mary Lynn and Linda Rising. *Fearless Change: Patterns for Introducing New Ideas.* Addison-Wesley, 2004.

Rainsberger, J. B. *JUnit Recipes: Practical Methods for Programmer Testing.* Manning Publications, 2005.

Ship, Howard M. Lewis. *Tapestry in Action.* Manning Publications, 2004.

Additional resources

Ambler, Scott W. *Agile Database Techniques: Effective Strategies for the Agile Software Developer.* Wiley, 2003.

Beck, Kent. *Test Driven Development: By Example.* Addison-Wesley, 2002.

Cohn, Mike. *Agile Estimating and Planning.* Prentice Hall PTR, 2005.

Duvall, Paul, Steve Matyas, and Andrew Glover. *Continuous Integration: Improving Software Quality and Reducing Risk.* Addison-Wesley, 2007.

Goetz, Brian, Tim Peierls, Joshua Bloch, Joseph Bowbeer, David Holmes, and Doug Lea. *Java Concurrency in Practice.* Addison-Wesley, 2006.

Meszaros, Gerard. *xUnit Test Patterns: Refactoring Test Code.* Addison-Wesley, 2007.

Newkirk, James W. and Alexei A. Vorontsov. *Test-Driven Development in Microsoft .NET.* Microsoft Press, 2004.

Schwaber, Ken and Mike Beedle. *Agile Software Development with SCRUM.* Prentice Hall, 2001.

Online resources

All URLs listed here were valid at the time of publishing. No doubt some of these will change over time.

Agical AB. RMock: Java Mock Object Framework to Use with JUnit. http://rmock.sf.net.

Agile Finland Community. Agile Finland Community Wiki. http://wiki.agilefinland.com.

Apache Community. Apache Ant Community Wiki. http://wiki.apache.org/ant.

———. Apache Ant: A Java-Based Build Tool. http://ant.apache.org.

———. Apache Ant Manual. http://ant.apache.org/manual.

———. Apache Maven: A Java-Based Build Tool. http://maven.apache.org.

———. Continuum: A Continuous Integration Server. http://maven.apache.org/continuum.

———. Jakarta Commons Lang: A Utility Library for the java.util API. http://jakarta.apache.org/commons/lang.

———. Jakarta Commons VFS: A Virtual File System API for Java. http://jakarta.apache.org/commons/vfs.

———. Wicket: A Component-Based Web Development Framework for Java. http://wicket.sf.net.

Ashley, Nick, Graham Tackley, and Sam Newman. dbdeploy: A Database Change Management Tool. http://dbdeploy.com/.

Atlassian Software Systems Pty Ltd. Bamboo: A Continuous Integration Server. http://www.atlassian.com/software/bamboo.

Atomic Object LLC. System Testing in Ruby. http://atomicobject.com/pages/System+Testing+in+Ruby.

Bossicard, Vladimir R. PrivateAccessor: A Utility Class for Overriding Access Modifiers in Java. http://junit-addons.sourceforge.net/junitx/util/PrivateAccessor.html.

Bowler, Mike. GSBase: A JUnit Extension of Test Utilities. http://gsbase.sf.net.

Cenqua. Clover: Code Coverage Analysis Tool for Java. http://www.cenqua.com/clover.

Cunningham, Ward. Fit: Framework for Integrated Test. http://fit.c2.com.

Diehl and Associates. Mckoi Database: A Lightweight, Java-Based Relational Database. http://mckoi.com/database.

Feathers, Michael. "The 'Self'-Shunt Unit Testing Pattern." January 2001. http://www.objectmentor.com/resources/articles/SelfShunPtrn.pdf.

———. "The Humble Dialog Box." August 2002. http://www.objectmentor.com/resources/articles/TheHumbleDialogBox.pdf.

———. "Working Effectively With Legacy Code." February 2002. http://www.objectmentor.com/resources/articles/WorkingEffectivelyWithLegacyCode.pdf.

Fowler, Amy. "A Swing Architecture Overview." http://java.sun.com/products/jfc/tsc/articles/architecture/.

Fowler, Martin. "Continuous Integration." May 1, 2006. http://www.martinfowler.com/articles/continuousIntegration.html.

———. "Mocks Aren't Stubs." January 2, 2007. http://www.martinfowler.com/articles/mocksArentStubs.html.

———. Passive View. July 18, 2006. http://www.martinfowler.com/eaaDev/PassiveScreen.html.

———. Supervising Controller. June 19, 2006. http://www.martinfowler.com/eaaDev/SupervisingPresenter.html.

Freeman, Steve, Tim Mackinnon, Nat Pryce, Mauro Talevi, and Joe Walnes. JMock: A Dynamic Mock Object Library for Java. http://www.jmock.org.

hsql Development Group. HSQLDB: A Lightweight, Java-Based Relational Database. http://www.hsqldb.org.

Hubbard, Charlie and Prashant Dhokte. PrivilegedAccessor: A Utility Class for Overriding Access Modifiers in Java. http://groups.yahoo.com/group/junit/files/src/PrivilegedAccessor.java (requires a Yahoo! account).

Jeffries, Ron. "Essential XP: Card, Conversation, Confirmation." August 30, 2001. http://www.xprogramming.com/xpmag/expCardConversationConfirmation.htm.

———. List of testing-related software. http://www.xprogramming.com/software.htm.

Koskela, Lasse. Bean Inject: Dependency Injection Framework for Java. http://www.laughingpanda.org/mediawiki/index.php/Bean_Inject.

———. Introduction to Code Coverage. January 2004. http://www.javaranch.com/newsletter/200401/IntroToCodeCoverage.html.

———. JspTest: A JUnit Extension for Unit Testing JavaServer Pages. http://sourceforge.net/projects/jsptest.

Martin, Robert C. "Design Principles and Design Patterns." January 2000. http://www.objectmentor.com/resources/articles/Principles_and_Patterns.pdf.

———. "SRP: The Single Responsibility Principle." February 2002. http://www.objectmentor.com/resources/articles/srp.pdf.

Meszaros, Gerard. xUnit Test Patterns. http://www.xunitpatterns.com.

Mort Bay Consulting. Jetty: An Embeddable Java EE Web Container. http://jetty.mortbay.com.

Mugridge, Rick. FitLibrary: An Extension Package for Fit and Fitnesse. http://sourceforge.net/projects/fitlibrary.

NetBeans Community. Jellytools Module: Jemmy Extension for Creating UI Tests for NetBeans IDE. http://jellytools.netbeans.org.

———. Jemmy: UI Testing Library for Java. http://jemmy.netbeans.org.

Payne, Bob. Agile Toolkit Podcast. Interview with Arlo Belshee at Agile 2005: "Promiscuous Pairing and the Least Qualified Implementer." http://media.libsyn.com/media/agiletoolkit/ArloBelsheeAgile2005.mp3.

Perrotta, Paolo. The Virtual Clock Test Pattern. March 1, 2003. http://www.nusco.org/docs/virtual_clock.pdf.

Potel, Mike. MVP: Model-View-Presenter, The Taligent Programming Model for C++ and Java. 1996. http://www.arsip.or.id/free_doc/m/mvp/mvp.pdf.

Pragmatic Programmers, LLC. "Tell, Don't Ask." http://www.pragmaticprogrammer.com/ppllc/papers/1998_05.html.

Rothman, Johanna. "What Does It Cost You To Fix A Defect? And Why Should You Care?" 2000. http://www.jrothman.com/Papers/Costtofixdefect.html.

Ruby on Rails Community wiki. Understanding Migrations. August 1, 2007. http://wiki.rubyonrails.com/rails/pages/UnderstandingMigrations.

Saff, David, Erich Gamma, Kent Beck, and Erik Meade. JUnit: A Simple Framework for Writing and Running Automated Tests. http://www.junit.org.

Schuh, Peter and Stephanie Punke. "ObjectMother: Easing Test Object Creation in XP." 2001. http://www.agilealliance.org/system/article/file/910/file.pdf.

SourceForge.net. Cobertura: Code Coverage Analysis Tool for Java. http://cobertura.sf.net.

———. CruiseControl: A continuous integration server. http://cruisecontrol.sf.net.

———. DbUnit: A JUnit Extension for Testing Database Code. December 28, 2006. http://dbunit.sf.net.

———. EMMA: Code Coverage Analysis Tool for Java. http://emma.sf.net.

———. Joda-Time: A Time and Date API to Replace the Standard java.util Classes. http://joda-time.sourceforge.net.

———. PMD: Static Analysis Tool for Java. http://pmd.sf.net.

———. SUnit: The Mother of All Unit Testing Frameworks. http://sunit.sf.net.

Splint Community. Splint: Static Analysis Tool for C. http://splint.org.

Tammo Freese. EasyMock: A Dynamic Mock Object Library for Java. http://www.easymock.org.

Urban{code}, Inc. AnthillPro: A Continuous Integration Server. http://www.urbancode.com.

World Wide Web Consortium. Logging Control in W3C httpd. July 1995. http://www.w3.org/Daemon/User/Config/Logging.html#common_logfile_format.

———. XML Path Language (XPath). November 16, 1999. http://www.w3.org/TR/xpath.

Yahoo! Inc. JUnit Group and Online Mailing List. http://groups.yahoo.com/group/junit.

index

A

B

C

H

I

J

K

L

S

T

X